WHAT PEOPLE SAY THEY DO WITH WORDS:

Prolegomena to an Empirical-Conceptual Approach to Linguistic Action

JEF VERSCHUEREN

Belgian National Fund for Scientific Research
and
University of Antwerp (UIA)

Volume XIV in the Series
ADVANCES IN DISCOURSE PROCESSES
Roy O. Freedle, Editor

ABLEX PUBLISHING CORPORATION
NORWOOD, NEW JERSEY

Copyright © 1985 by Ablex Publishing Corporation

All rights reserved. No part of this publication may be reproduced, stored in a retrieval system, or transmitted, in any form or by any means, electronic, mechanical, photocopying, microfilming, recording or otherwise, without permission of the publisher.

Printed in the United States of America

Library of Congress Cataloging in Publication Data

Verschueren, Jef.
  What people say they do with words.

  (Advances in discourse processes, v. xiv)
  Bibliography: p.
  Includes indexes.
  1. Semantics. 2. Pragmatics. I. Title
P325.V47 1985   401'.9   85-6211
ISBN 0-89391-197-6

Ablex Publishing Corporation
355 Chestnut Street
Norwood, New Jersey 07648

CONTENTS

Preface to the Series   vii

Preface   ix

PART I THEORETICAL AND METHODOLOGICAL PRELIMINARIES

Chapter 1 The Comparative Lexical Approach to Linguistic Action   3
1.0   Introduction   3
1.1   Speech-act theory at the breaking point?   4
1.2   Reflections on the study of social action   12
1.3   An empirical-conceptual approach to linguistic action   22
1.4   Epilogue: Linguistic expansionism   27

Chapter 2 Problems of Lexical Semantics   29
2.0   Introduction   29
2.1   Problem 1: What are lexical items?   30
2.2   Intermezzo 1: The object of investigation   33
2.3   Problem 2: How to describe the meaning of lexical items   36
2.4   Toward a solution of problem 2   45
2.5   Intermezzo 2: Abstractness in lexical semantics   53
2.6   Problem 3: How to avoid circularity   58
2.7   Problem 4: How to map semantic space   63
2.8   Epilogue: Pitfalls of comparison   67
2.9   Concluding remark   69

PART II FOUR EXPLORATORY EXERCISES

Chapter 3 The Semantics of Silence   73
3.0   Introduction   73
3.1   The frame of silence   74
3.2   Silence, meaning, context, and communication type   75
3.3   The codes of silence   83
3.4   The 'sound' of silence   89
3.5   Silence and its causes   96
3.6   The tacens and his motives   101
3.7   Silence and its interlocutors   108
3.8   Silence and its effects   111
3.9   The topics of silence   111
3.10   Silence and nonpropositional meaning   115
3.11   Silence and context   116
3.12   The illocutionary force of silence   118
3.13   Conclusions   118

Chapter 4 The Semantics of Lying   122
4.0   Introduction   122
4.1   The frame of lying   124
4.2   Lying and truth   125
4.3   The illocutionary force of lying   134
4.4   Lying and perlocutionary intent   138
4.5   The textual dimension of lying   141
4.6   Lying and value judgments   143
4.7   Note on human imagination   144
4.8   Conclusions   145

Chapter 5 The Semantics of Directing   148
5.0   Introduction   148
5.1   The frame of directing   152
5.2   The directivity of directing   153
5.3   Directing and its social settings   155
5.4   Directing and its goals   164
5.5   The directionality of directing   170
5.6   Directing and authority   180
5.7   Miscellaneous dimensions   183
5.8   Conclusions   184

Chapter 6 The Semantics of Forgotten Routines   186
6.0   Introduction   186
6.1   The expression of emotions and attitudes   188

6.2   Negative and positive responses   **195**
6.3   Fixed routine responses   **200**
6.4   Conclusions   **203**

PART III THEORETICAL AND METHODOLOGICAL EPILOGUE

Chapter 7 Provisional Conclusions   **207**
7.0   Introduction   **207**
7.1   Types of tentative results   **208**
7.2   Applying the semantic dimension approach   **211**
7.3   More pitfalls of comparison   **213**
7.4   Conclusion   **214**

Chapter 8 Perspectives: Basic Linguistic Action Verbs   **215**
8.0   Introduction   **215**
8.1   Programmatic statement   **215**
8.2   Primary operational criteria   **217**
8.3   Some words of caution   **222**
8.4   Secondary operational criteria   **223**
8.5   A provisonal list   **225**
8.6   Crosslinguistic comparison   **230**
8.7   Methodological afterthought   **232**

References   **235**

Index of English Linguistic Action Verbials   **243**

Index of Dutch Linguistic Action Verbials   **251**

Author Index   **257**

Subject Index   **261**

Preface to the Series

Roy O. Freedle
Series Editor

This series of volumes provides a forum for the cross-fertilization of ideas from a diverse number of disciplines, all of which share a common interest in discourse—be it prose comprehension and recall, dialogue analysis, text grammar construction, computer simulation of natural language, cross-cultural comparisons of communicative competence, or other related topics. The problems posed by multisentence contexts and the methods required to investigate them, while not always unique to discourse, are still sufficiently distinct as to benefit from the organized mode of scientific interaction made possible by this series.

Scholars working in the discourse area from the perspective of sociolinguistics, psycholinguistics, ethnomethodology and the sociology of language, educational psychology (e.g., teacher–student interaction), the philosophy of language, computational linguistics, and related subareas are invited to submit manuscripts of monograph or book length to the series editor. Edited collections of original papers resulting from conferences will also be considered.

Volumes in the Series

- Vol. I. Discourse Production and Comprehension. Roy O. Freedle (Ed.), 1977.
- Vol. II. New Directions in Discourse Processing. Roy O. Freedle (Ed.), 1979.
- Vol. III. The Pear Stories: Cognitive, Cultural, and Linguistic Aspects of Narrative Production. Wallace L. Chafe (ed.), 1980.
- Vol. IV. Text, Discourse, and Process: Toward a Multidisciplinary Science of Tests. Robert de Beaugrande, 1980.
- Vol. V. Ethnography and Language in Educational Settings. Judith Green & Cynthia Wallat (Eds.), 1981.
- Vol. VI. Latino Language and Communicative Behavior. Richard P. Duran (Ed.), 1981.
- Vol. VII. Narrative, Literary and Face in Interethnic Communication. Ron Scollon & Suzanne Scollon, 1981.
- Vol. VIII. Linguistics and the Professions. Robert J. DiPietro (Ed.), 1982.
- Vol. IX. Spoken and Written Language: Exploring Orality and Literacy. Deborah Tannen (Ed.), 1982.
- Vol. X. Developmental Issues in Discourse. Jonathan Fine & Roy O. Freedle (Eds.), 1983.
- Vol. XI. Text Production: Toward a Science of Composition. Robert de Beaugrande, 1984.

Vol. XII. Coherence in Spoken and Written Discourse. Deborah Tannen (Ed.), 1984.
Vol. XIII. The Development of Oral and Written Language in Social Contexts. Anthony D. Pellegrini & Thomas D. Yawkey (Eds.), 1984.
Vol. XIV. What People Say They Do With Words. Jef Verschueren, 1985.
Vol. XV. Systemic Perspectives on Discourse, Volume 1: Selected Theoretical Papers from the 9th International Systemic Workshop. James D. Benson & William S. Greaves (Eds.), 1985.
Vol. XVI. Systemic Perspectives on Discourse, Volume 2: Selected Applied Papers from the 9th International Systemic Workshop. James D. Benson & William S. Greaves (Eds.), 1985.
Vol. XVII. Structures and Procedures of Implicit Knowledge. Arthur C. Graesser & Leslie F. Clark, 1985.
Vol. XVIII. Contexts of Reading. Carolyn N. Hedley & Anthony N. Baratta (Eds.), 1985.
Vol. XIX. Discourse and Institutional Authority: Medicine, Education, and Law. Sue Fisher & Alexandra Dundas Todd (Eds.), 1986.
Vol. XX. Evidentiality: The Linguistic Coding of Epistemology. Wallace Chafe & Johanna Nichols (Eds.), 1986.

PREFACE

There isn't a more humbling experience than to open one's mind to the complexities of human language. The world is full of objects, some natural, some human-made, that most of us do not understand the first thing about. We know, however, that given a sufficient amount of time we are able to master every bit of technology used to construct even the most mysterious of artifacts, such as, say, airplanes. And though we can hardly expect ever to fully grasp the driving forces of nature, we can learn enough about them to control them to an amazing extent. But language, being both product and instrument of the human mind, constantly escapes the maze of our thoughts or, shall we say, its own grasp. This is why, after several years of studying theories of language and linguistic (inter)action, I felt compelled to have a look at what language can tell us about itself and its own activities. The resulting comparative lexical approach to linguistic (inter)action, or the study of metapragmatic terms, is theoretically justified and methodologically grounded in Part I of this book. Part II presents four pilot studies leading us into the realms of linguistic silence, deviations from the truth, verbal directing, and conversational routines. In Part III, the relevance of the approach is briefly discussed with reference to the results of our exploratory exercises, and suggestions are offered as to what the next step should be.

    A list of the people whose direct or indirect contribution to the creation of this work should be acknowledged is bound to remain as hopelessly incomplete and unfinished as the book itself. I am greatly indebted to many people: Charles Fillmore, without whose teaching and guidance none of this could ever have been written—nor conceived; Louis Goossens, who first introduced me to linguistics in general and pragmatics in particular, and who has witnessed and guided the growth of my ideas ever since; John Gumperz, whom I had not even met until a few months ago, but whose anthropological perspective forced me at once to make some important last-minute changes; Paul Kay, whose work is a major source of inspiration, and who has always been ready to listen to whatever I had to say; George Lakoff, whose critical, and at times skeptical, attitude has obliged me to formulate my ideas clearly enough for him to become convinced of their validity; Geoffrey Leech, who took the trouble to read a much earlier version and write down his comments; Tim McDaniel, who originally provided me with the wider perspective in which I am trying to situate this work; John Searle, whose philosophy of language is the intellectual starting point for whatever the purpose of this essay may be, and whose comments have always been useful; and Ann Verhaert, who has influenced my thoughts in more ways than she realizes, and who put her own work aside to prepare the final draft of the manuscript, no minor feat.

Thanks are also due to the Commonwealth Fund of New York for granting me a Harkness Fellowship, enabling me to start studying linguistics at the University of California, Berkeley, in 1975, and to the Belgian National Fund for Scientific Research, my employer ever since the end of my Harkness tenure.

Finally, I want to thank the publishers and editors of the following earlier publications for their permission to reprint revised versions in this book: Problems of lexical semantics, Lingua, 1981, 53.317-351 (Chapter 2); The semantics of forgotten routines, in F. Coulmas (ed.), *Conversational Routine*, (The Hague: Mouton, 1981) (Chapter 6); Basic linguistic action verbs, Cahiers de linguistique française (Genève), 1981, 2.71-88 (Chapter 8).

Berkeley
February 1982

ADDENDUM TO THE PREFACE

The final chapter of this book, in which suggestions are made for further research, has lost some of its timeliness, since more than three years have elapsed between writing and publication. In the meantime, an elaborate questionnaire has been prepared to carry out the project proposed, and research is in full progress.

Antwerp
March 1985

PART I

THEORETICAL AND METHODOLOGICAL PRELIMINARIES

CHAPTER 1

THE COMPARATIVE LEXICAL APPROACH TO LINGUISTIC ACTION

1.0 INTRODUCTION

1   Though renewed interest in language use has only recently surmounted the structuralist barriers erected by Bloomfield and maintained by Chomsky, linguistics has witnessed the emergence of quite a few 'theories' of linguistic action. Prevailing among them—though no longer dominant—is no doubt speech-act theory, which entered its incubation period with the late J. L. Austin's *How to do things with words* and finally hatched when J. R. Searle's *Speech acts* was published. Since then, hordes of scholars have been engaged in refining the theory, applying it to the so-called parasitic forms of discourse and to indirect speech acts, extending it to speech-act sequences and incorporating it into a wider speech-activity theory (what the Germans call *Sprechtätigkeitstheorie* as opposed to *Sprechhandlungstheorie*) or into the theory of action in general. In this chapter I shall argue that in spite of the bulk and diversity of the resulting literature,[1] nearly all speech-act scholars, whether linguists or philosophers, approach linguistic action from an essentially theoretical point of view, in a sense of 'theoretical' that even makes the adjective applicable to most of the sporadically occurring 'empirical' investigations of speech acts. It is not my intention to repudiate this approach. However, this book presents one of the possible alternatives, the comparative lexical approach, which I offer as an example of what I call the empirical-conceptual method. This alternative should be regarded as a necessary supplement rather than as a replacement.

---

[1] To get an idea of the voluminous and diverse literature on the subject, the reader should have a look at J. Verschueren (1978a) and its annual supplements in the *Journal of Pragmatics*.

2   The point of this introductory chapter is to elucidate the foregoing obscurities. First, I will point out some of the current threats to speech-act theory. Then, I will discuss their origins, with reference to some reflections on the study of social action in general. In this context the contrast between theoretical and empirical-conceptual methods will be explained. Further, the comparative lexical approach will be proposed to divert the threats and to give a new impulse to the study of linguistic action. Finally, I will argue that this new impulse is needed to free linguistics from a methodological straitjacket that could turn pragmatics into the dead end of linguistics.

3   As mentioned in the first paragraph, the proposal in question is not intended as a self-sufficient way of describing linguistic action. In principle, it is a one-sided approach meant to counterbalance the diagonally opposed methodology embodied in almost all inquiries into speech-act phenomena—with a few exceptions to be mentioned later. In practice, it cannot reach the acme of its perfection without constant interaction with the theoretical approach. This final point will not become absolutely clear until the very last chapter of this book, in which I address the question of what the logical next step should be to maximize the usefulness of the comparative lexical approach that, by then, will have been demonstrated by means of a more or less pure application in the four exploratory exercises of Chapters 3 through 6.

1.1 SPEECH-ACT THEORY AT THE BREAKING POINT?

1.1.1 Some Basic Notions

4   For the sake of the uninitiated reader I review the basic concepts of speech-act theory as they are habitually used.[2] A *speech act* is an act performed in or by using language; the intentional utterance of any sentence constitutes a speech act. Its main components are a *propositional content* (consisting of a reference and a predication) and an *illocutionary force* (i.e., its role as a statement, a request, an order, a promise, a question, etc.). The effect produced in a hearer by performing a speech act is its *perlocutionary effect* (e.g. convincing, persuading, pleasing, annoying, etc.). A speech act viewed under the aspect of its illocutionary force is called an *illocutionary act;* viewed under the aspect of the perlocutionary effect it produces it is a *perlocutionary act.*

5   Illocutionary acts are analyzed by means of formulating the constitutive *rules* for their felicitous performance: propositional content rules (specifying

---

[2]The following definitions are the 'orthodox' ones extracted from J. L. Austin (1962) and J. R. Searle (1969, 1975a, 1976). Many 'deviant' ones are to be found in the literature.

restrictions with respect to reference and predication; e.g., when making a promise the speaker predicates a future action to be carried out by him/herself); preparatory rules (expressing what the act implies or the conditions without which the act has no point; e.g., a promise only makes sense if the speaker believes that the hearer would prefer his/her doing the promised act over his/her not doing it); sincerity rules (formulating the psychological state of the speaker; e.g., a promise expresses the speaker's intention to carry out the action in question); essential rules (specifying the essence of the act; e.g., a promise counts as the speaker's undertaking of an obligation to do something). Often such rules are offered in the form of necessary and sufficient conditions, or *felicity conditions.*

6   Most, if not all, languages possess a number of verbs, such as TO PROMISE and TO ORDER, that describe types of illocutionary acts but that can also be used to perform the act in question as in 'I order you to leave the room' and 'I promise not to forget the book.' These are called *performative verbs*, and the two utterances presented are *explicit performatives* (as opposed to *primary performatives*, which use *illocutionary force indicating devices* of a less explicit nature, such as grammatical mood, adverbs, and the like). Verbs that cannot be used performatively but that can also describe types of illocutionary acts, together with the performative verbs, form the class of *speech-act verbs*.

7   Some speech acts, such as 'Can you pass me the salt?', have a double illocutionary layering: the ultimately intended force (i.e. the primary illocutionary force) is that of a request to pass the salt; but this is achieved indirectly by means of a secondary force (which is the force typically associated with the grammatical form of the utterance), namely that of a question. Hence, these are called *indirect speech acts*. Another classical example is 'The door is still open', which is a plain statement, but one that can, in certain situations (e.g. if the hearer is the speaker's servant), take the function of a request or even an order to close the door.

1.1.2 An Anthology of Controversies

8   After the publication of Searle's *Speech acts*, speech-act theory took less than five years to become a prodigious excrescence from the body of language studies, and one that grows every day. The continued, though somewhat weakened, attraction it exerts does not necessarily mean that it is in good health. On the contrary, I am about to present some problems that could soon prove to be fatal if no cure is found. I duscuss them under the following headings: the meaning-force controversy, the perlocution controversy, the seriousness-literalness controversy, the sequencing controversy, the classification controversy, and the indirectness controversy. Of course the controversies themselves do not constitute threats to the theory of speech acts. The trouble is in some of the solutions proposed, which menace the basic insights that made speech-act theory appealing in the first place.

The meaning-force controversy

9 Austin paraphrased the perlocutionary act as an act performed *by* saying something and the illocutionary act as an act performed *in* saying something. The act *of* saying something he dubs the locutionary act. Apart from its phonetic-phonological and its grammatical properties, a locutionary act is also characterized by a certain meaning (which Austin defines, in Frege's terms, as its sense and reference). In that way the term *meaning* acquired a technical sense (even though Austin did not intend it as such) in opposition to the *force* of an utterance, which is its status as an illocutionary act of some type.

10 Quite early in the development of speech-act theory, some scholars pointed out correctly that in the ordinary language sense of the word 'meaning', illocutionary force is part of meaning and cannot be placed in contrast with it. Though this argument, as it stands, cannot be exploited to refute Austin, who, like any other scholar, is free to posit his own terminological conventions, it is not futile. Its justification is the underlying question of whether illocutionary force can be distinguished from other aspects of meaning in any clear and consistent way. Usually such a distinction is taken for granted. Hence, the controversy between those who give a negative reply to the question and those who answer it in the positive is virtually absent from the literature. At first sight this absence of an overt *meaning-force controversy* conceals its potentially dangerous implications. But at a deeper level it reveals the extreme acuteness of the problem. The few who believed that there was no distinction between illocutionary force and other aspects of meaning have concluded that therefore illocutionary forces do not exist or at least that the concept is utterly useless (e.g. L. J. Cohen 1964). Such a conclusion is completely logical if one adheres to the principle that terminological clarity is an absolute prerequisite for fruitful thinking. And yet it deprives us of one possible way of talking about basic semantic phenomena such as the difference between 'He opened the door' and 'Did he open the door?' In other words, it deprives us of a notion that carried the promise of opening new horizons when it was first introduced and that has gone a long way by now in trying to fulfill that promise.

11 With the acceptance or rejection of the notion of illocutionary force, speech-act theory stands or falls. Therefore, the threat radiating from this controversy is not felt immediately: those who reject the notion tend to disappear from the speech-act camp without leaving a trace. The real trouble starts when speech-act theorists themselves begin to doubt the validity of the notion. It is hard to predict when this will happen. But sooner or later it may (the onset of this process may already be visible in occasional publications such as Berrendonner 1981, Harder 1978, etc.), because illocutionary force *is not* clearly distinguishable from other aspects of meaning. Explicit performatives should suffice to demonstrate this nondiscreteness: in such utterances the illocutionary force is also indicated in the propositional content and it is mainly due to this presence in the proposition that the utterances get their force; in other words, part of the propositional content functions as an illocutionary force indicating device.

The perlocution controversy

12 Next in line is the *perlocution controversy*. Remember that perlocutionary acts were defined as the production, by saying something, of any consequential effect in the hearer. By ordering somebody to leave the room you can make him/her leave the room; but you can also provoke laughter, annoy or anger your hearer, or cause his/her suicide. All these are perlocutionary effects—enough to drive any law-and-order-loving mind to despair. The contingent and capricious nature of perlocutionary effects has prompted most speech-act theorists to apply the time-honored practice of avoiding trouble; in other words, the perlocutionary aspect of linguistic acts has been omitted from most accounts. Some intended effects, such as the intention to make the hearer do something, which is inherent in the act of commanding, could not be shunned (but got relabeled as the *illocutionary point*, which is not to say that there is a one-to-one correspondence between intended perlocutionary effects and illocutionary points). But no systematic investigation has ever been made of the effects that are typically associated with particular types of illocutionary acts, let alone the less typical ones.

13 Whereas the meaning-force controversy only threatens speech-act theory from without, the perlocution controversy is a clear menace from within. Not all perlocutionary effects (even those typically associated with certain types of illocutionary acts) can be given an equally prominent place. Consider the subtle pragmatic difference between 'I tell you that P but I am not trying to make you believe that P' and 'I order you to do P but I am not trying to get you to do P': both are deviations from a standard situation, but this is more so for the order than for the statement. Yet the absence of a systematic investigation (in spite of a couple of shy but praiseworthy attempts as in T. Cohen 1973 and Davis 1979) is a gap that no bridge can span. This is where I disagree with Searle (personal communication) who would not deny that all types of illocutionary acts have an intended effect typically associated with them, but who regards these as *necessary by definition* for some illocutionary acts and optional for others; according to Searle, only the necessary ones (the existence of which is probably not beyond doubt) are worth considering in a theory of speech acts. Though the perlocution phobia is founded on the basically sound urge for controllable data, it veils fundamental aspects of linguistic action, such as the speaker's intention to make something known to the hearer when making a statement.

The seriousness-literalness controversy

14 The felicity conditions formulated for the performance of illocutionary acts usually bear on their performance in 'literal' and 'serious' discourse. In the

so-called parasitic forms of discourse, i.e. in the nonliteral ones (irony, metaphor, etc.) and in the nonserious ones (play acting, language teaching, etc.), these conditions are usually violated or suspended. A common and acceptable procedure is to describe such violations in terms of deviations from a standard. Recently, however, voices have been raised against this line of thought. It is argued that if a promise that the speaker does not intend to keep still counts as a promise, then it is wrong to regard the intention to carry out the promised action as a condition on the felicitous performance of the act of promising. If this conclusion is correct—I think it is not—then it is no longer possible to formulate felicity conditions at all: I am not aware of the existence of any that are immune against similar criticism. Therefore the *seriousness-literalness controversy* is capable of undermining the basic apparatus for describing speech acts.

15 The term 'felicity conditions' (and even more so its occasional substitute 'appropriateness conditions') has led people to believe that the rules formulated in speech act-theory (and in much of pragmatics in general) are prescriptive; e.g., see Riniker (1979). Though the terminology may be seen as descriptively capturing some of the prescriptive norms or standards in terms of which linguistic behavior is often perceived, it does not necessarily imply that the deviations (i.e. the 'parasitic forms of discourse') are inferior to the 'standard'. But in theory it might be equally justified to treat nonliteral and nonserious language itself as 'standard' since, for one thing, it is definitely more frequent. In practice, though, it is hard to see how this would work. This is not to say that vanguard studies of nonliteral and nonserious language (as opposed to rear-guard studies undertaken with an already existing speech-act theory as one's point of inspiration, such as Perret 1976; Pratt 1977; Searle 1975b, 1979b, and many others) could not constitute a valid heuristic procedure (in much the same way as Freud's observations of psychopathology, which led him to the formulation of his theories of the human mind—but without any comparable normative implications).

The sequencing controversy

16 Similar worries arise from the *sequencing controversy*. It is argued, quite correctly, that speech acts rarely occur in isolation and that the sequence to which they belong influences their semantic properties. In other words, speech-act theory is said to be inadequate (e.g., see Franck 1981; Levinson 1981) because its descriptions are static and lack the dynamics needed to account, for instance, for conversational interaction. But again, trying to incorporate contextual influences into the description of speech-act types instead of departing from a standard analysis that is allowed to change depending on the context is a maneuver that menaces the very possibility of speech-act analysis. It is not surprising, therefore, that some scholars have recently proposed to supplant speech-act theory with a totally new speech activity theory rather than to supplement it (e.g., see Schüle 1976).

17   The sequencing controversy is intimately related with disputes concerning *basic units* in the analysis of language in use. Speech-act theory posited the speech act as the basic analytical unit. For a number of pragmatic linguists (e.g. Ducrot 1973, Metzing 1975) the act of argumentation, chaining speech acts or propositions together, is basic; this motivates their interest in 'small words' such as *mais* (e.g. Anscombre & Ducrot 1977; Bruxelles et al. 1976), *donc* (e.g. Zenone 1981), etc. Also the text, which may vary in length from a single speech act to a fat volume, is a candidate (see, e.g., de Beaugrande 1980). Even a discourse, any instance of the interaction between two or more texts, is regarded as the basic unit of analysis by some scholars.

18   The attacks on speech-act theory presented in the previous paragraphs (14 ff.) are based on the practice of criticizing a theory for what it does not do; such criticism is usually misguided unless the theory criticized is *intended* to do what it does not do. Felicity conditions on speech acts are not meant (at least not in Searle's proposal) to cover cases of nonliteral and nonserious language, nor to explain the interaction of individual speech acts with their context or the text or discourse in which they are embedded. The conscious—and probably valid—policy is to describe standard forms. By failing to realize this, those who reject speech-act theory on those grounds throw the baby out with the bath water: the very fact that speech-act theory concentrates on standard forms enables it to shed light on all 'deviations'. It should be kept in mind that the term 'deviation' is not meant to imply 'inferiority' nor 'rarity'.

The classification controversy

19   Both Austin and Searle proposed a fivefold classification of illocutionary acts. Searle (1976) comes up with the following classes: representatives or assertives (the point of which is to represent a state of affairs; which have a word-to-world direction of fit, i.e. the intention is to make the words fit the world; in which a belief is expressed; and in which any proposition can occur), e.g. statements; directives (the point of which is to direct the hearer toward doing something; which have a world-to-word direction of fit; in which a wish is expressed; in which the proposition is a future act done by the hearer), e.g. orders; commissives (the point of which is that the speaker commits him/herself to doing something; which have a world-to-word direction of fit; in which an intention is expressed; in which the proposition is a future act done by the speaker), e.g. promises; expressives (the point of which is that a certain psychological state is expressed; which have no direction of fit; in which a wide range of psychological states can be expressed; in which the proposition ascribes a property or act to the speaker or the hearer), e.g. congratulations; declarations (the point of which is to bring something about in the world as specified in the propositional content; which have both a word-to-world and a world-to-word direction of fit;

in which no psychological state is expressed; and in which any proposition can occur), e.g. an excommunication.

20 In addition to those who present slightly modified versions of this classification, there are linguists (e.g. Ballmer & Brennenstuhl 1981) who maintain seriously that the number of distinct classes is around 600, and others (e.g. Van der Auwera 1980a) who contend that there are exactly three basic speech acts from which all the others can be derived. Let us call them the splitters and the lumpers, respectively. The splitters' attitude is based on some postulated principles of scientific taxonomies such as absolute discreteness (e.g. the unacceptability of overlap between categories) and on the use of the speech-act verb vocabulary of a natural language as one's point of reference. What the lumpers are doing is not really classifying speech acts but trying to determine the basic function of a couple of grammatical forms in such a way that the other uses can be derived from it. The illocutionary character of such functions is doubtful. Therefore, it is not surprising that they use terms such as 'indicative', 'interrogative', and 'imperative' as names for the categories they propose. But even so, the steps required to derive most illocutionary acts from one of the three basic types often strain logic. Both for splitting and for lumping theoretical justifications can be adduced. Yet these two poles of the *classification controversy* seem to move away from the central tenet of speech-act theory, namely an understanding of the phenomenon of illocutionary force. (For a more detailed discussion of the issues involved, see Verschueren 1983.)

The indirectness controversy

21 The lumper attitude, i.e. a strong though implicit preoccupation with grammatical forms, inevitably leads us to the *indirectness controversy*. The intuitive relevance of the notion of an indirect speech act is that in some cases people mean more than what they say. This is true not only with respect to the propositional content of utterances but also with respect to their illocutionary force. Such indirectness needs to be accounted for, which can be done in connection with the propositional content in terms of irony, metaphor, presupposition, some types of implicature, etc., and in connection with the illocutionary force in terms of indirect speech acts (which does not mean that indirect speech acts do not often involve 'unsaid' propositional meaning as well). However, if one adopts the grammar-based lumper position, one is forced to describe not only the request 'Can you pass me the salt?' as an indirect speech act because it is an imperative subtype disguised as an interrogative, but also the explicit performative 'I order you to leave the room' because it functions as an imperative even though its structure is indicative (see, e.g., Van der Auwera 1980b).

22 Leaving aside the issue of whether one should not regard certain propositional features (such as 'I order') as linguistic indicators of illocutionary force on a par with syntactic features (such as grammatical mood), we can regard the conclusion as logically correct. However, the claim of the indirectness (or, for that matter, the nondirectness) of explicit performatives is intuitively vacuous since the speaker does not mean more than what he/she says. If you say 'I promise to bring the book' but you do not bring it, you cannot reply to my accusation of your breaking your promise by saying 'I did not promise, I only stated that I promised to bring the book'. However troublesome vagueness may be, it is less harmful to scholarship than vacuity: though one can fill an empty bottle, no one has ever succeeded as yet in substantiating a vacuous claim.

23   The main argument in favor of the lumper view of explicit performatives is based on the notion of literal meaning: the literal meaning of 'I order you to leave the room' is said to be a statement meaning. The argument can easily be turned against this claim. The idea of literal meaning as being context-free has long been abandoned as a fiction (see, e.g., Searle 1978) and replaced by the meaning a word or an utterance has in some kind of neutral, unmarked, or minimal context. Neutrality and markedness in this sense are basically cognitive notions. A simple test to discover the typically associated minimal context for 'I order you to leave the room' would be to present the sentence to a number of informants and to ask them to construct a typical context for it. I am convinced that practically all of them would come up with a context in which 'I order you to leave the room' is an order rather than one in which it is a reply to a question such as 'What do you do if I make too much noise?'. Hence, the psychologically basic force of the utterance, i.e. the force it has in a maximally neutral context and which can thus be regarded as (one of) its literal force(s), is that of an order. Therefore, no indirectness is involved. I am not advocating the promotion of such tests as the single (or even the main) procedure to decide whether an illocutionary force is directly or indirectly conveyed. It is quite clear that the statement-meaning of 'I order you to leave the room' as a reply to 'What do you do if I make too much noise?' is also quite literal and direct (though the explicit performative reading cannot possibly be said to derive from the statement-sense in the way the indirect meanings of the classical examples of indirect speech-acts derive from their literal meanings, because, for one thing, the tense-value of 'I order' is different for the two cases). Moreover, strict adherence to the test might prove 'Can you pass me the salt?' to be literally and directly a request to pass the salt rather than an indirect speech act. Trying to solve these problems would lead us to a discussion of the different types of conventions involved in language and language use (as in Morgan 1978). All I am interested in here is demonstrating that the notion of literal meaning cannot be relied upon to support the lumper view of indirectness in language.

1.1.3 The Paradox

24   We are confronted with a true paradox. With respect to each of the controversies discussed, I have drawn attention to one or two possible solutions that

have been proposed at some point in the philosophical or linguistic literature. The paradox is this: though each of these solutions is logically sound, at least from some theoretical point of view, they are not compatible with the intuitively correct premises of speech-act theory. Let me recapitulate:
1. Illocutionary force, the fundamental concept of speech-act theory, can be rejected as a valid notion if one believes that it would only be valid if it could be clearly distinguished from other types of meaning. (See paragraphs 9 to 11.)
2. The need for studying the perlocutionary aspect of linguistic action can be opposed by those who want to restrict scholarship to the investigation of more controllable data. (See paragraphs 12 and 13.)
3. Felicity conditions can be discarded if one adheres to the principle that such conditions are acceptable only if they describe all occurrences of speech acts of a certain type, no matter whether they are serious and literal or not, and no matter what sequence they occur in. (See paragraphs 14 to 18.)
4. Searle's insightful classification of illocutionary acts can be rejected if one believes, as do the splitters, in the absolute discreteness of classes in a taxonomy or if one takes grammatical forms in semantic disguise rather than meaning categories as one's starting point, as do the lumpers. (See paragraphs 19 and 20.)
5. The lumpers' implicit but strong preoccupation with grammatical forms also leads to a rebuttal of the contention that explicit performatives are direct rather than indirect or nondirect representatives of the speech-act type they belong to. (See paragraphs 21 to 23.)

These attitudes could make speech-act theory collapse like a house of cards, though not all of them would play an equally important role in the process. Leaving perlocutionary effects untouched only makes the theory incomplete, but abstaining from a basically semantic or pragmatic approach to the classification of speech acts and the problem of indirectness makes the theory less relevant; and the theory is not possible at all without the notion of illocutionary force and the formulation of felicity conditions.

25 In the following paragraphs I shall inquire into the origins of these threats to speech-act theory, with direct reference to some reflections on the study of social action in general (of which linguistic action is one instantiation).

1.2 REFLECTIONS ON THE STUDY OF SOCIAL ACTION

1.2.0 Introduction

26 In spite of the lack of critical reflection that characterizes a great many scientific enterprises, it sometimes looks as if in the humanities and social sciences more attention is paid to methodological problems than to the application of the

proposed methods. Therefore, I would have hesitated to put down the following reflections concerning the social sciences had I not tried to apply the ideas I am defending (see chapters 3 through 6) and if I had no clear view on how to pursue them further (see chapter 8). The ideas themselves are not really new. More than 20 years ago they had already been formulated quite eloquently by the British philosopher Peter Winch. They originated in Max Weber's and Wilhelm Dilthey's visions (see, e.g., Dallmayr & McCarthy, 1977), and probably they can be traced back to the 18th-century philosopher Giambattista Vico, who is often regarded as an early precursor of modern anthropologists and ethnologists. Moreover, numerous applications are to be found in the work of American linguistic anthropologists of this century (see, e.g., Tyler 1969). Why, then, this excursus? First of all, because I believe that some social sciences, and in particular linguistics, have embarked on a one-way course and need to be reminded of some old 'truths'. A second, and less pragmatic, reason is that I hope to show, by means of my way of 'reminding', that also *Verstehen* can be an empirical matter, so that the antagonism between *Verstehen* and *Erklären* can be partly transcended.

1.2.1 Social Action and the Social Sciences

27   Most, if not all, social practices show both universal and particular aspects. If we accept this proposition—without, for the time being, pondering the nature of universality any further and without questioning the existence of universality outside the world of human conceptualization—we must conclude that there is a need for generalization and for dealing with the here-and-now in studies of social behavior. Generalizations can be made soon if a researcher acts as an observer operating with a preconceived framework of abstract and general concepts. The here-and-now can be grasped if an attempt is made to capture the culture-specific understanding of an action that the participants themselves have or, in other words, if one tries to penetrate the conceptual space associated with an action by the participants themselves. Ideally, these two methodological components should be blended into one coherent approach. In practice, they always *are* blended; thus, the framework of abstract and general concepts with which the object of investigation can be approached is, consciously or unconsciously, based on some researcher's previous observations of concrete and particular phenomena. Conversely, it is hard for a scholar to give up his/her habits of generalization, and probably he/she will never succeed completely in abstracting from the abstract and general concepts he/she has been confronted with. But rarely are the two components in balance. Hence the methodological spectrum of the social sciences is a continuum ranging from studies with a high degree of generality to investigations with a high degree of particularity, but with absolutely nothing at the two extremes of the continuum and hardly anything in the middle.

28   It is usually agreed upon that the ultimate aim of scholarship is to be able to make generalizations. Therefore, those studies tending more towards the use of a preconceived framework of abstract and general concepts somehow

seem to go more directly to the point; hence it is not surprising that this approach seems to be favored in the social sciences. I shall say that these investigations use a *theoretical* approach. If the balance leans more toward the culture-specific understanding of some kind of behavior, I shall say that an *empirical-conceptual* method is used. I realize that my usage of the term 'empirical' deviates from common practice; many so-called empirical investigations (e.g. most statistical and other data-oriented studies) apply a purely theoretical method in my terminology. That is why I prefer to introduce the more complex term 'empirical-conceptual'. The empirical-conceptual approach, which corresponds closely to what is usually called *Verstehen* with reference to the humanities and social sciences (as opposed to the biological and physical sciences), is *empirical* because it addresses itself to very specific phenomena that, as will be shown later, can be captured empirically—though in an indirect way—and it is *conceptual* because these phenomena are situated in the world of concepts.

1.2.2 Linguistic Action and Speech-Act Theory

29   In paragraph 1 I claimed that nearly all speech-act scholars, whether linguists or philosophers, approach linguistic action from an essentially theoretical point of view. In other words, they are rarely interested in the speech acts performed in a particular language—not to mention the way in which speakers of a particular natural language conceptualize and understand their own acts. Rather, their concern is mainly with speech-act universals, i.e. traits of linguistic action that are expected to be traceable in all languages. Even when universals are not directly envisaged and an attempt is made to investigate language-specific phenomena empirically, the approach is usually theoretical in the sense defined above; i.e., it is based on a preconceived framework of abstract and general concepts.

30   In order to prevent misunderstandings, I want to repeat my point about the impossibility of absolute generality or universality, with direct reference to speech-act theory. The point is especially clear with respect to existing classifications of speech-act types or, in the professional jargon, of illocutionary acts or illocutionary forces. Though Austin (1962) and especially Searle (1976), to cite the two best known examples, are explicitly interested in classifying the types of speech acts that can be performed in natural language as such—not in one particular language—they cannot avoid taking as their points of reference the English verbs used to perform those acts or to describe them. Thus, though an attempt is made to detach the universal claims from concrete data, they are at least partly based on them.

31   The uniformly theoretical and generalizing approach (only interrupted by a few poorly noticed papers to be mentioned later) is the underlying cause of the problems of speech-act theory. A natural outcome of such a lopsided approach is the relentless growth of mutually independent and often contradictory 'the-

ories'. There is nothing wrong with the existence of those theories as such: most of them can be successfully defended from some theoretical point of view. But (as in most cases where human endeavor gets thwarted by 'frame conflict'; see Schön 1979) because of their mutual independence, which results from differences in the theoretical points of departure (i.e. differences in the preconceived frameworks of abstract and general concepts), most issues remain unresolved.

32   I believe that the issues can be settled only by introducing a counterbalancing empirical-conceptual approach, i.e. by examining the way in which linguistic action is conceptualized by speakers of different natural languages. For instance, what is their notion of indirectness in language, and how do they classify (in a 'folk taxonomy' sense) speech acts? The similarities and differences with respect to such notions discovered between natural languages can constitute the basis for a reappraisal of the universals proposed by theorists. Incidentally, the particularity-oriented approach I am proposing should be thought of as *a possible empirical basis for the study of universals of linguistic action.*

33   The crucial question is now, Why should we not settle the unresolved issues by theorizing even more—and more carefully? Why do we have to cataract down into the pretheoretical world of facts? Does this not mean an intolerable regression of the scientific enterprise? In the next paragraphs the need for supplementing the theoretical method will be explained further.

1.2.3 Theoretical versus Empirical-Conceptual Approach

34   Though the question of whether universals exist in reality or only inside the world of our own conceptualizations is important in its own right, we do not really need an answer in order to justify talking about universals of behavior. Since generalization is one of the basic processes of our cognitive (scientific and prescientific) coping with reality, we can safely assume that what we call the theoretical approach is intrinsically justified and necessary. It seems that the vast majority of social studies have been conducted from this point of view. There are, however, some problems with it, as pointed out by Winch (1958) and reemphasized by McDaniel (1978), among others. One obvious restriction is the fact that abstract and general concepts can never capture the full meaning of social phenomena, which are themselves concrete, particular, and constantly subject to change. Deductive theorists would not really regard this as a problem. It is not so obvious why anyone would want to capture the particularity of social phenomena. The dispute is not necessarily an epistemological one. The main issue is, What kind of knowledge is most appropriate? The answer depends very much on what type of behavior one is trying to understand. The empirical-conceptual approach works on the assumption that what people say and think should be taken 'seriously', which is not always the case; when it is not, then the theoretical approach is particularly appropriate. Moreover, a theory-based method is needed to unmask motives of behavior that may be hidden to the

agents themselves. But even so, an epistemological aspect comes in. Though ultimately the search for universals may be our task, universals are intolerable if they are based on poorly understood particular facts—or if they do not have any correspondence with particularities at all.

35   A stronger plea for supplementing theoretical approaches with the empirical-conceptual method (and a clearer clue as to why it is 'conceptual') is rooted in the meaningfulness of social action. Social action is by definition meaningful in the sense that the participants in the action perceive it in terms of a background of shared meanings. To clarify this idea of shared meanings:

> I posit meaningful acts in the expectation that Others will interpret them meaningfully, and my schema of positing is oriented with respect to the Other's schema of interpretation. On the other hand, I can examine everything which, as a product of Others, presents itself to me for meaningful interpretation as to the meaning which the Other who has produced it may have connected with it. Thus, in these reciprocal acts of positing meaning, and of interpretation of meaning, my social world of mundane intersubjectivity is built; it is also the social world of Others, and all other social and cultural phenomena are founded upon it. (Schuetz 1967:468)

Similarly,

> Habermas argues that access to a symbolically structured object domain calls for procedures that are logically distinct from those developed in the natural sciences, procedures designed to grasp the 'meaning' that is constitutive of social reality. Social action depends on the agent's 'definition of the situation', and this is not solely a matter of subjective motivations. (McCarthy 1979:xi)

Thus there is a fundamental unity between the actor's *concepts* and the *practices* they serve to conceptualize. (Notice that this formulation implies the nonunity of the entities of which it is claimed that they are one; I have not found a way of avoiding this problem in English; therefore I would like the reader to condone further manifestations of the same linguistic flabbiness.) Action is always interpreted action. It was Gotthold Ephraim Lessing who remarked that it is unjust to give any action a different name from that which it used to bear in its own time and amongst its own people, even though it may be true that the actions are always the same in themselves, however different the times and the societies in which they occur.[3] This is because all actions have an 'understood context'. If there is such a strong unity between actions and concepts, then a full under-

---

[3] Actually, Winch (1958) starts his book with the following quote from Lessing (1778:423): 'Denn wenn es schon wahr ist, dass moralische Handlungen, sie mögen zu noch so verschiednen Zeiten, bei noch so verschiednen Völkern vorkommen, in sich betrachtet immer die nämlichen bleiben, so haben doch darum die nämlichen Handlungen nicht immer die nämlichen Benennungen, und es ist ungerecht, irgendeiner eine andere Benennung zu geben als die, welche sie zu ihren Zeiten und bie ihrem Volk zu haben pflegte.'

standing of social phenomena can be reached only if studies based on a preconceived framework of abstract and general concepts are supplemented with an attempt to penetrate the conceptual world of the participants in the action or behavior to be described. In other words (borrowed from Schuetz), the social scientist's 'second-level constructs' cannot be adequate without an understanding of the social actor's 'first-level constructs'.

1.2.4 The Unity of Practice and Concept

36   At this point it is certainly useful to illustrate the unity between concepts and practices. My examples, some of which are based on illustrations given by Winch (1958) and McDaniel (1978), show at the same time the failure of the theoretical approach to capture the particularity of social phenomena.

Consider, for example, the fixed rules of interaction between members of different castes in India. Employing his/her framework of comparative concepts, a theory-oriented researcher would characterize a 'caste' as a 'class without mobility'. There is nothing wrong with this description as such. But in that way the real cultural meaning that the caste system has for people in India would get lost: it is a hierarchical ranking of men and groups in terms of religious criteria of purity of which the hierarchy, the strict separation, and the division of labor are overt manifestations. (McDaniel quotes Dumont 1970 as an excellent attempt to penetrate this meaning of the caste system.)

To take an easier example, consider the practice of bathing. Bathing is not just a matter of cleaning oneself with water. In the United States and other parts of the Western world it is associated with hygiene and sex appeal. In a number of non-Western cultures it is associated with the purification of the soul.

Or take the conceptual apparatus that Freud developed to explain neuroses. If a psychiatrist wants to reveal the origin of neuroses among, say, the Trobrianders, it would be unwise for him/her to apply Freud's ideas without further reflection. First he/she would have to grasp many of their own culture-specific concepts, such as their concept of fatherhood.

37   Similarly, it is wrong for an anthropologist operating with Western standards of rationality and observing the frequent recourse to magic by a primitive culture to conclude that these people's behavior is basically irrational. The fact that the Azande, as Winch (1964) pointed out, blame all instances of bad fortune on witchcraft does not mean that they do not perceive reality clearly: they see as well as we do that the woman was not killed by a witch but by the roof of her hut that collapsed because of a tree that fell on it because of the strong wind. Or again, the constant use of magic by the Melanesian tribes studied by Malinowski (1954) does not prevent their minds from working with scientific accuracy: they know that rich crops depend mainly on precise and hard work and that safe sailing is in the first place a function of the application of certain principles of stability and hydrodynamics. So, why magic? Here is Malinowski's reply:

> Thus there is a clear-cut division: there is first the well-known set of conditions, the natural course of growth, as well as the ordinary pests and dangers to be warded off by fencing and weeding. On the other hand there is the domain of the unaccountable and adverse influences, as well as the great unearned increment of fortunate coincidence. The first conditions are coped with by knowledge and work, the second by magic. (1954:29)

If scientific experiments do not work, the experimenter's conclusion is usually that there was something wrong with the setup. Likewise with magic. The fact that it often does not work does not destroy the belief in it: if a ritual does not have the expected effect, its performance must have been improper somehow. Witherspoon (1977) reports that every time he witnessed the Navajos' rain dance, it started raining within 24 hours, but only once was the precipitation enough to be of any help. The Navajos' reaction was to smile and say 'How feeble-minded we've become'. (Thus it is not surprising that certain rituals make allowance for the possibility of failure. In this connection we think of the so-called poison oracle among the Azande, as described, e.g., by Winch 1964. To find out whether someone's witchcraft was the cause of some misfortune, poison is administered to a fowl. A yes-no question is formulated and the response value of the bird's death or survival (in terms of yes or no) is fixed in advance. Afterwards, the correctness of the oracle's response is checked by administering the poison to a second bird while asking whether the previous answer was correct or not.) It should be clear from such examples that detaching social behavior from the participants' own interpretation of it, though useful for certain purposes, is in general an unwarranted reduction.

38 It may be interesting to point out, in passing, that the idea of the unity between concept and practice is in keeping with one of the fundamental principles of *phenomenology*. Instead of departing from a single basic principle, such as Descartes' *cogito*, phenomenology takes as its starting point an entire field of original experiences, basic acts of consciousness. Such acts are always intentional: consciousness is always consciousness of something.

> If, then, an act of a certain structure is present, then by that very fact a certain object is also present; moreover, the character of this object is co-determined by the character of the act in which the object appears. The character, therefore, of the known object depends on the character of the act by which it is grasped. (Kockelmans 1967:32-33)

Applied to the topic of this chapter, this can be translated as follows: if social actors conceptualize their own practices, as they certainly do, the character of those practices must be partly determined by their own way of perceiving them.[4]

---

[4] The reader should resist the temptation to conclude from this digression that I am advocating a phenomenological approach to language. In spite of some similarity with respect to basic principles, any phenomenology of language will look substantially different from what I have in mind. Indeed, E. Husserl seems to have defended the idea of a general and a priori grammar, which would be an extremely theoretical approach (see Jakobson 1970:13).

39   Another field of scholarship (partly derived from phenomenological principles) that brings out how intricately concepts and actions are related is *ethnomethodology*. Probably it suffices to refer to some student experiments reported by Garfinkel (1972). Garfinkel asked his students to go home and try to give up some of their basic assumptions, for instance by imagining that they were paying boarders instead of part of the family. Dwelling on the results would be superfluous. It will be clear that in this way even the most common everyday actions can be shown to get a radically different meaning—i.e. to *be* radically different—if the tacit background assumptions, the ideas of the participants, are changed. Hence the importance ethnomethodologists attach to the discovery of implicit meanings in everyday conversations. That is why sociologists of the ethnomethodological tradition (see, e.g., Sudnow 1972) rather than linguists have started most of modern discourse analysis and conversational analysis (with 'classical' papers such as Sacks, Schegloff, & Jefferson 1974).

1.2.5 The Empirical-Conceptual Approach to Social Action

40   Once we have accepted as a necessity the attempt to understand the social agent's own views of what he/she is doing, we are confronted with a technical question: How can we achieve such understanding? Are we concerned with the type of contemplation that is often associated with *Verstehen*? Or are there any empirical procedures and observable data to rely on?

41   An apparent impediment is the impossibility for a scholar of abstracting from the general conceptual framework he/she has acquired. Following Gadamer's (1975) hermeneutical line of thought we can say that such a 'limitation' is no impediment at all, but rather the very prerequisite for understanding. Understanding results from a dialogue between one's beliefs and the observation of new phenomena. (How we can exploit this dialectic pattern in the study of linguistic action will not become totally clear until the last chapter of this book.)

42   There are, however, a couple of real problems. For one thing, as far as I can tell, there is no *direct* way of studying a person's conceptualization of his/her own actions. But it can be studied *indirectly* if one accepts that there is some kind of relationship between words and concepts. The existence of such a relationship is taken for granted by many scholars. Winch, for instance, after discussing the link between the actor's concepts and his/her actions, changes his topic to the link between words and social behavior: 'To give an account of the meaning of a word is to describe how it is used; and to describe how it is used is to describe the social intercourse into which it enters' (1958:123). Winch, whose ideas were strongly influenced by Wittgenstein (1953), illustrates this contention by quoting a book on social services in which it is claimed that it is the duty of a social worker to establish a relationship of friendship with her [sic!] clients, but that she must never forget that her first duty is to the policy of the agency by which she is employed. The notion of friendship used to exclude this sort of divided loyalty. According to Winch, this change in the notion of friendship re-

flects a change in social relationships. Indeed, a society in which one no longer makes a distinction between a friend and an acquaintance is probably a society that, because of its extreme mobility, is in need of instant friendship: make friends fast, otherwise the people you meet will be gone before you get around to knowing them.

43 If, then, there is a relationship between words and concepts, it should be possible to learn something about the conceptual space associated with certain practices by examining the words and expressions that the participants in the action have at their disposal to talk about those practices. The hermeneutic circle is playing tricks: it is not really possible to understand the one without understanding the other, and vice versa. But if we take this circle not as an evil spirit haunting our intellectual enterprise but as one of its inevitable structural features, then the proposed word-oriented procedure provides us with *an indirect way of approaching the practices we want to comprehend in an empirical-conceptual way*. After all, this kind of approach has already been used for decades by American linguistic anthropologists (see, e.g., Tyler 1969).

44 If the empirical-conceptual method is limited in the sense that the social agent's conceptual world can be approached only indirectly, we are now confronted with a second problem. My claim that an agent's conceptualization of his/her own behavior can be indirectly investigated by scrutinizing the words and expressions he/she has at his/her disposal to talk about the actions in question was predicated on the assumption that there is 'some kind of relationship between words and concepts'. But what kind of a relationship is it? To come back to Winch's example, it is clear that a person's belonging to a society with a changed notion of friendship does not mean that he/she is incapable of old-style friendship, or of conceiving it. We would not want to make the Whorfian mistake (which Alford (1978) and Silverstein (1979) have convincingly shown not to have been Whorf's error but the brainchild of his critics) of positing a one-to-one correspondence between words and concepts and claiming that language completely determines thought. In order to clarify the relationship between language and thought, one could compare language with Kuhn's (1962) notion of a scientific paradigm.[5] Though a language, in particular its lexicon, by no means determines the capacity of its speakers to draw distinctions, it does reflect the distinctions they *habitually* draw. The *reflection*, moreover, is not perfect: it is like the reflection on the surface of a pond rather than in a mirror. Though there will be some distortions, the *Gestalt* is recognizable. That Whorf also was in fact thinking about *conceptualization habits*, is suggested by the title of one of the classical articles containing his basic views: 'The relation of habitual thought and behavior to language' (1956).[6]

---

[5] I am borrowing the comparison from R. D. Van Valin (1976).

[6] The development of the 'radical' version of the Sapir-Whorf hypothesis, or the lin-

45 Reformulating paragraph **43** in those terms, we can say that since the lexicon of a language (conceived here as a collection of words and expressions) reflects the conceptual distinctions that its speakers habitually draw, it becomes possible to penetrate the conceptual space that the participants in an action associate with it by scrutinizing the words and expressions that their language provides for talking about the action in question. When doing this type of research, however, one should never lose sight of the limitations we have specified.

46 So far, our discussion of *linguistic reflections of conceptualization habits* has been restricted to the lexicon. It goes without saying that, in addition to words and expressions, speaking about forms of behavior in any language involves a number of other linguistic means that are equally or similarly indicative of an underlying network of concepts. Whorf liked focusing on grammatical structures. The same trend has reappeared in more recent work, such as Silverstein's (1979) paper 'Language structure and linguistic ideology'. Moreover, not only the fixed repertory of linguistic *means* that members of a community have at their disposal to define and describe a form of social action can be studied to penetrate the conceptual space associated with it. Equally valid conclusions can be drawn from the *way* in which certain activities are actually spoken about in given circumstances. A reliable source of data for conclusions concerning conceptualizations is the network of presuppositions or background assumptions characterizing any text or any conversation; see, e.g., Verschueren (1982a).

47 *Lexical* reflections of conceptualization habits can be particularly potent when they involve *metaphors*. The relationship between language and thought is crystallized in metaphorical usage. Comparing is an important thought process. When using metaphors to talk about a particular phenomenon, one compares it with another one. A large proportion of everyday repertory of words and expressions—even of what is normally regarded as 'literal'—is metaphorical in nature and, therefore, reflects comparative conceptualizations. Lakoff and Johnson (1980) have recently provided us with scores of examples showing how consistently metaphors (e.g. 'Time is money') pervade our everyday ways of speaking (e.g. one can 'waste' time or 'save' it, one can 'spend' one's time or use it 'profitably', something can 'cost' a lot of time, and time can be 'invested'). Especially— but not only—when comparisons remain more or less unconscious, as is the case with most so-called dead metaphors, they do not just *reflect* but also *influence* patterns of thinking, as a result of which they can also influence behavior. That is why Lakoff and Johnson (1980) call them 'metaphors we live by' and why Schön (1979) introduces the term 'generative metaphor'.

---

guistic relativity hypothesis, which reflects the ideas of neither Sapir (see, e.g., Sapir 1921) nor Whorf, would be an interesting topic of investigation for the history of the humanities and social sciences. It once induced me to start writing a paper—which never got finished— entitled 'Was Whorf really stupid?'.

1.3 AN EMPIRICAL-CONCEPTUAL APPROACH TO LINGUISTIC ACTION

1.3.0 Introduction

48 It should be clear (especially from paragraph **46**) that a wide range of empirical-conceptual approaches to social action in general and to linguistic action in particular are possible. For these prolegomena, and especially for the exploratory exercises of Part II, a choice had to be made. In the next section this choice is spelled out, its limitations clarified, and hints given on how to transcend those limitations. Afterwards, an overview of related previous work is presented. And finally, in an epilogue on 'linguistic expansionism', it is claimed that the approach proposed may help to save pragmatics from becoming the dead end of linguistics.

1.3.1 The Comparative Lexical Approach

49 Verbalizations of many aspects of social life have been investigated by cultural, especially linguistic, anthropologists. Linguistic action, however, has mainly been theorized about. It is true that verbs used in the performance and description of speech acts have been studied, but such studies were usually undertaken not only in view of the advancement of the theory (which is one of my ultimate aims as well) but also with strong theoretical prejudices; remember the attempts to classify speech-act types (e.g. Austin 1962; Fraser 1974; McCawley 1977; Searle 1976; Vendler 1972). As was recently pointed out by Pratt (1980) and convincingly shown by Rosaldo (1980), speech-act theory, the framework for most of those studies, does itself embody an ideology (in particular an excessively 'privatized' view of language) that is not necessarily applicable to other speech communities. This finding is entirely in keeping with the more general assumption, put forward by Harris (1980), that theories of language are geared to (the needs of) the societies in which they are created.

50 The existing theoretical approaches could be counterbalanced, for instance, by a systematic study of the words and expressions used to describe linguistic action, which is needed in order to lift part of the veil that is covering the language user's culture-specific and language-specific experience or conceptualization of his/her own speech activity. In other words, I am advocating one type of empirical-conceptual approach to linguistic action, namely a *lexical approach*. By undertaking this type of research, a significant—though not totally new—contribution to the study of linguistic action can be made. In the exercises of Chapters 3 through 6 (narrowing the topic of this book to a small number of relatively small subfields of the vast expanse of words and phrases used to describe linguistic action), an attempt will be made to keep the approach as theory-free as possible (though, for contrastive purposes, references will be made to the existing literature concerning the areas or aspects of linguistic action covered by those subfields). My hope is that thrusting the methodological balance to the opposite extreme may reveal more clearly than a 'mature' application would have done how a lexical approach can provide us with revealing data concerning linguistic action, on the basis of which the many unresolved theoretical issues can be tackled. Thus the exploratory exercises of Part II mainly serve a didactic purpose. Further research, however, will have to recognize the impossibility of abstracting completely from theories. Only such recognition can guard us against pitfalls similar, though opposite, to those that victimized speech-act theory. How pragmatic theories (or one coherent pragmatic theory) can be fruitfully used while an honest empirical-conceptual approach is being pursued is hinted at in Chapter 2 and further explained in Chapter 8.

51   Briefly, whereas theorists of linguistic action have been trying to explain *how people do things with words*, I propose to undertake a supplementary study of *what people say they do with words*. In this book we will be less interested in what people *actually* say than in what they *can* say about their verbal behavior. Trying to reveal the (lexically reflected) concepts they have at their disposal is probably the more basic question of the two in view of the fact that people do not always say what they mean. Let me formulate the enterprise in another different way. Trying to leave speech-act theory behind us—and, at best, we can only partly succeed—we shall take a guided tour through (certain aspects of) linguistic action with language itself as our guide.

52   Some additional remarks are called for. First, linguistic action provides us with an area in which the unity between action and concept is particularly clear, so clear in fact that it is almost tempting to postulate a complete overlap between words, concepts, and actions. The area I am thinking of is that particular subfield of the set of lexical items used to describe linguistic action that contains the truly performative verbs, i.e. the verbs that, if used in the first person singular simple present indicative active, are devices for the performance of the very same acts as the ones they describe when used differently. Since, in most contexts, saying seriously and literally 'I promise that P' constitutes an act of promising, the verb TO PROMISE is more than just a reflection of a conceptual category that happens to be associated with some type of verbal behavior. Somehow the word, the concept, and the action seem to be co-extensive; no doubt most speech-act theorists would hotly deny this because it shows the weakness of their universal claims based on concrete monolinguistic data. This strong link can probably be generalized to nonperformative speech-act verbs (i.e. all other verbs describing speech-act types) since, as I have shown elsewhere (see Verschueren 1977: Chapter 1), the two classes are not strictly separable; rather, there is a performativity continuum running through the complete set of speech-act verbs. The further a verb is removed from the truly performative type, the weaker the word-

concept-action overlap may be expected to become. Without pressing the point too strongly, I'd like to suggest that this is an area in which the limitations of the lexical approach (as specified in paragraph **42** and **44**) are themselves limited.

53   Second, the type of investigation I propose will lead us not only into the domain of linguistic activity covered by speech-act theory. Obviously, words and expressions describing linguistic action can focus on any of a large number of its aspects, not only on the speech-act type. In part II, I concentrate on four relatively small subfields of the words and expressions used to describe linguistic action, each of which is representative of a particular level of verbal behavior. Chapter 3 deals with the most marginal aspect of linguistic action imaginable, namely the semantics of silence, the absence of speech. The semantics of lying, related to propositional content, is next. Illocutionary force, the traditional domain of speech-act theory, is represented only in a chapter on directing. Chapter 6 deals with conversational routines, concentrating on those for which at least some languages do not provide a descriptive term.

54   Third, the relevance of the investigation can be expected to increase dramatically as soon as a comparative perspective is brought in. The enterprise is essentially open-ended because of the infinite possibilities of historical, crosscultural, and crosslinguistic comparison, but also because of the possibility of significant differentiation within one culture and one language at any particular time. What I am advocating is a *comparative lexical approach* to linguistic action: the comparative study of the sets of words (not only verbs but also nouns and maybe even adjectives and adverbs), idioms, and other fixed formulae and expressions used to describe linguistic action. In this book the applications are restricted to verbs and verblike expressions. The comparative aspect of the investigation is also restricted: the selected subfields are only studied contrastively in English and Dutch. A comparison between two less related languages (as in Rosaldo 1980 and Stross 1974) might have been more revealing, but if interesting conclusions can be drawn from a comparison between two languages that are so closely related, the same must a fortiori be true for all other confrontations. Moreover, the absence of dramatic differences obliges us to pay more attention to details. In Chapter 8 perspectives are opened on how to exploit the comparative aspect of the lexical, empirical-conceptual approach optimally.

1.3.2. Related Work

55   I do not want to create the impression that similar investigations have never been advocated or attempted before. After all, Austin is said to have defended a strongly verb-oriented approach himself, though he never got around to applying it extensively. Here are more examples to the contrary.

56   After arguing that speech-act descriptions have no place in linguistics—a position I would certainly not want to support—L. J. Cohen (1974), for instance, contends that linguists could shed light on the problem of speech acts by discussing the terms used in describing speech acts and by surveying the empirically detectable varieties of ways in which these terms function and the empirically detectable varieties of conditions for applying them. He even lists a number of relevant semantic dimensions of the words and phrases used in describing what people do with words. Unfortunately, his proposal has gone largely unnoticed so that further reflections on its relevance are hard to find.

57 Nevertheless, some attempts have been made, for instance by D. Lehmann (1976a, 1976b), H. Jessen (1979), the Berliner Gruppe (n.d.) which prepared a lengthy—still unpublished—manuscript on German speech-act verbs, and Ballmer and Brennenstuhl (1981). Other scholars such as J. Allwood (see 1976, 1978) have a definite interest in this kind of research but do not want to embark on it until they have constructed a satisfactory theory of linguistic action that can be taken as their point of departure. Also French linguists (e.g. Létoublon 1980), attracted by the interesting phenomenon of delocutivity[7] (originally pointed out by Benveniste 1966; see also Anscombre 1980 and Ducrot 1980), have taken an interest in speech-act verbs. As far as I can tell, however, none of these researchers derive their interest from a methodological commitment similar to mine. It is true that Ballmer and Brennenstuhl (1981) claim that the object of their book is 'to lay the foundations for a sound theory of linguistic behavior of human beings' (p. 3), but they construct their 8 model groups, their 24 models and typifications, and their 600 categories of speech acts completely a priori and only fill them up later with the speech activity verbs they find in English. (See Verschueren 1983.)

58 One scholar whose attitude is closer to mine is Meyer-Hermann. His recent work (e.g. 1978) shows a clear interest in what people say about linguistic activity for the sake of a better understanding of what linguistic action is. However, he concentrates on what they *actually* say rather than on the lexical reflection of the concepts they have at their disposal to talk about verbal behavior. Though I believe that the latter is the more basic of the two enterprises, they are both necessary and, in practice, mutually dependent. Another excellent example of this approach is Seitel's (1974) study of the metaphors and proverbs the Hayas use to talk about speech.

59 Inquiries in which an inference is drawn from the mere presence of certain lexical items to the way in which verbal behavior is conceptualized or experienced in a particular language community are rare. A marginal example is Kernan, Sodergren, and French's (1977) brief account of Belizian City Creole in which it is claimed that 'the proliferation of metalinguistic terms for types of

---

[7]Verbs are said to be 'delocutive' if they are derived from locutions (e.g. Latin SALUTARE, English TO OKAY).

speech acts is indicative of the cultural emphasis on speech and cultural appreciation of talented and elegant speech behavior' (p. 36).

60 More to the point is Stross' (1974) article on the metalinguistic terms of Tenejapa Tzeltal in which different forms of speaking are distinguished along the—for us unlikely—semantic dimensions of time (e.g. talking on Thursday, yesterday, last year, etc.), place (e.g. talking at home, in the field, etc.), and bodily posture (e.g. talking while lying down, etc.). And so is Rosaldo's (1982) study of Ilongot speech-act verbs, in which she shows a link between ways of thinking about language and about human agency and personhood; in particular, it is shown that the less 'privatized' views of the Ilongot result in a lower importance of representative acts, a higher importance of directive acts, and an almost complete absence of commissives, all of which is reflected in their lexicalization of linguistic action. These and similar studies belong to the tradition of the *ethnography of speaking* (see, e.g., Bauman & Sherzer 1974; Hymes 1974), which partly overlaps with the goals and methodological commitments of the empirical-conceptual approach to linguistic action. It is within this tradition that most of the studies relevant to the topic of this book are to be situated; see, e.g., Abrahams and Bauman (1971), Crumrine (1968), Feld and Schieffelin (1981), Finnegan (1969), Frake (1972), Gossen (1974), Kochman (1972), Mitchell-Kernan (1971).

61 Equally interesting is Reddy's (1979) insightful paper called 'The conduit methaphor—A case of frame conflict in our language about language'. Here is how he announces the theme of his article:

> In this paper, I am going to present evidence that the stories English speakers tell about communication are largely determined by semantic structures of the language itself. This evidence suggests that English has a preferred framework for conceptualizing about communication, and can bias thought process towards this framework, even though nothing more than common sense is necessary to devise a different, more accurate framework.' (p. 285)

Reddy claims that the basic view of linguistic communication that emerges from the English words and expressions used to describe it could be called the 'conduit metaphor': language is a channel through which thoughts are conveyed; the speaker puts his/her thoughts in at one end and at the other the hearer catches them; the thoughts are really in the words. He gives dozens of illustrations such as 'Try to GET your THOUGHTS ACROSS better', 'None of Mary's FEELINGS CAME THROUGH TO ME with any clarity', 'You still haven't GIVEN ME any IDEA of what you mean', 'Try to PACK more THOUGHT INTO fewer words' and 'That THOUGHT IS IN practically every other WORD'. Reddy claims that this metaphor distorts reality: a hearer never simply receives thoughts; instead, understanding results from an active process of interpretation, i.e. from hard work. In terms of the conduit metaphor, failure to communicate seems impossible as long as the speaker uses the 'right' words; success appears to be automatic. Reddy also elaborates on the dangerous impact such a distorted view can have on language-related behavior. I believe that he overstates his point a little in that he loses sight of the partial truth on which the conduit metaphor is based. If it were not true that somehow language is responsible for thought processes (in other words, that there *are* ideas in the words), then there would be no basis for him to contend that the metaphor can be perilous. But this does not undermine the importance of Reddy's claims.

1.4 EPILOGUE: LINGUISTIC EXPANSIONISM

62   Linguistic explanation procedures are characterized by a typically expansionistic mentality. If we regard the scale phonology-morphology-syntax-semantics-pragmatics as a hierarchy of levels of linguistic description, we can say that whenever arguments for a particular explanation include evidence from another level of description, this 'other level of description' is invariably higher up on the scale or completely outside the scale on a higher level of generality. Thus, a paper on syntax may refer to semantic or pragmatic data or theories, an article on language acquisition may look for an explanation in terms of cognition, a typological study may consider processing factors, a phonological problem may be explained on the basis of physiological phenomena, a grammatical problem may find a solution in sociocultural factors, etc. The view is even explicitly defended that such explanation procedures are necessary, and it is this view that dominated the semantic criticism of transformational grammar and that has caused the avalanche of pragmatic writings.

63   Pragmatics has blessed and complicated linguistics by bringing in social structures, cultural patterns, cognitive notions, psychology in general, and, occasionally, even parapsychology. But pragmatics is not only the universal benefactor that offers linguists a way out whenever they get stuck. There are also purely pragmatic notions that themselves require clarification and explanation. The most central one is the concept *linguistic action*.

64   The main problem of pragmatics seems to be that, by definition, it is the all-encompassing level of the hierarchical structure of linguistics. And since linguists, due to the common explanation procedure sketched, have never learned to go back to a lower hierarchical level to gain insight in their object of investigation, the notion of linguistic action has been mainly subjected to a theoretical or speculative approach in the sense described above and with the somewhat disastrous results discussed. This does not mean that the theoretical approach has not produced anything worthwhile. It definitely has; see, e.g., Habermas' article on universal pragmatics (1979). But theorizing becomes too easily circular, as we have demonstrated in connection with speech-act theory.

And if there is no way of breaking out of the circle—and there isn't, if the only possible direction of explanation is upward—then we must conclude that *pragmatics* is *the dead end of linguistics*, in which case the avalanche of pragmatic writings can only be expected—in keeping with the characteristic action of an avalanche—to cover up what it falls on top of, viz. what is interesting in language as a form of social behavior.

65 Dead-end streets are only dangerous when they are, at the same time, one-way streets. Fortunately, for linguistics there seems to be *an explanatory way back*. In particular, the proposed empirical-conceptual, lexical approach to linguistic action is an example of reversing the direction of explanation in linguistics: results of lexical-semantic investigations function as evidence for or against statements about a pragmatic notion.

66 Before offering the four illustrative applications of the comparative lexical approach to linguistic action (Chapters 3 through 6), some lexical-semantic questions must be addressed. This is done in the next chapter. In the meantime, I want to repeat my point that this study, though evidently particularity-oriented, should be regarded as an exercise preparing a potentially infinite series of wide-ranging comparative investigations (the concrete form of which is indicated in Chapter 8) that could be an *empirical basis* for reflections on *universals of linguistic action*. Because of the indirectness of the approach, the empirical-conceptual method, as applied to linguistic action (the subject matter of pragmatics), could be called *metapragmatics*. And *metapragmatic terms in natural languages* constitute its subject matter.

CHAPTER **2**

PROBLEMS OF LEXICAL SEMANTICS

2.0 INTRODUCTION

67 In the previous chapter I have issued a manifesto professing the belief that the existing theories of linguistic action (and in particular speech-act theory) suffer from some kind of anemia due to the lack of an acceptable decision procedure to settle unresolved issues, and that investigations of what people say they do with words could furnish us with (part of) such a procedure and hence increase the vitality of the theories. It was also announced that this essay would be restricted to the comparative study of some relatively small subfields of the English and Dutch words and phrases used to describe linguistic action. To the theoretical preliminaries of the first chapter (which should not be thought of as a full-fledged theory), some methodological preliminaries (which do not constitute a full-fledged methodology either) need to be added. Therefore, a few central problems of (comparative) lexical semantics will be addressed in the following sections:
1. What are lexical items? How does one decide which word groups, if any, should be treated as lexical items and which ones should not? The answers to these questions will enable us to define our object of investigation more precisely.
2. How can the meaning of lexical items be described? What are the limitations of componential analysis and semantic field theory as methods to describe the internal semantic structure of lexical items and their external semantic relationships, respectively, and how can they be transcended? In this context, the notions of prototype, basic level term, scene, and frame are introduced. Some reflections on abstractness in lexical semantics will be added.

3. How can one elude the danger of circularity in semantic analyses? The answer to this question will reveal the need for a coherent pragmatic theory when trying to maximize the benefits of the empirical-conceptual approach to linguistic action (see also paragraph **50** and Chapter 8).
4. How can analyses be represented? Here the notion of a semantic dimension (as opposed to a semantic class) will be brought in.

All of the problems scrutinized are bound to arise when undertaking comparative investigations of complex areas of the lexicon.

2.1 PROBLEM 1: WHAT ARE LEXICAL ITEMS?

2.1.1 Simple versus Complex Lexicalizations

68 In the first chapter, I advocated a comparative study of the sets of words, idioms, and other fixed formulae or expressions used in natural languages to describe linguistic action. Groups of words such as TO BEAT AROUND THE BUSH (i.e. 'talking without coming to the point') or the Dutch IEMAND IETS IN DE SCHOENEN SCHUIVEN (literally 'to shove something into somebody's shoes', meaning 'to accuse somebody unjustly of something'), the meaning of which cannot easily be derived from the senses of the component elements, we call *idioms*. The *other fixed formulae* or *collocations* are expressions with a more transparent meaning such as TO PRONOUNCE X AND Y HUSBAND AND WIFE (i.e. 'to marry X and Y). In that way idioms and other fixed formulae are by no means two completely separate classes of linguistic entities. Together they constitute what I shall henceforth refer to as *complex lexicalizations*. They are contrasted with *words* (i.e. monomorphemic words, derived words, and many compounds), which I call *simple lexicalizations*. Both simple and complex lexicalizations are *lexical items*.

69 There is a motivation, however trivial, for using the deverbative noun *lexicalization*. It is meant to keep reminding us that what we are talking about are not just linguistic entities but lexicalized (i.e. linguistically processed) forms of something else, viz. of parts of the conceptual space, associated with an area of experience, that has developed in a particular language community.

70 There is no clear-cut boundary between simple and complex lexicalizations. Most compounds are borderline cases. For instance, TO BADMOUTH (i.e. 'to criticize or disparage, often spitefully or unfairly') is sometimes characterized as an idiom. Yet I am inclined to include it in the class of simple lexicalizations. On the other hand, a DEAR JOHN LETTER (i.e. 'a letter that a girlfriend writes to break off an engagement or that a wife writes to ask for a divorce') is prone to be described as a compound word. Not only is it impossible to guess the meaning of this word group on the basis of an adequate understanding of its component elements. It has become such a unique semantic unity that, though the prototypical writer of a DEAR JOHN LETTER is a woman and in spite of the maleness of JOHN, even men can be said to write a Dear John letter to a woman. Furthermore, the formation seems to be getting productive in the sense that it is possible to hear a woman say, rather sarcastically, to a man, 'Thank you very much for that nice Dear John phone call of yours'. Yet I am inclined to regard a DEAR JOHN LETTER as a complex lexicalization. To justify these inclinations—which have no serious consequences—I rely on some rather arbitrary indices such as orthographical unity and unitary stress. Note, however, that the index of orthographical unity will not be used in cases such as prepositional verbs such as TO TALK ABOUT (SOMETHING) and phrasal verbs such as TO ORDER (SOMEONE) ABOUT, which are simple lexicalizations.

2.1.2 Why Study Complex Lexicalizations?

71   The first question a reader may be inclined to ask is, How can you justify including *groups of words* (such as TO BEAT AROUND THE BUSH and TO PRONOUNCE X AND Y HUSBAND AND WIFE) into your topic of investigation if you pretend to be doing *lexical semantics* (which is generally defined as the study of *word meaning*)? Bolinger (1975) offers a potential reply but adds a related problem:

> Since the lexicon purports to record all the pre-set meaning-bearing units of a language, ideally it would have to include every collocation as well as every word. In practice this is impossible—and probably in theory too. Practically, there would be no room. Theoretically, one would not know where to stop, because collocations shade off into more or less freely formed constructions and fluctuate too much from place to place and from individual to individual. Furthermore, there is no reliable way to test them, at least at the borders between collocations and constructions. (p. 105)

We will return to Bolinger's objection later. It is sufficient for now to note that it would be suspicious to find only categories with clear boundaries in the description of a phenomenon that is itself in constant fluctuation. An immediate corollary of this stance is the commitment to undertaking intrinsically endless jobs; note, however, that the apparent finiteness of certain types of investigation is rarely more than an illusion.

72   Let us return to the first question now. Whether including groups of words in the subject matter of lexical semantics is justified depends largely on one's purpose. In order to clarify this point, let me recall my reasons for undertaking the comparative investigations I advocate, in the form of a chain of beliefs (which have been defended in the first chapter). So far, linguistic action has mainly been approached from a theoretical point of view, i.e. with a preconceived framework of abstract and general concepts (as in philosophical speech-

act theory and most of the linguistic studies based on it). However, the nature of social practices (of which acts of speaking form one important subset) is partly determined by the concepts with which the participants in these practices associate them. The lexicon of a language is a reflection—however imperfect it may be—of the conceptual distinctions its speakers habitually draw; therefore, studying the lexical items speakers of different natural languages have at their disposal to describe linguistic acts may yield insights into people's conceptualization of linguistic action and thus into the nature of linguistic action itself. The necessity to take complex lexicalizations (i.e. word groups) into account is quite clear if we do not just think about a lexical semantic investigation in terms of the study of part of the lexicon as such, but as a reflection of underlying conceptualizations. Every lexicalization of reality or experience, whether simple or complex, is a unique reflection of some conceptualization habit. We have shown this in connection with a DEAR JOHN LETTER (paragraph 70). Further illustrations are not hard to find.

73   While further demonstrating the unique reflection of conceptualization habits in complex (as well as simple) lexicalizations, we can at the same time point out some different types of relationships between the lexical forms and the object or event they are applicable to.

First, there is the *exemplifying* relation. An illustration is, once more, our DEAR JOHN LETTER. A letter in which a wife asks for a divorce or a girlfriend breaks off an engagement is not likely to start with 'Darling' or 'Honey', but rather a distant mode of address will be chosen, such as 'Dear John' or, more general 'Dear X' where X stands for the hearer's given name. The term is exemplifying in two ways: it represents a particular mode of address (which is not the only one possible) and it picks out the name 'John' as an example.

Second, the relationship can be *analytical*, as when the expression TO RAISE ONE'S BLOOD SUGAR LEVEL is used instead of the verb TO EAT. The activity of eating is analyzed in terms of what it does for the body. Thus, as a matter of course, the expression is mainly used in circles where there is a strong (though often simply fashionable) preoccupation or obsession with health (which makes it particularly appropriate in Cyra McFadden's *The Serial*). There is a comparable formula in Dutch, namely CALORIEËN SLIKKEN (lit. 'to swallow calories'). Here the eating substance is analyzed. Saying 'I think it is about time for me to go and raise my blood sugar level' or 'Ik denk dat het tijd wordt nog eens wat calorieën te gaan slikken' (lit. 'I think it is about time again to go and swallow some calories') is somehow a euphemistic denial of the fact that what one is about to do is satisfying some primary bodily need or indulging in some earthly delights; it almost sounds like 'I am sorry, I simply have to, otherwise I wouldn't do such a thing'.

Third, there are *metaphorical* relations. A clear example of a metaphor is TO CASH IN ONE'S CHIPS meaning TO DIE. Even dead metaphors such as TO KICK THE BUCKET seem to preserve their metaphorical character (i.e. their relationship to literal meaning) to some extent. Though 'Harry's been dying for weeks now' is an acceptable sentence, *'Harry's been kicking the bucket for weeks now' is not, because of the association of abruptness carried by the verb TO KICK.

This list is no doubt incomplete. There are also complex lexicalizations in which there seems to be hardly any relationship between the lexical forms and the objects or events they describe. One has to look hard to find anything in TO DO A COLD TURKEY that makes it inherently suitable for expressing someone's withdrawing without medical help from an addictive habit such as drugs, alcohol, or cigarette smoking (though I have been told that people 'doing a cold turkey' tend to get goose bumps; thus, whether there is a conceptual relationship depends largely on one's knowledge of 'the world').

2.1.3 Word Groups versus Complex Lexicalizations

74   Though it may be clear why it is justified or even necessary to take fixed groups into account in lexical research, we are still left with Bolinger's objection. Bolinger is right that the borders between collocations and constructions are vague. What kind of criteria can one rely on to decide whether a group of words forms a lexical unity? The decision to treat a word group as a lexical item will always be based on a judgment of how strong a semantic unity the group forms. But 'strength of unity' can be viewed from two angles: the encoder's and the decoder's. The importance of this distinction is reflected in Makkai's (1972) contrast between idioms of decoding and idioms of encoding, and is re-emphasized in Fillmore's (1979) discussion of 'linguistic innocence'.

75   Consider TO TAKE A BATH, TO TAKE A WALK, TO HAVE BREAKFAST, TO HAVE A HAIRCUT. These are all transparent for the decoder of a message who knows the meaning of the individual words (including the very general sense that TO TAKE and TO HAVE can get). But why does one TAKE a bath and HAVE a haircut? The formation of these expressions is not completely predictable for an encoder who knows the meaning of the individual words. On the basis of this distinction we can propose the following criterion: If someone encoding his or her thoughts would be able to produce the group of words in question without having learned it as a unity, then we have to do with a simple group of words, a free construction; if previous learning can be expected to be required, then the combination of words is a lexical item even if someone decoding the message would have no trouble at all to interpret it without having come across it before.

2.2 INTERMEZZO 1: THE OBJECT OF INVESTIGATION

76   After setting up a terminological framework and explaining why we want to investigate complex as well as simple lexicalizations, another question crops up:

What classes of lexical items (in the sense of the traditional word classes) are used to describe linguistic action and are thus relevant to the type of investigation proposed?

Not only *verbs* are used to describe linguistic action, but also *nouns*. Though for many of the verbs in question (e.g. TO PROMISE) there is a corresponding noun (e.g. PROMISE), this is not always the case. For the verb TO URGE there is no corresponding noun URGE which describes the same linguistic act (though that gap would be at least partially covered by the noun EXHORTATION). Conversely, the Dutch noun ORDER has no one-to-one correspondence to any verb, but it describes linguistic acts that form a subclass of the acts described by the verb BEVELEN ('to order'). Therefore, both nouns and verbs are relevant to the study of what people say they do with words.

Adjectives provide us with pertinent information about the nature of certain linguistic actions through their combination possibilities with the nouns describing those actions. Note, for instance, that one can talk about A TRUE STATEMENT but not *A TRUE ORDER (unless TRUE is used in a different sense); A SOUND ARGUMENT but not *A SOUND PROMISE; A SOLID OFFER but not *A SOLID QUESTION; A BASIC QUESTION but not *A BASIC OFFER; or in Dutch EEN GAVE BEKENTENIS ('an unconditional confession') or EEN GAVE TOESTEMMING ('an unconditional permission') but not *EEN GAVE VRAAG ('an unconditional question'); EEN VAST AANBOD ('a solid offer') or EEN VASTE BELOFTE ('a firm promise') but not *EEN VAST BEVEL (lit. 'a solid order'). Adjectives always reveal a semantic dimension of the nouns they modify: the acceptability of the phrase THE TALL TREE exposes the fact that there is a tallness dimension to trees. Therefore, investigating such combination possibilities could yield some insights into the nature of certain types of verbal behavior.

Similarly, *adverbs* may prove useful in disclosing the most important dimensions of the acts described by the verbs or verblike expressions they can be used to qualify.

77   Though verbs, nouns, adjectives, and adverbs all deserve a place in the examination of what people say they do with words, there is no denying that when it comes to describing action (in this case, linguistic action), verbs and verblike expressions occupy a key position. This essay is no more than a pilot study on which severe limitations have to be imposed. The discussion in the subsequent chapters will therefore be confined to verbs and verblike expressions. Nouns, adjectives, and adverbs will only occasionally be treated when they are part of a complex verblike lexicalization.

78   Another comment on terminology is needed. In order to avoid the stylistically tiresome recurrence of the phrase 'verbs and verblike expressions' or 'verbs or verblike expressions' I create the term *verbials*, a neologism on the analogy of the word 'adverbial', which covers both adverbs and adverblike expressions. If a need arises to distinguish the two, I shall talk about *simple*

verbials (or simply *verbs*) and *complex verbials* on the basis of my earlier distinction between simple and complex lexicalizations. (Notice that the existing term 'verbal' would not have been suitable because its established meaning is 'a word that combines characteristics of a verb with those of a noun or adjective' and it covers gerunds, infinitives, and participles.)

The verbials used to describe linguistic action under one aspect or another, i.e. the objects for investigation in this essay, I call *linguistic action verbials*.

79   Now that we have confined our task to the Dutch-English comparative study of the verbials covering the small subfields of linguistic action specified in the first chapter (see paragraph 53), we ought to look for a criterion to decide on when a verbial can be rightfully included in the set of lexical items used to describe the action in question. As with most of the distinctions drawn so far, this criterion is going to be a hazy one.

Some verbs, such as TO ASK, have a type of verbal behavior as their primary meaning (though the meaning can be metaphorically extended, as in 'He is asking for trouble'). Evidently, these have to be accounted for.

Other verbs, such as TO THREATEN, denote actions that are not necessarily linguistic. Still, the linguistic part of their meaning is prominent enough to warrant unqualified inclusion.

Yet another class of verbs, such as TO PUT FORWARD, have an originally nonlinguistic sense of which awareness on the part of native speakers can still be assumed. But the metaphorical extension of their use to kinds of linguistic action has become so widespread and conventional that we can talk about dead or lexicalized metaphors. Hence, they should be dealt with.

Finally, we have verbs, such as TO KILL, that can only be used to describe verbal behavior if their meaning is very widely and actively extended metaphorically, as in the following song lyric: 'Killing me softly with his words'. Since the meaning of nearly all words can be extended in a similar fashion, the investigation would get totally out of hand if these were incorporated into the set of lexical items used in saying what one does with words.

Fuzziness is inevitable when it comes to making decisions about lexical items on the borderline between the third and last categories. Notice that the distinctions we have made here with reference to verbs apply also to complex verbials.

80   Briefly, in addition to idioms such as TO BEAT AROUND THE BUSH and other fixed formulae such as TO PRONOUNCE X AND Y HUSBAND AND WIFE, the set of linguistic action verbials will include performative verbs such as TO ORDER, TO PROMISE, TO STATE, nonperformative speech-act verbs such as TO THREATEN, TO BOAST, and a wide array of other verbs that can neither be used to describe nor to perform types of illocutionary acts, ranging from TO SPEAK (one of the most general linguistic action verbs) and TO WHISPER (a manner-of-speaking verb) to TO CONVINCE (describing a perlocutionary act), etc.

2.3 PROBLEM 2: HOW TO DESCRIBE THE MEANING OF LEXICAL ITEMS

2.3.0 Introduction

81 How should the meaning of lexical items (and in particular, of linguistic action verbials) be described? The question can be broken up in two interrelated parts. First, how can the internal semantic structure of verbials be brought to light? Second, how should the semantic relationships between the verbials covering a particular conceptual field be identified?

In the following sections, lexical decomposition, which is one of the possible responses to the first question, and the structuralist study of lexical fields, which was for a long time the favored solution to the second problem, are discussed briefly. Their limitations are considered and improvements proposed.

2.3.1 Problem 2, Part 1: Internal Semantic Structure

82 Saussure's distinction between *langue* and *parole* induced linguists such as Trubetzkoy to postulating abstract 'phonemes', which can be realized in different ways and which can be characterized in terms of a universal set of distinctive features such as ± voice, ± dental, etc. On the analogy of these structuralistic phonological notions, Hjelmslev and Jakobson proposed to analyze the meaning of words in terms of a set of universal *meaning components* or *semantic features*. In that way the meaning of MAN could be analyzed as + male, + adult, + human, and the meaning of WOMAN as − male, + adult, and + human. This semantic procedure is called *componential analysis* or *lexical decomposition*. The same principle was proposed—independently of the European tradition—by American anthropologists studying kinship terms and folk taxonomies (e.g. Goodenough 1956, 1965; Lounsbury 1964).

83 Componential analysis labors under a number of more or less serious difficulties. First, it is not too clear which pole of a binary contrast such as male-female should be taken as the descriptive point of departure. This problem is not too serious because the proponents of componential analysis can easily get away with a decision by declaring that the semantic features used should be regarded as *atomic concepts* that may, but need not, be lexicalized in individual languages; hence, a semantic feature such as ± adult must not be identified with the word ADULT. Nonetheless, componential analysts try to motivate their decisions by relying on the notion of *markedness*: since one normally asks 'How tall is John?' and not 'How short is John?' when making inquiries about John's size, 'tall' is regarded as the unmarked pole of the tall-short contrast, and therefore it is taken as the point of departure if the contrast is needed in semantic analysis.

Markedness (of which a more profound discussion is to be found in, e.g., Bolinger 1977 and Lyons 1977) is such a basic linguistic phenomenon that often it is even reflected in the morphology of the words in question: the contrast deep-shallow (of which 'deep' is the unmarked member because it refers both to the whole dimension and to one of its poles) is lexicalized in Dutch as *diep-ondiep* and in Spanish as *profundo-poco profundo* where the second item is a negation of the first.

84 But how can the meaning of semantic features be grasped if it is so objectionable to identify them with the corresponding words in natural languages? Especially for the components that are supposed to be atomic in the sense that they resist further decomposition, it is hard to see how their meaning can be explicated other than by means of such an identification. Obviously, this second problem cannot be smothered under terminological trickery.

Third, the alleged atomicity of certain semantic features is itself a point of dispute. Not only can many semantic features be further analyzed, often this can be done in more than one way. Thus, the feature + human could be analyzed either as + featherless and + biped, or as + hairless and + ape. Whether one wants to introduce such further analyses and, if so, one's choice of alternative depends largely on considerations of usefulness for the linguistic description.

Fourth, how detailed should an analysis in terms of semantic features become? Or, conversely, how abstract can it remain? A tentative solution to this problem was offered by Katz and Fodor (1963), when they distinguished between *semantic markers* (i.e. those meaning components that constitute the part of the meaning of a word that is systematic for the language to be described) and *distinguishers* (which constitute some further residue of meaning after all markers have been extracted). That such a neat distinction is hardly feasible was convincingly demonstrated by Bolinger (1965). (For a further discussion of abstractness in lexical semantics and its relation to the problems of universality and psychological relevance, see 2.5 and Verschueren 1982b.)

85 A fifth and equally serious problem is the dubitable existence of a universal set of semantic features belonging to some universal mental language from which speaking is always a translation to a particular natural language. Consider the rather random list of thirteen fundamental concepts proposed by A. Wierzbicka (1972, 1977, 1980): I, you, someone, something, world, this, want, don't want, think of, say, imagine, be part of, become. It is hard to detect any logic in this series, and any scholar will be able to think of concepts that are not readily analyzable in terms of Wierzbicka's Fundamental Thirteen. One concept most scholars would spontaneously add to the list is TO BE. But then we remember Witherspoon's (1977) claim that in Navajo TO GO appears to be a much more basic concept than TO BE. Maybe we ought to attribute the failure to construct an acceptable set of universal semantic primitives to the fact that, as Fortescue

(1979) points out, the language of thought, if conceived in terms of the view underlying the search for universal meaning components, is not a language at all. Though some contributions by cognitive psychologists (e.g. Miller & Johnson-Laird 1976) seem to suggest that psychological tests can be devised for detecting cognitively primitive concepts, even the usefulness of the search for a completely universal set is in doubt. Their level of abstraction is such that analyses in terms of them are hardly, if at all, intelligible. Consider

> X can be thought of as becoming a part of different parts of that part of the world

which Wierzbicka (1972:97) proposes as a semantic decomposition of 'X is moving'. It is a rare person who can detect, without any help, what the analysis is an analysis of.

86 When attempts were made to apply componential analysis or lexical decomposition to verbs, it was soon realized that the meaning components (which are then called *atomic predicates*) should be viewed as constituting a hierarchic semantic structure instead of a simple sum. A verb such as TO KILL, for instance, was thought to be analyzable as

> kill(x,y): CAUSE(x, BECOME(y, NOT ALIVE))

where x is the agent of TO KILL and y is the patient; read: 'x kills y means that x causes y to become not alive.'

87 One common criticism is that, for instance, TO KILL and TO CAUSE TO DIE cannot be substituted for each other: one can say 'Yesterday John caused Jim to die' even if Jim did not die until today; this is impossible with 'Yesterday John killed Jim'. Such criticism may reveal the need for time indexes in some lexical decomposition formulae, but scholars who maintain that atomic predicates, just like other semantic features, should not be confused with the corresponding words are of course immune to it.

If we abstract for a moment from the opacity and the dubious universality of the semantic primitives, which is a problem for the lexical decomposition of verbs as well as for other types of componential analysis, then we may ask whether the verbials used to describe linguistic action are also susceptible to the type of analysis under discussion.

88 The semantic complexity of notions such as promising, ordering, etc., is such that it cannot be captured in a lexical decomposition formula for the corresponding verbs (which is not to say that analyzing into components is impossible, but simply that the formalism does not work). Elsewhere (see Verschueren 1977) I used the decomposition paradigm to illustrate this complexity. Compare the following two formulae; the first one is a variation of the one given earlier for the verb TO KILL.

kill(x, y): CAUSE (x, COME ABOUT (DIE (y)))
order(x, y, P): CAUSE (x, COME ABOUT (DO (y, P)))

In the second formula, x is the speaker, y is the hearer, and P stands for a proposition, which in this case specifies a future act on the part of the hearer. The second formula is obviously incomplete as a description of the meaning of TO ORDER. At least the following elements need to be added: unlike the dying associated with killing, the doing associated with ordering is not a necessary outcome of the action but merely an intended one; the intention is carried out by means of uttering a sentence; it is the speaker's intention that his/her uttering that sentence will make the hearer do a certain action. Inserting all this additional information results in the following formula, in which Se stands for a sentence.

order(x, y, P): SAY (x, y, Se) ∧ INTEND (x, CAUSE ([SAY (x, y, Se)], COME ABOUT (DO (y, P))))

Put in plain words, 'x orders y to do P' means that 'x utters a sentence Se to y and x intends his uttering Se to y to cause it to come about that y does P'. However complex the formula is, it is not yet explicit with respect to several points: first, the two conjoined parts of the formula are part of the same act; second, the two occurrences of SAY (x, y, Se) are identical; third, the Se may be the surface expression of order (x, y, P); fourth, P is part of what Se expresses. But let us for a while expect a cooperative attitude from everybody so that making these points explicit in the formula would be redundant.

89 So far so good. But what happens if we try to construct comparable formulae for different speech-act verbs? Here is an attempt for TO REQUEST, TO STATE, and TO ARGUE.

request(x, y, P): SAY (x, y, Se) ∧ INTEND (x, CAUSE ([SAY (x, y, Se)], COME ABOUT (DO (y, P))))
state(x, y, P): SAY (x, y, Se) ∧ INTEND (x, CAUSE ([SAY (x, y, Se)], COME ABOUT (KNOW (y, P))))
argue(x, y, P): SAY (x, y, Se) ∧ INTEND (x, CAUSE ([SAY (x, y, Se)], COME ABOUT (KNOW (y, P))))

A serious problem emerges immediately. The formulae do not provide for any differentiation in meaning between TO ORDER and TO REQUEST and between TO STATE and TO ARGUE; yet, TO ORDER is not a synonym of TO REQUEST, nor are TO STATE and TO ARGUE synonymous. There is no obvious way in which the authority implied by TO ORDER and the expectation of the hearer's resistance against believing P in the case of TO ARGUE can be formalized in such a way as to obtain sufficiently differentiated decomposition formulae.

90 Lexical decomposition of speech-act verbs (by means of the formalism illustrated) does not lead us any further than the construction of a more or less general formula of the following kind, in which some basic semantic components of all speech-act verbs are brought together.

$$\text{SAV}(x, y, (P)): \text{SAY}(x, y, Se) \wedge \text{INTEND}(x, \text{CAUSE}([\text{SAY}(x, y, Se)], \text{COME ABOUT}(\text{ACCEPT}(y, SA'))))$$

Note that SAV stands for speech-act verb and SA' for all the aspects of the speech act in question, except (a) the effects x typically intends to bring about, for which ACCEPT (y, SA') stands (which should be read as 'y accepts or appropriately reacts to the speech act'), and (b) the fact that x utters a sentence Se by means of which he/she intends to bring about those effects, for which the rest of the formula stands. It should be clear that such formulae cannot make explicit the full meaning of individual speech-act verbs. First, in most cases it will not be possible to replace ACCEPT (y, SA') by a single word such as KNOW, DO, or TELL; though there is certainly an effect typically associated with acts such as promising (e.g. gratifying the hearer in one way or another), it is not always easy to describe, let alone to formalize. Second, a complete representation of SA' requires the formulation of most of the felicity conditions on the act in question, which is hardly feasible within the scope of a lexical decomposition formula. This is why attempts at decomposing verbs of communication, such as the following example from Miller and Johnson-Laird (1976:647):

(TO (TELL)) (x, w, y): Someone x 'tells' w 'to' someone y if w refers to some words W and:
(i) STATE (x, w)
(ii) PERCEIVE (y, W)
(iii) COMPREHEND (y, W)
(iv) KNOW (y, u)
(v) ALLOW (i), (ii) & CAUSE ((ii), (iii) & CAUSE (iii), (iv))

(where u refers to the meaning that the original listener, y, places on x's words), usually result in sets of conditions rather than genuine lexical decomposition formulae. In the discussion of Problem 3, this observation will lead us to an improved way of describing the internal semantic structure of lexical items as complex as linguistic action verbials (of which the speech-act verbs referred to in this paragraph constitute a subset). It will be seen that what is lacking in Miller and Johnson-Laird's descriptions is the background of an explicit theory of what the conditions are conditions on.

91 Our conclusion that we must look for an improved way of describing the internal semantic structure of linguistic action verbials does not mean that the idea of componential analysis or lexical decomposition has to be abandoned altogether. It would be wrong to dismiss the theoretical achievements of Nida (1975) and the practical ones of Bendix (1966). And evidently, any type of lexical semantic analysis will require a decomposition of some kind. But claims about the universality of sets of semantic features should be handled with care;

we should not shy away from identifying semantic features with words in natural language, as long as we are aware of the consequences; and we should forget about our desire to obtain nice formulae. Moreover, we should always remember that not everything can be explained in terms of features; for a nice illustration of what features leave unexplained, see Lyons (1977:333-335).

2.3.2 Problem 2, Part 2: External Semantic Relationships

92 How should the semantic relationships between linguistic action verbials, or lexical items in general, be identified? An obvious place to start looking for an answer is in the structuralist theory of lexical fields. But before a discussion of this linguistic tradition, it should be emphasized that there is no way of identifying sense components in the internal semantic structure of one word without implicitly or explicitly referring to the meaning of other words; all sense components, even if they are not part of a neat semantic dimension, contrast words with each other and thus express external semantic relationships as well as semantic properties of individual words. Therefore, it is not accidental that discussions of componential analysis and lexical fields often go together (as in Coseriu & Geckeler 1974; Lehrer 1974), and that, in America, componential analysis was first developed by anthropologists who were mainly interested in certain lexical fields (see Goodenough 1956, 1965; Lounsbury 1964). Thus the two parts of Problem 2 are strongly interrelated.

93 Saussurean structuralism regards a language as a unique system or network of functionally related elements within which each separate element derives its essence from its functional relation with the other elements. With respect to the vocabulary of a language this means that the meaning of each word depends on the existence of other words. This position inevitably leads to the conclusion that it does not make sense to try to define the meaning of one word separately. The meaning of each word covers a relatively small *conceptual area*, which is part of a wider *conceptual field*. The collection of words that together cover a complete conceptual field is called a *semantic field*, a *lexical field*, or a *lexical domain*. Within such a lexical field, the size of the conceptual area associated with a particular word is determined by the size of the conceptual areas of the surrounding words.

Since conceptual fields can be lexicalized (i.e. split up into conceptual areas) in different ways, the structure of the lexical fields to which certain words belong has to be taken into account when semantically comparing those words with their equivalents in different languages. Figure 1 illustrates this state of affairs.

94 There are three different types of lexical fields (see Vassilyev 1974). First, fields consisting of words belonging to the same part of speech, such as TOWER, STEEPLE, TURRET, PINNACLE, etc., are called *paradigmatic fields*. Second, we are confronted with a *syntagmatic field* if it consists of syntagmatically related words from different parts of speech; the syntagmatic relationships are based on essential semantic connections such as between BARK and DOG, HEAR and EAR, BITE and TOOTH, BLOND and HAIR. Finally, a *complex field* includes words from different parts of speech (i.e. the syntagmatic dimension) along with their paradigmatic correlates, as shown in Figure 2.

95 Semantic-field theorists have also drawn attention to the existence of *lexical gaps*. We can talk about a lexical gap whenever a particular language lacks a word to cover a certain conceptual area within a conceptual field that belongs to the experiential world of the language community involved. An example is to be found in Figure 3. Though a Dutch equivalent to SLEET may exist, it is absent from the competence of most speakers, and in most cases a paraphrase such as SMELTENDE SNEEUW ('melting snow'), which does not fit our criterion for lexical unity (see section 2.1.3), will be used. Figure 3 also reveals the hierarchical structure of the lexicon.

96 In this necessarily brief account of the theory of lexical fields, we can only mention some of its manifold problems. The simple fact that semantic-field theorists usually exclude complex lexicalizations and even compounds from their accounts should already arouse our suspicion. Let us review some of the trouble spots.

First, if the conclusion that it does not make sense to try to define the meaning of one word separately is so inevitable, how is it that people do it all the time? It is true that in the definition of a word there will always be sense components that implicitly carry along dimensions of contrast, but in everyday life we do not always feel obliged to even think about the words surrounding the one we want to define.

Second, how can the theory of lexical fields account for the semantic difference between two words that are not felt to be synonymous though they seem to cover an almost identical conceptual area, such as ANIMAL and BEAST. ADULT and GROWN-UP, or the French CRAINDRE and REDOUTER?

Third, does the absolute arbitrariness of the way in which conceptual fields can be lexicalized or split up into conceptual areas, which is implied in the theory of lexical fields and often claimed explicitly, reflect reality? Or are there any processes at work which make lexicalizations predictable up to a point?

Fourth, the practicability of semantic field theory depends on the possibility of defining the boundaries of word meanings; whether such strict boundaries exist is extremely doubtful.

97 The four problems mentioned can all be reduced to an inconsistency characterizing structuralism. On the one hand, it is postulated that every element within a linguistic system derives its essence from its functional relationships with other elements and that every individual element can only be described as a junction of relationships. On the other hand, orthodox structuralists believe that the language system is an independent being that can be described as such with-

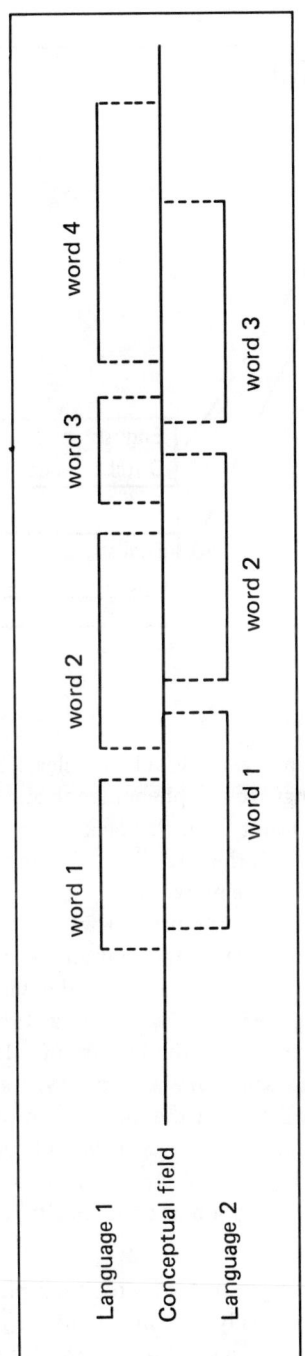

Figure 1

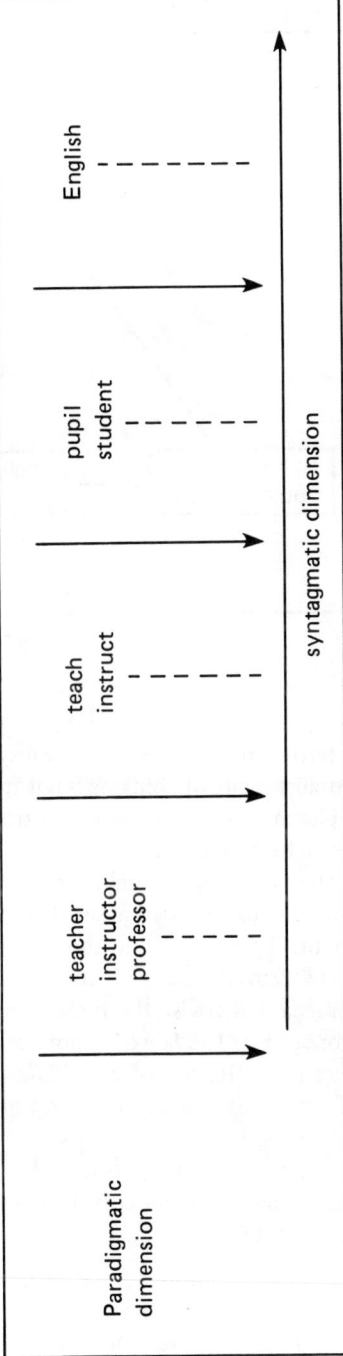

Figure 2

44 PROBLEMS OF LEXICAL SEMANTICS

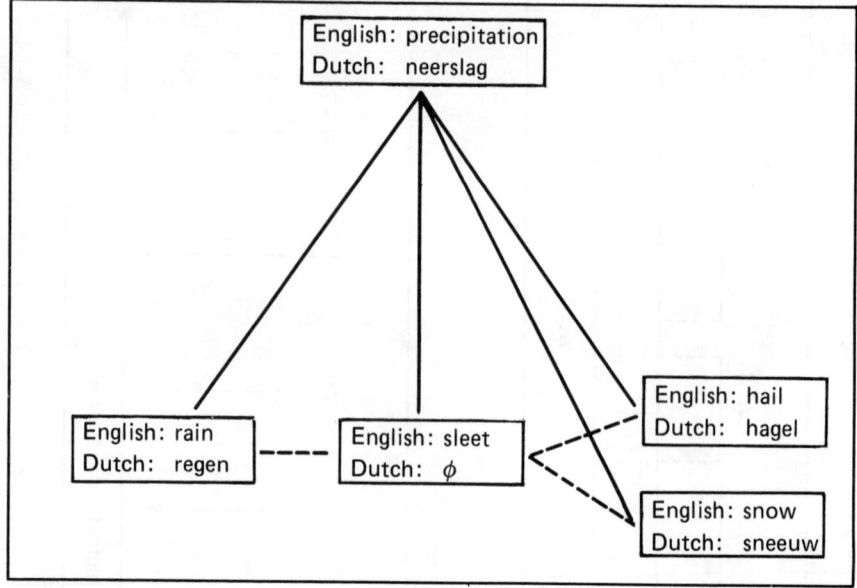

Figure 3

out referring to extralinguistic reality. The inconsistency should be clear: the structuralist mode of thinking is not applied to language as a phenomenon among other phenomena. How these four trouble spots result from this lack of consistency will be easy to understand after reading through the rest of this chapter.

The foregoing generalization, as it stands, may be more directly applicable to Bloomfieldian structuralism than to the European structuralism we are talking about. To be fair, one should admit that European structuralism has not completely overlooked all connections between language and extralinguistic phenomena. Otherwise the three giants Trier (e.g. 1931), Weisgerber (e.g. 1962) and Porzig (e.g. 1967) would not have been talking about the lexicon of a language as the reflection of a *Weltbild* (in much the same way as Sapir 1921 and Whorf 1956). But since they did not go any further than the observation of a certain 'reflection' function, it would not be unfair to say that, as far as lexical semantics is concerned, structuralism ignores the internal structure of extralinguistic reality, human cognitive processes, the expression of social reality, and linguistic context.

98 Insofar as componential analysis is itself a product of structuralism, it shares the latter's problems. One attitude the two usually have in common is the belief that an adequate description of the meaning of a word must be such that it covers the meaning that word has in all of its literal occurrences. In the case of semantic-field theory, this attitude was identified in terms of the requirement to

define the boundaries of word meanings. Fillmore (1975) dubs it the *checklist approach* to meaning: a word meaning is represented as a list of semantic features; if an object or event satisfies all the features in the list, the word can be used to refer to it; otherwise it cannot. The absurdity of such an approach will be demonstrated below (paragraph 105).

99 Not only European structuralists have engaged in the study of lexical fields. In the United States, linguistic anthropologists have done the same. Remember the works by Lounsbury and Goodenough, referred to earlier; another important work in this area is Berlin, Breedlove, & Raven (1973). It is their research that has inspired some of the solutions to our lexical semantic problems, as will appear from the following sections.

2.4 TOWARD A SOLUTION OF PROBLEM 2

2.4.0 Introduction

100 So far it has been claimed that lexical decomposition was inadequate to account for the internal structure of the verbials we want to describe, and lexical items in general, and that the structuralist approach to lexical fields cannot be expected to yield sufficient insight into the semantic relationships among them.

Psychologists such as Rosch (1977a, 1977b, 1978), sociologists such as Goffman (1974), linguistic anthropologists such as Berlin and Kay (1969), computational linguists such as Minsky (1977), Schank and Abelson (1977), and semanticists such as Fillmore (e.g. 1975, 1977, 1978) have created numerous concepts by means of which structuralist reductionism can be avoided: *scene, frame, schema, description, template, scenario, prototype, module, model, plan, script, basic-level term*. As in most innovative areas of research, there is considerable terminological confusion and conflict. In my search for an adequate methodology to analyze linguistic action verbials I have tried to handle the terms *prototype, basic-level term, scene, frame,* and *linguistic frame*.

2.4.1 Prototype Semantics

101 The lexicalization of the potentially infinite diversity of reality looks like a mission impossible for language. How then, can we explain its relative success?

Though the boundaries between categories of objects are mostly diffuse, yet reality is not an undifferentiated continuum of phenomena. Flying animals are nearly always feathered and only rarely furred. An object that looks like a chair is more frequently used to sit on than an object that looks like a pig. Such considerations led Rosch (1977a, 1977b) to believe that there exist 'intrinsically separate things' in the world. If the conclusion is correct, this fact may grease the wheels of the lexicalization process considerably.

Not only is reality structured, but moreover human perception operates according to some strict mechanisms. After an age-old belief in the arbitrariness of color terminology, for instance, Berlin and Kay (1969) have demonstrated quite convincingly that different languages show a strong conformity with respect to the focal point of the area of the color spectrum covered by a particular basic color term (whereas the boundaries of the area are always vague) and that there is a universal evolutionary pattern governing the acquisition of basic color terms by a language. Though the original study called for several modifications, it remains an example of the interaction between the internal structure of reality and the laws determining the human perceptual apparatus, in this case the uneven color sensitivity of the eye (discussed at length in Kay & McDaniel 1978).

102 Both phenomena, i.e. the internal structure of reality and the laws governing the perceptual apparatus, lead us to the notion of a *prototype*. The formation of prototypes, 'ideal' instances of a particular category, is one of the cognitive processes enabling humans to grasp the diversity of the world with their minds. This process is partly determined by the laws of perception and the structure of reality. An example of the first influence was mentioned with reference to color terminology. The second influence can be illustrated by saying that a pigeon or a sparrow is a more typical or 'better' example of a bird than is a chicken or an ostrich and that a dog or a cow is a more typical example of a mammal than is a whale. Briefly, for each lexicalized category human cognition contains a prototypical example (which does not have to be an actual member of the category itself, but which is a kind of 'mental image') that is used as a yardstick to decide whether a particular object can or cannot be referred to by means of the lexical item in question. If the deviation from the standard is too big, the word cannot be used.

103 This brief exposition may create the false impression that the prototype idea is valid only for nouns. But remember that color terms (functioning as adjectives or as nouns) have been adduced as examples already; the 'focal points' referred to are the prototypical examples of the colors denoted by the terms. To show that a similar analysis is feasible for verbs, I adopt an example given by Fillmore (1978); the verb TO CLIMB typically describes an *ascending* motion in a *clambering* fashion. I quote:

> A monkey climbing up a flagpole satisfies both of these conditions. The monkey climbing down the flagpole satisfies the clambering component only, but is nevertheless engaged in an action that can be properly called climbing. A snail climbing up the flagpole satisfies the ascending condition and can still be said to be climbing. But the snail is not privileged to *climb down* the flagpole, since that activity would involve neither clambering nor ascending. (p. 153)

So there is a clear prototype, deviations from which are possible. But if the meaning strays too far away from the standard, the word can no longer be used appropriately. Also, more abstract verbials can be approached in a similar fashion. Consider the speech-act verb TO CONGRATULATE. A typical congratulation is an expression of the speaker's being pleased about the hearer's success in doing or obtaining something important. The first aspect of this prototypical meaning is completely absent from many formal acts of congratulating. The second aspect is being tampered with in the following headline from the International Herald Tribune: 'Begin congratulates Sadat on *their* Nobel'. The most convincing example to date is Coleman and Kay's (1981) prototype analysis of the linguistic action verb TO LIE (which will be referred to again in Chapter 4).

104 Such a prototype approach to meaning, which takes into account the internal structure of reality, the laws of perception, and human cognitive strategies, immediately solves three of the problems pointed out in connection with the structuralistic semantic-field theory.

First, it demonstrates that there is no absolute arbitrariness in the lexicalization of conceptual fields. Second, it explains the age-old habit of defining the meaning of many words without direct reference to the surrounding lexical items in the same field: when doing so, the definer restricts him/herself to the prototypical meaning. Third, the nonexistence of sharp boundaries between the conceptual areas covered by related words in a particular lexical field is no longer a problem for lexical semantics. The main preoccupation of structuralist semantic-field theorists was to determine those boundaries, which turn out to be subject to strong interpersonal variation (within one language community as well as between different languages). With respect to the prototypical examples, there is a much greater consistency in the word use of a speaker, a much greater correspondence between the uses made of a lexical item by different speakers of the same language, and a striking similarity in the use of equivalent words in different languages. Evidently, we have encountered a fundamental property of word meaning, namely a psychological structure which is imposed on it (which could be represented as in Figure 4). Figure 4 cannot be used for the representation of the overall structure of complete lexical fields. As we shall see later, it can only be used to depict the patterning of lexical fields along a single (or at best a few) 'semantic dimension(s)'—a term to be explained below.

105 The prototype idea also reveals the absurdity of the checklist view still held by many linguists (most of those practicing lexical-field theory and/or com-

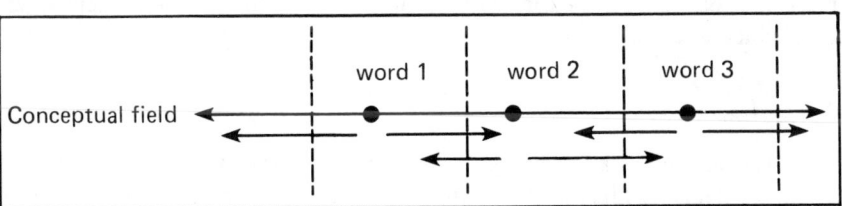

Figure 4

ponential analysis). To repeat, the checklist approach is based on the view that an adequate description of the meaning of a word must present the complete list of conditions under which the word can be used appropriately. The alternative is to give the 'typical' conditions, i.e. the prototype approach.

In trying to determine the meaning of the word BOAT, one could come up with a definition such as 'a man-made object that can be used for traveling on water'. A defender of the checklist approach, coming across a boat with a hole in it and deciding that he/she still wants to call it a BOAT (though it cannot be used for traveling on water anymore), would have to revise his/her definition: 'a man-made object that can normally be used for traveling on water, but in which there can also be a hole'. Further, he/she would have to determine how big the hole can be before the object in question is not a BOAT anymore, but simply a WRECK. The impracticality of the checklist approach is such that not even its proponents would want to be guilty of the absurdities mentioned. A defender of the alternative theory could simply stick to his/her definition and describe a boat with a hole in terms of deviations from the prototypical boat. It should be kept in mind that such 'deviations' are not necessarily 'defects'; for that reason the example is a bit misleading. Probably the best argument for the prototype approach is that, in practice, most analyses of word meanings are based on it, though often unconsciously.

106 It is this prototype approach to meaning that I want to advocate and that I shall make use of. Though the standard or typical uses of semantic units are more stable than the borders of their applicability, which can be expected to change very much from speaker to speaker, even the prototypes are subject to some interpersonal variability. This should not be surprising at all, given that prototypes are products of cognitive processes that serve to make perceived reality mentally manageable and given the fact that the world surrounding a member of a particular linguistic community is not necessarily identical to that of other members. Such variability does not make the specification of prototypes impossible. Judgments about prototypical meanings, however, must be regarded as *hypotheses* as long as they have not been verified by means of extensive psychological testing. Not everybody will agree with them, but the important thing is that such judgments can be made.

Since prototypes are basic tools in human categorization, this approach to the meaning of linguistic action verbials and lexical items in general is especially relevant if one is interested in word meaning for the sake of the conceptualization habits reflected.

2.4.2 Basic-Level Terms

107 Just as there is a psychological structure imposed on the semantic structure of lexical items (as illustrated in Figure 4), there is also a psychological structure imposed on lexical fields. Not all classificatory levels in the hierarchic structure of the lexicon play an equally important role in the cognitive processing of reality. The existence of a *cognitively basic level* emerges from simple tests of the following kind: If you show a guitar to someone and ask him/her 'What is this?', the reply is more likely to be 'a guitar' than 'a musical instrument' or 'a folk guitar'; if you present an apple to someone, the answer to the same question is more likely to be 'an apple' than 'fruit' or 'a golden delicious'. Therefore APPLE and GUITAR are called *basic-level terms*: the others are superordinate or subordinate terms. More examples are given in Table 1 (which is similar to those in Rosch 1977a).

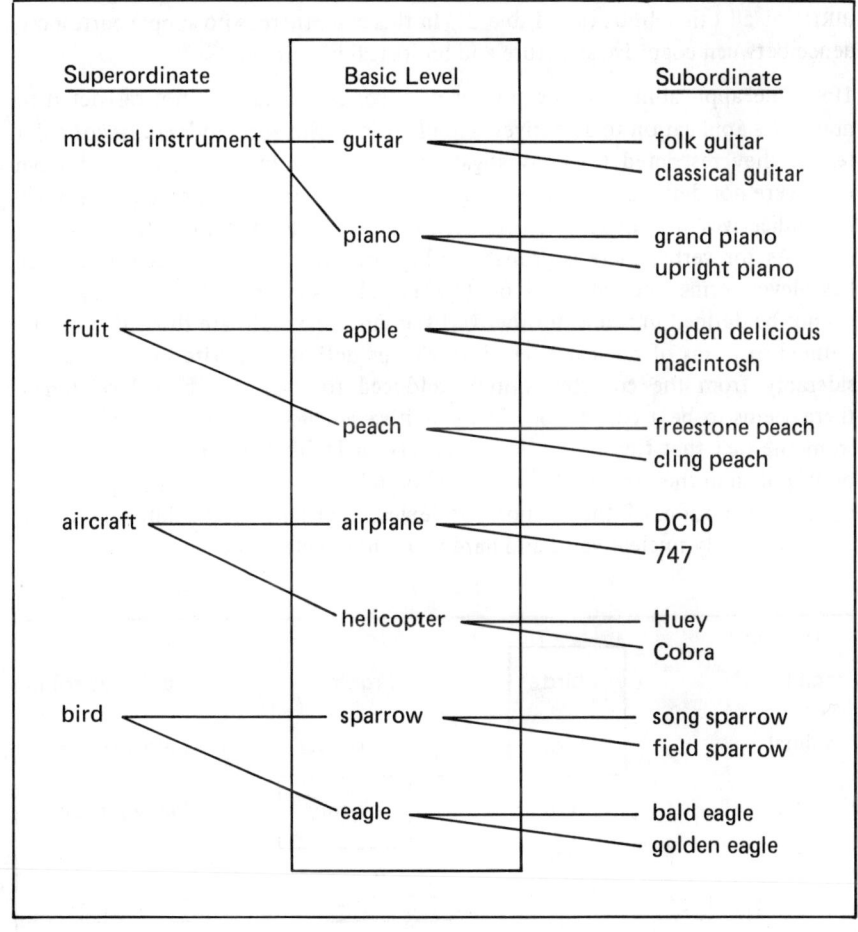

Table 1

108 Though it may be possible to discover the basic levels for the average member of a language community, they are, as are prototypes, subject to interpersonal differences. The variability, however, is not arbitrary: it depends on the degree of specialization or the knowledge someone obtains in a particular field. For instance, an aircraft engineer is likely to have DC 10 and 747 as basic-level terms rather than AIRPLANE. On the other hand, my limited knowledge of that field did not even allow me to fill in subordinates for HELICOPTER except for HUEY, which I accidentally got to know by reading about the Vietnam war, until, recently, COBRAs got into the news. Conversely, a life-long city-dweller is not unlikely to have BIRD as a basic-level term rather than SPARROW and ROBIN. Differences may be even more subtle: inhabitants of some pigeon-infested European cities may be expected to have PIGEON as a basic-level term for pigeons and BIRD for all other birds (see Table 2). In this case, there is no simple correspondence between cognitive structure and biological hierarchy.

109 The applicability of the notion of a basic-level term is not restricted to nouns. Its application to adjectives is implicit in Berlin and Kay's studies of color terms: they restricted their investigations to basic color terms, which, though they were not defined on a purely cognitive basis, might be regarded as the basic-level adjectives or nouns in the color lexicon. (See also paragraph **421**.)

As for verbs, there is probably a high degree of correspondence between basic-level terms and what Dixon (1971) calls *nuclear verbs*, i.e. verbs that cannot be defined in terms of other verbs; nonnuclear verbs are those that can be defined in terms of nuclear ones. Though this definitional criterion differs considerably from the cognitive criteria adduced to single out basic-level terms, there seems to be a correlation. The cognitive salience of nuclear verbs appears from the fact that the mother-in-law variety of Dyirbal (i.e. Dyalŋuy, which is only spoken in the presence of certain taboo relatives, and which is characterized by the restriction of the number of lexical items to an absolute minimum) contains mainly nuclear verbs and hardly any nonnuclear ones.

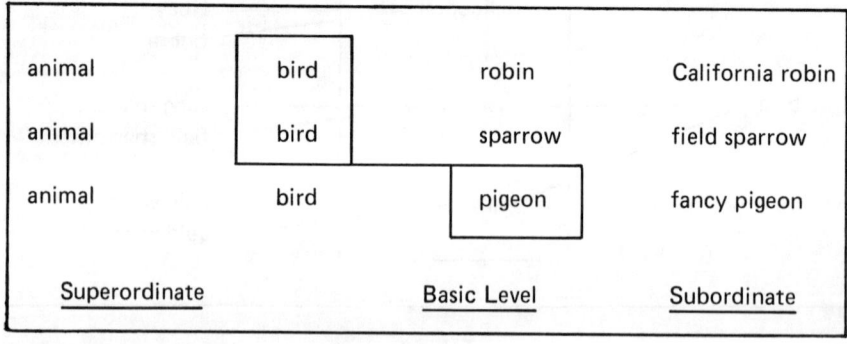

Table 2

110 But what about the relevance of basic levels to linguistic action verbials? No doubt some similar judgments can be made, but extreme caution is called for. Since the hierarchic structure of the lexicon is less clear for abstract concepts than for concrete objects, the psychological structure imposed on the hierarchy will be more difficult to detect also. Whereas judgments about prototypes are merely hypotheses as long as there is a lack of psychological testing, pre-experimental judgments about basic-level terms have to be regarded as extremely tentative hypotheses; at that stage it is safer to talk about the intuitively *most neutral terms* instead of basic-level terms (which is too much associated with Rosch's experimental methods).

2.4.3 Scenes and Frames

111 Words are not isolated entities. They are related not only to other words, but also to extralinguistic reality. The verb TO SELL, for instance, immediately evokes a commercial *scene* consisting of a buyer, a seller, money, and goods, between all of which there are relationships that are changed throughout the interaction. (For a detailed analysis, see Fillmore 1977.) Just as the human mind is forced to create prototypes to process the infinitude of stimuli presented by reality, so humans are also obliged to construct prototypical instances of scenes in order to be able to handle social reality cognitively. Such a prototypical instance of a scene I call a *frame*. Hence, to be precise, we would say that the verb TO SELL evokes a commercial frame, if we are interested in describing its prototypical meaning.

112 Lexical meanings are always partly determined by an association with such frames and/or nonprototypical scenes. Here is an example adapted from Fillmore (1977). We can say about John 'He spent three hours on land' and about Dick 'He spent three hours on the ground'. Though these sentences may be used to describe the nearly identical behavior of John and Dick in Antwerp on a rainy afternoon, yet they do not mean the same. The only reason is that ON LAND evokes the frame of navigation, whereas ON THE GROUND is associated with the frame of aviation.

Not only words with a clear lexical meaning such as LAND, GROUND, and TO SELL are connected with frames. Also, lexically empty items such as WHAT carry such associations. Consider the question 'What are you?'. The interrogative pronoun in this sentence used to be associated with the world of professions, the appropriate answer being 'a doctor', 'a teacher', 'a student', etc. But nowadays it is ambiguous in some social circles, since it may either evoke the professional world or the practice of astrology (in which case the appropriate answer is 'a Taurus', 'an Aquarius', etc.).

The notion of a frame provides us with a solution to the problem of how to account for the semantic difference between two words covering an almost identical conceptual area, such as ANIMAL and BEAST. In many contexts the two nouns simply evoke different frames.

Scenes and frames, too, are subject to interpersonal variability.

113 The set of linguistic choices—textual as well as grammatical and lexical—associated with a particular frame I call *linguistic frame*. Its lexical part is a *lexical frame*. It will be clear that the latter is not independent of the rest of the linguistic frame. To give a simple illustration (again borrowed from Fillmore 1977), even the choice of a determiner may influence the frame with which a noun is associated. Compare 'He did not give me a tip' and 'He did not give me my tip'. The indefinite article in the first sentence places TIP in the frame of generosity, whereas the possessive pronoun in the second sentence transposes it into a frame of obligatory payment. Hence, 'He did not give me a tip' is an accusation of bad manners, whereas 'He did not give me my tip' is an accusation of doing an 'illegal' thing. Another indication for the importance of linguistic frames is given by Leech (1974:105) when he claims that an Englishman will answer with less confidence and less consistency when asked about the synonymy of SCARED and FRIGHTENED in isolation than when in sentences such as 'John is scared of his father' and 'John is frightened of his father'. By thus connecting lexical meaning with other linguistic entities (on every level of structure), lexical semantics transcends yet another limitation of the structuralistic approach to semantic fields.

One might be tempted to identify lexical frames with what the structuralists called semantic or lexical fields. Such an identification would be wrong. Lexical frames are even more complex than complex lexical fields. The set of lexical choices associated with the commercial frame, for instance, includes not only TO BUY, TO PURCHASE, TO PROCURE, etc., but also TO SELL, TO PAY, TO CHARGE, etc., which approach the frame from a totally different point of view. (As a complex field, it does, of course, not only include verbs.) It is impossible to force all of these into a paradigmatic-syntagmatic scheme such as shown in Figure 2.

2.4.4 Interpersonal Variability

114 Summarizing, I am about to undertake a comparative study of a number of subsets of the verbials belonging to the lexical frame associated with linguistic action. When it comes to semantic analyses, the notions of frame, basic level, and prototype will be made use of (though to various degrees, as will be explained in the concluding remarks to this chapter).

In the foregoing discussion of these concepts, I have repeatedly drawn attention to interpersonal variability. Such variability is bound to make the job endless. An approach that obliges one to keep working forever is likely to be regarded as problematic. But frankly, I have never seen a phenomenon described completely, even with the most reductionistic approach imaginable. So where is the advantage?

Furthermore, the fact that success in communication is not automatic even if the speaker uses the 'right' words to express his/her thoughts, but rather depends crucially upon a laborious interpretation process, is veiled not only by the conduit metaphor (remember Reddy 1979) but also by all linguistic investigations based on the view that it is justified to abstract from the human (cognitive and social) aspects of a basically human phenomenon such as language. Such investigations actively support the conduit metaphor and may thus impede efficient communication. Not only are they out of touch with the actual character of the object of investigation (which makes them scientifically irrelevant), but they are also misleading in an acutely dangerous way (which could almost be said to make them socially irresponsible). The approach sketched above cannot be blamed on either of these two counts. I believe that we should not try to construct troubleproof theories; rather, we should institutionalize the troubles that reflect actual interpretation processes—for the sake of both the theory and the people who are confronted with it.

2.5 INTERMEZZO 2: ABSTRACTNESS IN LEXICAL SEMANTICS

2.5.0 Introduction

115 Being able to reduce lexical meanings to a limited set of atomic concepts, primary elements of human thought, or a cognitive alphabet is an age-old dream, the doctrinal status of which goes at least as far back as Leibniz. A relatively recent attempt to realize this dream by constructing a coherent system of semantic primitives is Wierzbicka's. The previously adduced example of her analysis of 'X is moving' in terms of her 13 fundamental concepts (see paragraph 85) illustrates the problem of abstractness in lexical semantics: the formula she comes up with is hardly intelligible. As shown before, the meaning of meaning components is always a problem in itself, whether one maintains (in accordance with orthodox componential analysis) that these components should not be associated with the corresponding words in natural language or that such an association is acceptable (as is explicitly stated in Wierzbicka's work). The more abstract the components get, however, the bigger the problem. And a real dilemma emerges since the general linguistic hunt for universality requires a high degree of abstractness, whereas abstractness carried to its extremes obstructs intelligibility and hence the meaningfulness of an analysis.

116 The solution to the problem of abstractness in lexical semantic investigations cannot be offered in this brief intermezzo. For one thing, it seems that a compromise between intellectual integrity and practical feasibility is always called for; the result can never be totally satisfying. Our intention is to pave the way for a solution by clarifying the question. The main tenet of this exposition is that the question of how abstract we can or should make our descriptions is not a purely theoretical matter, nor a mainly theoretical matter with great practical consequences, but a practical as well as a theoretical question. This means that the answer depends, to a significant extent, on the practical purpose of one's analyses, which determines the degree to which psychological relevance has to be aimed at. I shall try to sketch the answer to the question of abstractness as the constant search for the equilibrium between universality and psychological relevance.

2.5.1 Abstractness

117 What exactly does abstractness in lexical semantics mean? In particular, how can we compare degrees of abstractness? Two main parameters seem to play a part in this.

The first parameter is *analyzability* (touched upon in paragraph 84). In general we can say that the harder it is to analyze a meaning component, the more abstract it gets. For instance, + horse as a semantic component of MARE is not as abstract as + animate, − human, + mammal, and + ungulate, which can all be used in the further analysis of HORSE. Since analyzability is itself a controversial matter, a second parameter is more than welcome.

118 The actual wording of the second and probably more important parameter of abstractness, which is not totally independent of the first, depends on the descriptive method being used. If one uses componential analysis in the strictest sense of the word, the degree of abstractness of the resulting description is determined by the *position* of the used meaning components in the hierarchy of possible meaning components: the higher up in the hierarchy, the more abstract the component. The feature ± animate, for instance, is more abstract than the feature ± human, which in turn is more abstract than the feature ± male. Similarly, ± early could be said to be more abstract than ± young, ± primitive, ± fresh, and ± new.

If one does not want to hide behind the technicalities of componential analysis and if one starts (as Wierzbicka does) from a set of words that are regarded as carriers of primitive concepts from which all other concepts can be derived (which could be called the 'semantic primitive approach'), then the same parameter can be reduced to the *size* of that set.

119 In essence, the semantic primitive approach does not differ from the lexicographical method. Compare, for instance, the analyses that (1) Wierzbicka (1972) and (2) the *Longman Dictionary of Contemporary English* give of the word MARE.

(1) MARE = horse that could have inside her body something becoming the body of another horse
(2) MARE = female horse (or donkey)

Both definitions contain words that can and have to be further defined within the system of description relied on. For (1) these are HORSE and BODY; for (2) we are concerned with FEMALE and HORSE.

(1) X's BODY = the something that can be thought of as X
HORSE = an animal thinking of which one would say 'horse'
(2) FEMALE = of the sex that gives birth to young
HORSE = a type of large strong animal with mane, tail, and hard feet (hooves), which humans ride on and use for pulling and carrying heavy things

These definitions require further clarification. In (1), for instance, we encounter the word ANIMAL, which Wierzbicka would probably analyze as follows:

ANIMAL = something with a body that is not a human being

And HUMAN BEING gets an analysis of this sort:

HUMAN BEING = someone like you and me

Thus the whole concept of MARE has been reduced to semantically primitive concepts belonging to the proposed list of 13. *Longman's* definitions of FEMALE and HORSE, on the other hand, contain a whole string of unexplained words, in the definition of which yet other unexplained terms will appear. Hence, though the basic strategy is the same, the two approaches diverge with respect to the applied descriptive means: Wierzbicka, in her definitions, tries to reduce everything to 13 concepts, whereas *Longman* relies on about 2,000 'basic words'. The semantic primitive approach is therefore more abstract than the dictionary approach.

2.5.2 Universality

120 The evaluation of the degree of abstractness and the universality of an analysis shows a strong kind of parallelism. For universality as such, however, there is only one yardstick: universality itself. For the time being, linguistics is not advanced enough to pronounce unconditional judgments about the universal relevance of most meaning components. There are, however, a few indicators of universality, such as
  1. ease of identifiability in different languages,
  2. syntactic relevance, and
  3. wideness of distribution in the vocabulary.

Thus the semantic feature ± animate has a somewhat better chance of universal relevance than, for instance, ± male, since it is syntactically relevant for most languages (at least in the form of selection restrictions with a large number of verbs). The semantic feature ± male partly corresponds with a grammatical gender distinction but, first of all, the correspondence is usually incomplete and, second, gender distinctions are nonexistent in the grammars of a number of languages (such as Hungarian).

121 For the purpose of this exposition, a precise assessment of the degree of universality of a description is of no importance. From now on, universality will simply be regarded as *a requirement for every description*, but with the following proviso: an analysis for which it is not necessary to take other factors into account has to approach universality as closely as possible (and will therefore be relatively abstract). There are, however, other factors (which we'll go into immediately) that codetermine the required degree of abstractness and that thus may lower the level of universality.

2.5.3 Objectives and Psychological Relevance

122 That abstractness is not only a theoretical but also a practical matter appears clearly when we subject the different possible objectives or purposes of lexical semantic studies to close scrutiny. The two extreme possibilities are the following.

One's objective may be to construct *purely logical analyses* with a minimal number of meaning components and a minimal degree of redundancy. In that case, universality is the only target and the degree of abstractness should be as high as possible. This option, for instance, justifies the reduction—in the study of the linguistic action lexicon—of a QUESTION to a REQUEST FOR INFORMATION, which decreases the number of the required categories in a theoretically principled manner.

123 The other extreme is the study of (parts of) the lexicon of a language in view of the reflected conceptualization habits. In that case, the analyses will have to show relationships that are psychologically real for the speakers of the language(s) under investigation. As a result, the level of abstractness will go down. More specifically, an equilibrium will have to be found between the remaining requirement to produce descriptions that are as universal as possible and the additional requirement to make psychologically relevant judgments, which will usually be of a relatively language-specific nature.

Thus the descriptions and explanations will have to take into account, for instance, definitional relationships in natural language. By way of illustration, let us get back to our linguistic action example. Though a QUESTION can be logically reduced to a REQUEST FOR INFORMATION, the speakers of a number of natural languages will not be spontaneously inclined to produce this kind of definition. In English, for instance, the verb TO ASK is ambiguous between 'asking a question' and 'requesting'. The verb TO ASK itself is felt—most probably as a result of this ambiguity—to be a primary term in relation of TO RE-QUEST, and the reduction of TO REQUEST to ASKING SOMEONE TO DO SOMETHING can be expected to be psychologically more relevant and real than its logical reverse. (We'll come back to this example in Chapter 8.)

In other languages, the principle of psychological relevance can lead us yet in different directions. In Japanese, for instance, there is a word KIKU that is ambiguous between TO HEAR and TO ASK (in the sense of 'asking a question'). This leads us to a different—for the Japanese, psychologically real—meaning relationship that is also present, though somewhat more marginally, in western languages, as appears from terms such as the English noun HEARING (which is partly equivalent to the Dutch noun VERHOOR), and the Dutch and German verbs UITHOREN and AUSHORCHEN (meaning 'to pump for information').

2.5.4 A Practical Procedure and Its Application

124 In order to decide on the appropriate degree of abstractness for a given lexical semantic research project, in accordance with the foregoing considerations, one has to determine the exact objective of the investigations. It is on this purpose that the level of the required psychological relevance depends. If this level is high, then the degree of abstractness will go down; if it is low, then the abstractness will increase. Together with the raising or lowering of the degree of abstractness, the universality of the resulting description will go up or down, while the striving for the highest possible degree of universality remains a constant. This procedure is schematically presented in Figure 5.

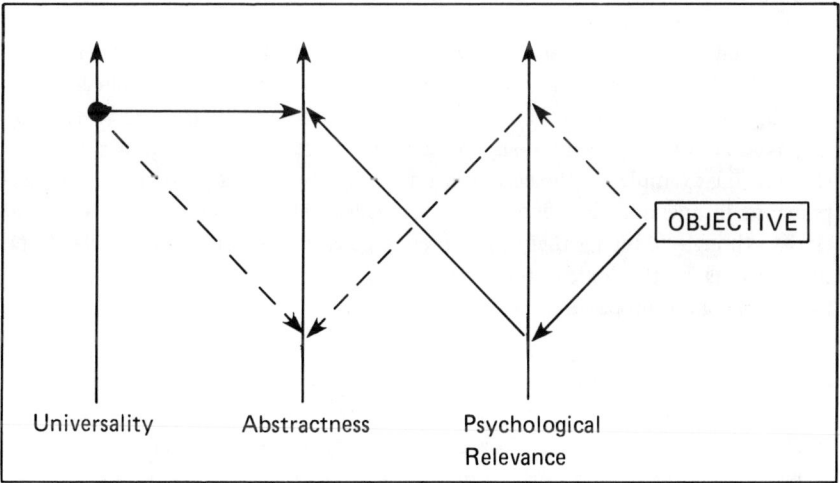

Figure 5

58 PROBLEMS OF LEXICAL SEMANTICS

125 An important practical question remains unanswered: Given a clear objective with its related level of the required degree of psychological relevance, how do we direct our investigations toward the appropriate degree of abstractness?

The question does not need an explicit answer if psychological relevance is the only thing one aims at; the only requirement is then that the degree of abstractness should not be so high as to obstruct psychological relevance. This is the case for the four exploratory exercises in Chapters 3 through 6, which only serve the didactic purpose of demonstrating that linguistic action verbials constitute a (psychologically) relevant basis for conclusions about conceptualization habits concerning linguistic action. The major remaining problem is to decide on a descriptive technique that would help us to avoid circularity. This will be dealt with in the next section.

The logical next step in the development of the empirical-conceptual approach to linguistic action (proposed in Chapter 8) requires explicit measures to find an equilibrium between abstractness and psychological relevance. These will be discussed in the final chapter of this book.

2.6 PROBLEM 3: HOW TO AVOID CIRCULARITY

126 There is always the danger of circularity in the attempt to describe the meaning of linguistic units: one can hardly avoid using language for it, i.e. using paraphrases every part of which is as much in need of an explanation as the element described. An investigation of linguistic action verbials, however, runs the risk of double circularity: language has to be used to describe the way in which language is described by means of language. Thus, this particular area of the lexicon shows some extra complexity.

I believe that the risk of circularity can be minimized. First, there is no circularity in ostensive definitions such as 'That is a tower' pronounced while pointing at a tower. Since we are concerned with lexical items used to describe linguistic actions, we can usually present some ostensive definitions simply by reproducing examples of the verbal acts described by means of the words and expressions in question. Needless to say, ostensive definitions do not provide real clarity; though adducing them can be regarded as a noncircular way of clarifying the meaning of the lexical items we are interested in, it is by no means a full-fledged semantic procedure.

127 The core of the approach to meaning I shall take is implicit in writings as divergent as Wittgenstein (1953) and Leisi (1973). The meaning of the semantic units referring to (an aspect of) a linguistic action can be presented by formulating the conditions to be satisfied in order for the description to be appropriate. Again there can be no circularity involved, since no paraphrases are needed. This

PROBLEMS OF LEXICAL SEMANTICS 59

approach is clearly pragmatic. Linguistic pragmatics is, after all, the study of the appropriateness conditions on the use of natural language.

We are talking about the appropriateness conditions on the use of the verbials we are investigating. But remembering the double linguistic layering of the enterprise (analyzing lexical items that are used to describe linguistic behavior) most, though not all, of them can be formulated in terms of conditions on or characteristics of the acts described by means of the verbials in question. The general form of the analysis should be this:

> A verbial V can be appropriately used in a description D of a linguistic action A if A satisfies condition C (or possesses characteristic C).

The symbols D (for the describing act), A (for the act described), and C (for the conditions on or characteristics of A necessary for D to be an appropriate description of A) will be used throughout. Because we shall have to talk about many describing acts, acts described, and conditions, they will be numbered consecutively ($D1$, $D2$, etc.) per section (sections are identified by double-numbered headings). In the few cases in which an appropriateness condition on the use of a linguistic action verbial cannot be formulated in terms of conditions on the act described, the symbol Cd will be used for it if it has to be formulated in terms of conditions on or properties of the describing act (as, e.g., when the verbial implies the describing speaker's value judgments). A few more symbols: S stands for speaker and H for hearer; the speaker and the hearer of A are abbreviated as Sa and Ha, and those of D as Sd and Hd.

128 In order to illustrate the procedure, let us have a look at the following partial description of the meaning of TO LIE (which is treated in more detail in Chapter 4). Remember that A stands for the act described, D for the describing act (containing the word the meaning of which has to be explicated), C for conditions on or properties of A, and Cd for conditions on or properties of D; Sa is the speaker of A and Sd is the speaker of D.

(A)   The earth is flat
(D) Sa lied
($C1$) The earth is round
($C2$) Sa believes that the earth is round
($Cd1$) Sd believes that the earth is round
($Cd2$) Sd believes that ($C2$) obtains
($C3$) Sa intends to deceive Ha
($Cd3$) Sd believes that ($C3$) obtains
($Cd4$) Sd regards saying A under conditions ($C1$) and ($C2$) as reprehensible

In other words, in order for TO LIE, in its prototypical sense, to be appropriately used in D as a description of A, conditions ($C1$), ($C2$), ($Cd1$), ($Cd2$), ($C3$), ($Cd3$), and ($Cd4$) (see also paragraphs **243** and **244**) have to obtain.

As mentioned in paragraph **90**, Miller and Johnson-Laird (1976), too, describe the meaning of verbs of communication in terms of sets of conditions. But since they lack an equally explicit theory of what the conditions are conditions on, and since they lose sight of the double layering of the enterprise, their analyses remain unsatisfactory.

129 It is not sufficient, however, to say that there can be conditions on A and on D. Our theory of what the conditions are conditions on needs to be much more explicit. It should, for instance, coherently describe all the phenomena presented in the following brief overview of appropriateness conditions so that it could be used as a heuristic procedure when analyzing linguistic action verbials. (For a further justification of the provisional distinctions I make, see Verschueren 1978b.)

Appropriateness conditions are not just attached to utterances as such. They can bear directly on some aspect of the *extralinguistic reality* surrounding the act described and/or the describing act (including properties of the *speakers* and *hearers* and their beliefs). The foregoing example concerning TO LIE includes only conditions of this type. But appropriateness conditions can also be attached to different levels of linguistic structure itself.

130 At the highest level of generality, we find a number of conditions attached to the use of *language* as such: If a speaker S tries to communicate with a hearer H by means of a language L, he/she must assume that H understands L, that H is not deaf, or that he/she can read, etc. This is part of what Searle (1969) includes in his 'normal input and output conditions'.[8] As with many other conditions their importance is only felt in case they do not obtain.

The next level is that of the *communication type*. Different types of communication are, for instance, conversation, literary writing, scholarly writing, advertising, etc. The maxims of quantity, quality, relation, and manner specified by Grice (1975)[9] were intended as conditions attached to a particular communi-

---

[8] Searle's formulation of his 'normal input and output conditions: 'Together they include such things as that the speaker and hearer both know how to speak the language; both are conscious of what they are doing; they have no physical impediments to communication, such as deafness, aphasia, or laryngitis; and they are not acting in a play or telling jokes, etc. It should be noted that this condition excludes *both* impediments to communication such as deafness and also parasitic forms of communication such as telling jokes or acting in a play' (1969:57). The problem of seriousness and literalness (which is referred to in this quote by means of the term 'parasitic forms of discourse' as opposed to serious and literal types of communication) is not to be situated at the level of language as such.

[9] For the sake of convenience I list Grice's (1975) maxims of conversation: *Cooperative Principle:* 'Make your conversational contribution such as is required, at the stage at which it occurs, by the accepted purpose or direction of the talk exchange in which you are engaged'; *Maxims of Quantity:* 'Make your contribution as informative as is required (for the current purposes of the exchange)' and 'Do not make your contribution more informative than is required'; *Maxims of Quality:* supermaxim: 'Try to make your contribution one that is true', plus 'Do not say what you believe to be false' and 'Do not say that for which you lack adequate evidence'; *Maxim of Relation:* 'Be relevant'; *Maxims of Manner:* supermaxim: 'Be perspicuous', plus 'Avoid obscurity of expression', 'Avoid ambiguity', 'Be brief (avoid unnecessary prolixity)', and 'Be orderly'.

cation type, namely conversation (though they can be generalized to some other types of communication as well, and though they are not equally valid for all types of conversation). Only if an act A is uttered within a communication type for which the maxim 'Try to make your contribution one that is true' is relevant, will it be appropriately described by means of TO LIE if it deviates from the truth as known to Sa.

Next is the *style* or *code*. A language is not an absolutely homogeneous instrument. Rather, closely related intentions can get very different expressions, as in 'Hi, Joe' versus 'Good morning, Professor Carruthers', both of which can be addressed to the same person. Different appropriateness conditions are attached to these different styles.

With the level of the *text* there is, for instance, a condition of coherence associated.

At the level of the *speech-act type*, we have to situate the whole apparatus of conditions on illocutionary acts worked out by Searle (1969). Many of these are specific applications of Grice's maxims of conversation. An act described by means of TO LIE will normally be an assertion subject to all the conditions attached to assertive speech-act types.

Then comes the occasion-specific *speech act*. This level is separate from the previous one for the following reason. Whereas, for instance, the speaker's intention to do a future act is a condition on the performance of a promise in general, the speaker's intention to come tomorrow is a condition on the occasion-specific utterance of the promise 'I promise to come tomorrow'.

In order for certain *sentence structures* to be appropriate, certain facts have to obtain. The wh-question 'When did George come back?' presupposes that George came back. Similarly, the cleft 'It was John who murdered the grocer' presupposes that someone murdered the grocer, and the pseudocleft 'What Henry did was to burn down the garage' presupposes that Henry did something.

Appropriateness conditions are also associated with smaller linguistic units. For some *noun phrases* such as definite descriptions to be appropriate, the object referred to has to be identifiable. Many *words* carry presuppositions (which constitute one type of appropriateness condition): a verb of transition such as TO AWAKE is only appropriate if the person who is said to awake was asleep before; a factive predicate such as TO REGRET presupposes that the regretted state of affairs obtains; similarly, many adverbials, such as AGAIN, etc., presuppose something. Even *sound features* such as a particular intonation pattern are only appropriate under certain circumstances.

131 A word of caution is called for. The foregoing illustrations may be misleading in that all the conditions presented were somehow conditions on standard forms of language. Needless to say, linguistic behavior deviates from this standard all the time. But there is a serious danger of confusion here. I claimed before that what I was mainly interested in was the prototypical or standard meaning of linguistic action verbials because I believe that the prototype ap-

proach to lexical meaning is the only tenable one. But what should be kept in mind is that a deviation from the standard conditions, specified in the previous paragraph, attached to some level of the linguistic structure of A may be a standard condition on the appropriate use of a verbial V in a description D of act A.

132 The reader should be warned against interpreting the attempt to formulate 'appropriateness conditions' as a return to linguistics as a prescriptive rather than a descriptive enterprise. As shown before (see paragraph 15), such an interpretation completely misses the point.

133 The conditions we are talking about are a matter of contextual appropriateness. Thus, a condition attached to a particular level of linguistic structure may be related to features of a different level of the same linguistic act, but also to features of the extralinguistic context including the speaker's intentions and the effects produced in the hearer. All these aspects of linguistic action are represented in Table 3.

As I have said before, the previous overview of appropriateness conditions on the basis of the different levels of linguistic structure to which they are attached mainly serves as a heuristic procedure and will not be immediately reflected in the ensuing expositions. Thus it may happen that, when specifying a condition C on the appropriate use of a verbial V in a description D of an act A, I shall be talking only about an aspect of the extralinguistic context of A or

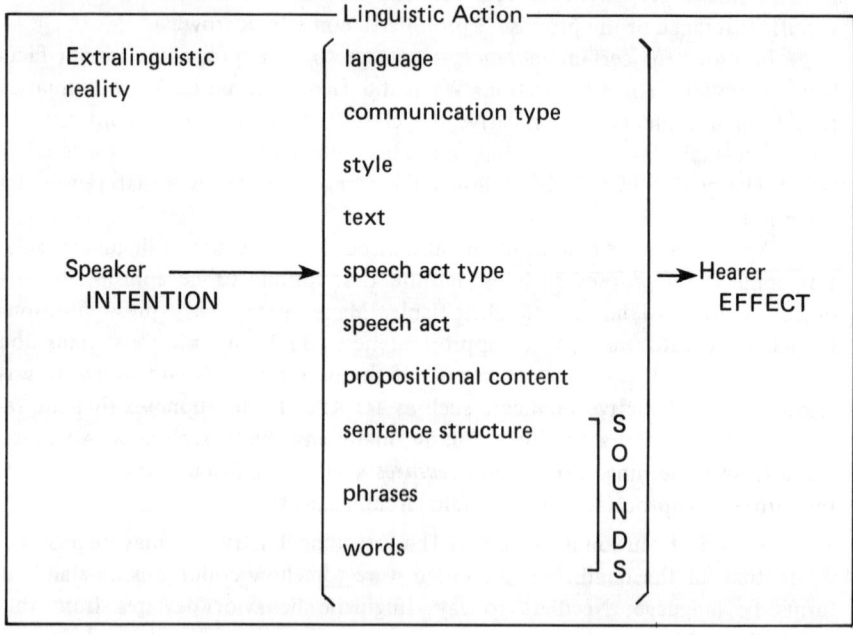

Table 3

of the communication type to which A belongs though in fact C is attached to the speech-act type or the propositional content of A. For instance, consider the condition that a speaker S must have authority over the hearer H in order for the verb TO COMMAND to be appropriately used in the description 'S commanded H to leave' of the act of uttering 'Leave!'. This condition is completely formulated in terms of an extralinguistic relationship between the speaker and the hearer, though it is a condition attached to the speech-act type.

In most cases, conditions will be attached to several of the levels of linguistic structure of the act to be described. But usually not all those conditions will be equally salient. These degrees of salience provide us with one criterion for identifying subfields within the vast lexical frame under investigation. Actually, this criterion was used in my selection of the subfields I concentrate on in this essay.

134 We have stressed the need for a coherent background theory that would allow us to formulate exactly what the conditions on the use of linguistic action verbials are conditions on (see paragraphs **128** and **129**). Though the foregoing overview of types of appropriateness conditions may be sufficient as a heuristic procedure for the purposes of this book (in which no really detailed analyses can be provided due to the size of the subfields of linguistic action to be dealt with), what is really needed for further in-depth studies is a *coherent pragmatic background theory*. Such a theory, which should spell out patterns of background assumptions, is presently being elaborated (though in somewhat different terms from the ones handled here in order to avoid the connotations of prescriptivism which some linguists attach to the term 'appropriateness'; the notion of 'linguistic adaptation' will be made central). Notice that the coherent pragmatic background theory is not a theory of linguistic action as such; it is only a tool that should help us to capture, in a more systematic way, conceptualizations of linguistic action as they are reflected in its lexicalization. Thus, the approach remains empirical-conceptual rather than becoming theoretical again, though (as predicted in paragraphs **50** and **67**, and as stressed in Chapter 8) theorizing of some sort has to come in.

2.7 PROBLEM 4: HOW TO MAP SEMANTIC SPACE

135 In the first chapter of this essay I have advanced my view of this enterprise as an attempt to map the conceptual space associated with linguistic action as reflected in the words and expressions used in different languages to describe it. But how can such a 'geography of the mind' be undertaken? Consider Figures 6 and 7 (both inspired by Bolinger 1975, pp. 190 and 212). Such mappings are quite straightforward. But notice that in Figure 7 there is only a dimension of 'hardness' at work. In Figure 6 there are three such dimensions, namely humanness, age, and gender; yet the diagram retains a high degree of simplicity. But what can we do with words that are much more complex and cannot be adequately

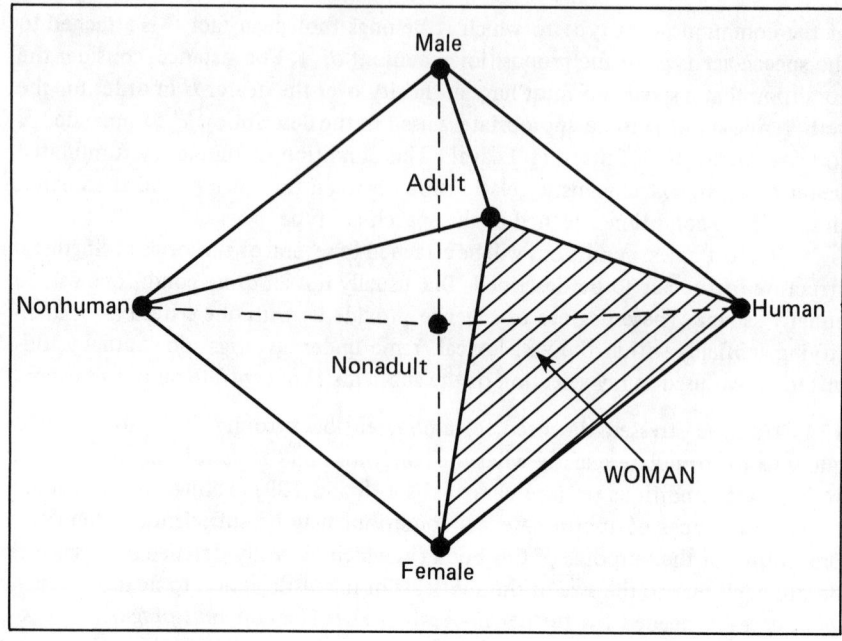

Figure 6. (Adapted from Bolinger 1975: 190.)

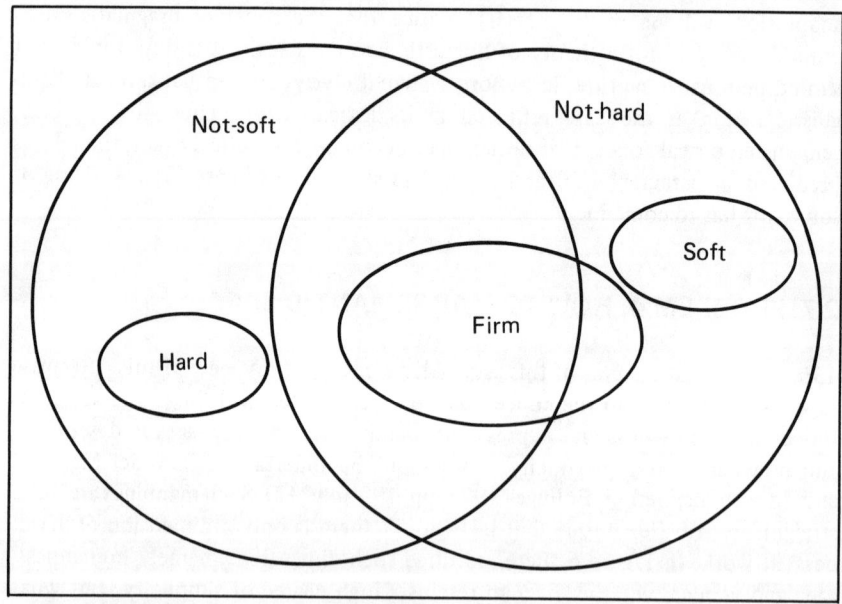

Figure 7. (Adapted from Bolinger 1975: 212)

accounted for in terms of a couple of features, such as our linguistic action verbials? Clearly, a comparable graphic representation is impracticable if its purpose is to be a satisfactory account of the differences in meaning between those verbials, and, in that way, to split them up into semantic classes.

136 Many attempts have been made to distinguish *semantic classes* of linguistic action verbials. Remember the attempts to classify speech-act verbs or the illocutionary forces they describe (see paragraphs 19 and 20). Though the number of semantic dimensions that have to be taken into account makes graphic representations of the type illustrated impossible, such classifications are feasible. There is, however, one condition: a decision has to be made as to the relative importance of the dimensions involved. Several different decisions can be made, depending on one's theoretical point of departure; and every decision is bound to prevent us from seeing certain things. Since the purpose of this investigation is to abandon theoretical biases as much as possible, I will not engage in the construction of classifications at all, which would be much less interesting than the discovery and analysis of the *semantic dimensions* along which linguistic action verbials can be compared. Not only does this enable us to remain faithful to the original intentions, it also makes graphic representations possible again. Most verbials under investigation will be presented in diagrams I call *semantic dimension comparison tables* (henceforth SDC tables).

137 The SDC tables take the following general form. At the center the semantic dimension will be presented by a list of acts (numbered A1, A2, etc.; those numbers will be substantiated in the text) and the relevant conditions (numbered C1, C2, etc.; again those numbers occur in the text) under which they are performed, i.e. those conditions relevant to the semantic dimension in question. To the left the Dutch verbials are listed to show clearly which acts performed under which conditions can be appropriately described by them; whenever necessary also the description *D* (also numbered as in the text) in which they are so used may be indicated; moreover, large dots often indicate (as in Figure 4) the prototypical uses of the verbials. To the right the same is done for English. As a result we get a visualized comparison of the relevant Dutch and English verbials with respect to a particular semantic dimension. The general form of these diagrams is depicted in Figure 8. Such diagrams are presented for most dimensions along which appropriateness conditions are formulated and compared. Needless to say, there are often several layers of overlapping words on each side of a single SDC table, and the area covered by a particular word does not have to be a continuous part of the dimension.

138 To make all this less abstract, consider Table 4, which represents a minute portion of the social setting dimension of Dutch and English verbs describing acts of directing. The two points on this part of the dimension in question are the following:

(C1) The social setting is of an unspecified 'official' nature
(C2) The act described is performed in a 'legal' setting

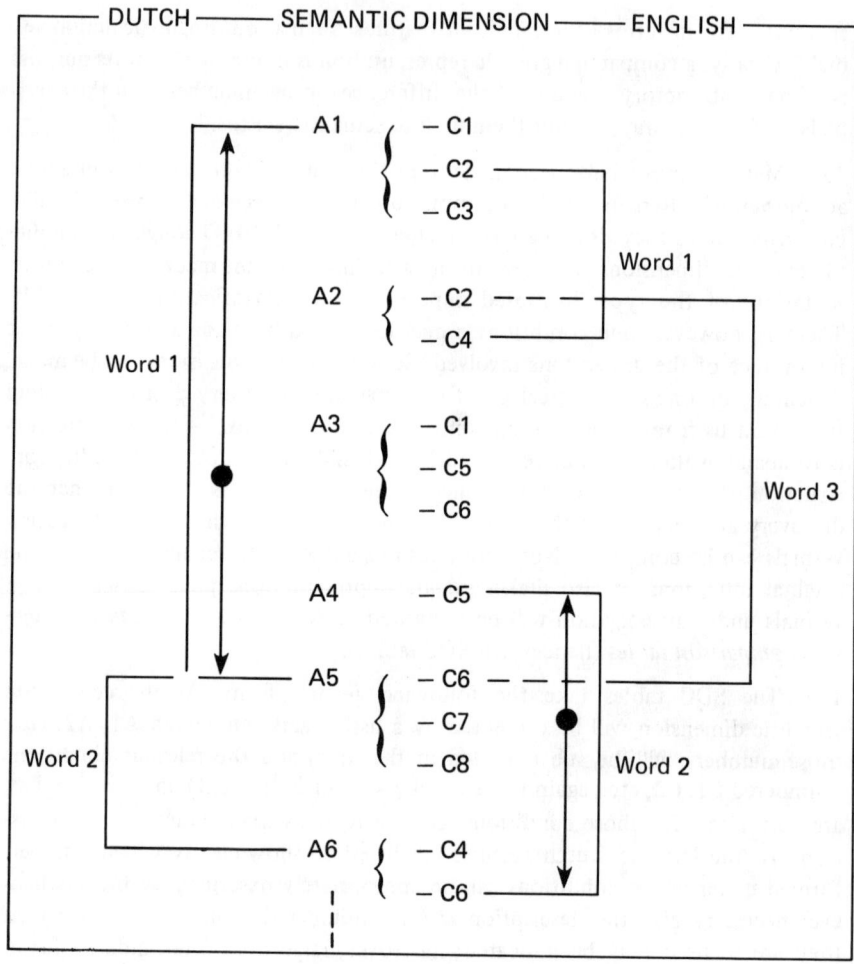

Figure 8

Further specification of acts described and describing acts would lead us too far. The example comes up again in Chapter 5.

139 Occasionally, it happens that a particular semantic dimension is relevant to the meaning of so many verbials that including them in the SDC table in question is physically impossible. In such cases the different *semantic patterns* (abbreviated SP) to which the verbials conform will often be numbered in the SDC table and a complete or representative list of the verbs and phrases belonging to each of the patterns distinguished will be given in the text. Thus a *semantic pattern* is defined as the way in which a word (or group of words) relates to a particular dimension of its meaning. Figure 9 depicts the general form of such simplified SDC tables.

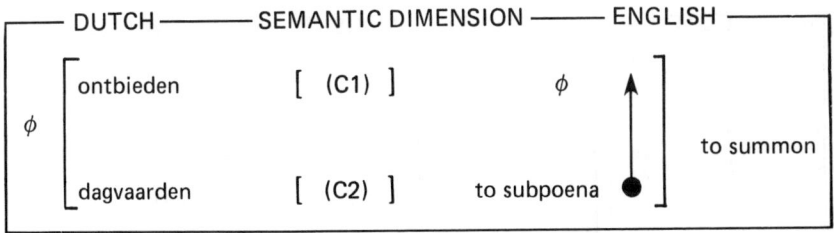

Table 4

Another way out when the number of relevant verbials is too large to squeeze into the tables is to simply give one or two examples. It will always be clear from the text which other verbials show the same semantic pattern as the examples given in the SDC table.

2.8 EPILOGUE: PITFALLS OF COMPARISON

140 After this review of some of the major problems involved in doing (comparative) lexical research, it may be interesting to point out a type of minor problem of comparison that is usually overlooked. To make the exposition as concrete as possible, how would I go about comparing parts of the lexicon of English and Dutch (which is what I do in the following chapters)? It happens that the varieties of these two languages that I have been confronted with most, are American English and the Flemish variety of Standard Dutch (spoken in the northern provinces of Belgium). There is a minor problem involved in any lexical comparison between American English and Flemish Standard Dutch, which has to do with the history of the two languages and the societies in which they are spoken.

Mobility is perhaps the basic structuring force in American society, resulting in a kind of cultural uniformity that, given the vast geographical, racial, and occupational differences, would be hard to imagine in less mobile European cultures. Apart from the language used by previously segregated groups such as American Blacks, there is also a quite impressive linguistic uniformity. Though the English spoken in the deep South sounds quite different from New York Jewish English—they are, after all, more than 1,000 miles apart—they are still mutually intelligible, whereas people in Limburg (the easternmost province of Flanders) do not understand the people in West Vlaanderen (the westernmost province of Flanders) if they speak their local dialect, and vice versa, though the two provinces are less than 100 miles apart (that is, less than the distance between New York and Philadelphia or between Los Angeles and San Diego). Because of the linguistic uniformity (and supported by a vague but strong principle of liberty), Americans can speak the same variety of English on all occa-

68 PROBLEMS OF LEXICAL SEMANTICS

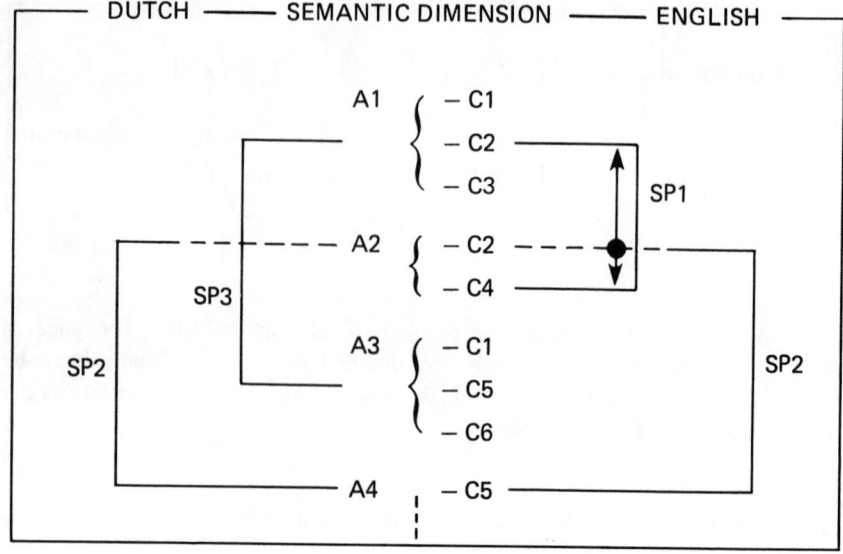

Figure 9

sions: at home, at work, addressing a friend, or addressing the whole nation. Their language is not just a means of communication scrupulously adapted to the circumstances but a means of expression with which they have become fused. As a result, though an American will not fail to respond when asked to make judgments about the formality or informality of linguistic expressions, in actual usage this contrast is becoming less and less relevant. Thus, the same Americans who euphemize about a basic activity such as eating by talking about RAISING ONE'S BLOOD SUGAR LEVEL, are likely to use a nice collection of four-letter words in the same conversation. Or again, the use of an expression such as TO PUT THE LID ON (which some dictionaries, even recent ones, characterize as slang) will cause no surprise at all in the discussion of the gross national product in a televised presidential campaign debate.

In Flanders, on the other hand, there was until recently a complete lack of linguistic uniformity. Even after Belgium became an independent country in 1830, the spontaneous growth of a standard language was prevented by the fact that for all purposes for which a standard language is needed, such as government, the press, science, and higher education, French was used (indeed, French was the only legally accepted language). Though a standard Flemish variety of Dutch has been used for all official purposes for several decades now, and though everybody understands it, most people have considerable difficulty speaking it: their language at home, and often at work, remains a regional dialect (which is maintained because of the still limited mobility of the society). The consequence is linguistic insecurity and an overanxiousness to use the right register and the right degree of formality in the right circumstances. Moreover, many speakers find it absolutely impossible to reach any degree of informality when using the standard language.

Consequently, since the patterns of usage of formal versus informal lexical items in American English and Flemish Standard Dutch differ considerably, an overall comparison (in which labels such as 'formal', 'informal' and 'slang' are used) is intrinsically distorted. There is no solution to such problems, which could be fascinating topics for further sociolinguistic research.

2.9 CONCLUDING REMARK

141 In this chapter, I hope to have succeeded in defining the object of investigation more precisely, in explaining the principles of lexical semantics underlying my approach, and in clarifying the way in which the analyses will be formulated and the results will be presented. Thus we should be ready now to take language as our guide for the tour through linguistic action. In view of the inevitable limitations of the investigation, some readers might be prompted to abandon the adventure altogether. But after all, curtailed insights are better than no insights at all.

142 As announced in the introduction to this chapter, the foregoing discussion of lexical semantic problems does not provide us with a full-fledged methodology to undertake wide-ranging comparative investigations of linguistic action verbials in view of the conceptualizations they reflect. For one thing, the required pragmatic background theory has not been worked out; only some sketchy observations (which may, however, be valuable from a heuristic point of view) have been made.

Similarly, no testing procedures have been developed to check our hypothesis about the prototypical meanings of linguistic action verbials or our intuitions about basic-level terms. The notion of a basic-level term itself will not figure prominently in the sample analyses of Chapters 3 through 6; its function in the empirical-conceptual approach to linguistic action will not be clarified in this book, though an (albeit minimal) role will be assigned to it in Chapter 8. Nor has a serious attempt been made to take into account the problems of complementation (i.e. a matter of linguistic framing) that are bound to influence the meaning of any verb or verblike element. Another way to pursue our ultimate interest in the conceptualization of linguistic action, viz. to study the metaphors revealed in its lexicalizations, has been completely neglected so far.

Yet, for the purposes of our exploratory exercises, the point of which is to show the relevance of the empirical-conceptual approach, we should be well enough equipped by now.

PART II

FOUR EXPLORATORY EXERCISES

CHAPTER **3**

THE SEMANTICS OF SILENCE

3.0 INTRODUCTION

143 In the theoretical preliminaries of the introductory chapter we announced a guided tour through (some types of) linguistic action with language, in particular the verbials it furnishes to describe what one does with words, as our guide. A good guide does not only take you to the obvious places that can be seen and recognized from miles away. Language fits that definition of a good guide. Immediately it draws our attention to an aspect of linguistic action that most theoreticians have ignored: the many ways of being silent. There is more to silence than the absence of speech. Silence can be golden, deathlike, tomblike, solemn, and even pregnant; but it is rarely neutral. That is, when silence is neutral it is rarely talked about or even noticed.

144 One can legitimately wonder whether silence is a linguistically significant category. Let us make a comparison. Though for a geologist the complete set of holes in the surface of the earth does not form a natural category, it consists of a number of subsets (e.g. volcanic craters, holes caused by the impact of meteorites, those caused by earthquakes, etc.) that do. Similarly, though all instances of linguistic silence, taken together, do not constitute a natural linguistic category, it is linguistically significant to get an overview of the complete set because it consists of a number of subsets the 'natural category' status of which would be hard to deny. Yet, the absence of speech has rarely been studied. Two of the exceptions are Mihailă's (1977) attempt to describe silence in speech-act terms, and Basso's (1972) anthropological account of motives for silence in Western Apache culture. The importance of silence, as reflected in Tzeltal metalinguistic terms, is mentioned *en passant* by Stross (1974:225). And silence *about* something is the implicit topic of Ochs Keenan's (1976) investigation of the way in which the inhabitants of a small Madagascar village deviate from the Gricean maxim 'Be informative'. The insights emerging from the following contrastive analysis of English and Dutch verbials used to describe linguistic silence will be compared with the findings and claims of these sporadic studies in the conclusions to this chapter.

145 For the sake of brevity I baptize all the verbials describing a person's being silent *verba tacendi* (Latin TACERE means 'to be silent'). And instead of having recourse to the quite informal OYSTER or CLAM, the silent person will be dubbed the *tacens*.

Due to the marginal position of the verba tacendi among the linguistic action verbials, this chapter differs from the others in one important respect. Ostensive definitions will be impossible here since acts of being silent cannot be reproduced on paper. Therefore, the acts referred to by means of the lexical items under investigation can only be described, whereas illustrations can be adduced when we come to the study of the other lexical subfields singled out in this essay.

3.1 THE FRAME OF SILENCE

146 Silence is no doubt the most marginal aspect of linguistic action imaginable. Yet it is certainly part of our talking about linguistic action. One would never make an assertion about someone's being silent unless he/she could have been expected to speak. Whereas the marginal character of silence within the frame of linguistic action is the reason why theorists of communication have usually neglected to talk about it, it provides us with two arguments to treat the verba tacendi in this essay, which, as announced, is intended to concentrate only on some *representative* subfields of the linguistic action verbials.

147 First, no matter what phenomenon one is trying to account for, the account is hopelessly inadequate if only its 'spectacular' aspects are dealt with and nothing is said about the inconspicuous ones. Let me try to clarify the relevance of this general statement for the problem at hand by carrying the metaphors of this undertaking as a kind of geography of the mind and as a guided tour a bit further. Someone who has visited Yellowstone National Park and the Grand Canyon but has no idea of the less impressive Midwestern landscape, or someone who has only seen New York City or San Francisco but has no idea of the kind of life going on in a less exciting small Midwestern town cannot be said to know the United States. Silence is the usually unnoticed and rarely appreciated Midwest of linguistic action. The area has to be included in any sample that purports to be representative.

148 Second, because of its marginality, silence is a reflection of all the major aspects of linguistic action. This is especially clear after a survey of the verba tacendi. Silence is not just the absence of linguistic sounds. There is also a meaning to it. It shows contextual links. There are social value judgments attached to silence. There is a speaker and a hearer involved—however strange this may sound. And so on. Briefly, *the frame of silence is the frame of linguistic action itself*. Whereas all other subfields of linguistic action verbials studied in this essay are centered around a few heavily emphasized aspects of verbal behavior, no such emphasis is clear with the verba tacendi. But let us now start listening to what the words have to say; in other words, let us start investigating what the lexical frame of silence has to tell.

3.2 SILENCE, MEANING, CONTEXT, AND COMMUNICATION TYPE

149 English contains dozens of verba tacendi. Yet none of the more or less neutral expressions (i.e. expressions carrying less presuppositions than most of the others used to describe linguistic silence) qualify as genuine lexical items (according to the criterion proposed in section 2.1.3). Thus TO BE SILENT is a transparent construction (both for the encoder and the decoder) combining a copula with an adjective. Similarly, NOT TALK, NOT SPEAK, and TO SAY NOTHING are transparent combinations of a simple verb of speaking with a negative particle or a (pro)noun. Since these expressions are conventional ways of talking, on a more or less basic level, about the kind of linguistic behavior in question, it would be wrong to say that we are confronted with a real lexical gap. Therefore, they will be used as a point of comparison with Dutch, which does contain genuine lexical items to cover the same 'neutral' silence meaning. In the resulting SDC tables, however, they will be put between square brackets in order to emphasize their different—if not totally absent—'lexicalization' status.

150 Though I am more interested in the semantic dimensions along which linguistic action verbials can be compared than in the semantic classes into which it is possible to group them, it may be helpful to observe that the set of verba tacendi seems to fall apart in three relatively natural categories (which, as shown below, can themselves be regarded as points of a semantic dimension). The contrast between the first two classes reflects the distinction between the form and the content of utterances or between the act of speaking as such and what one says. Let us call the lexical tools to describe the absence of acts as speaking as such *verba silendi*. Taking into account the reservation expressed in the previous paragraph, the basic ones in English are probably TO BE SILENT, NOT TALK, NOT SPEAK, and TO SAY NOTHING. Many other verba tacendi mean that the tacens refrains from talking about a particular subject (in which case he/she may either be completely silent or talking about something else): these I call *verba reticendi* (Latin RETICERE is synonymous with the transitive form of TACERE); the object in question will be referred to as the *tacendum*, pl. *tacenda*.

The basic English examples are TO BE SILENT ABOUT, NOT TALK ABOUT, NOT SPEAK ABOUT, and TO SAY NOTHING ABOUT. In addition to the verba silendi and the verba reticendi, there is a third category of words and expressions by means of which a person's being silent can be described. With the verba silendi they share the property of designating the absence of speech as such; a specification of what it is that is not being talked about is not necessary, though many of the verbials in question can take, or even require a complement. I am talking about what could be called the *verba cessandi*, verbials denoting a person's silence after he/she has been speaking (or writing) and sometimes implying that he/she will resume his/her linguistic activity after a brief interval. The complements they can take may specify the nature of the preceding discourse.

151 Observe that there is another set of verbials that describe linguistic actions related to silence. I am thinking of TO SILENCE, TO PUT TO SILENCE, TO HUSH, TO MUZZLE, TO DUMBFOUND, etc. These, however, are not verba tacendi (except for TO HUSH and TO MUZZLE in their sense as verba reticendi): they describe (usually linguistic) acts performed in order to cause somebody else to be silent. Therefore, they do not belong to my object of investigation in this chapter.

152 Remember that the purpose of paragraph **150** is not to set up a taxonomy of verba tacendi, which would be in contradiction with the overall aim of this work. Rather, I present the distinctions in order to demonstrate the kinds of verbials that I am about to analyze and to set up a terminology that will make the discussion easier. Moreover, the distinctions provide us with a kind of semantic dimension along which the 'basic' verba tacendi can be usefully compared.

By *basic verba tacendi* I mean those that are somehow neutral, unmarked; that is, those verba tacendi the applicability of which is governed by the least specific appropriateness conditions. If my linguistic intuitions had been backed by elaborate psychological testing, there might have been some reason for calling them basic-level terms (see section 2.4.2). Notice that I have not given an example of a basic verbum cessandi; it seems to me that there is no such thing in English: TO STOP TALKING is even less a lexical item than TO BE SILENT and its companions, and TO FALL SILENT is not 'neutral', as will be shown later.

153 From the few examples adduced so far, two facts about English verba tacendi emerge. First, the basic verba tacendi are always *complex* lexicalizations if lexicalizations at all (see paragraph **149**). Many simple lexicalizations will be encountered in the following discussion, but their meaning is always more specialized.

Second, English lacks a *general expression* for the absence of speech. In a way, TO BE SILENT is *too general*. It does not only contrast with SPEECH but also with NOISE. In addition it denotes not only the absence of speech but also a habitual reluctance to speak. Moreover, in its absence-of-an-act-of-speaking sense, TO BE SILENT does not necessarily mean that no words were uttered at all, though this is no doubt its central meaning; it is a more relative notion. If

Mr. Smith refrained from speaking on a certain occasion, the absolute absence of his speech activity would be accurately described by saying

(D1) Mr. Smith was silent

But the same sentence could be used if Mr. Smith had indeed been talking but if he had been more taciturn than he used to be or than was expected of him on such an occasion. In other words, TO BE SILENT is applicable to (A1) and (A2).

(A1) *Sa* utters no words at all
(A2) *Sa* utters few words (or fewer than usual under comparable circumstances)

Consequently, TO BE SILENT is not only applicable to situations in which a person abstains from using language.

154 On the other hand, TO BE SILENT is *not general enough*, in that not all silence acts can be described with it. In order to show this we distinguish two more possible types of such acts.

(A3) *Sa* utters no words about a particular topic
(A4) *Sa* discontinues his/her uttering of words

The attentive reader will have noticed that (A1) specifies the domain of the verba silendi, (A3) that of the verba reticendi, and (A4) the domain of the verba cessandi. TO BE SILENT, as it stands, can only be used in some marked descriptions of (A3) and (A4). I regard a description of (A3) as marked when (Cd2) instead of (Cd1) obtains, and a description of (A4) and (Cd4) instead of (Cd3) obtains.

(Cd1) The tacendum is expressed in the propositional content of D
(Cd2) The tacendum is not expressed in the propositional content of D
(Cd3) The discontinued discourse is not overtly indicated in D
(Cd4) The discontinued discourse is overtly indicated in D

Since the tacendum of a silence act can be anything, (D1) cannot be considered an adequate account of (A3) except, for instance, if (D1) is uttered in reply to a question such as 'Did Mr. Smith say anything about his forthcoming divorce?'. Because such a special context is required to avoid an expression of the tacendum in the propositional content of a description of (A3), any D describing (A3) and conforming to (Cd2) is marked whereas it would be unmarked or neutral when conforming to (Cd1). TO BE SILENT can only be used in such a marked description of (A3). However, only a small adaptation is needed to make TO BE SILENT applicable in D describing (A3) and conforming to (Cd1), namely the addition of the preposition ABOUT. But what about (A4)? It seems that verba cessandi such as TO FALL SILENT do not require an overt specification of the discontinued discourse in the D in which they are used to describe (A4): the fact that the silence act follows speech is clear from the verbial itself. Hence, D is unmarked if it conforms to (Cd3) but marked if (Cd4) is satisfied. Again, TO BE SILENT can only be used to describe (A4) in a marked D: (D1) does not mean that the utterance of words was discontinued. But in (D2), which satisfied (Cd4), TO BE SILENT is a verbum cessandi.

> (D2) He was silent for a couple of seconds (before he resumed the thread of his discourse)

Notice that even the addition of 'for a couple of seconds' may be sufficient as an overt indication of preceding discourse. In this case a small adaptation cannot make TO BE SILENT applicable in D describing (A4) and conforming to (Cd3). The verbial TO FALL SILENT can be used in an unmarked D of (A4), but it will be shown later that for other reasons it cannot be regarded as a 'basic' verbum cessandi (see paragraph 176).

155 Another verbial, TO SAY NOTHING (or NOT SAY ANYTHING), has two advantages over TO BE SILENT when it comes to deciding which term for the absence of speech is the most general. First, it excludes acts of type (A2) except in strongly hyperbolic speech; hence, it is a more absolute notion than TO BE SILENT. The relative character of TO BE SILENT is easy to understand if we remember that in one of its senses SILENT is synonymous with TACITURN, which is predicated of a person who is temperamentally disinclined to talk (though, of course, he/she talks whenever talking is inevitable).

Second, TO SAY NOTHING covers more acts of type (A3) than TO BE SILENT. The restriction to descriptions conforming to (Cd2), as well as the possibility of extending its use to descriptions satisfying (Cd1) by adding the preposition ABOUT, are identical. But imagine two ruffians torturing Mr. Smith to force some secrets out of him. If one of those brutes returns after having gone out for awhile and asks the other one 'Did he say anything?', the answer could be (D3).

> (D3) No, he didn't (say anything); he was just begging for mercy

In (D3) 'he didn't (say anything)' cannot possibly be replaced by 'he was silent' because that would be incompatible with 'he was just begging for mercy'. Thus TO BE SILENT can only be used in D describing (A3) and conforming to (Cd2) if condition (C1) is satisfied by (A3). TO SAY NOTHING, on the other hand, is applicable no matter whether (C1) or (C2) obtains.

> (C1) *Sa* utters no words at all
> (C2) *Sa* utters only words unrelated to the tacendum in question

(Notice the identity between (C1) as a property of (A3) and my previous formulation of (A1).) Here TO BE SILENT turns out to be a more absolute notion than TO SAY NOTHING. Is this not in contradiction with the difference in applicability of the two verbials to (A2)? The possibility of using TO SAY NOTHING in D describing (A3) and conforming to (Cd2) no matter whether (C1) or (C2) is satisfied by (A3) is due to the ambiguity of TO SAY SOMETHING between 'making an utterance' and 'stating something'. Its meaning can be even more specific: 'stating something about a specific subject'. Thus, for the ruffian's purposes

(D4) He did not say anything

would still be accurate if Mr. Smith had been making all kinds of statements such as

(A5) The weather is gorgeous today

or

(A6) I love peanut butter and jelly sandwiches

Sentence (D1) could not possibly replace (D4) with reference to the same acts. However, it might be possible to use (D5).

(D5) He kept silent

But just as TO FALL SILENT, the verbial TO KEEP SILENT is not a 'basic' verbum tacendi. Once more, this will be clarified later (see paragraph 179).

156 The negations of TO SPEAK and TO TALK cover (A1) and also (A3) in conformity with (Cd2) whether (A3) satisfies (C1) or (C2). Notice that, unlike TO SAY SOMETHING, the verbs TO SPEAK and TO TALK are not ambiguous between 'making an utterance' and 'stating something'. Yet they *are* ambiguous between 'making an utterance' and 'stating something about a specific subject'. That is why

(D6) He did not speak/talk

can replace (D4) in the torture situation sketched.

NOT SPEAK and NOT TALK pose an additional problem because of the ambiguity of TO SPEAK and TO TALK between 'to utter words', 'to conduct a conversation', and 'to deliver a speech, give a talk'. The second and third meanings explain why it is possible to say (D7) and (D8), respectively.

(D7) During the last five years of his life he never spoke/talked to anyone; only occasionally did he shout a greeting from inside his car
(D8) Because he did not speak/talk at the conference he had some time for a nice private conversation

Thus, NOT SPEAK and NOT TALK cover (A7) and (A8), neither of which can be included in any of the major types of silence acts distinguished so far: here the tacens abstains from engaging in a particular communication type.

(A7) *Sa* does not conduct a conversation
(A8) *Sa* does not deliver a speech/give a talk

None of the other verba tacendi discussed so far can be used in any way similar to (D7) and (D8).

Observe, finally, that adding ABOUT to NOT SPEAK and NOT TALK restricts their use to descriptions of (A3) conforming to (Cd1); in this respect they are similar to both TO BE SILENT and TO SAY NOTHING.

157 Whereas English possesses only complex lexicalizations (the lexical status of which is even dubitable) to express somebody's being silent in a more or less neutral way, many languages have *simple lexicalizations* at their disposal: Dutch ZWIJGEN, German SCHWEIGEN, French SE TAIRE, Latin TACERE and SILERE, Greek σιωπαω and σιγαω, etc. As announced, I only concentrate on the contrast between Dutch and English. ZWIJGEN is not only a simple lexicalization, its meaning is also *more general* than any of the English equivalents (without ever being too general): it covers the three major areas of the conceptual domain of the verba tacendi, i.e. the absence of speech as such, the absence of speech about a certain topic as in

(D9) Hij kon het niet langer ZWIJGEN
(He couldn't KEEP SILENT ABOUT it any longer)

and the act of discontinuing one's discourse. As shown, English simply lacks such a general term. Moreover, unlike TO BE SILENT, ZWIJGEN does not cover (A2), which I regard as outside the proper scope of the verba tacendi.

The semilexical units NIET SPREKEN ('not speak'), NIET PRATEN ('not talk'), and NIETS ZEGGEN ('to say nothing') have the same scope as their English counterparts. The meanings of these three verbials, as well as the meaning of ZWIJGEN, can be restricted, as with the English verbials, to descriptions of (A3) conforming to (Cd1) by adding the preposition OVER. For the description of (A3) conforming to (Cd1) Dutch provides another simple lexicalization, namely VERZWIJGEN, as in (D10).

(D10) Hij VERZWEEG zijn communistisch verleden
(He KEPT SILENT ABOUT his communist past)

(Note that ZWIJGEN, used as a verbum reticendi as in (D9), can always be replaced by VERZWIJGEN, whereas the reverse is not true.)

158 The differences between the basic verba tacendi in English and in Dutch are represented in SDC Table 1. A striking fact that emerges from the table is that for all the verbials that have (A1) as part of their meaning, (A1) is at the same time the focus of their meaning. The asymmetries between Dutch and English are no doubt clear.

How can A1-3-4-7-8 be regarded as a semantic dimension of the verba tacendi? I said earlier that due to the marginality of silence in the frame of linguistic action, the lexical frame associated with it is bound to reflect the whole spectrum of linguistic action itself. Thus there is an important *language dimen-*

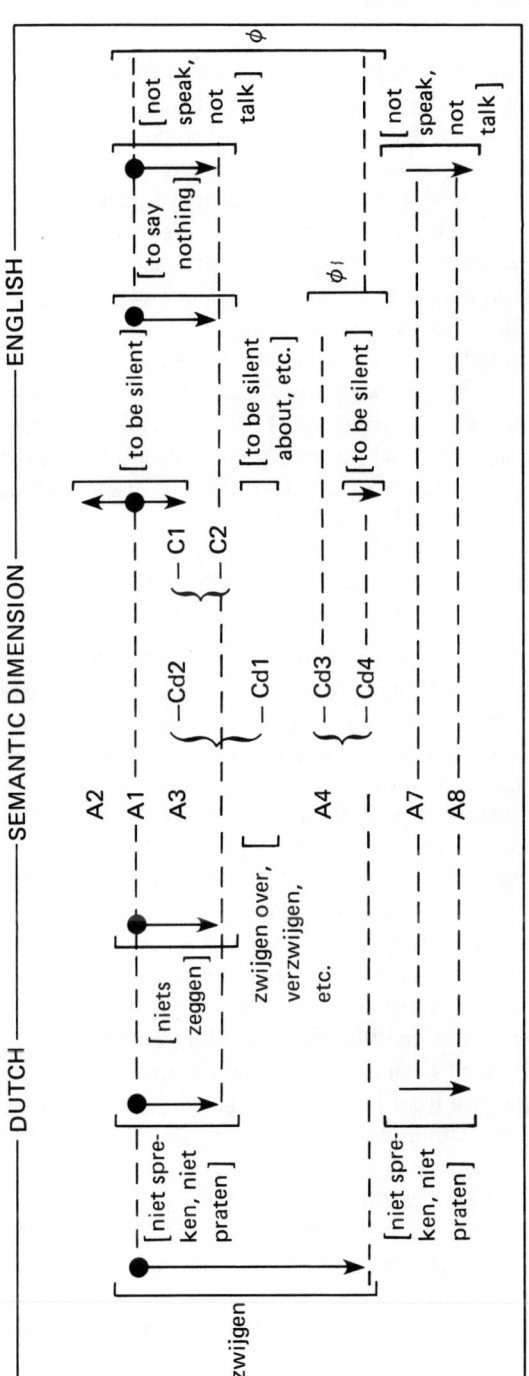

SDC Table 1

sion to the verba tacendi. Since the verbials discussed so far have all been said to be somehow 'basic' in the lexical frame of silence, (A1), (A3), and (A4)—and maybe also (A7) and (A8)—can be regarded as focal points in that language dimension of the verba tacendi: the simple absence of language, the absence of speech about a particular topic (which is related to the *meaning* aspect of linguistic action), the absence of speech in the *context* of surrounding utterances, and the absence of utterances belonging to a particular *communication type*.

Though the importance of (A1), (A3), and (A4) might have been realized by any theoretician studying acts of being silent, the importance of (A7) and (A8) would probably have been overlooked. Indeed, it appears arbitrary to single out the communication type within the realm of the different aspects and levels of linguistic action (see, e.g. paragraph **130**), and within the realm of the different communication types it seems even more arbitrary to single out the conversation type and the delivering of a 'speech'. Yet (A7) and (A8) occupy a salient place in our Western experience of linguistic action: they are our prototypes of dialogue and monologue, respectively. It would not cause too much surprise to find a highly ritual culture or subculture in which the equivalent of NOT SPEAK indicated the nonperformance of a particular ritual.

159 The previous paragraphs provide us with an additional argument for not starting out from a taxonomy of verba tacendi or, for that matter, of linguistic action verbials in general. Conceptualizations of linguistic action, as reflected in their lexicalizations, tend to be more complex than any theoretical taxonomy we could come up with; thus, they draw our attention to more of its aspects so that studying them first provides us with a better basis for thinking about linguistic action and ultimately for classifying its different manifestations. No doubt, the boundaries between the verba silendi, verba reticendi, and verba cessandi are fuzzy. A high percentage of the verbials to be investigated belong to more than one of these categories. Indeed, the meaning of the few 'basic' verba tacendi discussed so far was always spread out over more than one of the three types and often extended beyond the scope of all three. In some cases one could claim that the verbials in question have several different meanings. But there are obvious cases of mixed meanings. A typical example is the Dutch AFSTAPPEN VAN (lit. 'to step down from [a topic]'), which indicates at once silence about a particular topic and discontinuation of speech about that topic (as well as the taking up of another topic). Moreover, also the boundary between the verba tacendi and the verbials describing acts of putting someone to silence is vague; consider in this respect the verbs TO CENSOR and TO HUSH UP. Furthermore, there are probably borderline cases between the verba tacendi and the verbials of lying discussed in the next chapter: there may be occasions on which acts of keeping back information (i.e. the domain of the verba reticendi) should be considered acts of lying.

3.3 THE CODES OF SILENCE

160 The reader's attention should be drawn to the fact that all the verbials in the foregoing paragraphs explicitly concentrate on the absence of speech as an oral manifestation of language, and not on the absence of linguistic behavior as such. With respect to oral versus written communication, we can distinguish (A1) and (A2).

(A1) *Sa* abstains from speaking
(A2) *Sa* abstains from writing

Though all the basic verba tacendi represented in SDC Table 1 have (A1) as the focus of their meaning, some—if not most—of them can be applied metaphorically to (A2), as in (D1).

(D1) The novelist kept silent for almost a decade before publishing his last masterpiece

But this application *is* metaphorical. The only basic verba tacendi—the lexical unity of which is again nonexistent—centering on and restricted to (A2) are the negations of English TO WRITE and Dutch SCHRIJVEN. With respect to the codes of silence we get the quite symmetrical situation depicted in SDC Table 2.

161 With respect to the distinction between the absence of spoken versus written communication, the verba tacendi might be expected to show five different semantic patterns.

(SP1) The meaning is restricted to (A1)
(SP2) The meaning is restricted to (A2)
(SP3) The focus of the meaning is (A1), but it can be extended to (A2)
(SP4) The focus of the meaning is (A2), but it can be extended to (A1)
(SP5) The meaning includes (A1) and (A2) on an equal basis

These patterns are depicted in SDC Table 3.

162 How are the verba tacendi distributed across these theoretically possible patterns? An overview of the verba tacendi shows that the numerically best represented pattern is (SP5). The group includes, amongst many other verbials, TO BURY, TO CEASE, TO COME TO AN END, TO CONCEAL, TO END, NOT GIVE AWAY, TO KEEP BACK, TO KEEP UNDER ONE'S HAT, TO KEEP SECRET, TO MAKE NO SIGN, TO SECRETE, TO STOP, TO VEIL. Notice that in this group there are only verba reticendi and verba cessandi, with the possible exception of TO MAKE NO SIGN.

Also in Dutch the majority of verba tacendi show pattern (SP5). Some examples: AFSTAPPEN VAN (lit. 'to step down from'), EINDIGEN ('to end'), GEHEIMHOUDEN ('to keep secret'), ACHTERHOUDEN ('to keep back'), etc. Also

84   THE SEMANTICS OF SILENCE

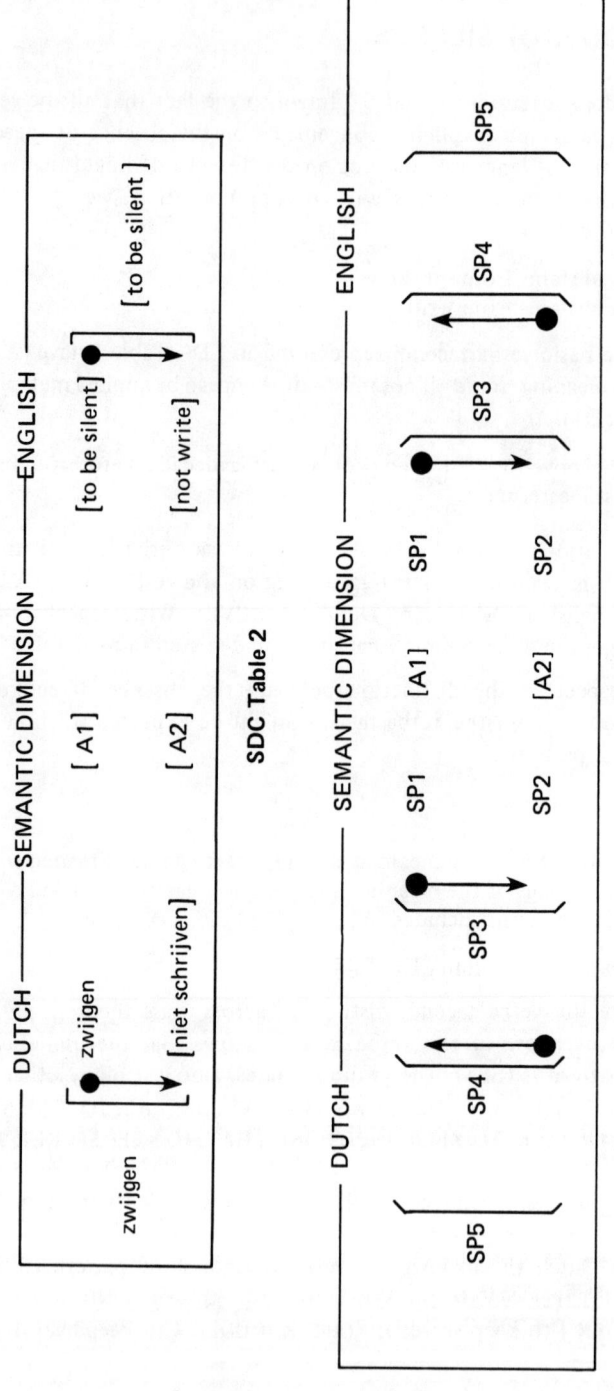

SDC Table 2

SDC Table 3

in Dutch the list only includes clear cases of verba reticendi and verba cessandi. I called TO MAKE NO SIGN a *possible* exception to this regularity. Consider its use in (D2) and its Dutch equivalent NIET VAN ZICH LATEN HOREN (lit. 'not let [somebody] hear about oneself') in (D3).

> (D2) I don't know his whereabouts; he's made no sign during the past three years
> (D3) Hij heeft al drie jaar niet meer van zich laten horen
> (lit. 'he has not let [us] hear about himself for three years already')

The context in (D2), as well as the reflexive VAN ZICH ('about oneself') in the Dutch verbial, show that it may be necessary to interpret the phrases as indicating the absence of (oral or written) communication about oneself rather than the absence of communication as such. This hypothesis may be further supported by the rough equivalence of (D2) with (D4) and of (D3) with (D5).

> (D4) I don't know his whereabouts; he's given no sign of life during the past three years
> (D5) Hij heeft al drie jaar geen teken van leven meer gegeven
> (He has given no sign of life for three years already)

But the rough equivalence of TO MAKE NO SIGN and NIET VAN ZICH LATEN HOREN with TO GIVE NO SIGN OF LIFE and GEEN TEKEN VAN LEVEN GEVEN could also be adduced as evidence to disprove the hypothesis: one might regard an act of 'giving no sign of life' as an act of refraining from communicating as such so that the 'hearer' cannot infer the tacens' being alive, rather than as an act of not communicating about oneself (or one's being alive). Hence, the four verbials in question are to be situated somewhere along the borderline between verba silendi and verba reticendi. That is, we have one more argument for not yielding to the temptation to make hasty taxonomic judgments.

But why the nearly absolute restriction of pattern (SP5) to verba reticendi and verba cessandi in both languages? Why are the verba silendi not normally neutral with respect to the oral versus the written code of silence? We are not yet in a position to venture a generalizing explanation—and we won't be within the scope of this essay. More comparative work is needed first in order to discover the universality or nonuniversality of the phenomenon. Only then will it be possible to decide where an explanation has to be found: in the nature of language as such, or in the cultural traits of particular linguistic communities.

163 Next on the scale of the number of representatives in the lexicon comes pattern (SP1). Some examples: NOT BREATHE A WORD, TO BUTTON ONE'S LIP, TO CLOSE ONE'S MOUTH, TO HOLD ONE'S TONGUE, TO KEEP QUIET, NOT SAY 'BOO', TO KNOCK IT OFF, TO SHUT ONE'S BAZOO, NOT UTTER A WORD. Dutch: BOE NOCH BA ZEGGEN (lit. 'to say neither boo nor ba'), GEEN BEK/ MOND OPENDOEN (lit. 'not open a beak/mouth'), ZIJN BAKKES HOUDEN (lit. 'to hold one's trap'), etc. Two remarks ought to be made.

First, there is a clear correlation between the formation of most (SP1) verbials and the restriction of their meaning to (A1). Most of them contain an explicit reference to part of the oral communication process (e.g. breathing, opening one's mouth, uttering sounds) or an instrument of oral communication (e.g. lips, tongue, mouth, etc.).

Second, the (SP1) verbials form the only set of verba tacendi that contains many slang expressions such as TO KNOCK IT OFF, TO SHUT ONE'S BAZOO, etc. Slang also occurs in verbials the meaning of which is patterned differently, but much less frequently. Hence, there is an interesting correlation between the oral code of the acts of silence to be described and the informal, slangy code of the appropriate describing acts. But again, an explanation will have to be based on further comparative data and on the observation of the existence or nonexistence of a comparable correlation with respect to non-silence aspects of linguistic action.

164 Pattern (SP3) comes next. Its representatives in the lexicon constitute the only remaining large group of verba tacendi. An example is the basic verbum tacendi TO BE SILENT and its Dutch equivalent ZWIJGEN, as will have appeared from SDC Table 2. I shall discuss some other examples in contrast with closely related (SP1) verbials. Consider the following two columns of verbials.

to fall silent	to be silent
to stand mute	to be mute
to button up	to keep buttoned up
not utter a word	not say a word
not say 'boo'	not say a word
to shut one's face/mouth/head	to shut up
to hem and haw	to beat around the bush

If I am not mistaken, the left column contains (SP1) verbials, whereas those in the right column all conform to (SP3). The meaning of TO BE SILENT has already been shown to be extendable to (A2). No such extension seems to be possible for TO FALL SILENT, the typical use of which is illustrated in (D6).

(D6) The politician made a desperate attempt to answer the press agent's question, but he soon fell silent

TO BE MUTE usually refers to (A1), but in (D7), uttered in response to 'I know you wrote to him about the irregularities you discovered, but did you get a reply?', the act described may be of the (A2) type.

(D7) No, he is still mute on the subject

An (A2) interpretation of TO STAND MUTE as used in (D8) is not possible.

(D8) He stood mute upon hearing about his superior's resignation

The next verbial, TO KEEP BUTTONED UP, can be used with reference to the absence of written communication, as in (D9), which is a reply to 'Did he answer your letter?'.

(D9) Yes, but he keeps buttoned up about the irregularities I discovered

TO BUTTON UP, on the other hand, is restricted to (A1). The (SP3) pattern of NOT SAY A WORD and the (SP1) pattern of the corresponding verbials NOT UTTER A WORD and NOT SAY 'BOO' will be clear from the fact that the latter two cannot replace the former in (D10).

(D10) In his letter he did not say a word about the irregularities I discovered

Also TO SHUT UP can be extended to (A2), as in (D11).

(D11) I want this letter to be mailed today, so I must shut up in a minute

Similar extensions are not possible for TO SHUT ONE'S FACE/MOUTH/HEAD. Finally, one can BEAT AROUND THE BUSH both orally and in writing, but one can only HEM AND HAW orally, though both verbials designate the same kind of silence about a particular topic brought about by talking about vaguely related but irrelevant things.

165 The interaction of three quite distinct parameters seems to be responsible for the differences in semantic pattern shown in the above pairs of verbials. First, there is the degree of *immediacy* of the linguistic *action* to be described. The immediacy of oral communication as opposed to the delayed interaction mediated by writing might explain why TO FALL SILENT, which implies the abrupt character of the silence described, is not normally used to describe 'silence in its written form'; there are exceptional cases, such as 'After writing one novel after the other for more than thirty years he suddenly fell silent', in which the abruptness is preserved. A second factor involved is the *formation* of the *verbials* (see also paragraph **163**). NOT UTTER A WORD and NOT SAY 'BOO' carry an explicit reference to the production of sounds, as does the imitative TO HEM AND HAW; whereas TO SHUT ONE'S FACE/MOUTH/HEAD and TO STAND MUTE focus on the instruments of oral communication. Therefore, their being restricted to (A1) is not surprising. The same factor may explain why TO BE SILENT, TO BE MUTE, and NOT SAY A WORD are in the first place concerned with the absence of speech instead of being neutral as to the (A1) or (A2) type of silence. Third, the degree of *formality* of the *description* is involved. TO BUTTON UP, NOT SAY 'BOO', TO SHUT ONE'S FACE/MOUTH/HEAD, and TO HEM AND HAW are all slangy. Also, the relation between slangy verba tacendi and the oral code of acts of silence has been observed before (see paragraph **163**). The restriction of the four verbials enumerated to (A1) is entirely in keeping with it. Moreover, the same correlation may explain why the pretty informal expressions TO KEEP BUTTONED UP, TO SHUT UP, and TO BEAT AROUND THE BUSH are in the first place concerned with the absence of speech rather than being neutral as to the (A1) or (A2) type of silence. This follow-up remark, as well as the one attached to the comments on verbial formation, indicates that none of the parameters discussed is self-sufficient to assign a particular semantic pattern to a verbial (after all, there are, e.g., informal verbials of writing, such as TO DROP A LINE); rather, an intricate interaction of these seems to be responsible. Again, a specification of this interaction will require a lot of further research. Quite similar arguments could be made for the equivalent Dutch verbials discussed in this paragraph.

166 Pattern (SP2) is extremely sparsely populated. We have already mentioned the semilexical NOT WRITE, which is the only basic verbial belonging here. I had to stretch my imagination to find a second and, admittedly, marginal example, namely TO DISCONTINUE in the sense of 'stopping the publication of' as in (D12). (But in practically the same sense one can talk about discontinuing a series of radio talks.)

(D12) The publishing company discontinued the unprofitable journal

One might be tempted to include verbials such as TO CLASSIFY and TO FILE AND FORGET in the list of (SP2) verba tacendi, but they do not belong here at all: they indicate not the absence of written communication but the use of writing as a medium to secrete information.

In Dutch there is only NIET SCHRIJVEN ('not write'). Including the Dutch equivalent to TO DISCONTINUE, namely DE PUBLIKATIE STOPZETTEN VAN ('stop the publication of'), requires an even greater stretching of the imagination because its semantic unity is so weak that it cannot possibly be regarded as a lexical item (however complex).

167 Finally, pattern (SP4) is, as far as I can see, completely empty, both in English and in Dutch. In this respect another interesting question arises. How is it that there is such an asymmetrical relationship between (A1) and (A2) that basic (A1) verbials such as TO BE SILENT can be extended to (A2), whereas the reverse is not true? I am not going to answer the question. Some readers may believe that it would be absurd even to assume that there might be a language in which the meaning of NOT WRITE would get extended to (A1). Yet there is no logical necessity in the restriction of NOT WRITE to (A2), as appears from the fact that words describing the reception and reproduction poles of written communication, such as TO READ and TO COPY, *do* get extended to the reception of oral language (transmitted by radio) as in 'Do you read me?' and 'I copy you'.

168 In connection with (SP2) we have hinted at a totally different aspect of the code of some acts of being silent. Some verba reticendi describe acts of withholding information or of being silent about a particulr topic that may be essentially brought about by linguistic means. I am thinking of verbials such as TO CONCEAL, TO COVER UP, TO HIDE, TO KEEP UNDER WRAPS, TO PUT THE LID ON, TO VEIL, and two mentioned already, TO CLASSIFY and TO FILE AND FORGET.

If language is used to hide information, that language has to appear either in speech or in a written form as well. Most of the verbials in question are neutral as to the code of the secreting language. Only TO CLASSIFY and TO FILE AND FORGET focus on the written code, though they may be metaphorically extended. Surprisingly enough, I have not been able to find any that focus specifically on the oral code of communication. So here the relationship between the two codes is reversed. Again, the stiuation in Dutch seems to be completely analogous.

3.4 THE 'SOUND' OF SILENCE

169 Absolute concepts are not susceptible to comparison or gradation. Thus, if two people are absent from a meeting it makes no sense to say that the one is more absent than the other or that both are very absent. Yet the absence of speech, just as speech itself, can be perceived as more or less intense or 'loud'. Moreover, as to speaking, there is an essentially temporal dimension to not speaking. Therefore, it should not surprise us that most of the expressions used to describe it contain some indication of duration. *Intensity* and *duration* are what I call the two 'sound'-related dimensions of silence. Their relevance to an understanding of the verba tacendi is discussed in this section.

170 In theory, it should be possible to distinguish among acts of being silent with high, average, or low intensity and among long, average, and short ones. The following semantic patterns of the verba tacendi might be expected to correspond to these degrees. They are represented in the SDC Tables 4 and 5.

  (SP1) The verbial describes a highly intense silence act
  (SP2) The verbial describes a silence act of average intensity
  (SP3) The verbial describes a silence act of low intensity
  (SP4) The verbial indicates a long silence
  (SP5) The verbial indicates a silence act with average length
  (SP6) The verbial indicates a short silence

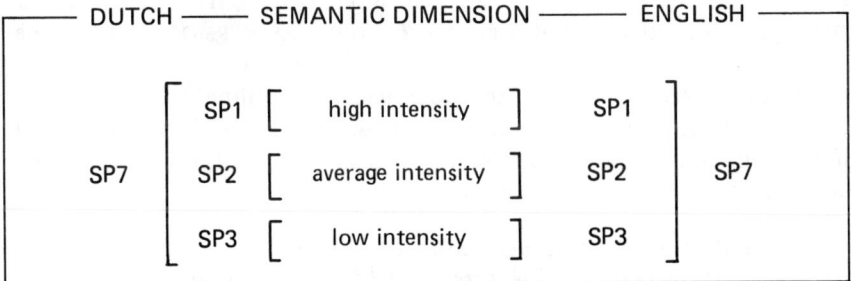

SDC Table 4

90 THE SEMANTICS OF SILENCE

$$\text{DUTCH} \quad \text{SEMANTIC DIMENSION} \quad \text{ENGLISH}$$

$$\text{SP8} \begin{bmatrix} \text{SP4} & [\text{long}] & \text{SP4} \\ \text{SP5} & [\text{average}] & \text{SP5} \\ \text{SP6} & [\text{short}] & \text{SP6} \end{bmatrix} \text{SP8}$$

SDC Table 5

However, only one of these degrees of comparison, the superlative, is reflected in the verba tacendi. In other words, patterns (SP2), (SP3), (SP5), and (SP6) in SDC Tables 4 and 5 characterize empty classes. All verbials that do not indicate highly intense silence acts are completely neutral with respect to intensity, i.e., they conform to (SP7).

(SP7) The verbial is applicable to a silence act with any degree of intensity

And those that do not indicate a long duration are neutral as to the temporal dimension, i.e., they conform to (SP8).

(SP8) The verbial is applicable to a silence act with any duration

Strictly speaking, the neutral (SP7) and (SP8) verbials are outside the scope of the two 'sound'-related dimensions of silence. Therefore, only the (SP1) and (SP4) verbials, i.e. those verba tacendi emphasizing the intensity and duration of the acts of being silent, are reviewed in the following paragraphs.

171 Some of the most common verbials for describing extreme cases of being silent contain a reference to death and the symbols of 'closedness'. In English the *reference to death* is present in TO MAINTAIN A DEATHLIKE/TOMBLIKE SILENCE and the metaphorical verbum reticendi TO BURY. Dutch, however, not only possesses the direct equivalents of these two (EEN DOODSE STILTE BEWAREN and BEGRAVEN), but has in addition ZO GESLOTEN ZIJN ALS EEN GRAF (lit. 'to be as closed as a grave'), ZWIJGEN ALS VERMOORD (lit. 'to be silent as if [one had been] murdered'), EEN GEHEIM MEE ONDER DE AARDE/ IN HET GRAF NEMEN (lit. 'to take a secret under the earth/into the grave'), and IETS DOODZWIJGEN (lit. 'to be silent about something until it is dead'). In all of these the death referred to is purely metaphorical, except in EEN GEHEIM MEE IN HET GRAF NEMEN. One can only say

(D1) Hij neemt heel wat geheimen mee in het graf
(He takes quite a few secrets with him into the grave)

if the person talked about has died. This again shows the marginality of the verba tacendi: here we are confronted with what is probably the only example of a linguistic action verbial that can be predicated of a deceased person. Notice that the literal equivalents of ZWIJGEN ALS HET GRAF, namely TO BE SILENT AS THE GRAVE and TO BE SILENT AS THE TOMB, as predicated of a conversational tacens, are not acceptable to many American speakers of English. Whereas the Dutch sentence

> (D2) Hij zwijgt als het graf
> (lit. 'he is silent as the grave')

is not at all uncommon, the English literal equivalents of the Dutch verbial are mainly used to describe silence as such, as in 'It's as silent as a tomb in here', though I remember reading the following sentence in a British novel: 'During the taxi drive she remained as silent as the tomb'.

172 Also with respect to the *symbols of 'closedness'* there are a couple of differences between English and Dutch. The most important English verbials in question are TO BE/BECOME MUM AS AN OYSTER, TO CLOSE UP LIKE A CLAM/AN OYSTER, and TO CLAM UP. In Dutch there is the comparable expression ZO GESLOTEN ZIJN ALS EEN OESTER (lit. 'to be as closed as an oyster'), but clams do not enter the picture and they are not even replaced by mussels, which are more common in the Dutch-speaking region of the world (maybe because the use of the word for mussel as a symbol for a weakling—for which one uses a jellyfish in English—is too strong a convention). However, Dutch extends its symbols well beyond the world of bivalve mollusks: ZO DICHT ZIJN ALS EEN POT/BRIEF (lit. 'to be as closed as a pot/letter'), POTDICHT ZIJN (lit. 'to be pot-closed'), ZO GESLOTEN ZIJN ALS EEN POT/PEPERDOOS/BRANDKAST (lit. 'to be as closed as a pot/pepperbox/safe'). Finally there is the less transparent image ZWIJGEN ALS EEN MOF (lit. 'to be as silent as a German'); MOF is a quite contemptuous term for 'German' (comparable to the American KRAUT), but it is hard to see an essential relationship between taciturnity and a German (whether he is a contemptible one or not).

173 TO BE SILENT AS A POST and TO BE SILENT AS A STONE, in which the intensity of silence is emphasized by the reference to typically *inanimate* and therefore silent objects, do not find any counterparts in Dutch, contrary to what one might have expected.

174 So far, we have presented an overview of those verba tacendi that derive the expression of intensity from the symbolic relationship between silence and death, 'closed' and inanimate objects. A second important series expresses highly intense silence by referring to the absence of basic speaking processes or the inactivation of certain organs of speech. The *absence of basic speaking processes* will be clear in most of the examples given in Table 1. The processes referred to are the production of words, as in NOT BREATHE A WORD, and the production of sounds, as in NOT LET OUT A PEEP, with somewhere in between NOT SAY

ENGLISH	DUTCH
not breathe a word	geen woord over zijn lippen laten komen (lit. 'not let a word pass through one's lips')
not let a word escape one	geen woord lossen (over iets) (lit. 'not let loose a word (about something)')
not utter/say a word	geen (stom) woord (meer) zeggen (lit. 'not say a (dumb) word (any more)')
not say 'boo'	boe noch ba zeggen (lit. 'to say neither boo nor ba')
not let out a peep	geen geluid uitbrengen (lit. 'not produce a sound') geen piep (meer) geven/laten (lit. 'not give/let out a peep (any more)') geen kik geven/laten (lit. 'not give/let out a sound'; KIK is a word for a very faint noise, which is used only in expressions such as these) kik noch mik geven (lit. 'to give neither KIK nor MIK'; MIK is semantically completely empty; its only function is to intensify the already intense GEEN KIK GEVEN) niet kikken (van iets) (lit. 'not produce any sounds (about something)')

Table 1

'BOO'. In this respect there is a complete parallelism between English and Dutch. The underlying rationale is no doubt that if higher-level processes would be referred to, the intensity of the silence could not possibly be highlighted: descriptions such as 'During the cocktail party, Smith did not utter a single full sentence' or 'He was not able to sustain a prolonged conversation' imply that there was not a complete absence of speech on Smith's part.

Closely related verbials that have not been entered into the table are the following: TO FORSWEAR SPEAKING/SPEECH, NOT HAVE A WORD TO SAY, GEEN WOORDEN VOOR IETS HEBBEN (lit. 'not have any words for something'), HET EERSTE WOORD OVER IETS NOG MOETEN ZEGGEN (lit. 'still have to say the first word about something'), and the quite colorful DE WOORDEN BLEVEN HEM IN DE KEEL STEKEN (lit. 'the words remained stuck in his throat') and HET WOORD STIERF OP ZIJN LIPPEN (lit. 'the word died on his lips').

175 On the other hand, the *inactivation of speech organs* (the favorite ones being the lips, the tongue, and the mouth as a whole) is involved in all the examples given in Table 2. Again, the parallelism between English and Dutch (except for TO MUZZLE ONESELF, which has no direct counterpart), is striking, though not surprising. About the only difference is that the button-and-zip-symbolism is missing in Dutch.

In contrast to the verbials in Table 2, there are also some that involve an unintentional inactivation of some organ of speech or of the organs of speech altogether. Surprisingly, however, one of these, TO HAVE LOST ONE'S TONGUE and the Dutch translation ZIJN TONG VERLOREN HEBBEN, is used typically in

ENGLISH	DUTCH
to seal one's lips to button one's lip to zip one's lip to bite one's lips	de lippen op elkaar drukken/klemmen (lit. 'to press the lips together') zich op de lippen bijten (lit. 'to bite one's lips')
to bite one's tongue to put a bridle on one's tongue to keep one's tongue in check	op zijn tong bijten ('to bite one's tongue') zijn tong in bedwang/toom houden ('to keep one's tongue in check/bridled')
not open one's mouth to keep one's trap/yap shut to shut one's bazoo/face/head	geen mond/bek opendoen (lit. 'not open a mouth/trap') zijn mond/bek/bakkes niet opendoen ('not open one's mouth/trap/yap')
to muzzle oneself	

Table 2

descriptions, such as (D3) and (D4), which are necessarily ironical and imply that the silence is quite voluntary.

(D3) He must have lost his tongue
(D4) Hij heeft zeker zijn tong verloren

The others, which do not carry such implications at all, are: TO STAND MUTE, MET VERSTIJFDE TONG STAAN (lit. 'to stand with a stiffened tongue'), VERSTOMD STAAN VAN (lit. 'to stand struck dumb because of'), SPRAKELOOS STAAN (lit. 'to be struck with dumbness'). A picturesque Dutch verbial in the same line of business is MET DE MOND VOL TANDEN STAAN (lit. 'to stand with the mouth full of teeth'): having teeth everywhere in one's mouth is a rather far-fetched but unquestionably effective image for the inactivation of the organs of speech and thus for being silent.

176 We are still left with a miscellaneous set of verbials describing intense acts of being silent that do not fit the schemes presented in the previous five paragraphs. First, there are some verba cessandi: TO BUTTON UP, TO CLOSE UP, TO DRY UP, TO DUMMY UP, TO FALL SILENT, and the Dutch DICHTKLAPPEN (lit. 'to smack closed') and STILVALLEN ('to fall silent'). In the case of verba cessandi, intensity is often associated with the sudden character of the discontinuation of speech, i.e. with the sharpness of the contrast between the silence and the speech it follows. It is because of the intensity of the silence act described by TO FALL SILENT that we did not want to regard the verbial as a 'basic' verbum tacendi.

Further, there are several verba reticendi such as NEVER LET ON, TO REFUSE COMMENT, TO REPRESS, TO SMOTHER, TO STIFLE, TO SUPPRESS, and the Dutch NIETS LOSLATEN (lit. 'not let anything loose'), OPKROPPEN (lit. 'to pile up in one's gizzard'), and EEN DIEP/GROOT GEHEIM VAN IETS MAKEN (lit. 'to make something into a deep/big secret').

Finally, there are a couple of additional Dutch verba silendi: IN ALLE/ZEVEN TALEN ZWIJGEN (lit. 'to be silent in all/seven languages'), and the less common GEEN SLAG AAN DE BAK KRIJGEN (the BAK referred to is a wooden container used to get sailors hot food from the ship's kitchen; the expression means 'not be able to reach the BAK' because of the pushing of the others so that one does not obtain food; its figurative meaning is 'not be able to say anything because of the excessive talking of others').

177 The intensity expressed by the verbials that we have just discussed is not merely a matter of intensity. It can be related to different aspects of being silent: the duration of the silence, the obstinacy of the person who keeps silent, the reason for being silent, and the meaning with which the silence is imbued. Explicit links will not always be made when we come to the investigation of these other dimensions, but let us not forget that such interrelationships exist.

178 The second 'sound'-related dimension to be dealt with is the *duration* of the silence. It should be noted at once that acts of being silent always have some duration. But whereas one can say 'He was silent for a second', it would be pretty weird to say 'He did not utter a word for a second', 'He did not open his mouth for a minute', or even 'He sealed his lips for five minutes' unless one wanted to joke about an excessively talkative person. The longer duration associated with NOT UTTER A WORD, NOT OPEN ONE'S MOUTH, and TO SEAL ONE'S LIPS becomes apparent through the incompatibility of the expressions with adverbials indicating a short period of time. Notice that these three verbials were included among those that express intense acts of being silent. As a matter of fact, silence cannot be intense unless it is relatively long. Therefore, all the verbials discussed with reference to the intensity dimension belong here as well. However, it is not true that all long acts of being silent are also intense: TO KEEP ONE'S MOUTH SHUT is, but TO KEEP QUIET is not.

In the following paragraphs we concentrate only on verba tacendi the form of which draws explicit attention to a longer duration. As a result, most of those discussed with reference to the intensity dimension are left out. The same principle would also exclude those verbials that derive their association with a longer duration only from their incompatibility with adverbials indicating a brief period of time. However, I have not been able to discover any verba tacendi that describe long silence acts and that neither carry an explicit reference to duration nor belong to those emphasizing the intensity of silence.

179 The most common indication of duration in English is the presence of the verb TO KEEP, as in TO KEEP BACK, TO KEEP BETWEEN US, TO KEEP BUTTONED UP, TO KEEP CLOSE, TO KEEP DARK, TO KEEP FROM, TO KEEP IN, TO KEEP IN IGNORANCE, TO KEEP IN PETTO, TO KEEP IN THE DARK, TO KEEP IT A DEEP DARK SECRET, TO KEEP IT UNDER ONE'S HAT, TO KEEP MUM, TO KEEP ONESELF TO ONESELF, TO KEEP ONE'S MOUTH SHUT, TO KEEP ONE'S OWN COUNSEL, TO KEEP ONE'S TONGUE BETWEEN ONE'S CHEEK, TO KEEP ONE'S TRAP/YAP SHUT, TO KEEP QUIET, TO KEEP SECRET, TO KEEP SILENCE, TO KEEP SILENT (the long duration of which was our reason not to regard it as a 'basic' verbum tacendi), TO KEEP SOMEBODY OUT OF SOMETHING, TO KEEP STILL, TO KEEP TO ONESELF, TO KEEP UNDER WRAPS, TO KEEP WITHIN THE BOSOM OF THE LODGE, TO KEEP WITHIN THESE WALLS.

Some other indicators are TO MAINTAIN, TO LEAVE, TO REMAIN, and TO SIT: TO MAINTAIN A SECRET, TO MAINTAIN (A DEATHLIKE/TOMBLIKE) SILENCE, TO LEAVE IN THE DARK (ABOUT), TO REMAIN SILENT (ABOUT/AS TO), TO SIT MUM, TO SIT ON. And finally there is the morpheme HOLD in TO WITHHOLD, and the verb TO HOLD in TO HOLD ONE'S PEACE, TO HOLD ONE'S TONGUE, TO HOLD OUT ON.

180 In Dutch there are three comparable indicators of duration, namely HOUDEN ('to keep, hold'), LATEN ('leave'), and BEWAREN ('to maintain, keep'), as in DE HANDEN IN DE MOUW HOUDEN (lit. 'to keep one's hands in one's sleeve'), IEMAND ERGENS BUITEN HOUDEN/LATEN (lit. 'to keep/leave someone out of something'), IETS ACHTER DE ELLEBOOG HOUDEN (lit. 'to keep something behind one's elbow'), IETS ACHTER DE HAND HOUDEN (lit. 'to keep something behind one's hand'), IETS ACHTER HOUDEN ('to keep something back'), IETS IN PETTO HOUDEN ('to keep something in petto'), IETS TUSSEN DE TANDEN HOUDEN (lit. 'to keep something between one's teeth'), IETS VOOR ZICH HOUDEN ('to keep something to oneself'), IETS IN DE MOUW HOUDEN (lit. 'to keep something in one's sleeve'), STILHOUDEN ('to keep still'), DE TONG VOOR DE TANDEN HOUDEN (lit. 'to keep the tongue in front of one's teeth'), IETS BEDEKT HOUDEN ('to keep something covered'), ZICH ERGENS BUITEN HOUDEN ('to keep out of something'), ZICH KOEST HOUDEN ('to keep mum'), ZIJN MOND/BEK/BAKKES/BABBEL/RAMMEL/SNATER/SNOET/SNUIT/ TOET HOUDEN (lit. 'to hold one's mouth/trap/yap, etc.') ZIJN TONG IN BEDWANG/TOOM HOUDEN (lit. 'to keep one's tongue in check/bridled'), ZIJN PIJPEN IN DE ZAK HOUDEN (lit. 'to keep one's pipes in one's pocket'); IEMAND VAN IETS ONKUNDIG LATEN (lit. 'to leave somebody ignorant about something'), IETS BUITEN BESCHOUWING LATEN (lit. 'to leave something out of account'), IETS MAAR BLAUWBLAUW LATEN (lit. 'to leave something blueblue'), TERZIJDE LATEN (lit. 'to leave something aside'), IETS IN DE DOOFPOT LATEN (lit. 'to leave something in the extinguishing-pot'); DE STILTE BEWAREN (lit. 'to maintain the silence'), EEN DOODSE STILTE BEWAREN ('to maintain a deathlike silence'), HET STILZWIJGEN BEWAREN (lit. 'to maintain the [act of] being silent'), EEN GEHEIM BEWAREN ('to keep a secret').

3.5 SILENCE AND ITS CAUSES

181 In the vast majority of cases, the act of being silent is deliberate. But the set of linguistic action verbials in English and in Dutch leaves room for instances of silence that lack this purposeful character. Thus, silence acts can be distinguished into those corresponding to (A1) and those describable in terms of (A2).

(A1) *Sa* is silent, but not deliberately
(A2) *Sa* is silent deliberately

What are the *causes* of the silence in cases where (A1) obtains? This question will occupy us in the next few paragraphs. Silence can be involuntary only if an *inability* to speak is involved. But this general cause needs further analysis: the inability itself can be caused by many different circumstances.

182 When we move from deliberate to nondeliberate silence, we find just across the border the acts of being silent that satisfy (C1), i.e. that are due to a general, temperamentally determined *disposition* not to talk.

(C1) *Sa* is temperamentally disinclined to talk

There are no verba tacendi that draw exclusive attention to this type of act. The verbials that can be used to describe it are ambiguous between an (A1)-(C1) act and an (A2) act of some kind. Consider, for instance, (D1).

(D1) Sally's pride was wounded, but she suppressed her feelings

The suppression of Sally's feelings can either be a conscious act performed for a particular reason or a temperamentally determined reflex. In the first case (D1) describes an act of the (A2) type; in the second case an (A1)-(C1) act is involved. The association of TO SUPPRESS with (C1) is probably due to the fact that the verb means not only 'to refrain from expressing' but also 'to exclude from consciousness', and excluding something from consciousness is, according to our heavily freudianized 20th-century world view, mainly an unconscious activity (in spite of *Webster's* definition of SUPPRESSION as 'the conscious intentional exclusion from consciousness of a thought or feeling', which is technically contrasted with the less conscious REPRESSION). The association with (C1) is even stronger in (D2) so that the ambiguity between (A1) and (A2) is almost— though not completely—resolved.

(D2) Sally's pride was wounded, but, as always, she suppressed her feelings

On the other hand, in (D3) the balance tips completely toward (A2).

(D3) Sally's pride was wounded, but somehow she managed to suppress her feelings

Notice that not only linguistic elements in the description can influence the deliberateness balance. The nature of the feeling to be expressed is also important. Consider (D4).

(D4) Sally was on the verge of getting as cross as two sticks, but she suppressed her feelings

In this case the suppression is almost necessarily deliberate, which implies that anger is regarded as a feeling easier to express or more difficult to control than, say, being hurt. In fact, anger and its expression are so firmly united in our Western mind that it would be hard to say (at least for most of the speakers of English I consulted) 'Sally was really pissed off, but she didn't show her feelings', whereas 'Sally was really hurt, but she didn't show her feelings' is quite likely to occur.

Similar verbs on the border between (A1) and (A2) are TO REPRESS, TO SMOTHER, TO STIFLE, and in Dutch ONDERDRUKKEN, VERSMOREN, and OPKROPPEN. I have the feeling that OPKROPPEN (lit. 'to pile up in one's gizzard') is more strongly associated with (C1) than any of the others.

183 Another source of involuntary silence is the tacens' *indecision*, as described in (C2).

(C2) *Sa* is unable to decide what to say (next)

Again, the most common verbial belonging here is ambiguous between (A1) and (A2), but (A1) is its central meaning: TO HESITATE, as used in (D5)

    (D5) Mr. Smith hesitated before continuing his talk

typically describes a silence due to indecision (which is not a voluntary state of mind); if the act described is willful, there is pretense involved. The same holds for the Dutch equivalent AARZELEN, but the meaning of a second equivalent, WEIFELEN, is completely restricted to (A1).

184 The inability to talk may also result from *astonishment, grief, shock,* or other *strong emotion*.

    (C3) *Sa* is unable to talk because of some strong emotion

The verbials TO BE MUTE and TO STAND MUTE belong here, as used in (D6) and (D7), respectively.

    (D6) After hearing the news of his wife's death, he was mute for several minutes
    (D7) The news was so unexpected that he stood mute for several minutes

These two verbials, however, can also be used to describe deliberate acts of being silent. Consider (D8).

    (D8) The mayor is still mute on the subject

And TO STAND MUTE may be predicated of a person arraigned by law who makes no answer, maintains silence, or refuses to plead directly or stand trial.

The Dutch expressions that use muteness as a metaphor exclude (A2) completely from their meaning: VERSTOMMEN (lit. 'to become mute'), VERSTOMD STAAN VAN (lit. 'to stand mute because of'), MET STOMHEID GESLAGEN ZIJN (lit. 'to be struck with muteness'), MET VERSTIJFDE TONG STAAN (lit. 'to stand with a stiffened tongue'), SPRAKELOOS STAAN (lit. 'to stand speechless').

Some more verbials satisfy (C3): TO DRY UP, which again is ambiguous between (A1) and (A2) as appears from the command 'Dry up!', TO FALL SILENT and its Dutch equivalent STILVALLEN, both of which are restricted to (A1), and the expression EEN KIKKER/ROGGESTAART IN DE KEEL HEBBEN (lit. 'to have a frog/raytail in one's throat'), which is ambiguous between the inability to speak because of hoarseness or because of some strong emotion, DE WOORDEN BLEVEN HEM IN DE KEEL STEKEN (lit. 'the words remained stuck in his throat'), HET WOORD STIERF HEM OP DE LIPPEN (lit. 'the word died on his lips'), and PAF STAAN VAN (lit. 'to stand surprised about').

185 An interesting question is what kinds of emotions are involved in producing the tacens' inability to speak. For one thing, all the (A1)-(C3) verbials imply that the emotion was caused by something unexpected; in other words, there is always *surprise* involved. Moreover, the surprise is almost necessarily of an unpleasant kind. If someone 'stood mute' or 'fell silent' upon hearing a piece of good news, bystanders would soon infer that the person in question was not glad at all; he/she is expected to say at least 'I can't believe it' (and to make some additional funny noises). Jumping to a conclusion, one might say that the vision underlying the Dutch and English lexical systems does not allow for the existence of joy unless it is expressed, whereas grief and sorrow are not in need of expression in order to exist. Joy is not the only emotion with which TO STAND MUTE, TO FALL SILENT, etc., are not generally associated. Another one is anger, which is also firmly connected with its expression because of what we referred to before as the relative ease with which it can be expressed or the effort it takes to control (see paragraph 182). A further explanation may be that unlike grief or shock, which may arise suddenly due to an unexpected piece of unpleasant news (remember the element of surprise), intense feelings of anger or wrath are considered to need more time to generate.

186 A further cause of the inability to speak may be a *lack of anything to say*.

(C4) *Sa* is unable to speak because he/she does not know what to say

This cause may be involved in an act described by means of TO DRY UP, TO FALL SILENT, and STILVALLEN. More specialized (A1)-(C4) verbials are NOT HAVE A WORD TO SAY, TO HAVE LITTLE TO SAY, and the Dutch GEEN WOORDEN VOOR IETS HEBBEN (lit. 'not have words for something') and MET DE MOND VOL TANDEN STAAN (lit. 'to stand with one's mouth full of teeth'). The last one of these indicates the tacens' defeat; metaphorically speaking, his/her conversational partners have checkmated him/her so that he/she is at a loss for things to say; of course, this does not yet make the image transparent.

187 A special case of not knowing what to say is the occasion on which one has *forgotten what one was going to say*.

(C5) *Sa* is unable to speak because he/she has forgotten what he/she was going to say

The verbials that can be used to express this quite specialized but not uncommon state of affairs are the same as for (C4): TO DRY UP, TO FALL SILENT, and STILVALLEN. This type of occasion is exemplified in (D9).

(D9) The play could have been good. It's a pity that one of the debuting actresses dried up in the second act and lacked the necessary presence of mind to improvise

In the example TO DRY UP simply means 'to forget one's lines' (which *Webster's* even lists separately as one of the meanings of TO DRY UP).

188 The next cause of silence to which explicit attention is drawn by some verbials is the *talking of others*.

100 THE SEMANTICS OF SILENCE

DUTCH	SEMANTIC DIMENSION	ENGLISH
(opkroppen, etc.)	(A1)–(C1)	(to suppress, etc.)
(aarzelen), weifelen	(A1)–(C2)	(to hesitate)
verstommen, etc.	(A1)–(C3)	(to be/stand mute)
geen woorden voor iets hebben, met de mond vol tanden staan	(A1)–(C4)	not have a word to say, to have little to say
ϕ	(A1)–(C5)	ϕ
geen slag aan de bak krijgen	(A1)–(C6)	not get a word in edgeways
een geheim mee in het graf nemen	(A1)–(C7)	to take a secret into the grave

stilvallen {(opkroppen…through…tanden staan)}

{(to dry up) / to fall silent} on English side covering C5–C7 group

SDC Table 6

(C6) *Sa* is unable to talk because of the excessive talking of others

Examples are NOT GET A WORD IN EDGEWAYS, Dutch ER GEEN WOORD TUSSEN KRIJGEN and GEEN SLAG AAN DE BAK KRIJGEN (the formation of which was explained in paragraph **176**).

189 The final—not to say terminal—cause of silence manifested in the verba tacendi is *death*.

(C7) *Sa* is unable to talk because he/she is dead

This cause of silence is clear in TO TAKE A SECRET INTO THE GRAVE and its Dutch equivalent EEN GEHEIM MEE IN HET GRAF NEMEN. The same cause is often implied by GEEN PIEP/KIK (MEER) GEVEN/LATEN (lit. 'not give/let out a peep/sound (anymore)').

The causal dimension of silence is represented in SDC Table 6. In the table, parentheses enclose verbials that show an (A2) meaning as well as an (A1) meaning.

3.6 THE TACENS AND HIS MOTIVES

190 This section deals with the second pole in the contrast between acts describable in terms of (A1) and those representing (A2).

(A1) *Sa* is silent, but not deliberately
(A2) *Sa* is silent deliberately

As noted before, in the vast majority of cases the acts of being silent are deliberate. Thus the question to ask is this: What are the tacens' motives or reasons for being silent? Whereas inability to speak was the one basic cause of all involuntary acts of being silent, it is hard to find a basic reason or motive for the willful ones. Not only is there a greater differentiation, often several reasons are intertwined.

191 Before giving an overview of the motives singled out by the verba tacendi, it is important to notice that the border between (A1) and (A2) is not clear. A troublesome case is TO FAIL TO MENTION; the presuppositions of TO FAIL and those often carried by the expression as a whole are contradictory. TO FAIL denotes an involuntary nonperformance of a certain activity because it presupposes a deliberate attempt to perform it. However, TO FAIL TO MENTION, as used in (D1) and (D2)

(D1) In his speech about American foreign policy he failed to mention the CIA's involvement in Chile
(D2) He told the police that he had been home at the moment of the crime. But he failed to mention that he had been at the scene of the crime fifteen minutes earlier and that he had seen the suspect

usually carries the implication that the silence act was conscious or even planned though it was performed as if through forgetfulness.

192 A second preliminary remark is that there are quite a lot of verba tacendi belonging to the (A2) category that do not single out any particular reason for the act of silence they describe: TO BECOME MUM, TO CLOSE, TO COME TO AN END, TO SAY NOTHING, TO MAINTAIN SILENCE, and the Dutch AFSTAPPEN VAN (lit. 'to step down from'), EINDIGEN ('to end'), NIETS ZEGGEN ('to say nothing'), HET STILZWIJGEN BEWAREN ('to maintain silence'), and many others are used to describe acts of being silent that can be performed for *any reason*. On the other hand, I have not been able to discover any (A1) verba tacendi that do not single out a particular cause for the involuntary silence described. The obvious rationale underlying the contrast is this: as any other activity, being silent is typically a willful act; therefore, if the act is involuntary, an explanation is always needed.

193 Along the lines of this contrast we could distinguish the following properties of the describing acts in which the verba tacendi are used.

(Cd1) The description does not single out a particular cause of the silence
(Cd2) The description singles out a particular cause of the silence
(Cd3) The description does not single out a particular motive for the silence
(Cd4) The description singles out a particular motive for the silence

Correspondingly, (A1) verbials could theoretically show patterns (SP1) or (SP2).

(SP1) The verbial satisfies (Cd1)
(SP2) The verbial satisfies (Cd2)

And (A2) verbials can show either (SP3) or (SP4).

(SP3) The verbial satisfies (Cd3)
(SP4) The verbial satisfies (Cd4)

These four patterns are represented in SDC Table 7. According to what we have said above, (SP1) is a completely empty pattern. (SP2) verbials have been discussed in the previous section on the causal nature of silence. This section on the tacens' motives is mainly concerned with (SP4) verbials.

194 A few more words need to be said about (SP3) verbials. Though they do not indicate any particular reason for the tacens to be or become silent, many of them refer to a strong *determination*, a refusal to speak or, in the case of verba silendi and reticendi, even obstinacy. (Probably the reader does not have to be reminded of the possible interrelationships between different semantic dimensions; in this case it is clear that verbials implying a strong determination often indicate a long duration and a high intensity as well.) Some examples are TO BE MUM AS AN OYSTER, NOT BREATHE A WORD, GEEN STOM WOORD ZEGGEN (lit. 'not say a dumb word'), IN ALLE TALEN ZWIJGEN (lit. 'to be silent in all

DUTCH	SEMANTIC DIMENSION	ENGLISH
ϕ	SP1 [(A1)-(Cd1)] SP1	ϕ
Paragraphs **182-189**	SP2 [(A1)-(Cd2)] SP2	Paragraphs **182-189**
Paragraphs **192-194**	SP3 [(A2)-(Cd3)] SP3	Paragraphs **192-194**
Paragraphs **195-204**	SP4 [(A2)-(Cd4)] SP4	Paragraphs **195-204**

SDC Table 7

languages'), etc. It is clear that often some strong emotion will be responsible for the generation of the determination or obstinacy. The nature of the emotion is never specified. But one may assume that, contrary to what we have discovered for the emotions involved in some of the involuntary acts of being silent, anger is one of the favorites here. On the other hand, joy is even more unlikely to underlie an (A2) act than an (A1) act.

Some (SP3) verbials do draw attention not to a strong determination as such but to a determination not to speak in spite of one's inclination to the opposite. I am thinking of TO BITE ONE'S LIP/TONGUE, TO MUZZLE ONESELF, TO PUT A BRIDLE ON ONE'S TONGUE, TO BUTTON/ZIP ONE'S LIP, and in Dutch OP ZIJN TONG BIJTEN ('to bite one's tongue'), ZICH OP DE LIPPEN BIJTEN ('to bite one's lips'), ZIJN TONG IN BEDWANG/TOOM HOUDEN ('to keep one's tongue in check/bridled'). Another example is ZIJN TONG GEWELD AANDOEN (lit. 'to do violence to one's tongue'). I present this one separately not only because it is an extremely clear case in point but also because it manifests very plainly the talkative character of Western culture: moving from nonaction to action certainly takes more effort than remaining in a state of rest; therefore, one could expect an expression that means literally 'to do violence to one's tongue' to describe the action of moving, against one's inclination, from not speaking to speaking; but quite the opposite is true: ZIJN TONG GEWELD AANDOEN is fighting one's inclination to talk in order to remain in a state of silence.

195 One of the most common reasons for being silent, which is manifested by many verba reticendi, is *concealment*.

(C1) *Sa* wants to conceal something

Some obvious examples: TO KEEP SECRET, TO CONCEAL, TO VEIL; GEHEIMHOUDEN ('to keep secret'), VERZWIJGEN ('to be silent about'), VERBERGEN ('to conceal'); etc. Concealment is often associated with subsidiary reasons or motives such as deception, solidarity, etc. The vast majority of (A2)-(C1) verbials do not restrict their meaning to a particular one of these, but a few of them do. Let us review those.

196 The following four subsidiary motives (which often interact) play a role in at least some verba tacendi:

(C1a) *Sa* wants to conceal something in order to deceive somebody
(C1b) *Sa* wants to conceal something out of solidarity
(C1c) *Sa* wants to conceal something out of discretion
(C1d) *Sa* wants to conceal something out of mercy

Though the *intention to deceive* can be supposed to be a very common reason for being silent about something, I have not been able to discover more than one verbial with which it is very strongly (though not even necessarily) associated: TO HOLD OUT ON as used in (D3), Dutch IETS ACHTERHOUDEN.

(D3) Ever since we married she's been holding out on me

The association with deception results from the fact that TO HOLD OUT ON means 'to withhold information to which someone has a right'; but even so, other reasons, such as fear, may be at work. How is it that for a common action such as withholding information with the intention to deceive, there are almost no verbials? Two phenomena may be responsible for this situation. First, our rules of politeness may curb our inclination to openly accuse a conversational tacens of deception. Second, and more importantly, our generally accepted rules of conversation dictate that we not make any claims for which there is insufficient evidence. Since silence is a completely intangible phenomenon, it is not possible to adduce it as evidence of any kind; in other words, the tacens can always get away with it by taking refuge in arguments based on forgetfulness and the like. Therefore, one usually does not have the courage to go any further than insinuating, as with TO FAIL TO MENTION, which, as mentioned before, literally describes the involuntary nonperformance of certain acts of speaking though it is often used in such a way that it implies the conscious and purposeful performance of an act of not mentioning something.

197 The three remaining subsidiary reasons for concealment manifested in some verba tacendi might be regarded as 'good reasons': they transform the acts described into cases of 'white silence' (if we are allowed to use the formation of a 'white lie' productively).

Solidarity is the underlying reason in NOT GIVE AWAY as used in (D4).

(D4) She did not give John away

Some other examples are NEVER LET ON, TO KEEP BETWEEN US/THEM, TO KEEP WITHIN THE BOSOM OF THE LODGE, TO KEEP WITHIN THESE WALLS, NOT LET IT GO FURTHER, and the Dutch NIET VERKLAPPEN and NIET VERRADEN (both of which are more or less equivalent to NOT GIVE AWAY).

Discretion is apparent as a motive only in TO BE THE SOUL OF DISCRETION and DE DISCRETIE IN PERSOON ZIJN (lit. 'to be discretion in person'). These verbials, however, are mainly used to describe a general disposition. If applied to a specific occasion as in (D5)

(D5) He was the soul of discretion last night

the implication is that the tacens talked about is not normally 'the soul of discretion'.

Finally, there is one Dutch verbial, IETS MET DE MANTEL DER LIEFDE BEDEKKEN (lit. 'to cover something with the coat of love') that reveals *mercifulness* as the tacens' reason to be silent about something; the tacens conceals some fact or event because the person(s) it is related to might be hurt if it were brought to light.

198 We have seen that bad intentions underlying acts of concealment are rarely focused on because of the difficulty of obtaining evidence for them and the generally accepted principle that one should not make accusations unless there is sufficient evidence. But when one praises someone, evidence is rarely asked for unless there is a strong suspicion that the person in question does not deserve the praise at all. Therefore, no such principles can be relied on to explain why there are so few verba tacendi focusing on good intentions underlying concealments. On the contrary, the following argument can be made. Since there are no such principles restricting the occasions on which one is allowed to ascribe 'good' properties or acts to someone, one could conclude from the small number of lexical tools at our disposal to describe cases of benevolent silence either that in our society 'white silence' is considered to occur once in a blue moon or that being silent because of solidarity, discretion, or mercy is not regarded as a really praiseworthy activity. In either case, the importance attached to speech is emphasized once more.

199 Next to concealment there are two types of *avoidance* in the spectrum of motives for being silent.

(C2) *Sa* wants to avoid a topic
(C3) *Sa* wants to avoid a confrontation

The most important (A2)-(C2) verbials are TO BEAT AROUND THE BUSH, TO HEM AND HAW; ROND DE POT DRAAIEN (lit. 'to turn around the pot'), and EEN SNAAR NIET AANROEREN (lit. 'not touch a [particular] string'). Closely related are TO SAY NEITHER YES NOR NO and ABRAHAMMETJE SPELEN (lit. 'to play little Abraham', which means 'to try to escape by telling half the truth'). The attempt to avoid a confrontation is implied by TO CHECK ONE'S SPEECH and TO HOLD ONE'S PEACE, as in (D6) and (D7).

(D6) From the moment the supervisor entered, all employees checked their speech

(D7) I did not agree with the teacher but held my peace as he was rather angry

The Dutch verbials OP ZIJN MOND PASSEN (lit. 'to guard one's mouth'), OP ZIJN WOORDEN PASSEN (lit. 'to guard one's words') and ZIJN WOORDEN AFMETEN (lit. 'to measure one's words') are comparable to TO CHECK ONE'S SPEECH; on the other hand, ZICH KOEST HOUDEN (lit. 'to keep quiet'; the adjective KOEST is a contracted form of the French 'Couche-toi!', and apart from its use in ZICH KOEST HOUDEN it is mainly used as an imperative addressed to a dog and means 'Lie down!' or 'Stop barking!') is closer to TO HOLD ONE'S PEACE.

200 Another reason for being silent or for being silent about something is the tacens' *indifference*.

(C4) *Sa* is silent (about something) because he/she regards the matter at hand as too unimportant

Both TO SAVE ONE'S BREATH and TO WASTE NO WORDS draw explicit attention to such indifference: the tacens regards talking as a waste of energy. TO SAVE ONE'S BREATH may suggest that the deeper reason for not talking about unimportant matters is to build up energy for later talking. Comparable Dutch verbials are NIET VEEL WOORDEN VERSPILLEN ('not waste many words') and NIET VEEL WOORDEN AAN IETS VUILMAKEN (lit. 'not dirty many words at something').

201 The expectancy of disappointment may induce a speaker to believe that a particular matter is not worth wasting any words on. *Disappointment* itself can also be the reason for willful silence.

(C5) *Sa* is silent because he/she feels disappointed

A feeling of disappointment presupposes a prior attempt to achieve something. Therefore, in the context of language it presupposes prior speech. As a result, the few verbials that fit (C5) are all verba cessandi. The verbials I am thinking of are TO ABANDON and TO QUIT, as used in (D8) to (D10).

(D8) The reporter abandoned asking questions after realizing that he would never get a reply
(D9) He abandoned trying to convince his friend
(D10) The senator quit speaking after the audience's rude reactions

The Dutch equivalent, OPGEVEN, may be more exclusively associated with disappointment, but its use is more restricted.

202 TO BREAK OFF, as used in (D11) and (D12), generally reveals a sudden *impulse* as the tacens' reason for discontinuing his/her speech.

(C6) *Sa* stops talking because of a sudden impulse to do so

THE SEMANTICS OF SILENCE 107

DUTCH	SEMANTIC DIMENSION	ENGLISH
geheimhouden etc.	(A2)-(C1)	
φ	(C1a)	to hold out on
niet verklappen, etc.	(C1b)	not give away, etc.
(de discretie in persoon zijn)	(C1c)	(to be the soul of discretion)
		to keep secret, etc.
iets met de mantel der liefde bedekken	(C1d)	φ
rond de pot draaien, etc.	(A2)-(C2)	to beat around the bush, etc.
op zijn woorden passen, etc.	(A2)-(C3)	to check one's speech
niet veel woorden aan iets vuilmaken	(A2)-(C4)	to waste no words, etc.
opgeven	(A2)-(C5)	to abandon, etc.
afbreken, etc.	(A2)-(C6)	to break off
in petto houden	(A2)-(C7)	to keep in petto
pauzeren, etc.	(A2)-(C8)	to take a break

SDC Table 8

(D11) The senator broke off in the middle of a sentence
(D12) The speaker was interrupted so often that he broke off and sat down

The impulse in question may be generated by any kind of emotion, such as surprise, anger, fear, and others. Similar verbials in Dutch are AFBREKEN ('to break off') and BOT STILZWIJGEN ('to stop talking abruptly').

203 The *postponement* of divulging a certain piece of information is yet another motive for keeping silent.

(C7) *Sa* wants to postpone divulging some information

It is revealed in TO KEEP IN PETTO, and Dutch IETS IN PETTO HOUDEN. The tacens keeps something in petto if he/she wants to reserve the tacendum in order to convey it at a more appropriate time or, in the case of an argument, to be able to use it more forcefully later on. (Originally 'in petto' was predicated of a cardinal appointed by the pope but not named in consistory.)

204 The final, and probably most trivial, reason for being silent revealed by the verba tacendi is the tacens' wish to *catch his/her breath*.

(C8) *Sa* wants some breathing time

This motive is manifested in TO TAKE A BREAK and its Dutch equivalent PAUZEREN (which does not mean that this is the only reason for taking a break). The implication is that the speaking will be resumed after a brief interval.

Both TO TAKE A BREAK and PAUZEREN are verba cessandi describing a break in a speech activity belonging to a particular communication type; in an everyday conversation, for instance, one does not 'take a break'. There is an additional (A2)-(C8) verbial in Dutch that is a verbum cessandi and at the same time a verbum reticendi; moreover, it is not restricted with respect to communication type, but it implies that the suspension of the speech activity is of a considerably longer duration. The verbial in question is ERGENS EEN SPELDJE BIJ STEKEN; a SPELD(JE) is a (little) pin; the pin referred to here is an object attached to a particular page of a book to indicate how far one has gotten; the expression means literally 'to attach a pin to something'; within the domain of the verba tacendi it means 'to suspend talking about a particular topic'.

The motivational dimension of silence discussed in this section is represented in SDC Table 8.

3.7 SILENCE AND ITS INTERLOCUTORS

205 Not only do verba tacendi inform us about the codes of silence, its 'sound' properties, its causes, and the tacens' motives; some of them even give away the nature of the tacens and his/her audience. There are several verba tacendi that describe acts of being silent directed at the public in general. I am thinking of

TO COVER UP, TO SIT ON, TO BLACK OUT, TO CLASSIFY, and TO FILE AND FORGET, as used in (D1) to (D6).

(D1) The banker tried to cover up his stealing some of the bank's money
(D2) The senator kept sitting on the plans until he knew for certain which way the winds were blowing
(D3) The wartime government blacked out all news
(D4) Dictators usually black out all criticism of the government
(D5) CIA officials classified all the information about their involvement in Chile
(D6) All the information about the CIA's involvement in Chile was filed and forgotten

All these examples conform to (C1).

(C1) The audience is the public in general

(C1) appears to be the only audience-oriented condition attached to any verbum tacendi.

206 Two corollaries follow from (C1). First, there would be no need to specify that the audience envisaged in the acts described in (D1) to (D6) is the public in general unless the tacendum is of general public interest and hence the tacens holds some kind of official function. Thus, the (C1) verbials also furnish information about the tacens. Depending on the character of the tacens, they can be divided into those satisfying (C1a) and those conforming to (C1b).

(C1a) The tacens is usually an impersonal official body
(C1b) The tacens may either be an individual holding an official function or an impersonal official body

TO COVER UP and TO SIT ON are of the (C1b) type, whereas TO BLACK OUT, TO CLASSIFY, and TO FILE AND FORGET satisfy (C1a). The anonymity of the tacens is especially clear in the case of TO FILE AND FORGET, which cannot even be used in the active voice as a verbum tacendi.

A second corollary of the special relationship between tacens and audience implied by (C1) verbials is that a certain motive, which has not yet been mentioned in the previous section, seems to be involved: the tacens withholds information from the general public because he/she believes that divulging it might weaken his/her position in public life.

Sometimes, (C1b) verbials may also be used to describe acts of being silent performed by an individual without the kind of official function referred to before, as in (D7), which conforms to (C1c).

(D7) The journalist kept sitting on some information that could have produced a second Watergate
(C1c) The tacens is an individual without official function

In this case also, the motivational structure of the act is transformed: the tacens withholds information from the general public because he/she believes that divulging it might either harm him/herself or weaken someone else's position in public life.

207 As far as I can tell, Dutch possesses only a single verbial that indicates that the audience is the public in general. The verbial in question is IETS IN DE DOOFPOT STOPPEN (lit. 'to put something into the extinguishing pot'), which means TO HUSH UP. These two verba tacendi presuppose previous discourse about the tacendum, and neither of them gives any further information about the character of the tacens. (Note that an act of hushing up is not necessarily directed at the public in general, though usually it is.)

208 There is only one more verbial relevant to the interlocutor dimension of the verba tacendi. TO DISCONTINUE, as used in (D8) and (D9) necessarily conforms to (C2).

(D8) The publishing company discontinued the unprofitable journal
(D9) The BBC discontinued the series of political debates
(C2) The tacens is a publisher or a broadcasting service

Its Dutch translations DE PUBLICATIE STOPZETTEN VAN (lit. 'to stop the pulication of') and DE UITZENDING STOPZETTEN VAN (lit. 'to stop the broadcasting of'), as said before, cannot be regarded as lexical items.

209 SDC Table 9 represents the interlocutor dimension, which is clearly marginal, and even more so for Dutch than for English. It is noteworthy that the only important manifestation of the dimension emphasizes public acts of being silent.

It should be noted, before going on to a next semantic dimension, that a number of verba tacendi require a complement specifying the person from whom a tacendum is withheld. They are TO KEEP FROM, TO KEEP IN IGNORANCE (ABOUT), TO KEEP IN THE DARK (ABOUT), TO LEAVE IN THE DARK (ABOUT), and a few others. But nothing about the person in question is predictable from the verbials themselves.

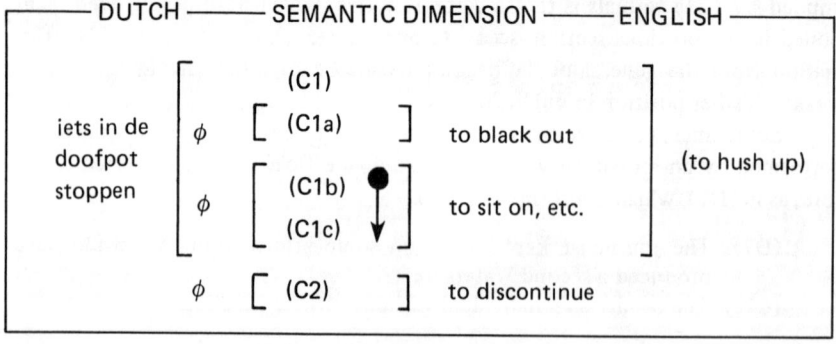

SDC Table 9

3.8 SILENCE AND ITS EFFECTS

210 Whereas causes of and motives for linguistic silence are to be found at the 'speaker' side of its interlocutor dimension, a dimension of effects could be expected at the 'hearer' side. However, the range of possible intended effects is left completely open by most verba tacendi. The only ones that are somewhat more specific are verba reticendi, such as TO KEEP SECRET, TO SECRETE, TO VEIL, TO COVER UP, TO SIT ON, TO FAIL TO MENTION, etc. Their quite general and totally negative implicit effect is to *leave the hearer uninformed* about (what the speaker thinks about) something. The only verba tacendi that make this kind of effect explicit (and that imply its achievement rather than simply its being intended) are the ones that require a complement specifying the person from whom a tacendum is withheld: TO KEEP FROM, TO KEEP IN IGNORANCE/IN THE DARK (ABOUT), etc. (see also paragraph **209**).

3.9 THE TOPICS OF SILENCE

211 The next semantic dimension to be discussed takes us into the realm of the 'propositional content' of acts of being silent. In other words, we shall be concerned with the tacenda, i.e. that which is not being talked about. As a result, only verba reticendi are studied in this section.

According to whether a tacendum, which may be either predictable or unpredictable from a given verbum reticendi, is to be specified as a complement to the verbial or not, we can distinguish four sets of verba reticendi.

(Cd1) The tacendum has to be specified; it is not predictable from the verbial

(Cd2) The tacendum has to be specified though it is more or less predictable from the verbial

(Cd3) The tacendum is not further specified because it is clear from the verbial

(Cd4) The tacendum cannot be specified though it is not predictable from the verbial

TO KEEP SECRET, TO BE SILENT ABOUT, TO WITHHOLD, NOT GIVE AWAY, and many others belong to the (Cd1) category, which constitutes the largest part of the verba reticendi both in English and in Dutch. The (Cd4) category is probably, and quite predictably, empty in both Dutch and English. Since only (Cd2) and (Cd3) verbials provide us with information about the tacendum, they are the only ones investigated in this section.

212 The variety of topics that can be talked about is without limit. And so is the variety of topics that one can choose not to talk about. The choice reflected in the lexicalization of the absence of speech, i.e. in the verba tacendi, can be expected to significantly further our understanding of the nature of linguistic silence as perceived in our linguistic communities.

213 The topics to which (Cd2) verbials draw our attention are all situated at either one of the two extremes of what could be called the 'privacy continuum' of talking matter. On the one hand there are matters of general public interest and on the other there are completely private ones.

(A1) *Sa* is silent about a private matter
(A2) *Sa* is silent about a matter of general public interest

The membership in the (Cd2)-(A2) category provides us with another example of the relationships among different semantic dimensions. In the previous section it was claimed that TO COVER UP, TO SIT ON, TO BLACK OUT, TO CLASSIFY, TO FILE AND FORGET, TO HUSH UP, and the latter's Dutch equivalent IETS IN DE DOOFPOT STOPPEN all describe acts of being silent directed at the public in general. There is no need for being so specific about the audience unless the tacendum itself is of public interest. Therefore, the same verbials belong to the (Cd2)-(A2) category.

214 The phrase 'matters of general public interest' covers a wide range of possible topics of speech; this is no doubt the reason why the verbials enumerated require a complement. Most (Cd2)-(A1) verbials are slightly more specific. They do not just indicate that the topic is a 'private matter', but most of them require some kind of feeling or emotion as a tacendum. The verbials TO REPRESS, TO STIFLE, TO MUFFLE, TO SUPPRESS, and TO SMOTHER, as well as their Dutch counterparts OPKROPPEN and VERSMOREN, all indicate that the tacens is silent about some feeling or emotion. Of course, a further specification is still necessary in the description because of the many sorts of emotion. Thus, one can smother one's rage, repress one's worries, stifle one's anger, etc. Notice that the range of tacenda is limited to unpleasant feelings. Apart from these emotional verbials, which describe acts of the (A1a) type, there is probably only one verbial, namely the Dutch IETS NIET AAN IEMANDS NEUS HANGEN (lit. 'not hang something on someone's nose'), that includes both (A1a) and (A1b) in its meaning, and there are none at all with a sense restricted to (A1b).

(A1a) *Sa* is silent about some (unpleasant) emotion or feeling
(A1b) *Sa* is silent about a non-emotional private matter

IETS NIET AAN IEMANDS NEUS HANGEN can be used for any act of not communicating something that the tacens regards as his/her own private business. Thus, 'Dat ga ik niet aan je neus hangen' (lit. 'I'm not going to hang that on your nose') is synonymous with 'That's none of your business'.

Notice that the (Cd2)-(A1a) verbials also get non-emotional complements, as in 'to smother a secret' and 'to muffle gossip'. It seems that in these cases the tacendum has to be a matter of general public interest as well. Thus, TO STIFLE, TO SMOTHER, etc., seem to incorporate both extremes of the 'privacy continuum'. It is hard to tell whether their (A1a) and (A2) meanings are on a par with each other or whether one is a derivative of the other.

215 Though the private-public contrast is still detectable in the (Cd3) verba tacendi, it plays a role only in some modified forms. For one thing, since (Cd3) verbials do not allow further specifications of the tacendum in the form of a complement, the verbial itself should give more precise information: it should be possible to calculate the nature of the tacendum on the basis of the verbial itself, combined with some contextual information. The most important topics of silence revealed by (Cd3) verba tacendi are presented in (A3) through (A7b).

> (A3) *Sa* is silent about everything that he/she regards as personal
> (A4) *Sa* is silent about other people's private matters (which may or may not be of public interest)
> (A5) *Sa* is silent about his/her ideas or plans (which are of potential interest to the hearer)
> (A6) *Sa* refrains from voicing his/her disagreement or disapproval
> (A7a) *Sa* is silent about a matter that is of interest to the hearer because it is the topic of conversation
> (A7b) *Sa* is silent about a matter that is of interest to the hearer because the latter has a right to know about it

A brief overview of the verbials in question follows.

216 Act (A3) differs from (A1) in that the former is an act of being silent about everything that the tacens regards as personal or private, whereas the latter is an act of being silent about one particular private matter. This fact can be reconciled with our previous statement that (Cd3) verbials should give more precise information about the topic of silence than (Cd2) verbials because the former do not allow further specifications of the tacendum in the form of a complement. The tacendum of a (Cd3)-(A3) verbial, being 'every personal matter', is linguistically more specific than 'a personal matter', though at the same time it is more general. The set of (Cd3)-(A3) verbials includes TO KEEP ONE'S DISTANCE, TO KEEP AT A DISTANCE, TO KEEP ONESELF TO ONESELF, TO STAND ALOOF, TO HOLD ONESELF ALOOF, and the Dutch OP EEN AFSTAND BLIJVEN ('to keep at a distance'), ZICH OP EEN AFSTAND HOUDEN (idem), GERESERVEERD BLIJVEN ('to remain reserved'). One of the ways in which the tacens may succeed in keeping his/her distance is by talking about nonpersonal things; this observation shows one of the many bridges between silence and nonsilence.

Observe that TO KEEP AT A DISTANCE and all three Dutch verbials may also describe acts of type (A8).

> (A8) *Sa* is silent about a certain topic of conversation that he/she regards as the other speaker's private business

Again, it is hard to decide whether the (A3) or (A8) meaning of these verba tacendi is derived from the other or whether they are on a par.

217 Silence acts of the (A4) type are described by one verbial only, namely TO BE THE SOUL OF DISCRETION, Dutch DE DISCRETIE IN PERSOON ZIJN (lit.

DUTCH	SEMANTIC DIMENSION	ENGLISH
iets niet aan iemands neus hangen	(Cd2) −(A1a)	φ
opkroppen, etc.	−(A1b)	to stifle, etc.
iets in de doofpot stoppen	−(A2)	to black out, etc. / to hush up
op een afstand blijven, etc.	(Cd3) −(A3)	to keep oneself to oneself, etc. / to keep at a distance
φ	−(A8)	φ
(de discretie in persoon zijn)	−(A4)	(to be the soul of discretion)
de kaarten duiken	−(A5)	to keep one's own counsel
φ	−(A6)	to hold one's peace
rond de pot draaien	−(A7a)	to beat around the bush
φ	−(A7b)	to hold out on

SDC Table 10

'to be discretion in person'). However, these two are marginal in the set of verba tacendi because they are not normally used to describe a particular act of being silent, but rather to indicate a general attitude or inclination.

A (Cd3)-(A5) verbial, reporting the tacens' silence about plans or ideas that are of potential interest to the hearer, is TO KEEP ONE'S OWN COUNSEL. Its Dutch equivalent is DE KAARTEN DUIKEN (meaning more or less 'not show one's cards') or NIET IN ZIJN KAARTEN LATEN KIJKEN (lit. 'not show one's cards').

Both (Cd3)-(A6) and (Cd3)-(A7b) are empty classes in Dutch. In English they are represented by TO HOLD ONE'S PEACE (the Dutch equivalent of which, ZICH KOEST HOUDEN, is much more general) and TO HOLD OUT ON, respectively.

Finally, (A7a) is described in English by TO BEAT AROUND THE BUSH and TO HEM AND HAW and in Dutch by ROND DE POT DRAAIEN (lit. 'to turn around the pot').

218 Two additional verbials that satisfy (Cd3) marginally are TO REFUSE COMMENT and TO SAY NEITHER YES NOR NO. Since the contextual information they carry is more important (and certainly less vague) than the propositional information, we shall come back to them in the section on silence and context.

The propositional dimension of the verba tacendi is given in SDC Table 10. Again, apart from some minor differences, the English and Dutch lexicons are quite symmetrical.

3.10 SILENCE AND NONPROPOSITIONAL MEANING

219 A person's silence may be imbued with a kind of meaning other than the topics or the propositions that the tacens is being silent about. This nonpropositional meaningfulness is generally indicated by means of adjectives as in TO MAINTAIN A DEATHLIKE/TOMBLIKE/GOLDEN/SOLEMN/PREGNANT SILENCE. DEATHLIKE and TOMBLIKE not only mark intensity, they also stress the sinister or ominous character of the silence. The absence of speech can be SOLEMN only when something serious happened, is happening, or is going to happen, usually as part of a (religious or secular) ceremony. Just as the 'calm before the storm' silence is PREGNANT when the silent people realize that a lot of (usually unpleasant) things could be said and are probably going to be said before long. When the silence is highly desirable to all parties, it may be said to be GOLDEN.

220 The same types of adjectives can be combined with STILTE ('silence') in Dutch: DOODS ('deathlike'), PLECHTIG ('solemn'), GELADEN (lit. 'loaded', equivalent to 'pregnant' in this context), etc. It is significant that there is almost no limit to the negatively colored adjectives that can be combined with 'silence' in both languages. Here are some more: OMINOUS and its equivalent ONHEIL-

SPELLEND; THREATENING and its Dutch counterpart DREIGEND; etc. On the other hand, it is hard to find any positive adjectives except for GOLDEN and SOLEMN, the latter of which is only semipositive since silence at a funeral is even more likely to be solemn than silence at a wedding ceremony. Moreover, the meaning of an inherently positive adjective such as PREGNANT (pregnancy being associated with 'joyful expectation', which is the literal translation of one of its Dutch lexicalizations) gets perverted in its combination with 'silence'. These facts emphasize once again our repeated conjecture that for Anglo-Americans and speakers of Dutch there is no such thing as joyful or pleasant silence—at least in the sense of silence as the absence of speech.

3.11 SILENCE AND CONTEXT

221 The contextual dimension of the verba tacendi was first introduced when the verba cessandi were defined (paragraph **150**). All verba cessandi presuppose preceding discourse. However, the nature of that discourse is rarely specified. Observe (D1) to (D9).

(D1) He abandoned stuttering, realizing it provoked ridicule rather than pity
(D2) He abandoned asking questions after realizing that he would never get a reply
(D3) He abandoned speaking after the audience's rude reactions
(D4) He abandoned his impolite speech after his father punished him
(D5) He abandoned writing poetry
(D6) He abandoned speech for several days
(D7) He abandoned his native speech and adopted the French tongue
(D8) He abandoned trying to convince his friends
(D9) He abandoned the subject when he did not get any response

The examples show that TO ABANDON, which denotes the discontinuation of previous speech, may focus on particular sound features, a certain speech-act type, a certain type of text, a particular style, a particular communication type, language in general, one individual language, a certain intention and a particular intended effect, and a particular subject. Thus, the verb is maximally general and does not carry information about the nature of the discourse the discontinuation of which it describes. Most verba cessandi are similar in this respect. The number of exceptions is extremely small.

222 An example of a verbum cessandi that carries specific information about the discontinued discourse is TO KNOCK IT OFF, as used in (D10).

(D10) John finally knocked it off

The use of TO KNOCK IT OFF presupposes that its user (e.g. the person uttering

(D10) regards the preceding discourse either as nonsensical or as inappropriate. In other words, condition (Cd1) obtains.

(Cd1) *Sd* regards the discontinued discourse as nonsensical or inappropriate

Consider (D11) and (D12).

(D11) After talking nonsense for hours, John finally knocked it off
(D12) John had been rude all night, but he finally knocked it off

In these two descriptions the possibilities are exemplified explicitly.

A Dutch verbum cessandi that provides specific information about the nature of the discontinued discourse is STAKEN (lit. 'to strike'), which can only be used to describe the discontinuation of conversations or other dialogic forms of communication.

The information carried by TO KNOCK IT OFF is mainly contained in its presuppositions. In the case of STAKEN, the information about the nature of the preceding discourse is supported by the valence of the verb: the subject is necessarily plural and the object has to be a substantive denoting a dialogic form of discourse.

223 Following discourse is as much a matter of context as preceding discourse. Combined, these two aspects of context yield three subclasses of contextualized acts of being silent.

(A1) *Sa* discontinues discourse
(A2) *Sa* discontinues discourse that is to be continued
(A3) *Sa* is silent before starting discourse

These three acts create several possible semantic patterns for verba tacendi. Not only are there three patterns corresponding to (A1), (A2), and (A3), respectively, but also the following ones: (A1) or (A2); (A1) or (A3); (A2) or (A3); (A1) or (A2) or (A3). But surprisingly, only (A1), (A2), and ((A2) or (A3)) are lexicalized. An obvious (A1) verb is TO FINISH, Dutch OPHOUDEN (MET SPREKEN). Most verba cessandi belong to this type. The (A2) pattern is only represented by TO PAUSE, Dutch PAUZEREN. The most striking gap in the lexical frame is the absence of (A3) verbials, which would form the logical counterpart to the verba cessandi. (A3) is only represented as one possible meaning of the ((A2) or (A3)) verb TO HESITATE, Dutch AARZELEN. The absence of (A3) verbials reflects the fact that pre-discourse silence is not noticed unless the hearer is waiting for the conversational tacens to talk, whereas postdiscourse silence is always noticed, whether or not more discourse is expected to follow. The lexical frame under discussion is represented in SDC Table 11.

224 Not only verba cessandi provide us with information about preceding discourse. For instance, both TO REFUSE COMMENT and TO SAY NEITHER YES NOR NO presuppose preceding discourse. One cannot 'refuse comment' unless

118 THE SEMANTICS OF SILENCE

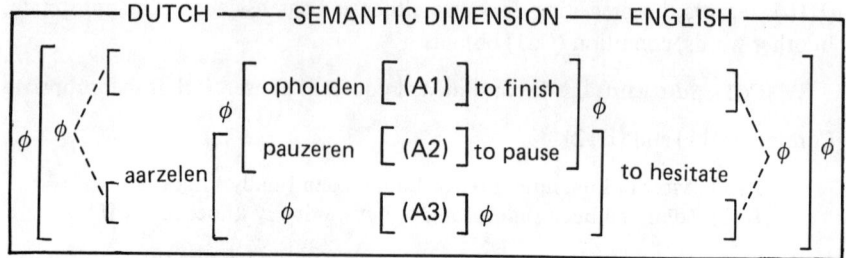

SDC Table 11

somebody asked to comment on some statement or state of affairs. And one cannot 'say neither yes nor no' unless somebody asked a question or made a proposal. Note, however, that in contrast with the verba cessandi, these two verba reticendi do not presuppose discourse on the part of the conversational tacens him/herself, but on the part of somebody else.

Other examples are hard to find. Thus it seems that there are no verba silendi that carry contextual information.

3.12 THE ILLOCUTIONARY FORCE OF SILENCE

225 A last, quite marginal, dimension of verba tacendi is the information they carry about the illocutionary force of the absent speech. Both TO FAIL TO MENTION and TO REFUSE COMMENT are clearly concerned with statementlike acts. The verbials TO REFUSE COMMENT and TO SAY NEITHER YES NOR NO also provide information about the illocutionary force of the preceding discourse. In the case of TO REFUSE COMMENT, a comment must have been asked for. In the case of TO SAY NEITHER YES NOR NO, the illocutionary force of the absent speech described even depends on the force of the preceding discourse: if a question precedes, then the absent speech is statementlike; if a proposal precedes, then acceptance and refusal is referred to by means of the 'yes' and the 'no'.

Once again, more examples are really hard to find, which justifies our claim about the marginality of this dimension of the verba tacendi, though it could be said that many verba reticendi typically describe nonperformed assertive speech acts.

3.13 CONCLUSIONS

226 The discussions in this chapter should enable us to make detailed semantic comparisons between 'equivalent' verba tacendi in English and in Dutch (and probably in many other languages as well) by comparing their positions with re-

spect to each of the semantic dimensions investigated. In most cases additional dimensions of meaning have to be taken into account. But I trust that the most important ones for the characterization of the contrasts and similarities between the sets of verba tacendi in English and in Dutch have been dealt with.

227 It is high time we wondered about the overall significance of this chapter on the semantics of silence. Undoubtedly it has revealed the importance of silence as an aspect of linguistic action (and hence I hope it may function as an incentive for further silence research): the whole structure of language and linguistic action, from its 'sound' properties via its meaning to its contextual architecture, is reflected in linguistic silence. In the process of uncovering the linguistic structure of the absence of speech, we have made numerous noteworthy observations, some of which were merely confirmations of pretheoretical intuitions, others being quite surprising, and still others being downright mysterious. Here is a partial list.

1. The language dimension of the basic verba tacendi reveals the conducting of a conversation and the delivering of a speech as the two fundamental communication types in the experience of linguistic action. (Paragraph **156**)
2. The absence of speech as such (i.e. the domain of the verba silendi) occupies the central position in our conceptualization of linguistic silence (as appears from SDC Table 1). (Paragraph **158**)
3. The verba tacendi reveal the primacy of the oral mode of communication. (Paragraphs **160** to **168**)
4. The verba tacendi that are neutral between oral and written communication are never verba silendi. (Paragraph **162**)
5. The metaphorical extension of the meaning of verba tacendi from the oral to the written code is irreversible. (Paragraph **167**)
6. There is a correlation between the code of the acts to be described and the code of the describing acts. (Paragraphs **163** and **165**)
7. The formation of verbials can determine their applicability. (Paragraph **165**)
8. The absence of speech is gradable along the two 'sound'-related dimensions of intensity and duration, but the superlative is the only point of the gradation scale that is really emphasized. (Paragraph **170**)
9. The verba tacendi reveal attitudes towards the expression of pleasant versus unpleasant feelings or emotions. (Paragraphs **182** and **184**)
10. The talkative character of Western culture is demonstrated repeatedly in various ways. (Paragraphs **194**, **198**, and **220**)
11. The verba tacendi lend support to the validity of the Gricean maxims of conversation (in particular 'Do not say that for which you lack adequate evidence') in our culture. (Paragraph **196**)

The list is completely random and most attentive readers will be able to supplement it.

228 Apart from the fact that English does not whereas Dutch does possess simple lexicalizations as basic verba tacendi and a quite general basic term to cover the domain of linguistic silence, most of the differences between the English and the Dutch sets of verba tacendi are of minor importance, though not uninteresting. The strong parallelism was, of course, predictable. It is necessary to carry out further comparative investigations in order to find out which ones of our conclusions are language-specific and which ones stand a good chance of being universals.

229 The foregoing cursory overview of some of the semantic dimensions relevant for the description of the verba tacendi in two closely related languages is already sufficient to support or to cast doubts on some of the claims made in the (extremely sporadic) theoretical writings about linguistic silence. For instance, Mihailă (1977) makes a basic distinction between 'absence of speech' and 'unpronounced speech'. Nothing in our data supports the conceptual relevance of this distinction for speakers of English and Dutch.

In the same article, it is claimed that the basic function of silence is to preserve a state of affairs. The rich causal, motivational, and topical variety emerging from the verba tacendi makes this claim look extremely simplistic.

Further, our data partly support Mihailă's belief that silence becomes pertinent as a linguistic activity only if it replaces a response or if speech is expected. But they also show that this is not the whole story. In the case of a temperamentally determined disposition not to talk, for instance, or in the case of a strong unpleasant emotion as the cause of silence, S's abstaining from speech may be exactly what is expected, and S's being described as having been silent may simply mean that nothing noteworthy happened.

Finally, Mihailă argues that silence, because of its obvious ambiguity, is hardly interpretable. Yet, the verba tacendi show that silence is interpreted constantly. How else could one explain that the same ambiguous silence can be described by TO CLOSE UP LIKE A CLAM, NOT HAVE A WORD TO SAY, TO STIFLE (SOMETHING), TO KEEP IN PETTO, TO FAIL TO MENTION, TO HOLD ONE'S PEACE, TO COVER UP, and so many other verbs and phrases the meaning of which is permeated with interpretative hints (which lose their implicit character in adjectives such as SOLEMN, PREGNANT, and the like). But even so, the ambiguity is there, which was said (in paragraph 196) to explain why judgmental interpretations are mainly restricted to hints and insinuations.

230 The major conclusion from our brief glance at the verba tacendi is that silence, which has only been studied sporadically (in the form of pauses and hesitations) by discourse analysts, deserves attention by linguists. Our finding that it forms an integral part of linguistic (inter)action is supported strongly by the few remarks in the literature about metalinguistic terms describing linguistic silence in non-Western languages. According to Stross (1974:225), Tzeltal even constructs its terms for silence on the basis of the morpheme K'OP, which has

the very general meaning of 'speech' so that 'Silence is felt to be an important component of the speech event': Č'ABAL K'OP (i.e. silence or near silence, during conversation or visit; pause in a conversation), Č'AYEM K'OP (i.e. speech or conversation that was audible but has faded out as the speakers have gone out of earshot; also, lost speech, lost words, speech that has slipped the mind of the speaker), KEHČEM K'OP (i.e. speech cut off in midstream by speaker but to be resumed).

231 Our preliminary results also enable us to formulate hypotheses about the lexicalization of linguistic silence in languages about which we have some anthropological data. For instance, Basso's (1972) account of silence in Western Apache culture, which pays exclusive attention to motives for being silent, suggests that silence is a very conscious act among the Apache and that the motivational dimension can be expected to be very well developed in their verba tacendi. To take a second example, Ochs Keenan's (1976) study of people's reluctance to be informative in a small Madagascar village might lead us to the hypothesis that verba reticendi can be expected to be prominent in their language; it would not even be surprising to find that talk about certain topics is lexicalized as the absence of silence rather than that silence about them is lexicalized as the absence of speech. But these are mere speculations, and further empirical-conceptual research is needed.

CHAPTER **4**

THE SEMANTICS OF LYING

4.0 INTRODUCTION

232 After surveying the apparently marginal area of silence, we shall now attempt to penetrate one of the cores of linguistic action, namely the domain of the propositional content. We shall do so by way of analyzing the verbials describing linguistic actions performed by a speaker who presents the propositional content of his/her speech act as reflecting a true state of affairs but who knows or believes that it deviates from the truth.

233 Though no further arguments are needed for our decision not to engage, from the start, in an endeavor to classify linguistic action verbials, we are now confronted with a particularly compelling one that should be mentioned. Even between the relatively marginal domain of silence and the quite central area of propositional content, there is no sharp boundary. Not only can acts of being silent about something be occasionally regarded as lying, there are also a number of linguistic action verbials that clearly cover portions of both domains without being ambiguous between two completely distinct senses. TO DISGUISE, for instance, is not only a verbum reticendi describing an act of being silent about some particular topic or fact; disguising can be done by lying. Suppose there is a politico-religious movement called Communists for Christ, which people are so suspicious of that it is forced to start operating through cover organizations, one of them being the Creative Thought Project. If a Communist for Christ introduces him/herself as a member of the Creative Thought Project, then he/she is not lying, but simply disguising his/her identity by being silent about it (which he/she can keep doing by assuming a different identity that, it is hoped, will not be associated with the 'real' one). Suppose, furthermore, that it is a well-known fact that Communists for Christ do not accept the authority of the Pope. If, then, our Communist for Christ claims that he/she accepts the authority of the Pope, then he/she is disguising his/her real convictions by lying. And if he/she makes the same claim after being asked whether he/she is a Communist for Christ, then he/she is disguising his/her identity by being silent about it *and* by telling a lie. Similarly, TO COVER UP describes acts that often combine silence about a particular tacendum (e.g. a crime) with a lie (e.g. a false alibi). Such marginal cases are left out of the subsequent account.

234 Not all linguistic actions in which the truth is distorted would be called lies. Within the scope of this chapter we shall not only discuss lying proper, but also exaggerating, understating, distorting, blackening, coloring, etc. Given this scope, it might be misleading to talk about 'verbials of lying'. Therefore, we introduce the term *verba mentiendi* (from Latin MENTIRE, meaning 'to lie') to cover the complete domain under investigation. The 'liar' will be called the *mentiens*. What is being 'lied' about will be referred to as the *mentiendum*, plural *mentienda*. Notice that in a case such as 'Yesterday I went to the moon' the mentiendum includes, strictly speaking, both the trip to the moon and yesterday's activities. Which one of the two aspects is focused on will depend on the context.

235 Remember that in the set of verba tacendi we included, albeit hesitatingly, some negations of non-silence linguistic action verbials such as NOT SPEAK and NOT TALK. One similar formation will be encountered in this chapter, namely NOT TELL THE TRUTH, which will be regarded as a complex lexicalization because it is a more or less conventional means of talking about untruthful linguistic acts. No comparable lexicalizations occur in the following chapters.

Whereas ostensive definitions (see paragraph 126) were impossible in the previous chapter because acts of being silent cannot be reproduced on paper, they will be used from this point on.

236 Unlike silence, deviations from the truth have been studied extensively. Not only is there a long-standing ethical tradition going from St. Augustine via Thomas Aquinas, Francis Bacon, Hugo Grotius, and Immanuel Kant to Warnock (1971) and Bok (1978). There are also numerous recent philosophical and linguistic investigations into the nature of lying and other deviations from the truth. To mention just a few, Baskett and Freedle (1974); Bolinger (1973); Chisholm and Feehan (1977); Leonard (1959); Siegler (1966); and Vincent and Castelfranchi (1981). Even the verb TO LIE has recently received close anthropological and linguistic scrutiny, from Coleman and Kay (1981) and Sweetser (1981). In the conclusions to this chapter, our preliminary empirical-conceptual findings are discussed with direct reference to some of these.

4.1 THE FRAME OF LYING

237 The linguistic actions described by verba mentiendi involve a conscious distortion of the truth. The notion of truth is ambiguous between truth as such (if such a thing exists) and what the speaker knows, believes, or thinks to be true. Given our lexical approach, a more tangible contrast is that between what is true for the user of a verbum mentiendi and what is true for the performer of the act described. If John believes that the earth is round and Jim believes that it is flat, and John is aware of Jim's belief, then John will not describe Jim's claim that the earth is round as a lie (even though the propositional content deviates from Jim's beliefs); instead, John will have to say that Jim told the truth (even though John realizes that Jim was trying to convey misleading information about his own world of beliefs). Such attempts at making an untrue statement are not describable in terms of a verbum mentiendi. They are simply mistakes. Thus, in the prototypical case, a verbum mentiendi is appropriately used only if the describing act D satisfies conditions (Cd1) and (Cd2), and if A, the act described, satisfies (C1).

(C1) Sa believes that what he/she presents as a true state of affairs is a distortion of the truth
(Cd1) Sd believes that what is presented in A as a true state of affairs is a distortion of the truth
(Cd2) Sd believes that (C1) obtains

These three conditions define the core of the lexical frame of lying (see also paragraphs **243** and **244**). As a result, the verba mentiendi discussed in this chapter do not include verbs such as TO ERR, which denote untruthfulness for which the speaker is not (completely) responsible, nor verbs such as TO FLATTER and TO BOAST, which may but need not imply deviations from the truth.

238 In the previous chapter we claimed that the verba tacendi, because of the marginality of silence as an aspect of linguistic action, reflected all the major aspects of linguistic action. In other words, the frame of silence was said to be the frame of linguistic action itself. This emerged very clearly from the salient role of what was called the language dimension of silence. Thus, studying the semantics of silence proved to be relevant as a way of gaining insight into our experience of language.

In a similar way, studying the semantics of lying may yield insight into truth as an aspect of language (or as an aspect of the propositional content of utterances). The most important semantic dimension of verba mentiendi will be shown to be the truth dimension. In other words, the frame of lying is the frame of truth itself.

4.2 LYING AND TRUTH

239 A natural expectation of what a truth dimension would look like could be in terms of the gradability of the notion of truth. One could expect there to be a continuum of verba mentiendi ranging from those indicating a minor deviation from the truth. Of course, such gradability is reflected in the set of verba mentiendi as appears from the contrast between TO LIE and TO COLOR (and the corresponding Dutch verbs LIEGEN and KLEUREN). However, the contrast is rarely this clear, since in most cases totally different semantic features play an important role. For instance, the fact that TO FIB appears to be weaker than TO LIE is not due to the gradability of the notion of truth; rather, it results from the type of falsehood involved: in the case of TO FIB, a trivial falsehood is referred to. On the other hand, TO LIE LIKE A TROOPER appears to be stronger than TO LIE, but this strength usually derives from the frequency implied rather than from the kind of gradability under discussion. Consequently, if there were only the gradability of truth, there would be very little to say about the truth dimension of lying.

Nevertheless, it is worth comparing, in passing, the sets of verbials available in English and in Dutch to describe highly intense acts of lying. Whereas the English repertoire does not go much further than TO LIE FLATLY and TO LIE LIKE A TROOPER, in Dutch we find considerable variation: LIEGEN ALS EEN KETTER (lit. 'to lie like a heretic'), LIEGEN ALS EEN ALMANAK (lit. 'to lie like an almanac'), TEGEN DE KLIPPEN/STERREN OP LIEGEN (lit. 'to lie up against the cliffs/stars'), LIEGEN ALSOF HET GEDRUKT STAAT (lit. 'to lie as if it had been printed'), LIEGEN DAT MEN HET ZELF GELOOFT (lit. 'to lie so that one believes it oneself'), LIEGEN DAT MEN ZWART/SCHEEL ZIET (lit. 'to lie so that one looks black/cross-eyed').

240 Apart from verbials such as TO LIE, TO COLOR, TO FIB, TO LIE LIKE A TROOPER, and many others, all of which simply indicate that the truth is being distorted, there are verba mentiendi that give information about *how* the truth is being distorted. The latter can be placed at the extremes of two scales, the quantity scale and the quality scale.

The set of verba mentiendi reflects four ways of distorting the truth. First, it is possible to make something look 'smaller' than it is. Second, one can make something look 'bigger' than it is. The basic verba mentiendi situated at these two poles of what I call the *quantity scale of truth* are TO UNDERSTATE (which does not always describe the figure of speech 'understatement') and TO EXAGGERATE. We shall call the first one a *quantity-diminishing verb*, the second one a *quantity-increasing verb*. It is interesting to note that Dutch lacks a basic equivalent to TO UNDERSTATE, though there is a quantity-diminishing verb such as VERKLEINEN (the adjective KLEIN means 'small'); however, we refrain from regarding this one as a basic quantity-diminishing verbum mentiendi because it is mostly quality-diminishing. Consequently, we seem to be confronted with a quite surprising lexical gap in the Dutch set of basic verba mentiendi. The Dutch equivalent of TO EXAGGERATE is OVERDRIJVEN.

The two remaining ways of distorting the truth consist in making something look 'better' than it is and making something look 'worse' than it is. The basic verba mentiendi situated at these two poles of the *quality scale of truth* are TO WHITEWASH and TO SLANDER (Dutch GOEDPRATEN and (BE)LASTEREN); We shall call the first one a *quality-increasing verb* and the second one a *quality-diminishing verb*.

The five types of verba mentiendi discussed so far are presented in Figure 1. TO LIE, TO COLOR, etc., are situated in the middle, with arrows directed at the two poles of the quality and quantity scales, because some instances of distorting the truth along these scales can be described in terms of lying, coloring, etc.

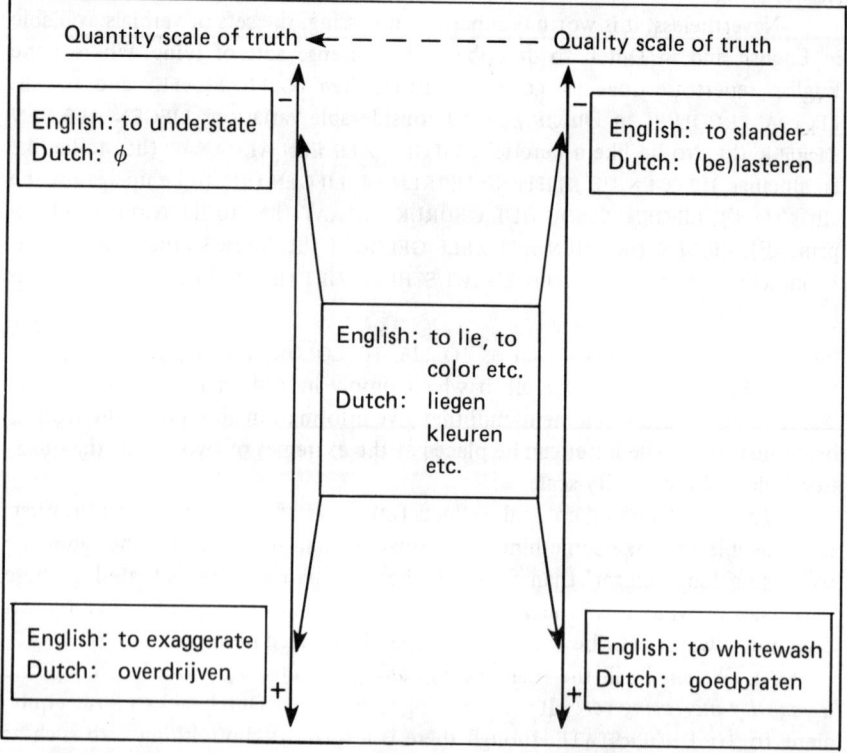

Figure 1

241 The quantity and quality scales of truth seem to show a curious one-directional interdependence relationship (indicated by means of the broken arrow in Figure 1). It is possible to whitewash somebody's 'bad' behavior by making an understatement about it or even by exaggerating its positive aspects. Similarly, one can slander someone by exaggerating his/her vices (though not as easily by making understatements about his/her virtues). But one cannot make an understatement *by* whitewashing, nor exaggerate *by* slandering. Why is the quality scale dependent on the quantity scale and not vice versa? Probably because it is not possible to take quality as a criterion for quantity, whereas in our culture quantity is continuously taken as a criterion for quality. This explanation would be entirely in keeping with the MORE IS BETTER value judgment Lakoff and Johnson (1980) discover in some chains of metaphors permeating the English language.

242 Once we leave the domain of the intuitively *basic* verba mentiendi, we discover a relationship between the like poles of the scales that opposite poles do not have. Indeed, the sets of quality-diminishing and quantity-diminishing verbs share one member in Dutch, VERKLEINEN, though none in English. Similarly, TO DRESS UP and TO EMBROIDER, as well as the Dutch BORDUREN ('to embroider'), belong to the quantity-increasing and quality-increasing verbs.

Just as the directionality of the dependence relationship discussed in the previous paragraph, the verba mentiendi enumerated here show that quantity is regularly taken as a criterion for quality. This state of affairs is reflected even more clearly in the verbs TO BELITTLE and KLEINEREN, which mean literally 'to make small' (the adjective KLEIN meaning 'small') but which can be used *only* as *quality*-diminishing verbs.

243 After indicating the main lines of force of the truth dimension of lying, our next task is to make a more detailed study of the English and Dutch verba mentiendi along this dimension. There are a number of general conditions on the standard appropriate use of the verba mentiendi that are not repeated for each verbial in the rest of this chapter. The conditions in question are (C1), (Cd1), and (Cd2), which have already been mentioned in the previous section (see paragraph 237) to define the lexical frame of lying.

(C1) S_a believes that what he/she presents as a true state of affairs is a distortion of the truth
(Cd1) S_d believes that what is presented in A as a true state of affairs is a distortion of the truth
(Cd2) S_d believes that (C1) obtains

Consequently, when we talk about an act A conforming to (C) and described by means of D, we mean that also (C1′), (Cd1′) and (Cd2′) obtain.

(A)   The earth is flat

(C) The earth is round
(D) *Sa* lied
(C1′) *Sa* believes that the earth is round
(Cd1′) *Sd* believes that the earth is round
(Cd2′) *Sd* believes that (C1′) obtains

In that way, redundant repetitions can be avoided.

244 One may be inclined to believe that (C1) and (Cd2) do not have to obtain in order for a distortion of the truth to be appropriately described by means of certain verba mentiendi such as TO EXAGGERATE. However, the validity of my general claim is probably sufficiently demonstrated by pointing out that an adequate response to the accusation 'You are exaggerating' is 'No, I really believe what I am saying'.

Why, on the other hand, do we not automatically include conditions such as (C2), (Cd3), ad (Cd4)?

(C2) *Sa* intends to deceive *Ha*
(Cd3) *Sd* believes that (C2) obtains
(Cd4) *Sd* regards saying *A* under conditions (C) and (C1) as reprehensible

(Cd4) has been adduced before (in paragraph 128) to illustrate the form of conditions directly attached to the description in which a descriptive verb is used. Why it is omitted here is explained in section 4.6 (on verba mentiendi and value judgments). Similarly, section 4.4 (on perlocutionary intent) provides an explanation for the omission of (C2) and (Cd3) at this point.

245 A simple case of deviating from the truth is (A1) if uttered in circumstances in which (C3) obtains.

(A1) John was home at the time of the robbery
(C3) In fact, John was not home at the time of the robbery

In any *D* describing (A1) conforming to (C3) one could use the verba mentiendi TO LIE, TO LIE FLATLY, TO TELL A LIE, NOT TELL THE TRUTH, TO SPEAK FALSELY, and in Dutch LIEGEN ('to lie'), LEUGENS VERKOPEN (lit. 'to sell lies'), LEUGEN VERTELLEN ('to tell lies'), DE WAARHEID GEWELD AANDOEN (lit. 'to violate the truth'), DE WAARHEID NIET ZEGGEN ('not tell the truth'). Let us call these *verbials of lying*.

246 All the (A1)-(C3) verbials mentioned, except TO LIE FLATLY, are also applicable to (A1) when it conforms to (C4).

(C4) John was almost home at the time of the robbery (in fact close enough to be sure that he could not have been at the scene of the crime when the crime was committed)

In addition to the (A1)-(C3) verbials, a large subset of the verba mentiendi, which cannot be applied to (A1) when (C3) obtains, are perfectly fit to describe

(A1) when (C4) applies, or at least to acts of a similar type: TO DISTORT, TO COLOR, TO BEND THE TRUTH, TO DEVIATE FROM THE TRUTH, TO GIVE A COLOR TO, TO GIVE A FALSE COLORING, TO MISREPRESENT, TO PREVARICATE, TO PUT A FALSE APPEARANCE UPON, TO PUT IN A FALSE LIGHT, TO SLANT, TO STRAIN THE TRUTH, TO STRETCH THE TRUTH, TO TWIST, TO WARP; and in Dutch KLEUREN ('to color'), IN EEN VALS DAGLICHT STELLEN (lit. 'to put in a false daylight'), VERDRAAIEN ('to twist'), VERKEERD VOORSTELLEN ('to misrepresent'), VERWRINGEN ('to twist'), EEN VERWRONGEN VOORSTELLING GEVEN VAN (lit. 'to give a distorted representation of'), DE WAARHEID TE KORT DOEN (lit. 'to wrong the truth'), VAN DE WAARHEID AFWIJKEN ('to deviate from the truth'), DE WAARHEID VERDRAAIEN/VERWRINGEN/VERKRACHTEN (lit. 'to twist/warp/rape the truth'). These are called the *verbials of distorting*.

In addition to the verbials of lying and distorting, there are all the quality- and quantity-diminishing and increasing verbials, which I shall now go on to list and illustrate.

247 To start with the *quality-diminishing* verba mentiendi, consider (A2) uttered in a context that satisfies (C5).

(A2) Mr. Kohl was a member of the Nazi party
(C5) Mr. Kohl has never been a member of the Nazi party (though perhaps he had some Nazi friends)

This act can be adequately described by means of TO SLANDER, as in (D1) or (D2).

(D1) *Sa* is slandering
(D2) *Sa* is trying to slander Mr. Kohl's good name

Similar quality-diminishing verbials (not all of which necessarily involve a distortion of the truth, though they are usually associated with it) are TO ASPERSE, TO BACKBITE, TO BADMOUTH, TO BESMEAR, TO BESMIRCH, TO BLACKEN, TO CALUMNIATE, TO CAST A SLUR ON, TO CAST ASPERSIONS ON, TO DEFAME, TO DEFILE, TO DENIGRATE, TO DISPARAGE, TO DRAG THROUGH THE MUD, TO GIVE A BAD NAME, TO LIBEL, TO MALIGN, TO RUN DOWN, TO SLUR, TO SMIRCH, TO SPEAK ILL OF, TO SPEAK SLIGHTINGLY OF, TO SULLY, TO TARNISH, TO TRADUCE, TO VILIFY; and in Dutch ACHTERKLAPPEN ('to backbite'), BEKLADDEN ('to besmirch'), (BE)LASTEREN ('to slander'), BEZWALKEN ('to besmear'), DENIGREREN ('to denigrate'), IEMAND IN ZIJN EER/GOEDE NAAM AANTASTEN (lit. 'to injure a person in his or her honor/good name'), IEMAND OVER DE HEKEL HALEN (lit. 'to pull someone across the hackle'; a hackle is a board with long metal teeth for dressing flax or hemp; the expression means 'to talk about and judge a person in a very sharp, merciless, and malevolent manner'), KWAADSPREKEN (lit. 'to speak ill'), VAN IEMAND KWAAD STOKEN (lit. 'to brew ill about someone'), IEMAND LELIJK/SLECHT MAKEN (lit. 'to make someone ugly/bad'), DOOR DE MODDER SLEUREN ('to drag through the mud'), DOOR HET SLIJK HALEN ('to drag through the mud'), IEMAND ZWART MAKEN ('to blacken someone').

248 Two aspects of the lexical frame associated with acts of the (A2)-(C5) type reflect one of the profoundest, though often unconscious, value judgments inherent in our linguistic culture. First, apart from TO CRITICIZE (Dutch BEKRITISEREN), I cannot think of any linguistic action verbial (except for a few exceptions to be mentioned at the end of this paragraph), either in English or in Dutch, that contains the meaning 'to say something bad or unfavorable about someone or something' and that is not, in all or most of its uses, associated with untruthfulness. (Even an apparently neutral verb such as TO BLAME often implies that the act it describes is not totally justified by the facts, and the victim of the blaming is often felt to be a black sheep; just consider the sentence 'Why do you blame me?'.) This is in sharp contrast with the large set of verbials meaning 'to say something good or favorable about someone or something' without being associated with a lack of truthfulness (such as TO PRAISE, TO LAUD, TO GLORIFY, TO HAIL, and many others).

Second, whereas the verbials of distorting can be used to cover the domains of the quality- and quantity-diminishing and increasing verbials (as will be clear from what follows), the verbials of lying can be easily extended to the conceptual domain of the quality-diminishing verbials (i.e. the acts of the (A2)-(C5) type) but not so easily—and in most cases not at all—to the area of the quality-increasing and the quantity-diminishing and increasing linguistic action verbials.

Both of these facts reveal a strong association of 'saying *bad* things about' with 'saying *untrue* things about.' Thus, the lexicon reflects a usually unconscious value judgment that is entirely in keeping with Freud's (1917:48) observation that 'society makes what is disagreeable into what is untrue'. How else can we explain that an expression such as TO DISH THE DIRT has come to assume the meaning of gossiping, which is strongly associated with untruthfulness? Dishing the dirt, even if the dirt is very real, is rarely appreciated, and therefore the truth is branded as untrue.

The 'rule' is even supported by its exceptions. Consider TO INFORM ON and its slang equivalents TO FINK/RAT/SNITCH/SQUEAL ON. Here 'saying bad things about' is not so much associated with lack of truthfulness as with low moral standards. Maybe it is exactly because of its association with low moral standards that 'saying bad things about' has come to be interpreted as 'saying untrue things about'.

249 The *quantity-diminishing* verb TO UNDERSTATE can be used to describe such acts as (A3) conforming to (C6).

> (A3) Once or twice a year Jim sends some money to the World Health Organization

(C6) In fact, at least twice a year Jim sends his complete monthly allowance to the World Health Organization

Another quantity-diminishing verb, with a quite specific meaning, is TO UNDERREPORT in the sense of reporting (e.g. to the Internal Revenue Service) an amount (e.g. as one's income) less than the actual one. In Dutch there seem to be no purely quantity-diminishing linguistic action verbials. There is, however, the verb VERKLEINEN, which is quantity-diminishing in form but which can be used either as a quantity-diminishing verb, as in (D3) describing (A3)-(C6), or as a quality-diminishing verb, as in (D4) describing (A2)-(C5).

(D3) *Sa* tracht Jims bijdrage te verkleinen
('*Sa* is trying to make Jim's contribution [look] smaller')
(D4) *Sa* tracht Mr. Kohls verdiensten als na-oorlogs socialist te verkleinen
('*Sa* is trying to belittle Mr. Kohl's merits as a postwar socialist')

English apparently lacks a verbial that can either be quantity- *or* quality-diminishing. TO BELITTLE can be used to describe some acts of the (A3)-(C6) type, as in (D5).

(D5) *Sa* is trying to belittle Jim's contribution

But in such cases it is a quantity- *and* quality-diminishing verb at the same time.

250 *Quantity-increasing* verbs such as TO EXAGGERATE and its Dutch equivalent OVERDRIJVEN can be applied to acts such as (A4) conforming to (C7).

(A4) Jim donates half his income to UNESCO
(C7) In fact, Jim sends a small contribution to UNESCO twice a year

Other quantity-increasing verbials are TO AGGRANDIZE, TO BLOW UP, TO DRAW THE LONGBOW, TO HYPERBOLIZE, TO MAGNIFY, TO TALK IN SUPERLATIVES, TO OVERLAUD, TO OVERPRAISE, TO OVERSTATE, TO OVERSTRESS; and in Dutch AANDIKKEN (lit. 'to thicken'), CHARGEREN ('to exaggerate in order to ridicule'), EXAGEREREN ('to exaggerate'; rarely used), OPBLAZEN ('to blow up'), OPSNIJDEN (lit. 'to cut up'), OPSCHROEVEN (lit. 'to screw up'), ER EEN SCHEPJE OP DOEN (lit. 'to add a little scoop'), MET SPEK SCHIETEN (lit. 'to shoot with bacon'), VERGROTEN (lit. 'to enlarge'), VAN EEN SCHEET EEN DONDERSLAG MAKEN (lit. 'to make a fart into a thunderbolt'), VAN EEN VLIEG/MUG/MUIS EEN OLIFANT MAKEN (lit. 'to make a fly/mosquito/mouse into an elephant').

Notice that it is possible to 'make something look bigger', i.e. to exaggerate something, by making it look *numerically* smaller. An example is the utterance 'In Belgium the sun shines once or twice a year'.

251 There are two different types of *quality-increasing* verba mentiendi. The first type, represented by TO EMBELLISH in English and its Dutch counterparts

VERFRAAIEN ('to embellish') and AANKLEDEN (lit. 'to dress'), is used to describe acts such as (A5)-(C8).

> (A5) We arrived in Los Angeles in the morning. The same day we visited Hollywood where we happened to see Peter Falk and Jane Fonda walking around
> (C8) *Sa* visited Hollywood, but he/she did not manage to see any well-known movie star

About *Sa*, who is inventing details to make his/her story nicer, one can say

> (D6) As usual, *Sa* is embellishing the story of his/her vacation

TO EMBELLISH, VERFRAAIEN, and AANKLEDEN describe acts of making look nicer or better something that may already have been good or nice to begin with.

A second type of quality-increasing verba mentiendi is used to describe acts of making look better something that was not good at all to start with. Consider (A6)-(C9).

> (A6) Jack's stealing is just a natural outcome of the deprivation he suffered during his childhood
> (C9) Jack is a thief (who may or may not have suffered deprivation during his childhood)

This type of act is described by TO WHITEWASH, TO DEODORIZE, TO GILD, TO GLOSS (OVER), TO MAKE SMELL LIKE ROSES, TO VARNISH, and the Dutch GOEDPRATEN (lit. 'to good-talk'), BEWIMPELEN (lit. 'to cover with a flag'), MOOIPRATEN (lit. 'to nice-talk'), VERGULDEN ('to gild'), VERBLOEMEN (lit. 'to turn into a flower'), VERGOELIJKEN (lit. 'to make good'), and WIT WASSEN (lit. 'to wash white', not to be confused with 'to whitewash').

252 We mentioned in paragraph 242 that TO DRESS UP, TO EMBROIDER, and the Dutch BORDUREN ('to embroider') are quantity- *and* quality-increasing verba mentiendi. Notice, however, that they do not cover the complete domain of the quality-increasing verbials but only the area of the (A5)-(C8) subtype. Also notice the curious fact that the Dutch verb AANKLEDEN (lit. 'to dress') is mainly quality-increasing and *not* both quality- and quantity-increasing as its literal English equivalent TO DRESS UP.

The fact that a distinction had to be made between (A5)-(C8) and (A6)-(C9), whereas no similar split was to be found in the set of quality-diminishing verbials (though it is quite conceivable to distinguish between making good things look bad and making bad things look worse), is another linguistic reflection of the habit to regard unpleasant things as untrue.

The preceding observations on the truth dimension of lying are summarized in SDC Table 1.

THE SEMANTICS OF LYING 133

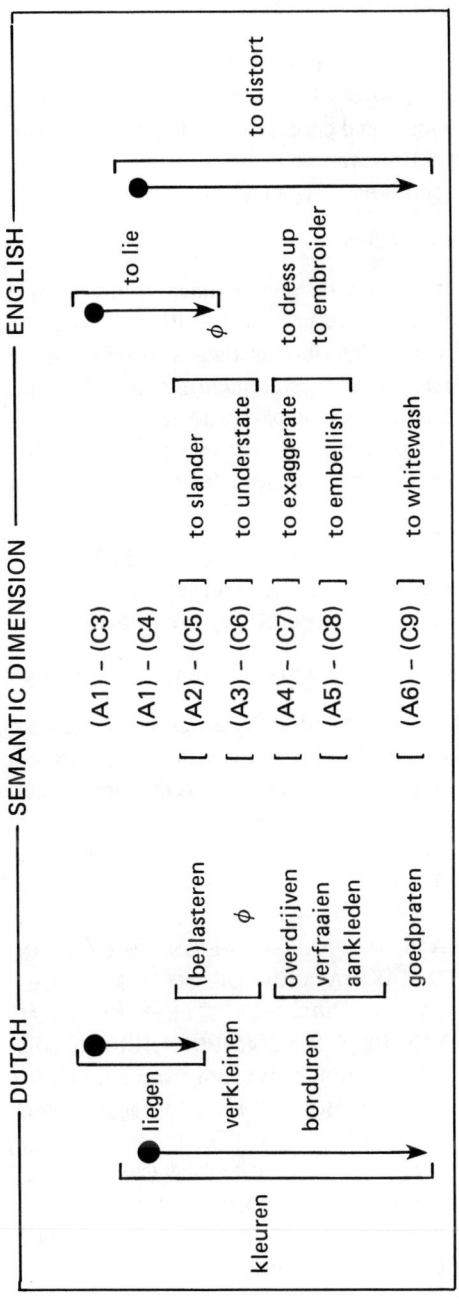

SDC Table 1

4.3 THE ILLOCUTIONARY FORCE OF LYING

253 The title of this section is misleading in the sense that lying cannot be said to possess an illocutionary force of its own. Lying is simply a matter of performing speech acts the propositional content of which deviates from the truth in any of several possible ways. However, all examples of verba mentiendi mentioned so far described acts of illocutionary type (A1).

(A1) *Sa* makes a statement

Therefore, though they cannot be said to have an illocutionary force of their own, they are not neutral with respect to illocutionary force: in Searle's terminology, the point of the acts described is always to represent or assert a certain state of affairs. This restriction to statementlike speech acts is not surprising. Though sincerity plays an important part with respect to other types of speech acts such as directives, commissives, and expressives, questions of truth (i.e. questions of the correspondence between 'reality' and propositional content) are less relevant.

254 Yet there is another set of linguistic action verbials that are closely related to the verba mentiendi mentioned so far but that describe acts of the type (A2), i.e., there is no illocutionary type specified by the verbials themselves.

(A2) *Sa* performs (a) speech act(s) with any illocutionary force

They can be regarded as verba mentiendi insofar as they can be used to describe statementlike utterances deviating from the truth. When they refer to acts of a different illocutionary type, they cease to be verba mentiendi because no deviation from the truth is involved, though sincerity is trifled with in some other way. Here is a partial list: TO PUT ON AN ACT, TO PUT UP A FRONT, TO PUT ON A (FALSE) FRONT, TO ACT, TO ACT/PLAY A PART, TO ACT/PLAY THE HYPOCRITE, TO CANT, TO AFFECT, TO ASSUME, TO SHAM, TO SIMULATE, TO DISSEMBLE, TO DISSIMULATE, TO FAKE, TO FEIGN, TO GAMMON, TO LET ON, TO MAKE A PRETENSE, TO MAKE A SHOW OF, TO MAKE FALSE PRETENSES, TO POSSUM, TO PRETEND; and in Dutch AFFECTEREN ('to affect'), DOEN ALSOF ('to act as if'), ZICH VAN DE DOMME HOUDEN (lit. 'to hold oneself stupid', meaning 'to act as if one does not know about something'), GEBAREN (lit. 'to gesture', meaning 'to let on'), HUICHELEN ('to feign', often 'to dissemble'), ONTVEINZEN ('to dissemble'), IN ZIJN ROL BLIJVEN (lit. 'to stay in one's role'), EEN ROL SPELEN ('to act a part'), SIMULEREN ('to simulate'), VEINZEN ('to feign'), VOORGEVEN ('to pretend'), VOORWENDEN ('to pretend'), FEMELEN ('to cant'), KWEZELEN ('to cant'), DE HYPOCRIET UITHANGEN ('to play the hypocrite'), etc. Whenever these verbials are discussed further on, only their (A1) meaning is referred to.

255 A number of verba mentiendi are applicable to certain specific subtypes of statementlike acts. One of these subtypes is the act of *accusing*, which is of the type (A1) conforming to (C1).

> (C1) The propositional content of *Sa*'s utterance ascribes to a person an act or property that is generally regarded as 'bad' or 'wrong'

An (A1)-(C1) verbial would be TO IMPUTE (something to a person); in Dutch there are the verbials AANWRIJVEN, AANTIJGEN, and IEMAND IETS IN DE SCHOENEN SCHUIVEN (lit. 'to shove something into somebody's shoes', meaning 'to accuse unjustly'). Almost all quality-diminishing verbials, though their meaning is wider, can be used in the sense of accusing unjustly.

256 The opposite of accusing is *praising*. There are two types of praising covered by specific verba mentiendi. The first type is (A1) conforming to (C2).

> (C2) The propositional content of *Sa*'s utterance ascribes to a person or object an act or property that is generally regarded as 'good' or 'right'

Some (A1)-(C2) verba mentiendi are TO OVERLAUD, TO OVERCOMMEND, TO OVERPRAISE, and the Dutch OVERROEPEN (lit. 'to overshout'). The second type of praising unjustly is (A1) conforming to (C2) plus (C3).

> (C3) The person about whom something 'good' is said or who has an immediate interest in the state of affairs talked about is (one of) *Sa*'s hearer(s)

Relevant verbials here are TO PLAY UP TO and the Dutch IEMAND NAAR DE MOND PRATEN (lit. 'to talk to someone's mouth' meaning 'to say what he/she likes to hear', which makes you wonder why the expression is not 'to talk to someone's ear'). Verba mentiendi that are neutral between (A1)-(C2) and (A1)-(C2+C3) are TO GIVE MOUTH HONOR TO, TO RENDER/GIVE/PAY LIP SERVICE and the Dutch EEN LIPPENDIENST BEWIJZEN ('to render lip service').

257 It is worth noting that whereas most quality-diminishing verbials such as TO CAST ASPERSIONS ON can be extended from a neutral (A1) to (A1)-(C1), it is impossible to extend the basic (A1) meaning of quality-increasing verbials such as TO WHITEWASH into the domain of praising unjustly. On the other hand, the quality-increasing verb TO EMBELLISH, as well as most quantity-increasing verbs such as TO EXAGGERATE, can be extended from (A1) to (A1)-(C2) and even (A1)-(C2+C3). But the quantity-diminishing verb TO UNDERSTATE, just as TO WHITEWASH, sticks to the neutral (A1) meaning. The interaction between the truth dimension and the illocutionary dimension in Dutch is completely analogous.

258 The third statementlike illocutionary-force type that some verba mentiendi draw explicit attention to is *swearing*. In other words, (A1) conforms to (C4) or (C5).

> (C4) *Sa* is taking an oath
> (C5) *Sa* is under oath

The Dutch EEN MEINEED AFLEGGEN ('to commit perjury') is restricted to (A1)-(C4). TO BEAR FALSE WITNESS and its equivalent EEN VALSE GETUIGENIS AFLEGGEN seem to be confined to (A1)-(C5); in some cases they do not belong to the domain of swearing at all. The English verbials TO PERJURE ONESELF and TO COMMIT PERJURY are neutral between (A1)-(C4) and (A1)-(C5): they can be used to describe either an act of swearing as such or an act of making an untruthful statement under oath (i.e. a statement made after swearing that what was to follow would be true).

259 The illocutionary dimension of the verba mentiendi, which is represented in SDC Table 2, shows that the question of truth is most relevant with respect to statementlike speech acts or assertives. Among the assertives, acts of accusing, praising, and swearing are focused on individually, which shows their salience. Praising untruthfully is salient because of its frequent occurrence in social interaction. Accusing and swearing are salient because the question of truth is absolutely central to these two acts. This is why the verb TO LIE and the other verbials of lying can be easily applied to acts of accusing unjustly and swearing falsely but not to overlauding or rendering lip service.

260 The centrality of the question of truth to assertive speech acts also emerges from the fact that the basic Dutch verb in this conceptual area, BEWEREN, is often associated with untruthfulness. BEWEREN means 'to state without proof or to maintain in spite of evidence to the contrary'. In that sense the Dutch verb is much closer to TO CLAIM than to TO STATE. There seems to be no Dutch assertive the meaning of which is as general and as neutral as the meaning of TO STATE and that is never associated with untruthfulness. Though the claim that this shows something about the credibility of Dutch statements would be hardly credible itself, we are at least confronted with a curious lexical gap. In practice, the gap is usually filled by the statement-specific use of the more general linguistic action verb ZEGGEN ('to say'), a use to which the English TO SAY can also be put; another common way out is to use VERKLAREN (English 'to declare'), but this is clearly not as basic a word as TO STATE.

261 Lying is a domain without explicit performatives. This results not only from the fact that lying has no illocutionary force of its own (though its domain is restricted to the assertive illocutionary act type) but also from some simple pragmatic constraints on the use of the verba mentiendi. Elsewhere (Verschueren 1977:13-14) I have shown that an act of boasting would destroy itself if the performative formula 'I boast' were to be used and that a moral judgment would be passed on an act of threatening by using the performative formula 'I threaten'. Similarly, Grice (1978:125) draws our attention to the fact that prefixing the phrase 'to speak ironically' to an ironical statement would destroy the irony (whereas 'to speak metaphorically' can be prefixed to metaphorical utterances). In the same way, adding 'I lie' to an untrue statement would turn it into a true statement, or at least it would destroy the possibility of deceiving the hearer. This final remark leads us toward the perlocutionary intent of lying.

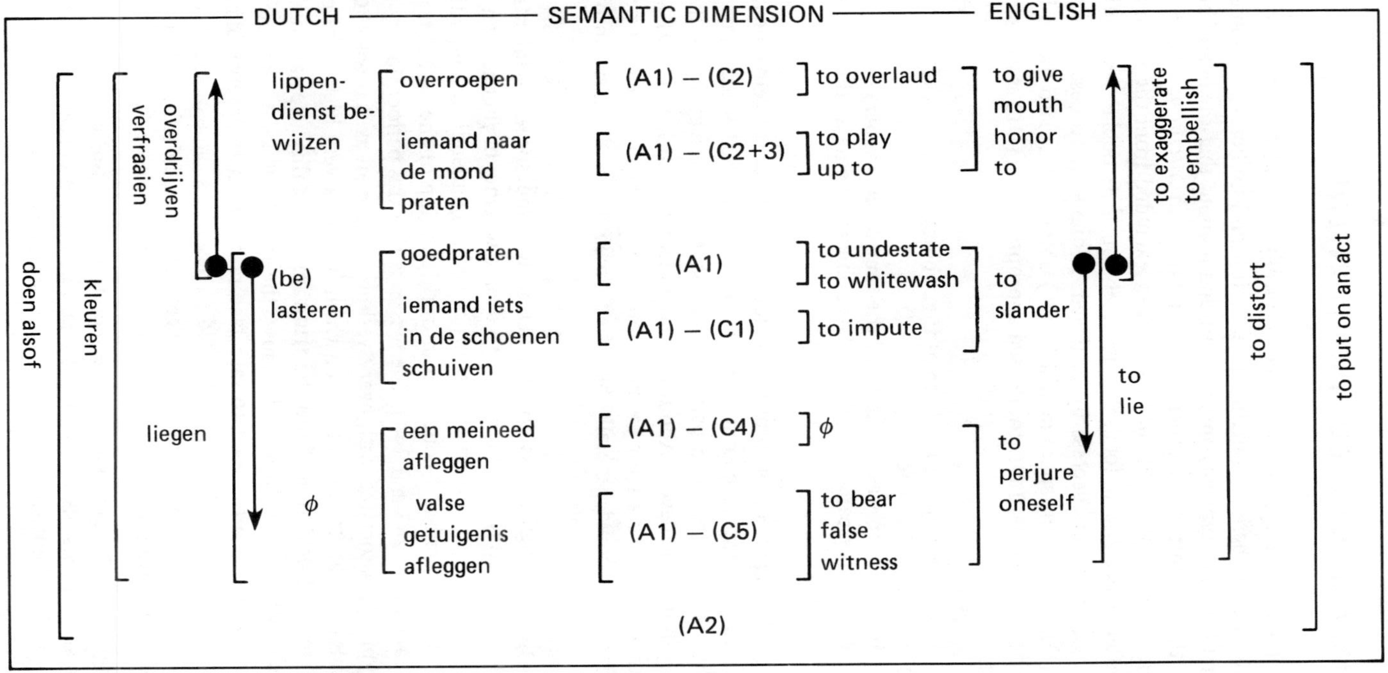

THE SEMANTICS OF LYING

SDC Table 2

DUTCH		SEMANTIC DIMENSION	ENGLISH
lippendienst bewijzen	overroepen	(A1) – (C2)	to overlaud / to give mouth honor
	iemand naar de mond praten	(A1) – (C2+3)	to play up to
(be)lasteren	goedpraten	(A1)	to understate / to whitewash / to slander
	iemand iets in de schoenen schuiven	(A1) – (C1)	to impute
	een meineed afleggen	(A1) – (C4)	φ
	valse getuigenis afleggen	(A1) – (C5)	to bear false witness / to perjure oneself
		(A2)	

overdrijven / verfraaien → to exaggerate / to embellish

liegen → to lie

kleuren → to distort

doen alsof → to put on an act

4.4 LYING AND PERLOCUTIONARY INTENT

262 The intended perlocutionary effect typically associated with statements is to make the hearer believe something or to inform him/her about something. Thus, if one lies, one typically intends to bring it about that the hearer believes something that is untrue. In other words, there is an *intention to deceive* involved. The verb TO DECEIVE has itself been excluded from the realm of the verba mentiendi because it focuses completely on a particular perlocutionary effect that is, moreover, necessarily achieved. If one were to describe (A1) by means of (D1) in circumstances in which (C1) obtains, (C2) also has to be fulfilled in order for TO DECEIVE to be used appropriately in (D1) as a description of (A1).

(A1) John was home at the time of the robbery
(D1) *Sa* deceived the police
(C1) In fact, John was not home at the time of the robbery
(C2) The police came to believe that John was home at the time of the robbery

Similarly, TO FLATTER has also been excluded from the set of verba mentiendi, though it may be used to describe untruthful statements, because, just as TO DECEIVE, it really focuses on a particular perlocutionary effect that in this case may or may not be achieved. About the verba mentiendi such as TO LIE we can only say that they have a strong association with a typically intended perlocutionary effect that could generally be called deception or the creation of false beliefs.

263 Though the judgment as to whether it was the speaker's intention to deceive his/her hearer(s) may be crucial to decide whether his/her act can be described by means of TO LIE and most other verba mentiendi, the intention to deceive was not entered as a condition in our definition of the lexical frame of lying (see paragraphs 243 and 244). The reason is that this perlocutionary intent is not as typically associated with every verbum mentiendi as it is with TO LIE. Even verbials such as TO LIE FLATLY, which implies a very high score on the gradability scale of deviations from the truth, may lack this association. In circumstances in which both *Sa* and *Ha* know 'the truth' and know that the other knows it, a 'flat lie' is often used to save face rather than to deceive. Similarly, TO LIE LIKE A TROOPER is frequently used to describe a game of social interaction comparable to the boasting and bragging common in Afro-American culture—intent to deceive is not a significant feature of this type of activity.

264 Though there is this one basic effect typically associated with many—though not all—verbials discussed in this chapter, there is considerable variation among the verba mentiendi along the perlocutionary dimension. There are mainly two parameters for the differentiation. First, the type of false belief may be further specified. Second, different types of further effects may be aimed at via the false belief induced. These two parameters are now considered.

265 Most verba mentiendi give no further specification of the false belief that the speaker is trying to induce in the hearer. Consequently, most of them are neutral with respect to this part of the perlocutionary dimension. Probably there is only one class of exceptions constitued by verbials such as TO CANT, TO ACT/ PLAY THE HYPOCRITE, and the Dutch KWEZELEN ('to cant'), FEMELEN ('to cant'), and DE HYPOCRIET UITHANGEN ('to play the hypocrite'). As an illustration of their use, consider (D2) and (D3) as descriptions of (A2)-(C3) and (D4) and (D5) as descriptions of (A3)-(C4).

- (A2) It is hard to understand why so many young people should die, but I think we should not try to judge God's decisions
- (D2) *Sa* is canting again
- (D3) *Sa* is playing the hypocrite again
- (C3) *Sa* does not believe that God exists, or at least he thinks that if God exists he must be a super-cruel being in order to let so many young people die

The second example:

- (A3) Let this incident not be a reason for declaring war; they are, after all, our brothers
- (D4) *Sa* was canting about brotherly love
- (D5) *Sa* was playing the hypocrite again
- (C4) *Sa* wants vengeance; he is only waiting for a better moment

These two examples show that the kind of belief typically intended to be generated by means of canting and playing the hypocrite is the hearer's belief that the speaker is a virtuous or pious person. In other words, (C5) should be a characteristic of (A2) in order for (D2) and (D3) to be appropriate descriptions of (A2), and (C6) should be a characteristic of (A3) in order for (D4) and (D5) to be appropriate descriptions of (A3).

- (C5) *Sa* wants *Ha* to believe that he/she is a pious, God-fearing person
- (C6) *Sa* wants *Ha* to believe that he/she is a virtuous, peace-loving person

I have not found other verba mentiendi that give equally specific information on the perlocutionary intent at the level of the beliefs that the speaker wants to arouse.

266 There is a perlocutionary level beyond the beliefs that the speaker wants to arouse when making an untruthful statement. The intention may be to produce a further effect by means of generating a certain false belief. Also, at that level many verba mentiendi do not provide any specific information. But this parameter yields a somewhat stronger variation than the previous one.

For one thing, the four types of verba mentiendi specifying the way in which the truth is being distorted (quality-increasing, quality-diminishing, etc.) also single out, as a direct corollary, different intended effects. Thus, the typically intended effect of an act describable in terms of a quality-increasing verbial such as TO WHITEWASH is to create a favorable attitude toward something or someone by making the hearer believe that it/he/she is 'better' than it/he/she is in reality. The typically intended effect of an act describable in terms of a quality-diminishing verbial such as TO SLANDER is to create an unfavorable attitude toward something or someone by means of making the hearer believe it/him/her to be 'worse' than it/he/she is in reality. Similarly, the typically intended effect of an act describable in terms of a quantity-increasing verbial such as TO EXAGGERATE is to impress the hearer by making him/her believe that the blown-up representation given matches reality. Conversely, acts describable by means of quantity-diminishing verbials such as TO UNDERSTATE are typically intended to yield the reverse effect of impressing.

267 It should be noted that understating, in actual discourse, is very often not intended to make the hearer believe the propositional content. Thus 'He is full of understatement' may mean that the person in question is full of humor and that he achieves his humoristic effects by means of understatements (as figures of speech). Does this invalidate our analysis? By no means. This observation simply points to a more general problem. Making a statement the propositional content of which does not match reality or the 'truth' is not necessarily lying. Consider (A4) uttered in circumstances to which (C7) obtains.

(A4) John is a genius
(C7) In fact, John can hardly produce two coherent sentences

(A4) can either be an instance of lying or an instance of irony. What distinguishes the two is the speaker's perlocutionary intent. In the case of irony, it is not the speaker's intention to make the hearer believe that John is a genius; quite the opposite is true. Humorous understatements differ from lie-like understatements in the same way. This observation shows the necessity of formulating the typically intended perlocutionary effect of acts within the domain of the verba mentiendi.

268 There are a couple of quantity-increasing verbs the intended effect of which deviates from the general intention of 'impressing' formulated in paragraph **266**. Not only are their effects different in type, they are also much more specific.

First, the Dutch verb CHARGEREN means 'to give an exaggerated representation of something in order to ridicule it'. I have not found an exact equivalent in English, though TO CARICATURE is close.

Second, the verb TO OVERCHARGE denotes acts intended to make someone pay more for something than it is really worth by making him/her believe that the charged price reflects its real value. In Dutch only circumscriptions such as TEVEEL AANREKENEN ('to charge too much'), which can hardly be regarded as lexical items, can be used to describe such acts.

269   There are also some verbials that do not belong to any of the four sets of verba mentiendi singling out the way in which the truth is being distorted; they specify an intended effect to be achieved via the arousing of false beliefs in the hearer.

First, verbials such as TO PLAY UP TO and its equivalent IEMAND NAAR DE MOND PRATEN (lit. 'to talk to someone's mouth') describe acts typically intended to gratify or flatter the hearer by making him/her believe that the speaker holds beliefs that the hearer would want him/her to hold.

Second, TO BEAR FALSE WITNESS and its equivalent EEN VALSE GETUIGENIS AFLEGGEN describe acts typically intended to influence judgments (in or out of court) by inducing false beliefs in the hearer.

Finally, the Dutch ABRAHAMMETJE SPELEN (lit. 'to play little Abraham') is used to talk about acts of telling part of the truth (and thus holding back the other part or lying about it) in order to escape from further questioning, which may be achieved if the hearer comes to believe that what the speaker says is the whole truth.

These remarks conclude our overview of the salient points on the perlocutionary dimension of acts of lying.

4.5 THE TEXTUAL DIMENSION OF LYING

270   There are several ways in which the verba mentiendi reflect the textual dimension of lying. For one thing, there are quite a few verba mentiendi that denote linguistic actions and that almost necessarily consist of more than one speech act.

Many of the verbials that have been said not to give any information about the illocutionary type of the acts described belong here. Acts described by means of TO PUT ON AN ACT, TO PUT UP A FRONT, TO MAKE FALSE PRETENSES, and the Dutch DOEN ALSOF ('to act as if'), EEN ROL SPELEN ('to act a part'), etc., are rarely restricted to one single speech act. Usually a whole text, of any kind, is involved.

Similarly TO DRESS UP, TO EMBELLISH, and TO EMBROIDER often require a suprasentential segment of linguistic action, as will be clear from their usage in (D1) to (D3).

(D1)   He dressed up the story of what he did on vacation
(D2)   He kept inventing details to embellish his story
(D3)   He embroidered the story of his adventures in Hollywood

The Dutch equivalents BORDUREN ('to embroider'), VERFRAAIEN ('to embellish'), and AANKLEDEN ('to dress up') behave in a similar fashion.

The verb TO STORY can also be used as a verbum mentiendi. But it is quite remarkable that this verb can be used to refer to one single untrue statement, in spite of the fact that a story normally consists of a sequence of speech acts, as appears from (D1) to (D3). Thus, TO STORY is used quite appropriately in (D4) as a description of (A1) given that (C1) obtains.

(A1) I am nearly 30 years old
(C1) *Sa* is over 40
(D4) *Sa* storied about his/her age

A comparable Dutch verbial, SPROOKJES VERTELLEN (lit. 'to tell fairy tales'), can also be used as a verbum mentiendi. But unlike TO STORY it rarely refers to a single speech act.

271   A second group of text-sensitive verba mentiendi requires not only that the linguistic action described consists of more than one speech act but also that these speech acts could be separately characterized as lies. Most of the intensified verba mentiendi, such as TO LIE LIKE A TROOPER and the Dutch TEGEN DE STERREN OP LIEGEN (lit. 'to lie up against the stars'), belong here. It would be hard to predicate of a certain speaker that he/she lied like a trooper if he/she uttered only one untrue statement.

272   There are a couple of Dutch verbials that basically indicate a person's general inclination toward lying. They are WAT AFLIEGEN ('to lie a lot'; we are really concerned with a lexical item here, since AFLIEGEN has no meaning of its own when in isolation) and VAN ALLE KATTEN KWAAD WETEN (lit. 'to know something bad about all cats'). But just like TO LIE LIKE A TROOPER and other intensified verba mentiendi, they can also be used to describe multiple acts of lying. This will not be hard to understand for WAT AFLIEGEN, but the use of the second verbial in its act-sense instead of its inclination-sense requires an illustration. Consider (D5).

(D5) Hij wist weer van alle katten kwaad
      (lit. 'Again he knew something bad about all cats')

(D5) is an adequate description of a speaker's linguistic activity during a tea-time conversation in which he/she claimed, without proof or evidence, that Jane was about to get her third divorce, that Jim passed his exam because his father paid a large sum of money to the professor in question, that Kate had an affair with an official of the Internal Revenue Service so that she did not have to pay any taxes, etc. (Again, the verbial in question shows the strong tendency to associate 'saying bad things about' with 'saying false things about'; see paragraph 248.)

273   Some verba mentiendi may presuppose discourse preceding the untruthful statement described. For instance, the use of ZICH VAN DE DOMME HOUDEN (lit. 'to hold oneself dumb'), which means 'pretending not to know anything about a certain matter', often implies previous questioning about that matter by the hearer. In this case even the type of preceding speech act is made explicit.

Others may presuppose either preceding or following discourse. One can describe the taking of an oath by means of EEN MEINEED AFLEGGEN (lit. 'to take a false oath') only if the oath in question bears on a lie uttered before or after the oath was taken. Again, the nature of the preceding discourse or the following discourse, which in this case must contain a lie, is made explicit.

274 A final set of verba mentiendi that relate acts of distorting the truth to other linguistic actions includes TO MISQUOTE, TO FALSIFY, TO TWIST SOMEONE'S WORDS, and the Dutch VERVALSEN ('to falsify') and IEMANDS WOORDEN VERDRAAIEN/VERWRINGEN/VERVALSEN ('to twist someone's words'). In this case previous linguistic utterances (usually by someone else) are misrepresented. Needless to say, TO MISQUOTE is only a verbum mentiendi in case it refers to a voluntary action with the intention to deceive.

4.6 LYING AND VALUE JUDGMENTS

275 When defining the lexical frame of lying (see paragraphs 243 and 244), we considered the possibility of adding a condition of the type (Cd):

(Cd) Sd regards saying A when the propositional content of A represents a state of affairs falsely and when Sa believes it does, as reprehensible.

In a very real sense, judgments as to whether an assertion should be called a lie or not depend very often on the reprehensibility of the act rather than on the distortion of the truth (as the speaker sees it) as such. This is not true to the same extent for all verba mentiendi, which is why it was not entered as a condition in the definition of the lexical frame as a whole.

276 Though there are supposed to be such things as WHITE LIES (in Dutch LEUGENS OM BESTWIL, lit. 'lies for the best'), negative value judgments (as formulated in (Cd)) are attached to practically all verba mentiendi. That is to say, neither Dutch nor English provides us with instruments for talking favorably about distorting the truth. The only verbials that present distortions of the truth as excusable acts include TO FIB, TO KID, TO PULL SOMEONE'S LEG, and the Dutch JOKKEN ('to fib') and IEMAND BIJ DE NEUS NEMEN (lit. 'to grab someone's nose', meaning 'to pull someone's leg'). TO FIB and JOKKEN describe acts that are excusable because of the unimportance or triviality of the facts lied about. The acts referred to by means of TO KID, TO PULL SOMEONE'S LEG, and IEMAND BIJ DE NEUS NEMEN are excusable because of the humor involved. But the very fact that these few exceptions merely present some acts of lying as *excusable* stresses the general negative attitude towards distortions of the truth.

277 Two more indicators of these value judgments may be adduced. First, there are a couple of fixed expressions used to describe acts of saying something in favor of a distortion of the truth, namely TO COLOR A LIE and TO GILD A LIE. Now, TO COLOR and TO GILD imply distortions of the truth themselves.

Since I know of no other fixed verbials describing acts of saying something favorable about a lie and not carrying the same implication, we might dare to formulate the conclusion that, whenever something favorable is said about a lie, this is generally regarded as a distortion of the truth and, therefore, that lies are generally regarded as inherently 'bad' and lacking praiseworthy features.

Second, the lexical items available for describing the end of a lying-sequence (i.e. admitting that what was said before was all lies) imply that lying is an activity that one usually does not stop deliberately. (Here we disregard the neutral phrase TO STOP LYING because it is not a lexical item, and because it does not necessarily imply that the truth was revealed at the end of the lying-sequence.) I am thinking of verbials such as UIT ZIJN ROL VALLEN (lit. 'to fall out of one's role') and DOOR DE MAND VALLEN (lit. 'to fall through the basket'), both of which refer to a failure to uphold one's lies or pretenses. Again, the explanation is to be found in a negative attitude toward lying. A mentiens tries to maintain his/her false representation of the truth in order to avoid being judged and losing face.

278 Together with the importance of questions of truth for statements, which was revealed in the section on the illocutionary force of lying, the overwhelming prominence of negative value judgments attached to distortions of the truth supports the relevance—for our cultures—of Grice's (1975) conversational maxim of quality 'Try to make your contribution one that is true'. Though under innumerable circumstances the question of truth becomes irrelevant, as several authors have shown and as Grice certainly realizes, the verba mentiendi show beyond any doubt that truth is one of the basic parameters in terms of which statementlike utterances are conceptualized.

4.7 NOTE ON HUMAN IMAGINATION

279 The propositional content of linguistic actions describable in terms of verba mentiendi is always a product of the human mind or human imagination, since the speaker knows or thinks it does not match reality. There is, however, a set of lexical items that strongly emphasizes this imagination aspect of lying; in other words, these items explicitly present the mentiendum as a product of the human mind. They are TO CONCOCT, TO COOK UP, TO FABRICATE, TO FANTASIZE (ABOUT), TO INVENT, TO MAKE UP, TO MANUFACTURE, and TO TRUMP UP. Here are some illustrative sentences showing their use as verba mentiendi.

(D1) They concocted an alibi for their friend
(D2) Whenever he arrived late he cooked up an elegant excuse
(D3) He fabricated a complicated explanation for his being late
(D4) At tea-time she always keeps fantasizing about her neighbors
(D5) What he did not know, he invented
(D6) He made up most of the story

(D7) The historian was evidently manufacturing all the evidence he adduced
(D8) Whenever he was late he trumped up a new excuse

Notice that these verbs are often ambiguous between a purely mental activity and the linguistic activity of putting creations of the mind into words. Though imagination or mental activity is much appreciated in our society, a pejorative connotation is attached to the verbs mentioned as soon as they are used as verba mentiendi. This phenomenon provides us with additional support for the thesis that strong negative value judgments are attached to lying in our culture and that Grice's maxim of quality shows a strong factual salience in our experience of linguistic activity.

280 Similar verbials are to be found in Dutch: FABRICEREN ('to fabricate'), FANTASEREN ('to fantasize'), FINGEREN (lit. 'to produce fiction', meaning 'to make up'), VERZINNEN ('to make up'), UITVINDEN ('to invent'), VERDICHTEN (lit. 'to turn into poetry', meaning 'to invent'), and the picturesque expression UIT ZIJN DUIM ZUIGEN (lit. 'to suck from one's thumb', meaning 'to invent').

Notice that most of these imagination-oriented verbs belong to the set of verba mentiendi that usually refer to more than one single speech act. On the truth dimension they are to be situated among the verbials of lying proper.

4.8 CONCLUSIONS

281 In this chapter we have touched upon the most important semantic dimensions along which English and Dutch verba mentiendi seem to be comparable: the truth dimension (which is no doubt the basic one), the illocutionary dimension, the perlocutionary dimension, the textual dimension, and finally the dimension of value judgments and the role of imagination. This is not to say that no additional semantic dimensions will have to be taken into account when further comparing the meaning of individual verbials within the domain of lying.

282 As I did at the end of the previous chapter, I shall now give a relatively small and random list of noteworthy observations that forced themselves upon us in the process of scrutinizing the lexical field associated with linguistic acts of distorting the truth.
1. The gradability of the notion of truth is a relatively unimportant parameter of the truth dimension of the verba mentiendi. (Paragraphs 239 and **240**)
2. From the set of verba mentiendi, it appears that the different ways in which the truth can be deviated from are conceived in terms of a fourfold contrast: quality-increasing, quantity-increasing, quality-diminishing, quantity-diminishing. (Paragraph **240**)
3. There is a one-directional dependence relationship between the quantity scale of truth and the quality scale. (Paragraph **241**)

4. The lexicon reflects the general habit of taking quantity as a criterion for quality. (Paragraph 241)
5. Only the like poles of the two truth scales share descriptive verbials. (Paragraph 242)
6. The verba mentiendi reflect the following attitude prevailing in our culture: what is disagreeable is regarded as untrue. (Paragraph 248)
7. Questions of truth are most relevant in connection with assertive speech acts. (Paragraphs 253 to 261)
8. The acts of praising, accusing, and swearing are salient points in the area of the representative speech acts when it comes to the question of truth. (Paragraphs 255 to 259)
9. Deception is an effect typically intended by utterers of untrue statements; this reinforces the independent claim that there is a typically intended effect associated with all assertives, namely making the hearer know or believe something. (Paragraphs 262 to 269)
10. It is shown that negative value judgments are usually attached to distortions of the truth; together with item 7, this strengthens the linguistic relevance of Grice's conversational maxim of quality with respect to statement-like utterances. (Paragraphs 275 to 278)

283 Apart from the quite surprising gap for a basic quantity-diminishing verb in Dutch, differences between the sets of Dutch and English verba mentiendi are minimal. Of course all the generalizations summed up in the previous paragraph should be subjected to further comparative research. An especially promising topic for further investigation would be the universality or nonuniversality of the two scales of truth (the quantity scale and the quality scale) in terms of which different types of deviations from the truth are conceptualized and their interrelationships.

284 Particularly striking about the foregoing overview of the semantic dimensions along which the domain of the verba mentiendi is structured is the poverty of the motivational dimension (which has been presented here only in terms of perlocutionary intents), the absence of a topic-related dimension (over and above the simple distinction between trivial and nontrivial topics that emerged in paragraph 276), and the overpowering prominence of negative value judgments. This probably results from our ethical tradition, which, though it has occasionally presented justifications for certain types of lies, can in general be said to start from and to lead to the maxim that 'what is not true we should never try to persuade anyone to believe' (St. Augustine); that every lie is a sin, though not necessarily a mortal one (Thomas Aquinas); that 'there is no vice that doth so cover a man with shame as to be found false and perfidious' (Francis Bacon); that 'to be truthful in all declarations is a sacred and absolutely commanding decree of reason, limited by no expediency' (Immanuel Kant); or that, no matter how difficult the circumstances, one should always make an attempt at 'thinking up honest ways to deal with problems' because trust and integrity 'can thrive only on a foundation of respect for veracity' (Bok 1978:257, 263).

285 In everyday life we are, of course, constantly confronted with lies. Lies are considered routine in business, in government, in the medical world, maybe also in academics. And deviations from the truth are made to serve all kinds of purposes. Yet, the ethical tradition, condemning this kind of verbal behavior, seems to have blocked the development of a rich motivational and topic-related dimension in the verba mentiendi. Whenever a distortion of the truth is felt to be justified, the majority of verba mentiendi are simply not likely to be used to describe the behavior in question. Thus, a valid hypothesis might be that the verbials within the domain under investigation could show more variety in motivations for distorting the truth and in the subject matter of the distortions in cultures that lack a similar long-standing 'philosophical' tradition and in which there would not be this conflict between practice and theory. Whether such cultures exist is an interesting topic for empirical research.

286 The prominence of negative value judgments explains some of the problems encountered by Coleman and Kay (1981) in their experimental study of the prototype meaning of the verb TO LIE. They found that participants in the experiments sometimes seemed to base their judgments as to whether a given act was a lie or not on the graveness of the consequences and the moral implications rather than on the parameters they wanted to investigate (viz. factual truth, speaker's belief, and intention to deceive).

CHAPTER **5**

THE SEMANTICS OF DIRECTING

5.0 INTRODUCTION

287 We are now entering a second central area of linguistic meaning, the realm of illocutionary force. Within this vast area we single out speech acts of a directive kind. What types of acts are encompassed by the general term 'directive' is elucidated in the following paragraphs. The verbs and expressions used to describe linguistic actions of a directive kind are referred to as *verbials of directing*.

Whereas linguistic silence has so far been little noticed by students of language and lying has mainly been the topic of philosophical—especially ethical—considerations (though quite a few linguistic studies are to be found), many dozens of articles, in the tradition of linguistic pragmatics, have been devoted to directive linguistic behavior—so many, in fact, that listing them here would be futile. For references, the reader is referred to Verschueren (1978a) and its annual supplements in the *Journal of Pragmatics*.

288 One aspect of the subsequent treatment of the verbials of directing will no doubt arrest the reader's thoughts. Though this chapter is supposed to explore a subfield of the vast area of illocutionary force, we shall not explicitly discuss an illocutionary dimension of the verbials of directing. The reason is that illocutionary force itself is the criterion for including a verbial in the subject matter of this chapter. The different shades in force that present themselves depend on a large variety of factors that have to be dealt with in terms of different semantic dimensions. The overview of directive speech-act types in the next few paragraphs could be regarded as an outline of the illocutionary dimension in question. The individual discussion of other dimensions afterward will clarify the different shades of illocutionary force pointed out.

289 Though primarily a matter of illocutionary force is at stake, some of the linguistic action verbials to be investigated do not describe what would traditionally have been called an 'illocutionary act'. Instead, many of them refer to larger configurations of linguistic acts such as text-level structures. These configurations of speech acts, however, can be said to possess a force similar to individual directive speech acts. It should be kept in mind that when I use 'a directive act' in this chapter, this phrase can frequently be replaced by 'a set of directive acts' or 'a series of acts with a directive force'. Its permeating different levels of linguistic structure shows how fundamental directing is as a function of language.

290 According to Searle's (1976) classical definition of directive speech acts, the point of a directive is to get the hearer to do something; there is a world-to-word direction of fit; the speaker expresses a wish; and the proposition specifies a future act to be done by the hearer. Not surprisingly, this definition is geared to the central instances of directing, namely commands and requests. This means that it would be wrong to adopt it as a rigid criterion for including or excluding a verb or expression in or from the set of verbials of directing. The result would be the exclusion of many verbials about which we intuit that they refer to linguistic actions that possess a directive force of some kind; we would be left with TO COMMAND, TO REQUEST, TO BEG, and their synonyms. It would be equally wrong, after using our intuition to round up the verbials of directing, to force their meaning into the mold of Searle's definition. For instance, it is impossible to describe every directive speech act as an attempt to get the hearer to do something. But how can a linguistic action that is not, strictly speaking, an attempt to get the hearer to do something, be regarded as an act of directing? The answer will, it is hoped, reveal itself in the course of the following introductory and sketchy overview of directives that deviate somehow from the central instances of commanding and requesting. The overview is meant to shape the reader's expectations as to the lexical domain covered by this chapter.

291 A first type of directive that departs from the central cases outlined by Searle's definition is commonly described by means of TO PROHIBIT and its synonyms. Prohibitions direct the hearer to not doing something instead of doing something. In this case the deviation is minimal. The act is clearly directive.

A second deviant type: TO ASK, when used to describe the asking of a question (instead of as an equivalent of TO REQUEST), refers to acts the propositional content of which does not specify the future act to be done by the hearer. What is expected from the hearer is a response to the question. This is clear from the verb itself.

TO DARE in the sense of to challenge to do something requiring boldness and skill stands apart from the central directives in that it does not usually imply the speaker's belief that the hearer is able (or bold enough) to do what he/she is trying to get him/her to do. Such an implication is traditionally assigned (as a 'preparatory condition') to acts of commanding and requesting.

292 Also, acts of threatening can be directive. I am not thinking about unconditional threats such as 'I'll kill you' but about conditional ones such as 'If I ever see you with my sister again, I'll kill you'. The latter is clearly an attempt to keep the hearer away from the speaker's sister, and the act as a whole can be described by means of TO THREATEN as in '*S* threatened *H* into staying away from *S*'s sister' or '*S* threatened to kill *H* if he ever saw *H* with *S*'s sister again'.

Also in this case the future act to be performed by the hearer is not specified in the propositional content. Moreover, threatening is never purely directive. In its unconditional form it is simply commissive and lacks directive aspects. In its conditional form it is at the same time commissive (though not as strongly as a promise, since the 'obligation' it creates to inflict harm is unlikely to lead towards the speaker's being reproached in case he/she does not act in accordance with his/her commitment).

Notice that a description such as '*S* threatened *H*' focuses completely and exclusively on the commissive aspect of threatening. This means that a complement is needed to bring out the directive character of the act. This is also true for the Dutch equivalent DREIGEN or BEDREIGEN. The form BEDREIGEN can be used only in a structure such as '*S* threatened *H*'. DREIGEN is used in descriptions of the type '*S* threatened to kill *H* if he ever saw *H* with *S*'s sister again'. Neither of them can be used in a structure such as '*S* threatened *H* into staying away from his sister'. Thus, TO THREATEN and DREIGEN can focus both on the directive and the commissive aspects of conditional threats, whereas BEDREIGEN does not allow for a directive aspect at all. Therefore, BEDREIGEN is left out of account in this chapter. There is another closely related verb in Dutch, namely AFDREIGEN, which is one of the Dutch equivalents of TO BLACKMAIL; it means 'trying to get the hearer to give something by means of threatening'. In this verb both aspects of the conditional threat are united.

293 There are two more types of directives that are in fact mixtures between directives and some other type of linguistic action. Both of them derive their lack of centrality in the area of directives from their being mixed classes *and* from the fact that they cannot really be paraphrased as 'attempts to get the hearer to do something'.

The first of these mixed classes is represented by TO ADVISE and TO WARN. Usually acts of advising and warning are partly—if not primarily—assertive. In what sense can they be said to be directive? A piece of advice is an indication of a preferable course of action. Its directive force does not necessarily derive from a wish on the part of the speaker—though in some circumstances it may—but rather from the fact that a particular course of action is presented as preferable because it is to the hearer's benefit. On the other hand, warning is an indication of an event or course of action to be avoided because it could be detrimental to the hearer.

294 A second mixed class is more troublesome, not because it is less clearly directive than advising and warning, but simply because of recent attempts to declare it a monolithic commissive. The acts in question can be described by means of TO PERMIT and its equivalents. The argument goes like this: when giving his/her permission to do something, the speaker commits him/herself to not obstructing a particular action on the part of the hearer; hence, a permission is a kind of promise; therefore, it is a commissive rather than a directive. This is a decent argument in favor of the claim that a permission is commissive. But it presents no evidence *against* classifying permissions as directives. Unless one accepts that every type of speech act can belong to only one class. But that is one of the main errors it is hoped this essay will help to abolish.

Yet permitting is not a central type of directing. It cannot be described as an 'attempt to get the hearer to do something'. What, then, makes it directive at all?

295 Like advising, a permission is an indication of a certain course of action. Unlike advising, permitting does not imply that the speaker presents that course of action as preferable to the hearer. But permitting implies that the hearer him/herself prefers his/her doing the action over his/her not doing it. Moreover, the speaker not only *indicates* a course of action that the hearer regards as desirable, but he/she also uses his/her authority over the hearer to *open the way to* that course of action. The latter aspect emerges very clearly from some equivalents of TO PERMIT such as TO GIVE THE GO-AHEAD (which can be used to describe a speaker's permitting to start with the execution of a plan). Thus, in a very real sense, a person giving the permission to do something is *regulating* another person's behavior and using his/her authority to do so. In other words, permitting might even be said to be more strongly directive than advising or warning.

296 What about the wish on the part of the speaker, which is characteristic of the central instances of directing? It was not necessarily present in advising and warning. In contrast, a weak form of wishing is always present in permissions: if S did not want H to do P at all, he/she would simply forbid him/her to do it, which he/she can do by virtue of the same authority that is applied when permitting. This type of wanting is, admittedly, quite weak because it does not even require the speaker's belief that the course of action in question is advantageous to anyone. But what it boils down to is that the speaker, just as when he/she is commanding (with authority), is willing to take the *responsibility* for an act to be performed by the hearer. Since S has power over H's doing or not doing P, he/she can be held responsible if H does P. This willingness to take responsibility, or this weak form of wanting H to do P, makes permitting directive. But at the same time it is the very basis of the commissive aspect involved. The same kind of commitment characterizes all authoritative acts of directing. Recalling Nürnberg, where officers were convicted of ordering soldiers to shoot people, should convince anyone of the truth of this claim. And if it is true that both commanding and permitting share this type of commitment, its presence in permissions is certainly no adequate ground for excluding acts of permitting from the realm of the directives. This paragraph probably contains the strongest indication given so far of the dangers of theoretical classifications of speech acts.

297 Just as with commanding and requesting, the propositional content of a linguistic act of permitting specifies a future act to be done by the hearer. This fact pulls permissions away from other commissives, which usually contain a proposition specifying an act to be done by the speaker. Thus one could say that the directive aspect of permissions is quite explicit, whereas the commissive aspect remains largely implicit. One could object that an utterance such as 'You may go to the movies tonight' is quite explicitly and overtly commissive because it *means*—due to the presence of 'may'—'I commit myself to not obstructing your going to the movies tonight'. But such a claim would already be based on a semantic analysis that uses as a premise the belief that permissions are primarily commissive.

298 The discussion in the foregoing paragraphs should not be misinterpreted as an attempt to decide whether acts of permitting are primarily commissive or primarily directive. In this, as in many cases, I regard such attempts as irrelevant. The important thing to realize is that permissions have both a directive and a commissive aspect. The classes of speech acts proposed in the literature are rarely mutually exclusive because they are based on criteria of classification that are always arbitrary to a certain extent and because there is no logical impediment to the co-occurrence of several different functions of language. The reader will recall that this realization was the very incentive to the investigations reported in this essay, and it vindicates our decision to study, for the time being, semantic dimensions rather than semantic classes. There are two reasons, one theoretical and one practical, why in spite of this decision some class terminology is still being used. First, it links this essay with earlier research. Second, an uncompromising inquiry directed at semantic dimensions would have to take as its point of departure the complete set of linguistic action verbials; practical considerations dictate that I limit the object of investigation; in this chapter a subfield is singled out on the basis of what has been regarded up to now as a major class of illocutionary acts.

5.1 THE FRAME OF DIRECTING

299 The introductory overview of some directive speech-act types leads us toward the following definition of verbials of directing: all verbs and verblike expressions that describe linguistic actions by means of which a speaker typically directs or influences a hearer's subsequent behavior. Directing is not only one of the fundamental functions of language, it is also one of the vital roles in social life; for the performance of this role the directive function of language is usually put into action.

Whereas silence was to be situated in the frame of language and lying in the frame of truth, directing belongs in one of the most basic frames of social interaction in general. It involves parameters such as authority and wishing, which will be reflected as semantic dimensions in the verbials of directing. The verbials can also be expected to reveal the specific areas of social interaction in which directing is a major function. Let us go ahead and find out what the words have to say.

5.2 THE DIRECTIVITY OF DIRECTING

300 It will be clear from the introduction that not all acts denoted by verbials of directing are equally strong as directives. I would like to call these differences in strength *degrees of directivity*. Though there is some interaction with other dimensions, such as the authority involved, these degrees of directivity depend mainly on the strength of the *wish* or *wanting* expressed by the speaker. As with all other dimensions involving similar types of gradability, it is not possible to mark off really discrete points. What we can do, however, is to indicate the two extremes of the scale and try to arrange some basic verbials of directing with respect to these. The extremes are, of course, (A1) and (A2).

(A1) *Sa* expresses a strong wish for *Ha* to do (not do) *P*
(A2) *Sa* expresses a weak wish for *Ha* to do (not do) *P*

Though it is clear that TO COMMAND, TO ORDER, and TO PROHIBIT are quite high up on the scale, there are directives expressing even stronger wishes, namely TO BEG and TO PLEAD. At the other end of the scale we approach a zero wish with TO ACQUIESCE (in the sense of permitting) as used in (D1) describing (A3) conforming to (C1), (C2), and (C3).

(A3) Okay, you can go to medical school
(C1) *Sa* is *Ha*'s father
(C2) *Sa* has been trying to get his son to take over his business
(C3) *Ha* has been trying for months to get his father's permission to go to medical school instead of taking over his business
(D1) *Sa* finally acquiesced in his son's going to medical school

In this instance, the speaker's wish for the hearer to do *P* is even weaker than with regular permissions. But though it is clear from the context that his son's going to medical school was originally *against Sa*'s wishes, for (A3) the argument holds that if *Sa* did not want his son to go at all, he would keep resisting the decision (which he could do on the basis of some kind of parental—and financial— authority, which *Ha* accepts because otherwise he would not have asked his father's permission in the first place).

301 Before discussing the degree of directivity of any further individual cases briefly, I submit a tentative picture of the scale in question, namely SDC Table 1.

154   THE SEMANTICS OF DIRECTING

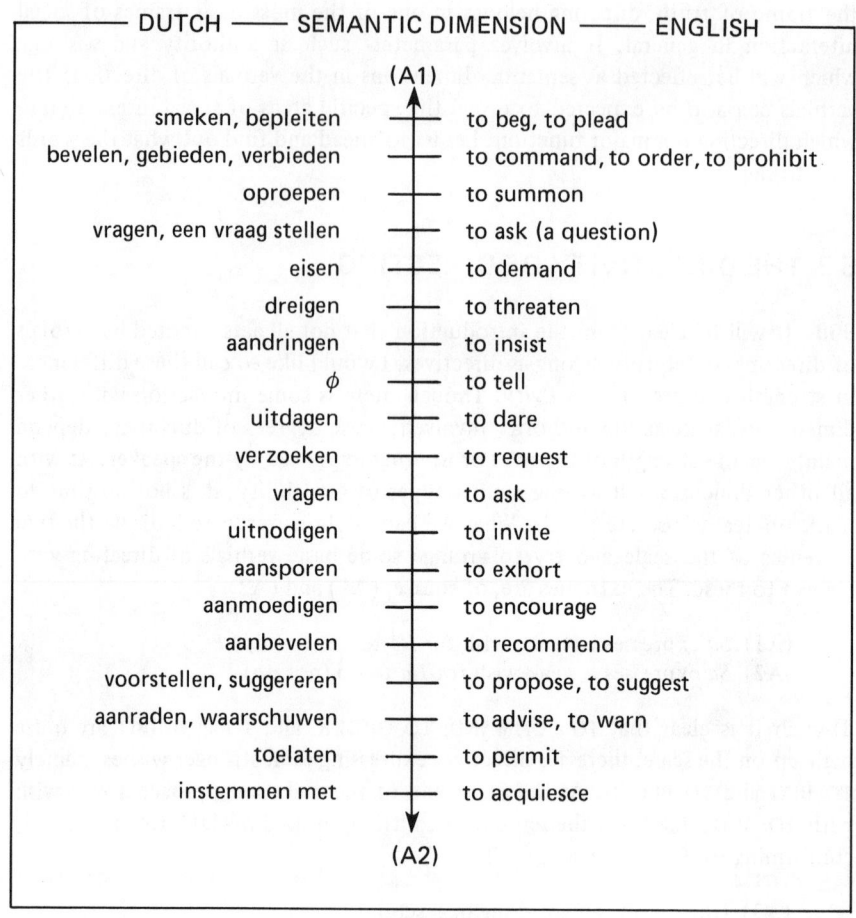

SDC Table 1

Needless to say, the elusive character inherent to matters of gradability is responsible for the tentativeness of the picture. There are no claims attached to the actual sequence of verbs on the scale; I do not even want to contend that the sequence is an accurate representation of my own judgment and intuition. All that counts is the approximate placement of the verbs on the scale.

In the following paragraphs I shall draw attention to some of the more striking aspects of the SDC Table.

302 What may strike the reader first is the position of TO ASK in the sense of TO ASK A QUESTION, Dutch VRAGEN or EEN VRAAG STELLEN. Asking a question is high up on the scale. But is its directivity so strong that it warrants its placement as high up as TO DEMAND and considerably higher up than TO INSIST and TO REQUEST? I believe that asking a question always involves a strong wish to get a reply. This is true even in the course of cocktail conversations, in which both the topic of conversation and the truth of the statements made are, to a large extent, irrelevant. Not answering a question is always a rupture in the social interaction between two interlocutors; usually it is taken as a lack of consideration or even as an insult. In this sense, asking a question is comparable to demanding. Both imply the speaker's belief that he/she has a right to what he/she wants the hearer to do (which is an unspecified kind of act in the case of TO DEMAND and a linguistic act in the case of TO ASK A QUESTION). TO INSIST is less strongly directive, and so is TO REQUEST: the wish implied is still strong, but not necessarily based on a right, and not strong enough to cause a disruption of the social interaction if the acts of insisting and requesting are not acted upon.

303 TO SUMMON and TO INVITE both describe acts of a speaker trying to get a hearer to go or come to some place. In spite of the near synonymy, they are quite far apart in SDC Table 1. The difference in the degree of directivity is probably the main difference between them: summoning is 'ordering to come', whereas inviting is 'asking to come'.

304 There are many ways of translating TO TELL, as used in (D2) describing (A4) conforming to (C4).

>(A4) If you wait a minute, I'll find you a table
>(C4) *Sa* and *Ha* are in a restaurant; *Sa* is the waiter, *Ha* is the customer
>(D2) The waiter told the customer to wait until he found a table for him/her

But there is no Dutch verbial available with exactly the same degree of directivity, which is somewhere between requesting or asking and ordering.

5.3 DIRECTING AND ITS SOCIAL SETTINGS

305 Directing has been said to be one of the basic functions in social interaction. It is not surprising, therefore, to find that the majority of verbials of directing contain strong clues to the social setting or settings in which the acts they describe occur. Such clues are absent from many of the basic verbs, such as TO COMMAND, TO ASK, TO TELL, TO INVITE, TO SUGGEST, TO ADVISE, etc.; after all, it is because of their not being specific or of their being 'neutral' with respect to a number of semantic dimensions that they can be said to be more 'basic' than the others. It is certainly not too bold to assume that the ensuing overview of the less neutral verbials of directing will single out some areas of social interaction in which directing other people's behavior is a prominent activity. The semantic dimension under investigation in this section deals with the different frames of action with which linguistic acts of directing are associated.

306 A large number of verbials situate the act described in a vaguely *'official'*

setting, without further specifications. In other words, (C1) applies to the act described.

(C1) The social setting is of an unspecified 'official' nature

Some examples are: TO ACCREDIT (in the sense of 'to authorize'), TO APPLY FOR, TO APPOINT, TO ASSIGN, TO AUTHORIZE, TO BLACKLIST, TO CERTIFY (in the sense of 'to license', which is a type of permission), TO CHARGE (in the sense of imposing a certain duty or task), TO COMMISSION, TO CONVENE (in the sense of causing to come together), TO CONVOKE, TO GIVE CARTE BLANCHE, TO GIVE FULL POWER, TO GIVE AN OPEN MANDATE, TO GIVE OFFICIAL SANCTION, TO LICENSE, TO MEMORIALIZE (in the sense of 'to petition'), TO PETITION, TO POST (in the sense of assigning to a specific position or station), TO PRESENT A PETITION, TO QUALIFY, TO SUSPEND, TO VOUCHSAFE (in the sense of granting as a privilege, allowing, permitting), TO WARRANT (in the sense of 'to authorize'); Dutch AANSTELLEN ('to appoint'), EEN AANVRAAG INDIENEN ('to make an application'), AANVRAGEN ('to apply for'), AANZEGGEN ('to announce as an official order'), AUTORISEREN ('to authorize'), BEKRACHTIGEN ('to give official sanction'), BELASTEN MET ('to charge'), BENOEMEN TOT ('to appoint'), BIJEENROEPEN ('to convene'), CARTE BLANCHE GEVEN ('to give carte blanche'), CONVOCEREN ('to convene, to convoke'), GELASTEN ('to order officially and solemnly'), MACHTIGEN ('to authorize'), ONTBIEDEN ('to invite officially and authoritatively'), OPDRAGEN ('to charge'), ORDONNEREN (equivalent to GELASTEN but rarely used), PETITIONEREN ('to petition'), SCHORSEN ('to suspend from membership or from duty'), SOLLICITEREN NAAR ('to apply for'), VEROORLOVEN ('to allow officially'), EEN VERZOEKSCHRIFT INDIENEN (lit. 'to hand in a written request' meaning 'to petition' or 'to memorialize'), VOLMACHT GEVEN ('to authorize'), EEN VOORSTEL INDIENEN (lit. 'to hand in a proposal').

The Dutch and the English lists presented are quite parallel. One of the finer differences, however, is the following: GELASTEN and ONTBIEDEN describe orders and invitations, respectively, of an unspecified official nature. No comparable English verbials seem to exist: all the English verbials of directing that describe official acts of ordering and inviting situate the act in a more specific official context; examples of these are adduced in the next few paragraphs.

307 Many verbials of directing situate the act described in a specific official setting. The most frequently specified official contexts are listed in (C2) through (C6).

(C2) The act is performed in a 'legal' setting
(C3) The act is performed in a 'religious' setting
(C4) The act is performed in a 'commercial' setting
(C5) The act is performed in a 'military' setting
(C6) The act is performed in a 'political' setting

We shall supply an overview of the verbials focusing on linguistic actions of a directive kind conforming to each of these five conditions. The reader is advised to keep in mind that classifying a verb or verblike expression as, for instance, a (C2) verbial does not mean that it can be applied *only* to a directive linguistic action performed in a legal context. It means only that the verbial in question is strongly associated with that context.

308 By far the largest group is the set of (C2) verbials that situate the acts described in a *legal* setting. The prominence of this frame of action in the domain of directing is not surprising. After all, regulating people's behavior is what the law is all about.

Here is a list of verbials focusing on legally directive linguistic acts: TO APPEAL, TO ASSERT/VINDICATE A CLAIM/RIGHT/TITLE TO, TO BAN, TO CITE (in the sense of calling upon to appear before a court), TO CLAIM, TO CROSS-EXAMINE, TO CROSSINTERROGATE, TO CROSS-QUESTION, TO DECREE, TO ENJOIN, TO EXAMINE (in the sense of interrogating closely), TO INTERDICT, TO ISSUE A WRIT/INJUNCTION, TO LAY CLAIM TO, TO LAY DOWN THE LAW, TO LEGALIZE, TO LEVY, TO MAKE MANDATORY, TO MAKE REQUISITION, TO MANDATE, TO NEGATIVE, TO OBTEST (in the sense of invoking as a witness), TO ORDAIN, TO OUTLAW, TO PROSCRIBE, TO PUT ONE'S VETO UPON, TO PUT UNDER AN INJUNCTION, TO PUT UNDER AN INTERDICT, TO PUT UNDER THE BAN, TO READ THE RIOT ACT (in the sense of ordering a mob to disperse), TO RECLAIM, TO REGULATE, TO REQUISITION, TO RULE, TO RULE AGAINST, TO SANCTION, TO STIPULATE, TO SUBPOENA, TO SUMMON, TO TRY (in the sense of interrogating an accused person), and TO VETO.

309 Some members of the foregoing list call for further comment. TO SUMMON can be used to illustrate my earlier observation that inclusion of a verbial in the list does not imply that it cannot be used to account for acts performed outside the legal frame of action. The verb refers to an official and authoritative invitation that can be issued either by a court or not. Thus, its uses in (D1) as a description of (A1) and in (D2) as a description of (A2) are both acceptable.

(A1) You are requested to appear in court as a witness in the Cutler murder trial
(D1) *Sa* summoned *Ha* (as a witness)
(A2) You are requested to appear before Mr. Allworthy at 9:00 A.M.
(D2) *Sa* summoned *Ha* to appear before Mr. Allworthy

But since summoning is strongly associated with the courtroom situation, one can hardly regard TO SUMMON as neutral with respect to the type of official setting in which the acts it can be used to describe are performed. In Dutch, DAGVAARDEN would be used in (D1) and ONTBIEDEN in (D2); hence, the former requires an act satisfying (C2), whereas the latter specifies only that (C1) obtains. Though ONTBIEDEN is quite neutral with respect to the type of official setting, it may be interesting to point out that, most probably because of the existence of DAGVAARDEN, ONTBIEDEN is hard to apply to acts of the (A1) type. In English there is, of course, also the verb TO SUBPOENA, which is completely restricted to acts of the (A1) type. The minute portion of the social-setting dimension of directing under consideration here is illustrated in SDC Table 2.

310 The reader may have wondered why TO CLAIM and TO REQUISITION have been included among the (C2) verbials. Consider (D3) and (D4).

(D3) He claimed his bags at the station
(D4) During the war the army requisitioned most hotels

The acts of demanding denoted by these two verbs are based on the speaker's belief that he/she has a right to what he/she asks. Such belief can only be based on laws, written or unwritten. That is how a legal setting comes in.

TO READ THE RIOT ACT in its original sense of ordering (a mob) to disperse is only obliquely related to a legal frame of action: the speaker must be a person invested with the authority to execute the law. Needless to say, its extended meaning of giving a strong warning, which is more prominent now, is not related to a legal setting.

Finally, the directive verbial that is most explicitly related to a legal context, TO LAY DOWN THE LAW, is more commonly used in its metaphorically extended sense of giving strict orders (as a teacher, a parent, etc.) than as a description of a directive act to which (C2) obtains.

311 The main (C2) verbials in Dutch are AANSPRAAK MAKEN OP ('to claim'), IN DE BAN DOEN ('to ban'), BUITEN DE WET STELLEN ('to outlaw'), DAGVAARDEN ('to subpoena'), DECRETEREN ('to decree'), EEN EIS INSTELLEN ('to demand'), HEFFEN ('to levy'), INVORDEREN ('to claim'), AAN EEN KRUISVERHOOR ONDERWERPEN ('to crossexamine'), LEGALISEREN ('to legalize'), MANDATEREN ('to mandate'), SANCTIONEREN ('to sanction'), SOMMEREN ('to admonish'), STIPULEREN ('to stipulate'), TERUGVORDEREN ('to reclaim'), TOEWIJZEN ('to assign'), VERBANNEN ('to ban'), VERHOREN ('to try'), VERORDENEN ('to ordain, to decree'), ZIJN VETO UITSPREKEN OVER ('to veto, to

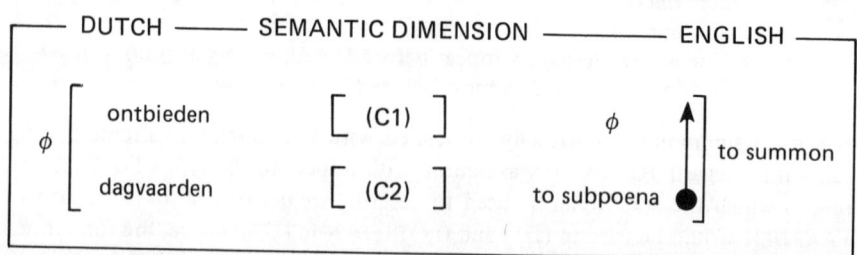

SDC Table 2

pronounce one's veto upon'), VORDEREN ('to claim'), and WETTIGEN ('to legalize').

312 When comparing the Dutch list with the English one, a number of conspicuous facts emerge. For instance, why are EEN EIS INSTELLEN, SOMMEREN, and TOEWIJZEN listed as (C2) verbials, whereas their translations, namely TO DEMAND, TO ADMONISH, and TO ASSIGN, are not considered to focus on a legal setting for the acts they describe? The answer is simply that they refer to acts of demanding, admonishing, and assigning in a legal context, for which no direct English equivalents can be given. The Dutch equivalent of TO DEMAND is EISEN, which differs from EEN EIS INSTELLEN (lit. 'to institute a demand') only in that the latter refers to an official judicial way of demanding.

SOMMEREN, as used in (D5) and (D6), is an act of admonishing to fulfill a certain duty or to comply with a request; the act is based on judicial authority on the part of the speaker or on a legal right.

(D5) De politie sommeerde de menigte uit elkaar te gaan
('The police admonished the mob to disperse')
(D6) De winkelier sommeerde zijn klanten tot betaling
('The shopkeeper admonished his customers to pay')

If the more common equivalent to TO ADMONISH, namely AANMANEN TOT, had been used, there would not have been direct legal implications.

TOEWIJZEN is used to refer to judicial acts of assigning, as appears from description (D7).

(D7) Na de scheiding wees het gerecht haar de kinderen toe
(lit. 'After the divorce, the court assigned the children to her')

This sentence means 'After the divorce, the court granted her the custody of the children'. TOEWIJZEN draws the attention to both the rights and the duties involved, whereas 'granting custody' emphasizes the rights.

313 Many verbials of directing focus on the legal setting of the act described. This would probably not be the case in languages spoken in societies that lack an elaborate legal system. However, there are no societies without laws. But in more 'primitive' societies, behavior is regulated by religious-ethical codes rather than by what we would call 'civil law'. Indeed, in many cases it may be impossible to separate these two types of regulating institutions. The traces of such a situation are still to be found in the English and the Dutch verbials of directing: a considerable number of them are ambiguous between an emphasis on the frame of civil law and the frame of ecclesiastical law. Nevertheless, civil law clearly dominates, which is no doubt in keeping with regular observations of the directing forces in our Western societies. My hunch is that, depending on the nature of the society, in the directive verbial section of the lexicon of every language a prominent place is occupied by verbials situating linguistic acts of directing in a legal or religious setting. This is a hypothesis to be tested by further crosscultural and crosslinguistic research on linguistic action verbials.

314 These observations lead us to the verbials of directing implying a religious context; in other words, (C3) obtains.

(C3) The act is performed in a religious setting

Among those that are clearly ambiguous between (C2) and (C3) we find TO ENJOIN (which is especially strongly associated with the legal and ecclesiastical context in its prohibition sense), TO INTERDICT (which describes ecclesiastical or judicial prohibitions), TO ISSUE AN INJUNCTION (which refers to an ecclesiastical or judicial order or prohibition), and TO ORDAIN (which denotes an order or appointment based on a court decision or on the authority of the church). For all of these except TO INTERDICT (Dutch EEN INTERDICT UITSPREKEN OVER, lit. 'to pronounce an interdict on'), it is hard to find Dutch equivalents carrying the same implications with respect to the social setting.

Notice that we have listed only clearly ambiguous cases in this paragraph. There are, in addition, many (C2) verbials the use of which can be extended without difficulties to (C3) contexts.

315 Some verbials focusing on (C3) contexts are TO CATECHIZE (i.e. giving systematic religious instruction by means of asking questions, receiving answers, and offering explanations or corrections), TO CENSURE (the meaning of which can easily be extended to nonreligious and nonethical settings), TO EXCOMMUNICATE (i.e. to shut off by an ecclesiastical sentence from communion with the church), TO PRECONIZE (i.e. to approve a high ecclesiastical appointment publically by papal proclamation in consistory), TO PUT ON THE INDEX, and TO TABOO; Dutch CATECHISEREN ('to catechize'), CENSUREREN ('to censure'), EXCOMMUNICEREN ('to excommunicate'), PRECONISEREN ('to preconize'), OP DE INDEX PLAATSEN ('to put on the index'), and TABOE VERKLAREN ('to taboo', lit. 'to declare taboo'). Here the parallelism between Dutch and English is complete.

Apart from TO ORDAIN, TO CATECHIZE, and TO PRECONIZE, all the verbials listed in this and the previous paragraph refer to acts that are or can be prohibitive in nature. The predominance of *negative directives* is certainly not unrelated to the prohibitive nature of christian ethics. After all, eight of the Ten Commandments are prohibitions.

316 The (C3) verbials discussed so far describe acts of directing the behavior of people. Within a religious or semireligious frame of action, people also try (or used to try) to direct the behavior of supernatural beings, i.e. gods, devils, or spirits. Thus, acts of directing situated in a religious context can conform either to (C3a) or (C3b).

(C3a) *Ha* is/are (a) human being(s)
(C3b) *Ha* is/are (a) supernatural being(s)

Whereas (C3)-(C3a) defines a religious or religious-ethical context, (C3)-(C3b) points at a religious-magical setting. Some (C3)-(C3b) verbs are TO CONJURE (in the sense of summoning a supernatural being to appear or to disappear; Dutch BEZWEREN), TO CONJURE UP, TO EXORCISE (Dutch UITDRIJVEN). Also, TO INVOKE (Dutch OPROEPEN) is often used in a (C3)-(C3b) sense but can hardly be said to imply a religious-magical setting as part of its central meaning.

317 Next in line is the world of *commerce*. (C4) verbials describe attempts to get money, goods, or services; to get someone to use or buy something; or to make someone accept a particular price or condition for a commercial transaction.

(C4) The act is performed in a 'commercial' setting

Some relevant verbials are TO ADVERTISE, TO BARGAIN, TO BOOK, TO CANVASS (in the sense of seeking orders, contributions, or subscriptions), TO CHARGE (in the sense of asking as a fee or payment), TO COMMISSION (as used in (D8)), TO HAGGLE, TO HIGGLE, TO INDENT, TO MAKE RESERVATIONS, TO ORDER (as used in (D9)), TO PROMOTE, TO PUBLICIZE, TO PUT IN AN ORDER FOR, TO RESERVE.

(D8) Most of his prominent contemporaries commissioned Rubens to paint their portraits
(D9) He ordered a cheeseburger and a coke

The Dutch set of (C4) verbials is quite analogous: ADVERTEREN ('to advertise'), AFDINGEN ('to bargain'), AFPINGELEN ('to haggle'), BESTELLEN ('to order'), BESPREKEN ('to book, reserve'; the original sense of this verb, in which it is still used, is 'to talk about'; another one of its derived but prominent meanings is 'to review'), RECLAME MAKEN VOOR ('to advertise'), RESERVEREN ('to reserve'), WERVEN ('to canvass'). A (C4) verb without a parallel in English is AANPRATEN, which means 'to talk into buying or using'.

318 When asked to sketch a prototypical directing or commanding situation, informants can be expected to call attention to a *military* frame of action. Yet there are almost no (C5) verbials of directing.

(C5) The act is performed in a 'military' setting

Indeed, the Dutch verb COMMANDEREN, which must originally have been associated with military commands, has come to be used almost exclusively in a semi-ironical sense to describe directing behavior based on assumed—as opposed to real—authority; in many cases it can be translated by 'to order about'.
There seem to be only a couple of verbs focusing on (C5) contexts, but even the use of these few can easily be extended outside the military world: TO CONSCRIPT (i.e. to enroll into service by compulsion) and TO DRAFT; in Dutch INLIJVEN ('to conscript, draft'). TO CALL UP (Dutch OPROEPEN) is

frequently used in the same sense, but it is less strongly associated with the military.

Curiously enough, these typically military commands are directed at nonsoldiers. The (C5) situation could be subdivided into (C5)-(C5a) and (C5)-(C5b).

(C5a) *Ha* is not a soldier
(C5b) *Ha* is a soldier

I have not been able to discover verbials in Dutch describing military commands directed at soldiers. As far as English is concerned, I am aware of the existence of only one, namely TO ORDER UP (which also has the nonmilitary meaning of ordering someone to go or come upstairs). Its military sense is illustrated in (D10).

(D10) The general ordered two battalions up to strengthen a weak point in the line

It means 'to order from a position in the rear to the front line'.

Is there any explanation for the discrepancy between the conceptualization of the military world as a prototypical directing situation and the lack of verbials of directing focusing on the military setting? The solution is probably to be found in the very fact that the situation *is* so prototypical: if a military command is a command *par excellence*. there is no need to call it differently.

319 Some verbials focus on *political* acts of directing, i.e. (C6) obtains.

(C6) The act is performed in a 'political' setting

It is not surprising that the (C4) and (C6) sets share a member, namely TO CANVASS (Dutch WERVEN), which means in the (C6) setting 'to solicit votes or seek political support in an election campaign'.

A typical (C6) verb is TO INTERPELLATE (Dutch INTERPELLEREN), meaning 'to question formally about a governmental policy or decision'. A couple of other verbials of directing situate the act described in even more precise social contexts, namely those specified in (C6a) and (C6b), the specificity of which increases progressively.

(C6a) The act is performed in a 'diplomatic' setting
(C6b) The act is performed in a frame of 'international political-economical diplomacy'

A (C6)-(C6a) verb is TO ACCREDIT in the sense of appointing as ambassador; there is no Dutch counterpart. The (C6)-(C6b) verbials I am thinking of are TO EMBARGO and TO LAY AN EMBARGO ON (Dutch EEN EMBARGO LEGGEN OP), in the sense of a governmental prohibition for the departure or entry of foreign ships or for importing or exporting.

320 We are still left with a clutter of verbials of directing specifying different social contexts. Another more or less official setting is mentioned in (C7).

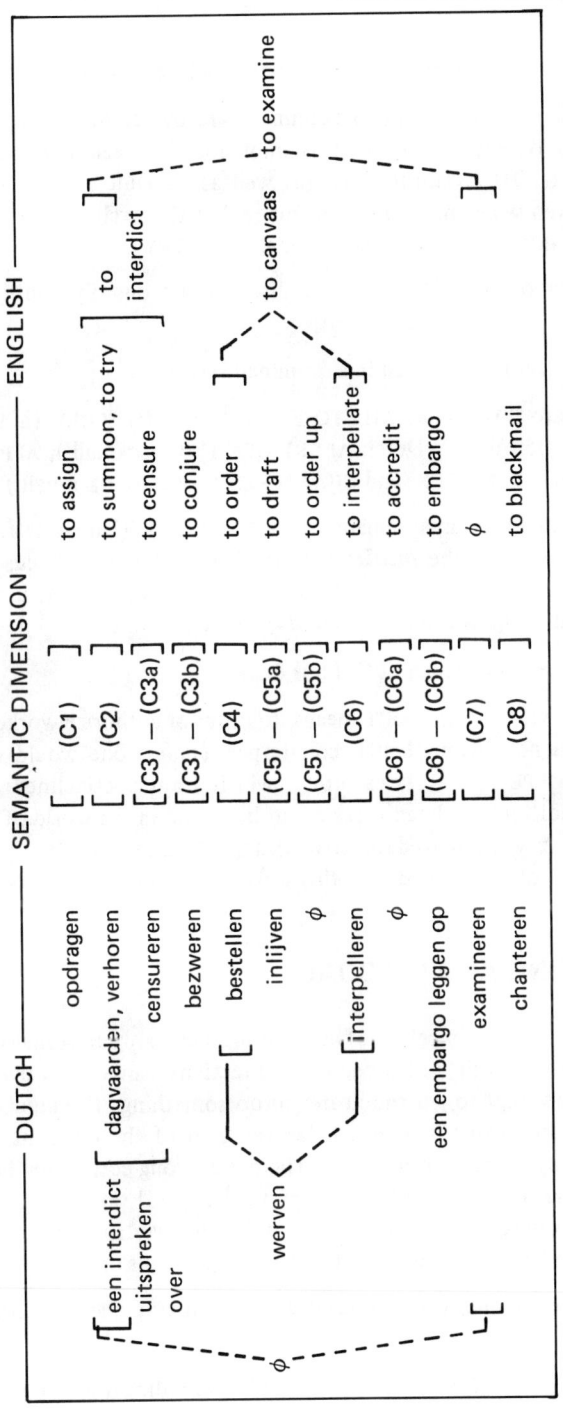

SDC Table 3

164   THE SEMANTICS OF DIRECTING

(C7) The act is performed in an 'educational' setting

The Dutch verb EXAMINEREN ('to examine') is restricted to acts satisfying (C7). The English equivalent TO EXAMINE is ambiguous between a legal and an educational context. TO INTERROGATE (as well as its Dutch equivalent ONDERVRAGEN) is even wider in usage. Remember that the exclusively legal counterpart to EXAMINEREN was VERHOREN (English TO TRY).

321   A number of verbials situate the directive act described in the world of crime.

(C8) The act is performed in a 'criminal' setting

The examples are TO BLACKMAIL, TO EXTORT, and TO SCREW (in the sense of practising extortion upon); Dutch AFDREIGEN ('to blackmail'), AFPERSEN ('to extort'), CHANTAGE PLEGEN, and CHANTEREN (both 'to blackmail').

322   A few isolated cases remain: TO INTERVIEW (Dutch INTERVIEWEN) points at the world of the *media*; a *medical* setting is often focused upon by TO PRESCRIBE (Dutch VOORSCHRIJVEN); and TO CALL OUT as used in (D11) is to be situated in the world of *industrial relations*.

(D11)   The union called out all bus drivers

In such a context, TO CALL OUT means 'to order or authorize workers to go on strike'; there is no obvious Dutch counterpart (unless one would regard TOT STAKING OPROEPEN as a lexical unity, which I am not inclined to do). No doubt some additional isolated cases could be found in the world of sports (e.g. TO CALL has a very specialized directive meaning in card games).
The results of the discussion in this section are summarized in SDC Table 3.

5.4   DIRECTING AND ITS GOALS

323   Directing can be conceived of as orienting somebody to some course of action. Only in cases with a high degree of directivity can such activity be paraphrased as an attempt to get the hearer to do something. The course of action toward which the hearer is oriented, i.e. the goal of the directing activity, is specified in many verbials of directing. There is a strong correlation between the verbials situating the act described in a particular social setting and those specifying its goal. Consequently, there is a significant overlap between the sets of verbials discussed in this section and those in the previous one.

324   The most commonly emphasized goals of directing are specified in (A1) through (A3).

(A1) *Sa* directs *Ha* toward an act of responding (i.e. of performing a linguistic act

(A2) *Sa* directs *Ha* toward an act of coming or going somewhere
(A3) *Sa* directs *Ha* toward an act of giving or granting (*Sa*) something

The set of (A1) verbials includes TO ANGLE FOR, TO ASK (ABOUT), TO ASK A QUESTION, TO CATECHIZE, TO CROSSEXAMINE, TO CROSSINTERROGATE, TO CROSS-QUESTION, TO ELICIT, TO EXTRACT INFORMATION, TO EXAMINE, TO FISH FOR, TO GRILL, TO INQUIRE, TO INQUISITION, TO INTERPELLATE, TO INTERROGATE, TO INTERVIEW, TO MAKE INQUIRY, TO MAKE INQUISITION, TO PICK THE BRAINS OF, TO POSE A QUESTION, TO PRY/PRIZE OUT, TO PUMP, TO PUMP FOR INFORMATION, TO PUT A QUESTION TO, TO PUT ON THE GRILL, TO PUT QUERIES, TO QUERY, TO QUESTION, TO QUESTIONNAIRE, TO QUIZ, TO ROAST, TO SHOOT QUESTIONS AT, TO TAKE UP/CARRY ON AN INQUIRY, TO TRY, TO WORM OUT OF; Dutch EXAMINEREN ('to examine', in the educational setting), INFORMEREN ('to ask for information'), INTERPELLEREN ('to interpellate'), INTERVIEWEN ('to interview'), AAN EEN KRUISVERHOOR ONDERWERPEN (lit. 'to subject to a crossexamination'), ONDERVRAGEN ('to interrogate'), ONTLOKKEN ('to elicit'), ONTWRINGEN (lit. 'to wrench out of'), OP DE ROOSTER LEGGEN ('to put on the grill'), UITHOREN (lit. 'to hear out', i.e. 'to pump'), UITVRAGEN (lit. 'to ask out', i.e. to interrogate), VERHOREN ('to examine', in the legal setting), VISSEN NAAR ('to fish for'), EEN VRAAG STELLEN ('to ask a question'), VRAGEN ('to ask'), VRAGEN AFVUREN OP ('to shoot questions at').

This whole chapter deals with linguistic acts of directing. The foregoing list of (A1) verbials represents a subclass of such acts aimed at the production of other linguistic acts. They differ from most of the others in that their propositional content does not specify or even hint at the actions to be carried out by the hearer. Such specification is not necessary because of the interrogative mood and other markers that signal the type of directive behavior under investigation. If this type of directive behavior is important enough to justify the emergence of a special grammatical mood, it should not surprise us that (A1) verbials occupy an important place among the verbials of directing. Moreover, ethnomethodologists have shown us clearly enough that eliciting responses is the most salient type of control the speaker usually tries to exert over the course of linguistic interaction.

325 The (A2) verbials, describing acts of trying to get the hearer to come or go somewhere, include TO BAN, TO BEG LEAVE, TO BID (in the sense of inviting), TO BID COME, TO CALL, TO CALL AWAY, TO CALL BACK, TO CALL IN, TO CALL OUT, TO CALL TOGETHER, TO CALL UP, TO CITE (in the sense of summoning), TO CONJURE, TO CONJURE UP, TO CONVENE, TO CONVOKE, TO DEMAND (in the sense of asking to see, as in 'The crowd demanded the star', or summoning to court), TO DRAFT, TO EVOKE, TO EXORCISE, TO EXTEND AN INVITATION, TO GIVE LEAVE, TO INVITE, TO INVOKE, TO MUSTER (as in 'They did not muster much of a crowd'), TO OBTEST (in the sense of invoking as a witness), TO ORDER UP, TO RECALL, TO REQUEST THE PLEASURE OF SOMEONE'S COMPANY,

TO REQUEST THE PRESENCE OF, TO SEND AFTER, TO SEND FOR, TO SUBPOENA, TO SUMMON, TO WARN OFF; Dutch BEZWEREN ('to exorcize'), BIJEENROEPEN ('to call together'), BINNENROEPEN ('to call in'), CONVOCEREN ('to convoke'), DAGVAARDEN ('to summon'), INROEPEN ('to call in'), INVITEREN ('to invite'), LATEN HALEN ('to send for'), MEELOKKEN ('to entice someone to come along'), MEETRONEN ('to entice someone to come along'), ONTBIEDEN ('to invite'), OPROEPEN ('to draft' or 'to call up'), TERUGROEPEN ('to call back'), TE VOORSCHIJN ROEPEN (lit. 'to call/order to appear'), TRONEN ('to entice someone to go or come somewhere'), UITDRIJVEN ('to exorcize'), UITNODIGEN ('to invite'), VERBANNEN ('to ban'), VERZOEKEN ('to invite'), WEGTRONEN ('to entice to go away').

The prominence of the (A2) verbials among the verbials of directing may be surprising. What makes coming and going into such an important activity that it is the focus of so many verbials of directing? The fact itself is interesting to observe, even though the answer to the question may be relatively simple. Not only is movement a basic category of voluntary action (voluntary action being the only reasonable object for acts of directing), it is such a salient cognitive category in general that for some languages such as Navajo (according to Witherspoon 1977) the principal verb is 'to go' rather than 'to be' (which is commonly regarded as the principal verb of so many other languages).

326   The third prominent area in the goal dimension of the verbials of directing is the set of (A3) verbials describing acts of trying to get the hearer to give or grant (the speaker) something. The set includes TO APPEAL TO ONE FOR, TO APPLY FOR, TO ASK FOR, TO BEG, TO BLACKMAIL, TO CLAIM, TO DEMAND, TO EXACT, TO EXTORT, TO LAY CLAIM TO, TO MAKE DEMANDS/A DEMAND, TO MAKE REQUISITION, TO PRAY FOR, TO PUT IN A CLAIM, TO PUT THE BITE ON (which means 'to ask for money, favors, etc.' as in 'John put the bite on his friend for several tickets to the dance'), TO REQUEST, TO REQUIRE, TO REQUISITION, TO SCREW, TO SOLICIT, TO STIPULATE FOR, TO SUE FOR, TO SUPPLICATE, TO WHEEDLE SOMETHING OUT OF A PERSON; Dutch AANSPRAAK MAKEN OP ('to lay claim to'), EEN AANVRAAG INDIENEN (lit. 'to submit an application'), AANVRAGEN ('to apply for'), AFBEDELEN (lit. 'to beg off'), AFDREIGEN ('to extort by means of threatening'), AFDWINGEN ('to extort'), AFPERSEN ('to extort'), AFSMEKEN (lit. 'to beg off'), AFTROGGELEN ('to wheedle something out of a person'), BEDELEN ('to beg'), BEDINGEN ('to stipulate for'), BIDDEN OM ('to pray for'), CHANTAGE PLEGEN (lit. 'to commit blackmail'), CHANTEREN ('to blackmail'), EISEN ('to demand'), EEN EIS INSTELLEN ('to put in a claim'), OPEISEN ('to claim, demand'), OPVRAGEN ('to claim'), RECLAMEREN 'to claim'), SCHOOIEN ('to beg', but a derogative term), SOLLICITEREN NAAR ('to apply for'), TERUGEISEN (lit. 'to demand the return of'), TERUGVORDEREN ('to demand the return of'), VORDEREN ('to demand'), VRAGEN OM ('to ask for').

What the (A3) verbials describe is probably central in the area of directing other people's behavior. This cannot be concluded from a comparison of the three sets of goal-specific verbials listed so far. However, a close look at the remaining goal-specific verbials of directing reveals that about half of them refer to acts of the (A3) type with an even further specified goal. They are presented in the next paragraph.

327 (A3a) through (A3g) can all be paraphrased as attempts to get *Ha* to undertake an action from which *Sa* will profit in some tangible way, i.e. to engage in an activity of 'giving' or 'granting' in a broad sense.

(A3a) *Sa* directs *Ha* toward buying *Sa*'s products
(A3b) *Sa* directs *Ha* toward paying something
(A3c) *Sa* directs *Ha* toward making or keeping something for *Sa*
(A3d) *Sa* directs *Ha* toward voting for *Sa*
(A3e) *Sa* directs *Ha* toward mailing something to *Sa*
(A3f) *Sa* directs *Ha* toward marrying *Sa*
(A3g) *Sa* directs *Ha* toward having sexual intercourse with *Sa*

The principal (A3a) verbials are TO ADVERTISE, TO CANVASS, TO PROMOTE, TO PUBLICIZE, and TO RECOMMEND; Dutch AANBEVELEN ('to recommend'), AANPRATEN (lit. 'to talk a person into buying something'), AANPRIJZEN ('to recommend'), ADVERTEREN ('to advertise'), RECLAME MAKEN VOOR ('to advertise'), WERVEN ('to canvass').

(A3b) verbials are TO CHARGE, TO DUN, and TO LEVY; Dutch HEFFEN ('to levy') and AANREKENEN ('to charge'). There seems to be no obvious Dutch equivalent for TO DUN in the sense of making persistent demands for money, as used in 'The grocer dunned the customer monthly by mail for payment of his bill' or in 'dunning for contributions'.

The (A3c) verbials include TO BESPEAK, TO BOOK, TO COMMISSION, TO INDENT (in the chiefly British sense of 'to order by an indent, i.e. an official requisition, as for supplies'), TO MAKE RESERVATIONS, TO ORDER, TO RESERVE, TO PUT IN AN ORDER FOR; Dutch BESPREKEN ('to book, reserve'), BESTELLEN ('to order'), RESERVEREN ('to reserve'). The actual 'giving' toward which *Sa*'s utterance is directed is of course delayed in acts of the (A3c) type.

Attempts to get someone's vote can be described by means of the (A3d) verb TO CANVASS, Dutch WERVEN. Note that the same word applies to seeking political support and trying to attract buyers.

Whereas (A3c) verbials refer to acts of 'giving' that are delayed, the 'giving' indicated by (A3e) verbials is indirect, namely through the mail. The relevant lexical items are TO SEND FOR and TO ORDER, Dutch AANVRAGEN and BESTELLEN.

In the remaining two sets, the object of the 'giving' is quite specific. In the case of (A3g) verbials such as TO IMPORTUNE (in the sense of making advances towards), TO SEDUCE, and TO SOLICIT, Dutch EEN AANZOEK DOEN ('to solicit') and VERLEIDEN ('to seduce'), *Sa* is after *Ha*'s body. In the case of (A3f) verbials such as TO POP THE QUESTION and TO PROPOSE, Dutch EEN AANZOEK DOEN and IEMANDS HAND VRAGEN (lit. 'to ask someone's hand') *Ha*'s whole life is at stake.

328 The remaining sets of goal-specific verbials of directing are all relatively small. The acts they describe are listed in (A4) through (A16).

(A4)   *Sa* directs *Ha* toward not buying, using, etc., something
(A5)   *Sa* directs *Ha* toward taking on a certain duty
(A6)   *Sa* directs *Ha* toward going on strike
(A7)   *Sa* directs *Ha* toward making war
(A8)   *Sa* directs *Ha* toward writing something down
(A9)   *Sa* directs *Ha* toward keeping something where it is
(A10) *Sa* directs *Ha* (a mob) toward dispersing
(A11) *Sa* directs *Ha* toward attacking somebody
(A12) *Sa* directs *Ha* toward accepting a lower price than he/she wanted originally
(A13) *Sa* directs *Ha* toward changing his/her party or opinions
(A14) *Sa* directs *Ha* toward hurrying up
(A15) *Sa* directs *Ha* toward stopping his/her (professional) activities temporarily
(A16) *Sa* directs *Ha* toward a rebellion of some kind

We can briefly list the most important lexical representatives.

329 (A4) verbials include TO BAN, TO BAR, TO BLACKLIST, TO CENSURE, TO OUTLAW, TO PROSCRIBE, TO PUT ON THE INDEX, TO TABOO; Dutch BUITEN DE WET STELLEN ('to outlaw', lit. 'to place outside the law'), CENSUREREN ('to censure'), OP DE INDEX ZETTEN ('to put on the index'), TABOE VERKLAREN (lit. 'to declare taboo'). Notice that in acts of the (A4) type, *Ha* is never an individual, but a large group of people; the objects the verbials take refer to what the group of people in question is not supposed to buy, use, etc.

The (A5) verbials include TO ACCREDIT (in the sense of 'to order to proceed on an official mission'), TO APPOINT, TO ASSIGN, TO CHARGE, TO COMMISSION, TO MANDATE, TO ORDAIN, TO POST, TO PRECONIZE, TO SET, and TO STATION; Dutch AANSTELLEN ('to appoint'), BELASTEN MET ('to charge'), BENOEMEN TOT ('to appoint'), MANDATEREN ('to mandate'), OPDRAGEN ('to charge'), OPLEGGEN ('to charge'), TOEWIJZEN ('to assign').

I know of only one (A6) verb, namely TO CALL OUT, as in 'Bus drivers may be called out in support of their recent wage claim'. The Dutch equivalent, TOT STAKING OPROEPEN, cannot be regarded as a lexical item.

Another one without an obvious Dutch counterpart is the (A7) verb TO DEFY in its quite specific meaning of 'to challenge to combat'.

The main (A8) verb is TO DICTATE, Dutch DICTEREN, in the sense of 'to speak or read for a person to write down or transcribe'.

THE SEMANTICS OF DIRECTING   169

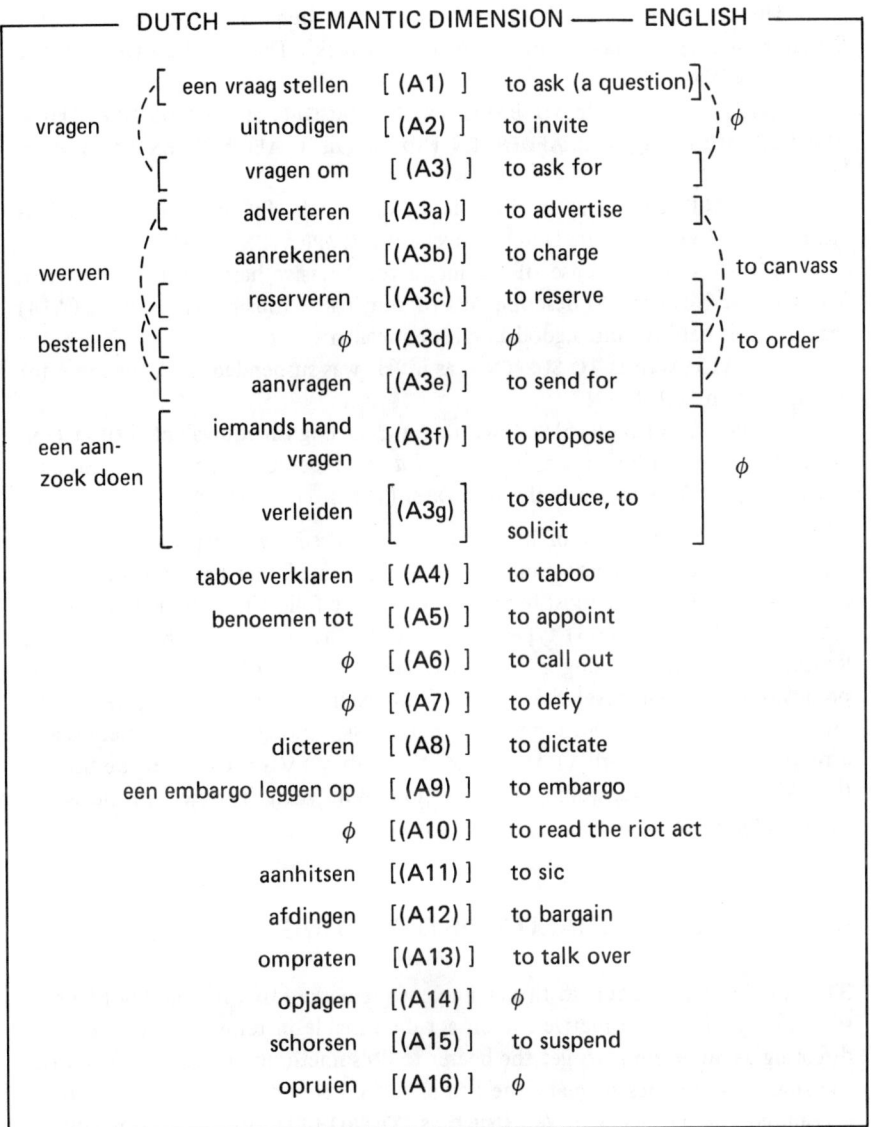

SDC Table 4

TO EMBARGO and TO PUT AN EMBARGO ON, Dutch EEN EMBARGO LEGGEN OP, are (A9) verbials.

TO READ THE RIOT ACT in the sense of ordering *Ha* (which cannot be an individual but which is generally a mob) to disperse is an (A10) verbial. Apparently, a Dutch counterpart is lacking.

170 THE SEMANTICS OF DIRECTING

The set of (A11) verbs is again a one-member class. The verb TO SIC, Dutch AANHITSEN, means 'to incite to an attack'. The *Ha* of an (A11) act is typically *Sa*'s dog.

(A12) verbs include TO BARGAIN, TO HAGGLE, and TO HIGGLE; Dutch AFBIEDEN ('to bargain'), AFDINGEN ('to bargain'), AFPINGELEN ('to haggle, higgle').

TO TALK OVER, as in 'Fred is trying to talk Bill over to our side', is clearly an (A13) verbial; its Dutch equivalent is OMPRATEN.

OPJAGEN in the sense of 'to incite to excessive haste' is an (A14) verb. The same verb is used to describe acts of starting or rousing game. In its (A14) meaning it is hard to find a good English equivalent.

An (A15) verb is TO SUSPEND, as in 'He was suspended from the army for a year', Dutch SCHORSEN.

Finally, a Dutch (A16) verb without a clear English equivalent is OPRUIEN, which always describes an act of inciting *Ha* to a rebellion of some kind. Similar, at least in one of its senses, is the verb OPZETTEN.

330 The goal dimension of linguistic acts of directing is represented in SDC Table 4. In the table some comparisons are indicated that have not been mentioned so far. By far the most important one is the following. Though in English, acts of the (A1) and (A3) types are joined by the common verb TO ASK, the lexical link is not as strong as in Dutch. TO ASK in its (A3) sense requires the preposition FOR whenever the object of the asking is indicated; as a result, the (A3) verbial is TO ASK FOR rather than TO ASK. Though in Dutch there is also a prepositional (A3) verb VRAGEN OM, the verb VRAGEN can itself be used in the (A3) sense without adding a preposition, even when the object of the asking needs to be made explicit.

5.5 THE DIRECTIONALITY OF DIRECTING

331 In the introduction to this chapter, we remarked that it would not be possible to regard every directive speech act describable in terms of the verbials of directing as an attempt to get the hearer to do something. Indeed, in some cases the speaker even tries to make the hearer *not* do something. Such cases can be accounted for by means of verbs such as TO PROHIBIT. In this section, speech acts directing the hearer toward *not* doing something will be said to display a *negative directionality*, as opposed to the *positive directionality* of attempts to make the hearer *do* something. Thus, directive speech acts can be divided into two types, (A1) and (A2).

(A1) *Sa* tries to get *Ha* to do something
(A2) *Sa* tries to get *Ha* not to do something

At first sight, one could expect the verbials of directing to fall into two corresponding categories, with TO COMMAND in the (A1) category and TO PROHIBIT in the (A2) category. But an attempt to place all our verbials in one of the categories soon turned out to be in vain. The lexicon is patterned in a much more intricate way, which I am about to sketch.

332 With respect to the directionality dimension, all verbials of directing can be placed on a nine-point scale. At the two extremes are the *exclusively positive* and *exclusively negative* ones. Next are those that are *intrinsically positive* and those that are *intrinsically negative*. I regard a verbial of directing as intrinsically positive if it shows positive directionality whenever combined with a complement with a positive propositional content and negative directionality whenever the propositional content of the description in which it is used is negative. Conversely, a verbial of directing is intrinsically negative if it signals negative directionality when combined with a positive propositional content and positive directionality when the propositional content of the description in which it is used is negative. As a result, the first set nearly always indicates a positive directive, whereas the second set nearly always describes a negative one. Examples will be given soon.

Further toward the center of the scale, we should find verbials tending towards the positive side and some tending towards the negative side. The remaining sets can be expected to be (a) those that can be either positive or negative, with equal probability; (b) those that can be positive and negative simultaneously; (c) those that are neither negative nor positive.

The nine-point scale of the dimension under discussion should be formulated directly in terms of semantic patterns displayed by the verbials (since an *act* of directing can itself only be positive or negative):

(SP1) The verbial describes (A1) exclusively
(SP2) The verbial describes nearly always (A1)
(SP3) The verbial describes usually (A1)
(SP4) The verbial describes either (A1) or (A2)
(SP5) The verbial describes (A1) and (A2) simultaneously
(SP6) The verbial describes neither (A1) nor (A2)
(SP7) The verbial describes usually (A2)
(SP8) The verbial describes nearly always (A2)
(SP9) The verbial describes (A2) exclusively

The relevant verbials can now be listed systematically. But before doing so, some preliminary remarks will be made.

333 An intuitively plausible expectation would be to find TO COMMAND at the positive extreme of the scale and TO PROHIBIT at the negative one. However, these verbials are not exclusively positive and negative, respectively. Consider (D1) through (D4).

(D1) He commanded the soldier to scrub the floor
(D2) He commanded the soldier not to leave the building

(D3) He prohibited the soldier to leave the building
(D4) He prohibited the soldier not to scrub the floor

Of these descriptions, (D2) and (D4) are less likely to occur than the others; indeed, (D4) will probably only be found in a logic handbook. But the point is that both are possible: (D2), with TO COMMAND, describes a negative directive and (D4), with TO PROHIBIT, a positive one. Thus TO COMMAND and TO PROHIBIT fit our definition (in the previous paragraph) of *intrinsically positive* and *intrinsically negative* verbs of directing.

334 At this point one question crops up immediately: if TO COMMAND and TO PROHIBIT are not exclusively positive and negative, respectively, are there any (SP1) and (SP9) verbials at all? In fact, there are as many exclusively positive and negative verbials of directing as there are intrinsically positive and negative ones. But the acts describable in terms of the exclusively positive and negative ones have rarely been regarded as central cases of linguistic directing. An exclusively positive verb is, for instance, TO INVITE in its original sense of requesting *Ha*'s presence or participation. Someone's being present or his/her participating is always a positive act. In its derivative sense of requesting formally or politely, TO INVITE is of course a (SP2) verb. Another (SP1) verb is TO ORDER, as in 'He ordered a meal'; in its other, noncommercial senses, TO ORDER also belongs to the (SP2) set. A (SP9) verb would be TO BAN in the sense of prohibiting (by legal means or social pressure) the performance of some activities or the dissemination or use of something: an act of banning in this meaning can only be directed at a nonaction.

335 By far the most numerous sets are the (SP1) and (SP2) verbials. This means that the lexicon reflects a definite tendency toward focusing on the positive aspect of directive behavior. The main English (SP1) verbials are TO ADVERTISE, TO ANGLE FOR, TO APPLY FOR, TO APPOINT, TO APPROVE, TO ASK (A QUESTION), TO ASK FOR, TO ASSIGN, TO BESPEAK, TO BID (COME), TO BLACKMAIL, TO CALL (in the sense of commanding or requesting to come), TO CALL AWAY, TO CALL BACK, TO CALL FOR, TO CALL FORTH, TO CALL IN, TO CALL ON, TO CALL OUT, TO CALL TOGETHER, TO CALL UP, TO CANVASS, TO CATECHIZE, TO CERTIFY (in the sense of licensing to do something, as in 'to certify a teacher'), TO CHARGE, TO CITE (in the sense of calling upon officially or authoritatively to appear before a court), TO CLAIM, TO CLAMOR FOR, TO COMMISSION, TO CONJURE (UP), TO CONVENE, TO CONVOKE, TO CROSSEXAMINE, TO CROSS-INTERROGATE, TO CROSS-QUESTION, TO DEMAND (in the sense of claiming), TO DICTATE (in the sense of speaking or reading for someone to write down), TO DRAFT, TO ELICIT, TO EXTRACT INFORMATION, TO EVOKE, TO EXACT, TO EXAMINE, TO EXTEND AN INVITATION, TO EXTORT, TO FISH FOR, TO FOMENT (in the sense of inciting, as in 'to foment riots, revolutions'), TO GIVE A FREE HAND, TO GIVE THE GO-AHEAD, TO GIVE THE GREEN LIGHT, TO GRILL, TO IMPORTUNE in the sense of making advances towards), TO IMPOSE, TO IMPOSE ON

ONE FOR, TO INQUIRE (AFTER), TO INQUISITION, TO INTERPELLATE, TO INTERROGATE, TO INTERVIEW, TO INVITE (in the sense of asking to come over), TO INVOKE, TO LAY CLAIM TO, TO LEVY, TO MAKE INQUIRY, TO MAKE INQUISITION, TO MAKE REQUISITION, TO MAKE RESERVATIONS, TO MANDATE, TO MUSTER, TO OBTEST (in the sense of invoking as a witness), TO ORDER (as in 'to order a meal'), TO ORDER UP, TO PICK THE BRAINS OF, TO POP THE QUESTION, TO POSE A QUESTION, TO POST, TO PRECONIZE, TO PROMOTE, TO PROPOSE (in the sense of asking to marry), TO PRY OUT, TO PUBLICIZE, TO PUMP (FOR INFORMATION), TO PUT A QUESTION TO, TO PUT IN AN ORDER FOR, TO PUT ON THE GRILL, TO PUT QUERIES, TO QUERY, TO QUESTION, TO QUESTIONNAIRE, TO QUIZ, TO READ THE RIOT ACT (in the sense of ordering to disperse), TO RECALL, TO REQUEST THE PLEASURE OF SOMEONE'S COMPANY, TO REQUEST THE PRESENCE OF, TO REQUISITION, TO ROAST, TO SCREW, TO SEDUCE (in the sense of enticing into partnership in sexual intercourse), TO SEND AFTER, TO SEND FOR, TO SET (in the sense of appointing or assigning to an office or duty, as in 'to set pickets around the camp'), TO SHOOT QUESTIONS AT, TO SIC, TO SOLICIT (in the sense of offering sexual intercourse), TO STATION, TO SUBMIT, TO SUBPOENA, TO SUMMON, TO TAKE UP AN INQUIRY, and TO WORM OUT OF.

Notice that the (SP1) verbials include all those describing acts directed at *Ha*'s responding verbally, such as TO ASK A QUESTION. No need to explain why these are exclusively positive. Another goal-specific category that is completely represented at the positive extreme of the directionality scale is the one encompassing the lexical items used to account for acts of directing *Ha* toward coming or going somewhere. The same is true for the category of verbials describing attempts to make *Ha* give or grant (*Sa*) something.

336   The Dutch set of (SP1) verbials is AANPRATEN ('to talk a person into buying, doing something'), AANSPRAAK MAKEN OP ('to claim'), AANSTELLEN TOT ('to appoint'), AANVRAGEN ('to apply for' or 'to send for'), EEN AANZOEK DOEN (in the sense of 'to pop the question' or try to seduce), ADVERTEREN ('to advertize'), AFBEDELEN (lit. 'to beg off'), AFDREIGEN ('to extort by means of threatening'), AFDWINGEN ('to extort'), AFPERSEN ('to extort'), AFPINGELEN 'to haggle, higgle'), AFSMEKEN (lit. 'to beg off'), AFTROGGELEN ('to wheedle out of a person'), BEDELEN ('to beg'), BELASTEN MET ('to charge with'), BENOEMEN ('to appoint'), EEN BEROEP DOEN OP ('to call on'), BESPREKEN ('to book'), BESTELLEN ('to order', as in 'to order a meal'), BEZWEREN (in the sense of 'to conjure up'), BIJEENROEPEN ('to call together'), BINNENROEPEN ('to call in'), CHANTAGE PLEGEN ('to blackmail'), CHANTEREN ('to blackmail'), CONVOCEREN ('to convoke'), DAGVAARDEN ('to subpoena'), DICTEREN ('to dictate' in the sense of reading or speaking for someone to write down), EISEN (in the sense of 'to claim'), EEN EIS INSTELLEN ('to put in a claim'), EXAMINEREN ('to examine' in the sense of 'to subject to an examination', in the educational setting), HEFFEN ('to levy'), INFORMEREN ('to ask for information'), INROEPEN

(both in the sense of 'to call in' and 'to call on'), INTERPELLEREN ('to interpellate'), INTERVIEWEN ('to interview'), INVITEREN ('to invite', in the sense of asking to come over), INVORDEREN ('to claim'), AAN EEN KRUISVERHOOR ONDERWERPEN ('to subject to a crossexamination'), LATEN HALEN ('to send for'), MANDATEREN ('to mandate'), MEELOKKEN ('to entice to come along'), MEETRONEN ('to entice to come along'), ONDERVRAGEN ('to interrogate'), ONTBIEDEN ('to invite officially'), ONTLOKKEN ('to elicit'), ONTWRINGEN (lit. 'to wrench out of'), OPEISEN ('to claim'), OPGEVEN ('to assign'), OPJAGEN ('to entice to hurry up'), OPROEPEN (in the sense of 'to draft'), OPRUIEN ('to incite to rebellion'), OPVRAGEN ('to claim'), PRECONISEREN ('to preconize'), RECLAME MAKEN VOOR ('to advertise'), RECLAMEREN ('to claim'), RESERVEREN ('to reserve'), SCHOOIEN (pejorative for 'to beg'), SOLLICITEREN NAAR ('to apply for'), TERUGEISEN ('to demand the return of'), TERUGROEPEN ('to call back'), TERUGVORDEREN ('to demand the return of'), TE VOORSCHIJN ROEPEN (lit. 'to call, order to appear'), TOEWIJZEN ('to assign'), TRONEN ('to entice to come or go somewhere'), UITDRIJVEN ('to exorcise'), UITHOREN (lit. 'to hear out', i.e. 'to pump for information'), UITNODIGEN (in the sense of asking to come over, 'to invite'), UITVRAGEN (lit. 'to ask out', i.e. 'to interrogate'), VERHOREN ('to examine', in the legal setting), VERLEIDEN ('to seduce'), VERLOKKEN ('to entice, seduce'), IN VERZOEKING BRENGEN ('to seduce'), VISSEN NAAR ('to angle for'), VORDEREN ('to demand' in the sense of asking to give), EEN VRAAG STELLEN ('to ask a question'), VRAGEN (in the sense of asking a question), VRAGEN AFVUREN OP ('to shoot questions at'), WEGTRONEN ('to entice to go away'), DE WEG WIJZEN (lit. 'to show the way', i.e. 'to give directions'), WERVEN ('to canvass').

337 The intrinsically positive (SP2) verbials are equally numerous, but it is harder to relate them to categories specified previously in the discussion of different semantic dimensions. In this class all the traditional central examples of directive linguistic action verbs are encountered (but *not only* those). The English set is TO ACCEDE, TO ACCREDIT, TO BLACKMAIL, TO BRIEF, TO ACQUIESCE, TO ADJURE, TO ADMONISH, TO ADVISE, TO ADVOCATE, TO AGREE, TO ALLOW, TO ALLURE, TO APPEAL TO ONE FOR, TO APPLY PRESSURE, TO APPROVE, TO ASK (in the sense of requesting), TO ASSENT, TO AUTHORIZE, TO BEG, TO BESEECH, TO BULLY (SOMEONE INTO DOING SOMETHING), TO CAJOLE, TO CALL (in the sense of requesting, as in 'He called for an investigation of the facts'), TO CALL ON/UPON, TO CHALLENGE, TO COACH, TO COAX, TO COMMAND, TO CONJURE (in the sense of entreating earnestly or solemnly, as in 'I conjure you to weigh my case well), TO CONSENT, TO COUNSEL, TO CRAVE (in the sense of asking earnestly, as in 'He craved his superior's pardon'), TO DARE, TO DECREE, TO DEFY, TO DELIVER AN ULTIMATUM, TO DEMAND, TO DICTATE (in the general sense of speaking commandingly and imposing orders), TO DIRECT, TO DROP A HINT, TO EGG (ON) (in the sense of provoking to action, as in 'They egged their governments on to spend hundreds of millions'), TO ENCOURAGE,

TO ENDORSE (in the sense of expressing definite approval of), TO ENTICE, TO ENTREAT, TO EXHORT, TO GIVE CARTE BLANCHE, TO GIVE FULL POWER, TO GIVE AN OPEN MANDATE, TO GIVE AN ORDER, TO GIVE A PIECE OF ADVICE, TO GIVE LEAVE, TO GIVE OFFICIAL SANCTION, TO GIVE PERMISSION, TO GIVE THE WORD (OF COMMAND), TO GOAD, TO GRANT, TO HINT, TO IMPETRATE, TO IMPLORE, TO IMPORTUNE (in its general sense of making frequent and troublesome requests, or begging), TO INCITE, TO INDUCE, TO INSIST ON, TO INSTIGATE, TO INSTRUCT, TO INVEIGLE (as in 'He used the most subtle means to inveigle the author into the office'), TO INVITE (in the general sense of requesting politely), TO ISSUE A COMMAND, TO LAY DOWN (THE LAW), TO LEGALIZE, TO LICENSE, TO LURE, TO MAKE A DEMAND, TO MAKE A REQUEST, TO MAKE OBLIGATORY/ MANDATORY, TO MANIPULATE, TO OBTEST (in the sense of beseeching), TO OKAY, TO ORDAIN, TO ORDER, TO PERMIT, TO PERSIST, TO PERSUADE, TO PETITION, TO PLEAD, TO PRAY, TO PRESCRIBE, TO PRESENT A PETITION, TO PRESS, TO PRICK, TO PROD, TO PROMPT, TO PROPOSE, TO PUT A FLEA/BUG IN SOMEONE'S EAR (i.e. to give a hint or secret information to make someone act, as in 'He saw Mary at the jeweler's admiring the diamond pin; so he was able to put a bug in Henry's ear'), TO PUT THE PRESSURE ON, TO PUT THE SCREWS TO, TO QUALIFY (in the sense of licensing), TO RECOMMEND, TO REGULATE, TO REQUEST, TO REQUIRE (in the sense of asking authoritatively), TO RULE, TO SANCTION, TO SAY THE WORD, TO SEDUCE (in the sense of persuading into disobedience, disloyalty, etc.), TO SET (in the sense of 'to decree'), TO SET CONDITIONS, TO SOLICIT (in the sense of inciting or strongly urging), TO SPUR, TO STAND ON, TO STIPULATE, TO SUBSCRIBE, TO SUE, TO SUGGEST, TO SUPPLICATE, TO TELL, TO TEMPT, TO TROUBLE SOMEONE FOR, TO URGE, TO VOUCHSAFE, and TO WHEEDLE.

338 No doubt there are surprises for the reader of these lists. For instance, how can we explain that TO GIVE A FREE HAND, TO GIVE THE GO-AHEAD, and TO GIVE THE GREEN LIGHT seem to be exclusively applicable to positive directives, whereas a very similar verbial such as TO GIVE CARTE BLANCHE, though intrinsically positive, seems to allow for negative directionality as well? To take another example, why is the Dutch EEN BEROEP DOEN OP definitely a (SP1) verbial, whereas the English equivalent most commonly used to translate it, namely TO CALL ON, had to be listed in the (SP2) set? We have hardly started to make any systematic observations of this kind. It is quite natural, therefore, that explanations are still far off in the future.

339 The Dutch (SP2) verbials include AANBEVELEN ('to recommend'), AANDRINGEN ('to urge'), AANHITSEN ('to egg on'), AANMANEN ('to urge'), AANMOEDIGEN ('to encourage'), AANPORREN ('to incite'), AANPREKEN ('to recommend strongly'), AANPRIJZEN ('to recommend'), AANRADEN ('to advise'), AANSPOREN ('to incite'), AANSTICHTEN ('to instigate'), AANSTOKEN ('to foment, instigate'), EEN AANVRAAG DOEN/INDIENEN ('to make an application'), AANVUREN ('to incite'), AANWAKKEREN ('to foment'), AANWIJZINGEN GEVEN

('to give directions'), AANZEGGEN ('to order officially', a sense in which the verb is rarely used), AANZETTEN ('to incite'), EEN AANZOEK DOEN (OM) (in the sense of making a solemn, serious request), VAN ADVIES DIENEN ('to counsel'), ADVISEREN ('to advise'), AUTORISEREN ('to authorize'), BEKRACHTIGEN ('to sanction'), BEPALEN ('to rule'), BEPLEITEN ('to plead for'), BEPRATEN ('to persuade'), EEN BEVEL GEVEN ('to give an order'), BEVELEN ('to order'), BEWEGEN TOT ('to incite'), BEZWEREN ('to adjure'), BIDDEN (OM) ('to pray for'), BILLIJKEN ('to approve of'), BRENGEN TOT ('to incite'), CARTE BLANCHE GEVEN ('to give carte blanche'), COMMANDEREN ('to command'), DECRETEREN ('to decree'), DICTEREN ('to dictate' in its general sense of speaking commandingly or imposing orders), DRUK UITOEFENEN OP ('to put pressure on'), EISEN (to demand'), EEN EIS STELLEN ('to make a demand'), GEBIEDEN ('to order'), GOEDKEUREN ('to approve'), IEMAND HET MES OP DE KEEL ZETTEN (lit. 'to put the knife on someone's throat', meaning 'to put the screws to'), IEMAND IETS IN HET HOOFD PRATEN (lit. 'to talk something into somebody's head'), IEMAND IETS OP HET HART DRUKKEN (lit. 'to press something on to someone's heart', i.e. to urge a person to), IEMAND LASTIG VALLEN MET ('to importune' in the sense of urging with frequent or unreasonable requests), IEMAND VOOR IETS WINNEN (lit. 'to win someone for something'), INBLAZEN ('to suggest', lit. 'to blow in'), INGEVEN ('to suggest'), INSTEMMEN MET ('to accede'), INSTRUEREN ('to instruct'), INWILLIGEN ('to accede to'), LEGALISEREN ('to legalize'), MACHTIGEN ('to authorize'), MACHTIGING GEVEN TOT ('to authorize'), MANIPULEREN ('to manipulate'), MISRADEN ('to advise wrongly'), OPDRAGEN ('to order'), OPHITSEN ('to instigate'), OPLEGGEN ('to charge with'), OPPEREN ('to suggest'), OPROEPEN (in the sense of calling on), OPSTOKEN ('to instigate'), OPZWEPEN ('to incite', lit. 'to whip up'), ORDONNEREN ('to order', rarely used), OVERHALEN TOT ('to persuade'), OVERREDEN ('to persuade'), PETITIONEREN ('to petition'), PLEITEN VOOR ('to plead for'), RAAD GEVEN ('to advise'), OP ZIJN RECHTEN STAAN ('to assert one's rights'), REGLEMENTEREN ('to regulate), SANCTIONEREN ('to sanction'), SMEKEN ('to beg'), SOMMEREN ('to demand authoritatively'), STAAN OP ('to insist', lit. 'to stand on'), STIPULEREN ('to stipulate'), SUGGEREREN ('to suggest'), TARTEN ('to dare'), TOEGEVEN ('to accede'), TOELATEN ('to permit'), TOELATING GEVEN ('to give permission'), TOESTAAN ('to permit'), TOESTEMMEN IN ('to accede'), TOESTEMMING GEVEN ('to give permission'), UITDAGEN ('to challenge'), EEN ULTIMATUM STELLEN ('to deliver an ultimatum'), VASTLEGGEN ('to set'), VERGUNNEN ('to permit'), VERGUNNING GEVEN/VERLENEN ('to give permission'), VEROORLOVEN ('to permit'), VERORDENEN ('to decree, ordain'), VERZOEKEN ('to request'), EEN VERZOEKSCHRIFT INDIENEN ('to request formally and in writing'), VOET BIJ STUK ZETTEN ('to insist'), VOLMACHT GEVEN ('to authorize'), VOORSCHRIJVEN ('to prescribe'), VOORSLAAN ('to suggest, propose'), EEN VOORSTEL INDIENEN ('to make a proposition'), VOORSTELLEN ('to suggest, propose'), VOORWAARDEN STELLEN ('to make conditions'), VRAGEN ('to ask'),

ZICH WENDEN TOT ('to call on'), WETTIGEN ('to legalize').

340 Again, questions exist to which we do not know the answer. For instance, why is OPLEGGEN a (SP2) verb, whereas its most common English equivalent, TO CHARGE, is exclusively positive? The trivial answer is, of course, that their meanings do not overlap completely. But is this purely accidental, or is there a deeper rationale? Though I am unable to answer the question, the intuitive similarity in meaning makes me reluctant to accept the accident hypothesis without further scrutiny.

Another potentially interesting fact is the difference in semantic patterning between TO ASK and Dutch VRAGEN. When discussing the goal dimension of the verbials of directing, we were forced to distinguish between two types of asking: TO ASK in the sense of 'asking a question', as in (D5), and TO ASK FOR in the sense of requesting *Ha* to give or grant (*Sa*) something, as in (D6). The directionality dimension of directing imposes a third type on us: TO ASK simply in the sense of 'requesting', as in (D7).

(D5) He asked where the station was
(D6) He asked for money
(D7) He asked me to go home

In all three cases Dutch VRAGEN could be used, though in the case of (D6) the preposition OM may be added. Both TO ASK in (D5) and TO ASK FOR are (SP1) verbials, whereas TO ASK, as well as VRAGEN, in the (D7) sense is a (SP2) verb.

341 Let us jump immediately to the opposite pole of the scale, i.e. the exclusively and intrinsically negative verbials of directing. Both sets are much smaller than the corresponding positive ones. Some English (SP9) verbials are TO BAN (as in 'to ban a political party/a book', implying a categorical civil or ecclesiastical prohibition), TO BAR (as in 'barring the use of poison gas in war'), TO BLACKLIST, TO CENSURE, TO EMBARGO, TO EXPOSTULATE (in the sense of reasoning earnestly with a person for purposes of dissuasion), TO INTERDICT, TO LAY AN EMBARGO ON, TO REMONSTRATE (in the sense of expostulating), TO NEGATIVE (in the sense of refusing assent to), TO PROSCRIBE, TO PUT ONE'S VETO UPON, TO PUT ON THE INDEX, TO PUT UNDER AN INTERDICT, TO PUT UNDER THE BAN, TO READ THE RIOT ACT (in the sense of issuing a peremptory warning to cease doing something or not to do something again, as in 'Three boys were late to class and the teacher read the riot act to them'), TO SUSPEND, TO TABOO, TO VETO.

The reader may have noticed that almost all the verbials of directing specifying the act (not) to be performed belong either to the (SP1) or the (SP9) category. This is hardly surprising, because the behavior toward which *Ha* is directed is either a positive or a negative act. As a result, if the act in question is specified, its being positive or negative is likely also to be specified, and hence the directionality of the verb is fixed.

Some Dutch (SP9) verbials are CENSUREREN ('to censure'), OP DE INDEX PLAATSEN ('to put on the index'), EEN INTERDICT UITSPREKEN OVER (lit. 'to pronounce an interdict about'), SCHORSEN ('to suspend'), TABOE VERKLAREN (lit. 'to declare taboo'), UITSLUITEN (in the sense of not admitting), ZIJN VETO UITSPREKEN OVER ('to veto').

342 The list of intrinsically negative (SP8) verbials can be equally short: TO DISALLOW, TO DISCOURAGE, TO FORBID, TO INHIBIT (in the sense of prohibiting from doing something), TO OUTLAW, TO PROHIBIT, TO RULE AGAINST, TO RULE OUT (notice that TO RULE was listed as a (SP2) verb), TO DISSUADE; Dutch, AFBRENGEN VAN ('to dissuade'), AFRADEN ('to advise against'), BUITEN DE WET STELLEN ('to outlaw'), IEMAND IETS UIT HET HOOFD PRATEN (lit. 'to talk something out of a person's head', i.e. 'to dissuade'), ONTMOEDIGEN ('to discourage'), ONTRADEN ('to advise against'), VERBIEDEN ('to prohibit').

Whereas the central instances of positive directives such as TO ORDER and TO COMMAND were found to be (SP2) verbs, the central negative example, TO PROHIBIT, turns out to be a (SP8) verb. So far the symmetry is complete.

343 Moving in the direction of the center of the directionality scale we come across the (SP3) and (SP7) slots. In those slots we should find verbials that are not intrinsically negative or positive but that, in a vague probability-of-occurrence sense, tend toward the negative or positive poles. At the negative side we find (SP7) verbials such as TO ADDRESS A WARNING TO, TO CAUTION, TO GIVE FAIR WARNING, TO ISSUE A CAVEAT, TO UTTER A CAVEAT, and TO WARN; Dutch, WAARSCHUWEN ('to warn') and EEN WAARSCHUWING GEVEN ('to give a warning'). No doubt a description such as (D8) is more likely to occur than (D9), though both are acceptable.

(D8) I warned him not to stay there
(D9) I warned him to go home

Therefore warning, as a directive, tends toward the negative pole of the directionality scale. But TO WARN is not intrinsically negative, because its directionality is positive, not negative, when it is followed by a positive complement; it is negative when a negative propositional content signals the act toward which *Ha* is directed.

344 To preserve the symmetry of the scale, one would expect TO ADVISE to fill the (SP3) slot. But TO ADVISE was, quite correctly, listed as an intrinsically positive directive. Thus the (SP3) slot remains empty. This shows that there must be more to warning than (usually) negative advising; the Dutch lexicon shows, moreover, that negative advising (reflected in the verb AFRADEN, as opposed to AANRADEN), belongs to the (SP8) rather than the (SP7) set. How then, can we explain that TO WARN tends toward the negative pole of the scale though it does not behave like intrinsically negative directive verbials but rather like intrinsically positive ones? The question will remain unanswered in this essay.

THE SEMANTICS OF DIRECTING 179

DUTCH	SEMANTIC DIMENSION	ENGLISH
vragen ⎡ vragen	(SP1) ⎡	to ask (a question)
⎣ uitnodigen	⎣	to ask for
⎡ vragen	(SP2) ⎡	to invite
verzoeken		to ask
⎣ bevelen	⎣	to request
φ	(SP3)	to order
commanderen ⎡ ompraten	(SP4)	φ
⎣ φ	(SP5)	to enjoin
φ	(SP6)	φ
waarschuwen	(SP7)	φ
verbieden	(SP8)	to warn
een interdict uitspreken over	(SP9)	to prohibit
		to put under an interdict

Bracketed groupings (English side): SP1–SP2 "to ask"; SP4 "to order about".

SDC Table 5

345 Every act of directing pushes *Ha* to either doing or not doing something. Thus it comes as no surprise to find that there are no (SP6) verbials either. This leaves us with (SP4) and (SP5). There are some English verbials that can be used to describe either positive or negative acts of directing with equal probability: TO ENJOIN, TO ISSUE A WRIT/AN INJUNCTION, TO MENACE, TO PUT ONE'S FOOT DOWN, TO PUT UNDER AN INJUNCTION, TO THREATEN, and TO WARRANT (in the sense of giving authority or power for doing or forbearing to do something). Dutch, DREIGEN ('to threaten') and OMPRATEN (which can be either 'to persuade' or 'to dissuade'). Notice that apart from the pair TO THREATEN-DREIGEN, the English and Dutch sets of (SP4) verbials do not contain equivalents.

346 I have not been able to discover any verbials of directing that are necessarily of the (SP5) type. However, there are quite a few that can satisfy either (SP4) or (SP5), depending on the context. All of them indicate series of directive acts (which in the case of the (SP5) interpretation, are a mixture of positive and negative ones) rather than a single one. The English examples include TO CALL THE SHOTS, TO CALL THE SIGNALS, TO PLAY/CALL THE TUNE, TO MAKE THE RULES, and TO ORDER ABOUT/AROUND, Dutch, COMMANDEREN (which is often used more or less in the sense of 'to order about'), IEMAND DE WET STELLEN (more or less equivalent to 'to make the rules'), and RINGELOREN (similar to 'to order about').

The directionality dimension of directing is summarized in SDC Table 5. Keep in mind that in the case of the (SP4) slot, the verbials on both sides of the dimension are not necessarily each other's equivalents.

5.6 DIRECTING AND AUTHORITY

347 Though authority can be expected to be one of the major phenomena involved in acts of directing and to be necessary to understand in order to grasp the nature of such behavior, its discussion in the literature on speech acts is restricted to some cursory statements, such as Searle's claim that the distinction between a request and a command is simply that the latter implies authority on the part of the speaker whereas the former lacks such an implication. The purpose of this section is neither to provide support for these cursory statements nor to refute them. My intention is simply to show that authority really constitutes a complex semantic dimension in the lexical frame of directing. Authority is not just either absent or present. Nor is the authority dimension simply a matter of gradability. The verbials of directing force us to distinguish a whole range of different *types* of authority.

348 Very clear cases of directive verbials implying authority of some sort are TO ORDER (Dutch BEVELEN) and TO COMMAND (Dutch BEVELEN). They can be used to describe linguistic acts of the type (A1) conforming to (C1).

(A1) *Sa* directs *Ha* toward some action
(C1) *Sa* has authority over *Ha*

A less salient but equally clear example is TO TELL, as used in (D1).

(D1) The waiter told us to wait

The main difference between TO TELL and TO ORDER or TO COMMAND seems to be that the former implies authority of a somewhat weaker type, though essentially of the same kind. In the (C1) category also belongs TO PERMIT (Dutch TOELATEN).

349 The reader may have noticed that both TO ORDER and TO COMMAND have BEVELEN as a Dutch equivalent. Also, TO TELL can be translated by means of BEVELEN under certain conditions, but in the case of (D1) it is hard to find a good Dutch equivalent at all. The most likely translation for (D1) would be (D2),

(D2) De kelner deed ons wachten

which means literally 'The waiter made us wait'; a good lexical equivalent seems to be lacking.

350 The number of verbials applicable to directive acts conforming to (C1) is extremely large. But what about all the others? Do they all imply a simple negation of (C1)? Take, for instance, TO ADVISE (Dutch AANRADEN) and TO WARN (Dutch WAARSCHUWEN). It is clear that a piece of advice and a warning also involve a type of authority, which could be called *knowledge authority*, as opposed to the *power authority* underlying orders and commands. In other words, in the case of advising and warning, *Sa* has authority over *Ha* as a result of knowing more. Therefore, (C1) has to be made more specific.

(C1a) *Sa* has power authority over *Ha*
(C1b) *Sa* has knowledge authority over *Ha*

(It is by virtue of the concept of 'knowledge authority' that an expert in a particular field can be called an 'authority' in that field.) Directive acts conforming to (C1a) are describable in terms of TO ORDER, etc., whereas those satisfying (C1b) can be accounted for by means of TO ADVISE, etc.

351 So far so good. But are there also mixed categories of acts, conforming both to (C1a) and (C1b), or are these two mutually exclusive? And if they are not mutually exclusive, are these mixtures also reflected in the lexicon? In other words, are there any (C1c) verbials?

(C1c) *Sa* has both power and knowledge authority over *Ha*

A clear case seems to be TO INSTRUCT (Dutch INSTRUEREN).

352 A next question to ask is, Should all directive acts that are not describable in terms of (C1a), (C1b), or (C1c) verbials be regarded as conforming to (C2)?

(C2) The act involves no authority

There are no doubt a large number of (C2) verbials, including TO HINT, TO SUGGEST, TO INSIST, TO ASK (in its requesting sense), and maybe even TO REQUEST. There is no need to list them all here.

353 But we have not yet reached the end of the authority story. Not only are there different kinds of authority that the speaker may have over the hearer. The lexicon imposes a fact on us, the formulation of which might have been regarded as contradictory in purely theoretical approaches to directive linguistic behavior. It turns out that in some cases of directing, the hearer has authority over the speaker. How can a speaker, who holds a subordinate position, direct the hearer, his or her 'superior'? In other words, how can there by any acts satisfying (C3)?

(C3) *Ha* has authority over *Sa*

The mystery disappears when looking at some obvious (C3) verbs, such as TO PETITION (Dutch EEN VERZOEKSCHRIFT INDIENEN) and even TO BEG (Dutch SMEKEN). Both verbs are used to describe acts of trying to get the hearer to do (or allow) something, and in both cases the decision to perform the act or not is completely in the hearer's hands. There is a clear *reversal of authority*, and still the speaker's behavior remains directive.

354 Is there also a distinction between power and knowledge authority when the authority is on the hearer's side? In other words, is there a distinction between (C3a) and (C3b) verbials?

(C3a) *Ha* has power authority over *Sa*
(C3b) *Ha* has knowledge authority over *Sa*

The examples given so far, TO PETITION and TO BEG, are no doubt of the (C3a) type. But there are, indeed, (C3b) verbials as well. Consider, for instance, TO ASK (in the sense of asking a question, Dutch VRAGEN). When asking a question the speaker's attempt to get an answer (at least a helpful or correct answer) fails unless the hearer has what we call knowledge authority over the speaker: with respect to the subject matter of the question he/she is supposed to know more than the speaker. The same holds for TO CONSULT (in the sense of asking for advice, Dutch RAADPLEGEN) and many others.

355 There seems to be only one point where there is no symmetry between speaker and hearer authority, namely (C3c).

(C3c) *Ha* has both power and knowledge authority over *Sa*

I have not been able to find any (C3c) verbials, either in English or in Dutch.

In this section I have refrained from giving extensive lists of examples, but no doubt the reader will be able to select lots of additional examples for the six points on the authority dimension from the long lists provided in previous sec-

DUTCH	SEMANTIC DIMENSION	ENGLISH
bevelen, verbieden	(C1a)	to order, to prohibit
aanraden, waarschuwen	(C1b)	to advise, to warn
instrueren	(C1c)	to instruct
voorstellen, aandringen, verzoeken	(C2)	to suggest, to insist, to request
een verzoekschrift indienen, smeken	(C3a)	to petition, to beg
vragen, raadplegen	(C3b)	to ask (a question), to consult
φ	(C3c)	φ

SDC Table 6

tions. The authority dimension is visualized in SDC Table 6.

5.7 MISCELLANEOUS DIMENSIONS

356 The five semantic dimensions discussed so far are certainly not the only ones we need to understand the patterning of directive verbials in the English and Dutch lexicons, but they are certainly among the most important ones. In this section I want to draw attention to a couple of additional dimensions that deserve further research.

357 A relevant dimension for further investigation could be the specification of the hearer of the directive utterances (or, if you wish, the *directee*). The hearer can be an individual, a mob (as implied by TO READ THE RIOT ACT in one of its senses), the public in general (as in TO DECREE), even spirits (as in TO CONJURE UP) and dogs (as in TO SIC). Of course, such hearer specifications are often connected with, for instance, the social setting in which the directive act is situated. Along the hearer dimension a particularly interesting case is TO SEND FOR, as used in (D1) as a description of (A1).

(A1) Go and get the doctor, quickly!
(D1) *Sa* sent for the doctor

In this case there is, in addition to the immediate hearer *Ha* who is told to go and get the doctor, a second or *delayed hearer*, namely the doctor, who is requested to come. Unlike other cases where there is more than one hearer, the different status of the two directees of (A1) turns the utterance into a *double directive*.

358 A second neglected but potentially relevant line of research is the study of the *value-judgment* dimension. For one thing, many verbials of directing pass value judgments on the act toward which *Ha* is directed. For instance, both AANSTOKEN and AANVUREN mean TO INCITE, but the former implies that the act toward which *Ha* is directed is questionable, whereas the second one implies that it is praiseworthy. In this respect Dutch seems to show sharper contrasts than English; the questionable character of the act is often implied by TO INSTIGATE, but not always; and I have not been able to find an English directive verbial implying the unquestionably praiseworthy character of the act.

Value judgments are also passed on the linguistic act of directing itself. Verbs such as AFTROGGELEN (i.e. TO WHEEDLE SOMETHING OUT OF SOMEONE), AFDWINGEN (i.e. TO EXTORT), AFDREIGEN (lit. 'to extort by threatening', i.e. TO BLACKMAIL) and TO SCREW (in the sense of practising extortion upon) all imply disapproval, with judgments ranging from 'blameworthy' to 'criminal'.

5.8 CONCLUSIONS

359 Nothing in this chapter can be regarded as conclusive; it barely touches the surface of the semantics of directing. Let us recapitulate some of the main points.
  1. This chapter, as a whole, reveals how fundamental a function of language directing is.
  2. The dangers of purely theoretical classifications were demonstrated even more clearly than before; directive meaning is shown to spill over into the domains of the representatives and the commissives. (Paragraphs **290** to **298**)
  3. Commanding and ordering turn out not to be the strongest types of directives. (Paragraph **300**)
  4. Asking a question is shown to be more strongly directive than insisting and requesting. (Paragraph **302**)
  5. The verbials of directing single out a number of areas of social interaction in which directive behavior is prominent. (Paragraphs **305** to **322**)
  6. A discrepancy has been noted between the conceptualization of the military world as a prototypical directing situation and a lack of verbials focusing on the military setting. (Paragraph **318**)
  7. The verbials indicate that 'responding', 'moving to or from a place', and 'granting or giving something' are conceived as the basic types of acts towards which people direct each other linguistically. (Paragraphs **323** to **330**)
  8. Though the act toward which a hearer is directed can only be positive or negative (i.e. doing something or not doing something), this two-sided directionality is reflected in a six-fold distinction that is required to under-

stand the semantic patterning of the verbials of directing. (Paragraphs 331 to 346)
9. The lexicon shows that warnings are not just negative pieces of advice. (Paragraphs 343 and 344)
10. The verbials of directing shed light on the nature of the authority that is often involved in directive behavior; for one thing, they show that a distinction is necessary between different types of authority. (Paragraphs 347 to 355)
11. Contrary to what one would expect, it turns out that even cases in which the hearer has authority over the speaker with respect to the action to be performed can be genuine cases of directing. (Paragraph 353)

Each of these observations can be taken as the point of departure for extensive further investigations.

360 As in the previous two chapters, differences in Dutch and English lexicalizations have been found to be relatively unimportant, if not rare. This was quite predictable given the close relationship between the two languages and the strong cultural ties between the communities in which they are spoken. Yet our cursory comparison between the two sets of verbials of directing has led us to the observation of phenomena that have rarely been discussed, even in excellent theoretical classifications of directive forms of linguistic behavior such as Hindelang (1978) and in spite of the bulky literature on the subject. On the other hand, of some theoretical distinctions no traces have been found in the Dutch and English lexicalizations of the domain in question. The reader will have no trouble finding specific instances of this when consulting the relevant literature.

361 Especially in an area such as directive linguistic behavior, in which social settings and social relationships (such as authority) play a crucial role, a comparison with culturally diverse linguistic communities looks extremely promising. In one of the only 'exotic' studies of verbials of directing, Rosaldo (1982) claims that the Ilongot, in general, view language much less as an expression of an individual mind than we do. Rather, their linguistic behavior, in which directives are very frequent and prominent, whereas commissives are virtually absent, seems to be experienced much more directly as the constant affirmation and challenging of relationships in their ongoing social life. Thus, it would be reasonable to predict that their verbials of directing would show less variation along the directivity dimension (which was said to depend mainly on degrees in the speaker's wishing or wanting), and that the social-relationships dimension would not be restricted to different types of authority. To mention just one possibly significant difference, Rosaldo's data seem to indicate that even regular commands and requests are conceptualized by the Ilongot as involving knowledge authority rather than (or at least in addition to) power authority; giving orders to children, for instance, is regarded as a way of teaching them. But again, all these claims and questions are topics for further empirical-conceptual research.

CHAPTER **6**

THE SEMANTICS OF FORGOTTEN ROUTINES

6.0 INTRODUCTION

362 So far, we have already used the comparative lexical approach to further our understanding of the linquistically marginal area of conversational silence. We have also tried to penetrate the experience of truth, a central feature of propositional meaning, by way of studying the verbials used to describe representative speech acts in which the propositional content distorts the truth in one way or other. In the previous chapter, we have scratched the surface of the vast area of illocutionary meaning by canvassing the verbials describing speech acts of the directive type.

This final sample study enters an area marginal in one respect, but very central in another. The topic of investigation is the area of conversational routines. I am referring not only to formulaic expressions (as described by Tannan and Oztek 1977) and politeness formulas (Ferguson 1976), but also to routine utterances of a less fixed nature and with different social functions. Thus I shall not only (not even maily) be talking about expressions such as 'God bless you' (uttered when someone sneezes), which is formulaic in nature and which constitutes a form of linquistic politeness; but I shall also pay attention to a number of quite flexible, nonformulaic responses to acts of insisting, giving permission, requesting, advising, etc., that are not necessarily induced by politeness.

363 The centrality of conversational routines in linquistic action is beyond doubt. Without them, conversation would cease to exist. Further, the occurrence of formulaic expressions and politeness formulas appears to be a universal phenomenon, though their actual shapes vary crosslinguistically and crossculturally.

Moreover, their importance emerges from the fact that omitting them (e.g. by neglecting to greet a person one knows) or failing to acknowledge them (e.g. by not responding to a greeting inevitably creates tensions in interpersonal relalationships. These observations lead naturally toward the following question: In what sense could we say that conversational routines (including formulaic expressions and politeness formulas) are marginal?

364 The production of conversational routines involves a high degree of *automaticity*. Whereas in the standard case lying requires a conscious messing around with the propositional content of a statementlike utterance, and whereas commanding involves a conscious act of the will, replying 'You're welcome' to 'Thank you' is largely automatic. Therefore, if we agree that a human action typically results from a conscious impulse of the will, we have to conclude that routine utterances are less central instances of linquistic action than, say, lies or commands or even many acts of being silent.

365 This observation is not meant to distract from the importance (emphasized in paragraph **363**) of routine utterances as aspects of conversational interaction. But it may help us understand why, as Ferguson (1976:137) puts it, "this universal phenomenon has been very little studied by linguists or anthropologists or other students of human behavior" (which is somewhat less true now than it was when Ferguson wrote his article; think, e.g., of recent publications such as Coulmas 1981). It may also explain why, for a number of these routines, many languages lack descriptive verbials. If, for instance, John says 'God bless you' when Jane sneezes, there is no easy way for speakers of English to describe what John *did* or, in other words, what type of linguistic act he performed. A description such as 'John wished that God would bless Jane' would be hopelessly inadequate; no native speaker of English would take it seriously. The problem remains the same for the alternative and equivalent formula 'Gesundheit', which could not be accounted for by claiming that 'John wished Jane health'. One would have to take refuge in the phrase 'John said "God bless you"' or 'John said "Gesundheit"', which does not yield any insight into the nature of the act performed because the linguistic action verb TO SAY (as will be shown again in Chapter 8) is so general that it can be prefixed to any utterance (in directly or indirectly reported speech). The automaticity with which routine acts are performed may explain why there are many gaps in the lexical frame associated with them: their being performed more or less unthinkingly diminishes their cognitive salience, which is reflected in the absence of a lexicalization.

366 It is the set of nonlexicalized conversational routines that I call *forgotten routines*. This chapter is an overview of some major gaps in this area in English and in Dutch.

The foregoing tentative explanation (in terms of the automaticity involved) of why some types of routine utterances are easily 'forgotten', however attractive it may be, still leaves us with mysteries. In fact, it might even make some things harder to comprehend. For instance, how is it that certain types of routines (e.g. greetings) are so salient that they get their own descriptive verbials, whereas others can hardly be described at all in a given language? Sometimes it will be possible to present a hypothetical answer to this question; sometimes it will not. But in all cases the question is relevant.

There is something peculiar about a semantic discussion of lexical gaps. What I hope this chapter will lead to is a partial understanding of the types of conversational routines that are easily 'forgotten' in the sense mentioned and that, therefore, require special study. We will be skimming through an area of semiconscious linguistic action in which some of language's most fundamental properties may be hidden.

6.1 THE EXPRESSION OF EMOTIONS AND ATTITUDES

367 A large proportion of linguistic routine acts can be situated in the domain of what Searle (1976) called *expressives*, i.e. the class of speech acts the illocutionary point of which is that a certain psychological state, emotion, or attitude is expressed. Of course, this area shades off into the other traditional classes, for speech acts of which the expression of a psychological state is not a prominent aspect (e.g. Searle's declarations) are rare.

In English and in Dutch, as in many other languages, there are specialized linguistic action verbials to describe the expression of some emotions. For others, there are no such lexical items. This first contrast between lexicalized and nonlexicalized linguistic actions, which is amply illustrated in the following paragraphs, will lead us to some interesting conclusions as to why expressives were made into a separate class of speech acts.

368 Let us first consider some of the ways in which sorrow (or regret) and pleasure can be expressed.

(A1) I am sorry that you could not come over for a visit
(A2) I regret that you could not come over for a visit
(A3) I am sorry for having been so rude to you
(A4) I regret that I have been so rude to you
(A5) I am sorry that your father died
(A6) I am glad that I have gotten the fellowship
(A7) I am glad that you've gotten the fellowship
(A8) (I am) glad/pleased to meet you

Descriptions (D1) to (D8) correspond to acts (A1) to (A8), in the same order.

(D1) *Sa* said/stated/claimed that he/she was sorry that ... *or: Sa* expressed his/her regret that ...
(D2) *Sa* said/stated/claimed that he/she regretted that ...
(D3) *Sa* apologized for having been rude

(D4) *Sa* apologized for having been rude
(D5) *Sa* commiserated/condoled *Ha*'s father's death
(D6) *Sa* said/stated/claimed that he/she was glad that he/she ...
(D7) *Sa* congratulated *Ha* on getting ...
(D8) *Sa* greeted *Ha*

It will be clear that the phrase '*Sa* said/stated/claimed ... ' could have been employed in all the foregoing descriptive acts. Notice, however, that this phrase, which can introduce any type of reported statementlike utterance, would not normally be used by a speaker of English who was asked to tell what *Sa* did when uttering (A3), (A4), (A5), (A7), and (A8). Instead, the specialized expressive linguistic action verbs TO APOLOGIZE, TO COMMISERATE, TO CONDOLE, TO CONGRATULATE, and TO GREET would be used. Notice, moreover, that English lacks such specialized verbials for the description of (A1), (A2) and (A6). In other words, there is no verbial available for describing (A1), (A2), and (A6) *as expressions of emotions*, i.e. verbials that focus on the emotive aspect of these acts. Thus, some expressions of psychological states are lexicalized whereas others are not. The discrepancy is striking because sometimes identical formulas are used for the lexicalized and the nonlexicalized expression of identical emotions. A case in point is the formula 'I am sorry', which always expresses a feeling of regret but which introduces what would be described as a simple statement in (A1), whereas it triggers the descriptive verbials TO APOLOGIZE and TO COMMISERATE in (D3) and (D5). Similar things happen with 'I regret' and 'I am glad'.

369 A completely analogous picture emerges from Dutch. The formula 'I am sorry' can be replaced by the impersonal phrase 'Het spijt mij' (lit. 'it sorrows me') in (A1), (A3), and (A5); 'I regret' can be translated as 'Ik betreur' in (A2) and (A4); and 'I am glad' is equivalent to 'Ik ben blij'. In (D1), (D2), and (D6) the phrase '*Sa* zei/beweerde ... ' ('*Sa* said/claimed ... '), which can introduce any type of reported statementlike utterance, would be used, whereas the verbials ZICH VERONTSCHULDIGEN ('to apologize'), ZIJN DEELNEMING BETUIGEN ('to commiserate'), GELUKWENSEN ('to congratulate'), and GROETEN ('to greet') would be used in the remaining describing acts.

This complete parallelism shows that probably we are not dealing with one of the whimsical features of natural language. But before attempting to formulate an explanation, we shall take a look at some more comparable data.

370 Consider the following acts in which liking and disliking are expressed.

(A9) I (don't) like working late
(A10) I like your plan very much
(A11) I don't like the way you dress

Act (A9) can be described as in (D9).

(D9) *Sa* said/stated/claimed that he/she liked/did not like working late

Though the same statement-formula '*Sa* said/stated/claimed ... ' could be used to account for (A10) and (A11) in all circumstances, there is another possibility as well. Imagine that *Sa* is *Ha*'s employer. Thus condition (C1) applies to (A10) and (A11).

(C1) *Sa* has authority over *Ha* (with respect to the topic of *Sa*'s utterance)

In such circumstances we are likely to get (D10) and (D11) as descriptions.

(D10) *Sa* approved of *Ha*'s plan
(D11) *Sa* disapproved of the way *Ha* dressed

Again, we are confronted with linguistic actions in which identical psychological states are expressed by means of identical formulas, though for only some of them English provides us with descriptive verbials.

Once more, the parallelism with Dutch is striking. The verbs GOEDKEUREN (lit. 'to judge good', i.e. 'to approve') and AFKEUREN ('to disapprove') would be used in (D10) and (D11). Moreover, the distinction between (A9) on the one hand and (A10) and (A11) on the other, is reinforced by the fact that the verb HOUDEN VAN ('to like') can be replaced by GOEDVINDEN (lit. 'to find good'), which is ambiguous between liking and approving, in (A10) and (A11), but not in (A9).

A minor difference between English and Dutch is that whereas TO APPROVE and TO DISAPPROVE are not necessarily linguistic action verbs (i.e. they can be used to describe the attitudes rather than their expression), GOEDKEUREN and AFKEUREN can be used *only* to describe the *expression* of approval and disapproval.

371 The divergence of human emotions and attitudes is unlimited. So is the number of their linguistic forms of expression. In this paragraph I offer a random selection of the remaining ones. Unlike those discussed so far, the following ones do not constitute *pairs* of lexicalized and nonlexicalized forms of expression. Yet they do present exactly the same problem in the sense that, for no obvious reason, some of them are lexicalized whereas others are not. The expression of a wish and the expression of gratitude are two examples of lexicalized expressives. Consider (A12) and (A13).

(A12) I wish I could go
(A13) I'm truly grateful for your hospitality

These two can be described by means of the linguistic action verbs TO WISH and TO THANK as in (D12) and (D13).

(D12) *Sa* wished he/she could go
(D13) *Sa* thanked *Ha* for his/her hospitality

In contrast, there are no emotion or attitude-oriented verbials associated with the expression of hope as in (A14), the anticipation of pleasure as in (A15), disappointment as in (A16), surprise as in (A17), and concern or worry as in (A18).

(A14) I hope he arrives on time
(A15) I am looking forward to receiving your reply
(A16) I am disappointed that he did not come after all
(A17) I am surprised that he came
(A18) I am concerned/worried that/about . . .

Both in English and in Dutch these can only be described as statements. (A12) and (A13) are also lexicalized in Dutch: the verbs WENSEN ('to wish') and (BE)-DANKEN ('to thank') would be used in (D12) and (D13).

Notice that TO WISH (Dutch WENSEN) is a borderline case in the sense that its use as a linguistic action verb is extremely limited. An act such as (A12) is likely to be described by means of '*Sa* expressed the wish that he/she could go' rather than by means of (D12). But in the case of (A14) through (A18), similar paraphrases are the *only* way out.

The data presented so far are summarized in SDC Table 1 (with TO WISH and WENSEN in parentheses because of their marginal character). We should now start looking for explanations.

372 What needs explaining is the fact that some linguistic expressions of emotions or attitudes can only be described as statements, whereas others are lexicalized in such a way that they seem to take on a totally different speech-act status. In other words, the problem is that some of these expressions, *as expressions of emotions or attitudes*, are simply forgotten in the conceptualization underlying the sets of linguistic action verbials in English and in Dutch. The best place to look for an explanation is in the pairs of identical formulas expressing identical emotions, which are sometimes lexicalized and sometimes not, i.e. in (A1) through (A11).

373 Let us take, for instance, the formula 'I am sorry'. What distinguishes its use in (A1) from (A3) and (A5)?

(A1) I am sorry that you could not come over for a visit
(A3) I am sorry for having been so rude to you
(A5) I am sorry that your father died

I believe that the major difference is that whereas in (A1) *Sa* is simply conveying about him/herself information that may or may not interest *Ha*, in both (A3) and (A5) the speaker's psychological state expressed is of crucial importance to the hearer. (A3) presupposes that *Sa* has been rude to *Ha*; therefore, all further interaction between the two interlocutors depends crucially on *Ha*'s coming to know whether *Sa* feels sorry about his/her previous behavior or whether he/she can expect similar behavior in the future. Similarly, (A5) presupposes that *Ha*'s father died; whether *Sa* feels sorry (for *Ha*) about this unfortunate event partly defines *Sa*'s attitudes toward *Ha*, and therefore it is important for *Ha* to know *Sa*'s feelings. My hypothesis is that the importance of the emotions expressed

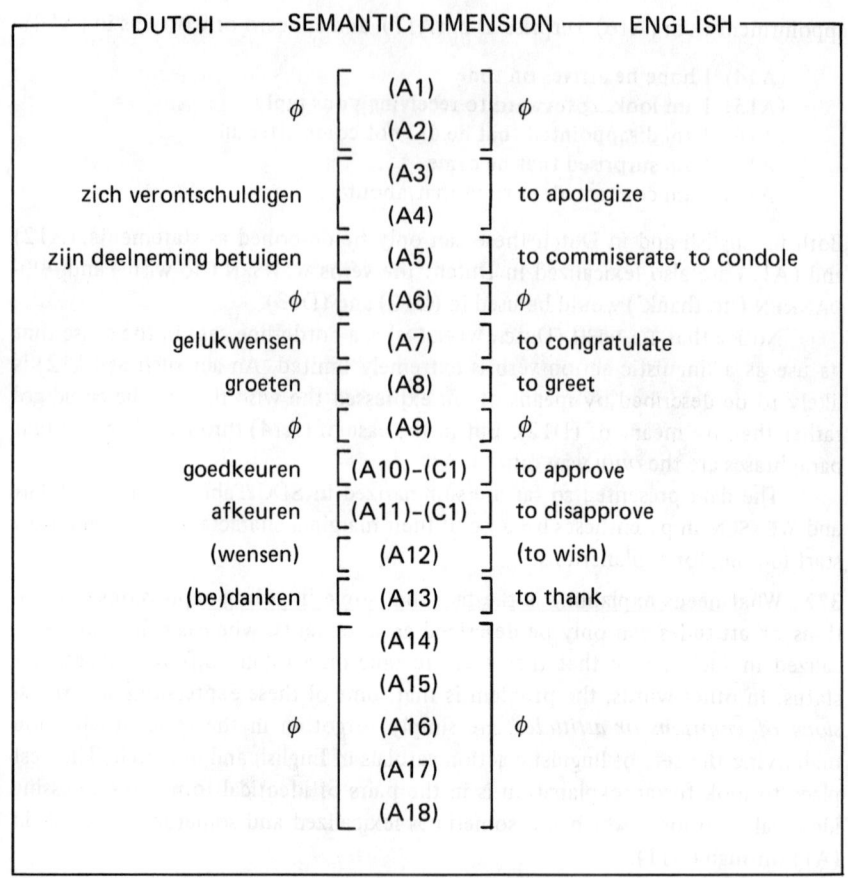

SDC Table 1

in (A3) and (A5) for the relationship between *Sa* and *Ha* and for their social interaction increases the cognitive salience of these expressions within the domain of linguistic activity to such an extent that their conceptualization and lexicalization *as expressions of emotions* becomes inevitable. An act such as (A1) lacks this cognitive salience and is therefore 'forgotten' in the lexicalization process, though both the emotion expressed and the formula used are identical with (A3) and (A5).

374 In Searle's typology of speech acts, (A1) would simply be described as a statement (an assertive), whereas (A3) and (A5) would be said to be expressives. Thus, if my hypothesis is correct, the distinguishing trait of expressives is not the expression of a psychological state as such (because the point of (A1) as well is to express a psychological state) but the expression of a psychological state important to the hearer. Our lexical data support the validity of the distinction be-

tween assertives and expressives while enabling us to formulate the distinction more accurately.

375 We still have to check the validity of our explanation for the rest of our data. The contrast between (A2) and (A4) can be put in the same terms as that between (A1) and (A3). Also, the congratulation (A7) and the greeting (A8) differ from the statement (A6) in that the attitudes expressed are important to the hearer. Exactly the same holds for the difference between the approval (A10)-(C1), the disapproval (A11)-(C1), and the simple statement (A9).

But what about the unpaired examples (A12) through (A18)? The importance to *Ha* of the gratitude expressed in an act of thanking, as in (A13), is evident. On the other hand, the hope in (A14), the disappointment in (A16), the surprise in (A17), and the concern in (A18) do not show the same kind of relevance to the hearer. This does not mean that sentences starting 'I hope . . .', etc., are always just statements. Consider (A19).

(A19) I'm giving a party tomorrow. I hope you can come

In this case, 'I hope you can come' is clearly an act of inviting *Ha* to come to the party; an invitation is a directive speech act. The only points I want to make are that sentences starting with 'I hope . . .', etc., though they clearly constitute the expression of a psychological state, cannot be described by means of a linguistic action verbial focusing on the psychological state expressed, because no such verbials are available, and that the lexical gaps in question result from the fact that the expression of the feelings expressed lacks an inherent importance for the relationship between speaker and hearer.

So far, the hypothesis seems to work. There are, however, two troublesome cases, namely (A12) and (A15).

376 The first problematic case is (A15), which is a widely used phrase to end a letter.

(A15) I am looking forward to receiving your reply

One might want to argue that the anticipation of pleasure expressed in (A15) is important to the reader of the letter. Of course it is. But upon closer investigation the problem turns out to be imaginary. The anticipation of pleasure is only important to *Ha* in the same way as the hope expressed in 'I hope you can come' (as in (A19)). That is, the verbalized psychological state does not matter as such. What really counts for *Ha* is its implication. The expression of *Sa*'s hope that *Ha* would be able to come, and therefore the sentence 'I hope you can come', counts as an invitation. Similarly, *Sa*'s looking forward to receiving *Ha*'s reply implies that *Sa* wants *Ha* to reply, and therefore (A15) counts as a polite request to reply. The directive overtones of (A15) and (A19) dominate so strongly that it would be surprising to get a description emphasizing the expressive aspect of these acts.

377   The only real problem is (A12), which can be described by means of TO WISH used as a linguistic action verb (though, as said before, such usage is extremely marginal).

(A12) I wish I could go

What makes wishing so different from hoping that (D12), as a description of (A12), can be interpreted as an account of the *linguistic action* performed, whereas (D14), as a description of (A20), can be regarded only as an account of the *psychological state* expressed in the act?

(A20) I hope I can go
(D12) *Sa* wished he/she could go
(D14) *Sa* hoped he/she could go

In other words, what makes TO WISH into a linguistic action verb (in one of its marginal senses), whereas TO HOPE can only refer to a state of mind? Obviously, there is no difference in importance to the hearer between the expression of a wish and the expression of hope. It is even hard to see any difference between a wish and hope as states of mind. I want to suggest that in this case the hearer-oriented principle I formulated is overcome by a second principle, one idiosyncratic to acts of wishing. What makes TO WISH into a linguistic action verb may be the belief that a state of affairs can be created by putting one's wishes into a linguistic form (e.g. a magical formula, a prayer, etc.). As a result, the meaning of the verb TO WISH is extended from a state of mind to the linguistic expression of that state of mind.

378   The belief that verbalizing one's wishes may bring about the desired state of affairs, and the resulting strong association of wishes (as mental acts) with their expression (as linguistic acts) and with the desired state of affairs itself (brought about by the formulation of the wish), may explain another peculiarity of the verb TO WISH. Wishing normally concerns a state of affairs that does not yet obtain, as in 'wishing someone a happy New Year', which is done at the beginning of a year. However, 'wishing someone a happy birthday', though not entirely synonymous with 'congratulating someone on his/her birthday', has as its object a state of affairs that in most cases does already obtain. This extension of the meaning of TO WISH could be explained as follows. Take T_1 to be the time at which a wish is uttered and T_2 as the time at which the state of affairs that is the object of the wish obtains. In the paradigm case of 'wishing someone a happy New Year', T_2 is later in time than T_1. Now, imagine someone wishing that it would stop raining. If one believes that uttering a wish can bring about the desired state of affairs, then T_1 and T_2 could nearly coincide: immediately after someone's wish that it would stop raining, it might indeed stop raining. This quasi-identification of the act with its object makes it possible to understand how wishing got extended to circumstances in which its object is already present. This extension is very nicely reflected in the fact that the Dutch verb

for TO CONGRATULATE, in all its occurrences, is GELUKWENSEN (lit. 'to wish happiness').

But whatever the explanation for its behavior, TO WISH remains marginal as a linguistic action verb. Due to its marginal character, it does not present a real threat to our hypothesis about the lexicalization of expressions of emotion.

6.2 NEGATIVE AND POSITIVE RESPONSES

379 The subject matter of the previous section could be called the *expressive dimension* of forgotten routines. We have discussed the types of psychological states for the linguistic expression of which languages such as English and Dutch do not provide descriptive verbials. Now we go into the *textual dimension* of forgotten routines. We present an overview of the gaps in the lexical apparatus to describe *responses* to diverse types of speech acts. In this section the overview is limited to responses to speech acts of a directive nature. All of the responses can be either negative or positive. Thus we are concerned with two types of acts, (A1) and (A2).

(A1) *Sa* responds positively to a speech act performed by *Ha*
(A2) *Sa* responds negatively to a speech act performed by *Ha*

The nature of the preceding discourse can be specified in the form of conditions on these acts. Consider (C1).

(C1) The act performed by *Ha* is a suggestion, such as 'I suggest we take the night train'

Examples of responses can be given as follows: (A3) is a response of the (A1)-(C1) type; (A4) is a response of the (A2)-(C1) type.

(A3) Let's do that
(A4) I don't feel like it

These two responses could be described as in (D1) and (D2).

(D1) *Sa* agreed to take the night train
(D2) *Sa* disagreed about taking the night train

Thus, the verb TO AGREE can refer to the positive responses to suggestions, whereas TO DISAGREE denotes, amongst other things, negative responses to suggestions. Consequently, if (C1) obtains, both types of responses are lexicalized in English. Dutch provides the verbial AKKOORD GAAN ('to agree') for (A3); however, its negation, NIET AKKOORD GAAN ('to disagree'), would be rarely used for (A4); instead, the verb AFWIJZEN (more or less equivalent to 'to decline') would be more likely to occur, as in (D3).

(D3) *Sa* wees het voorstel af
(lit. '*Sa* declined the suggestion')

380 Let us go on to a second type of preceding discourse.

(C2) The act performed by *Ha* is an act of insisting, such as 'I insist that you come home with me'

A possible (A1)-(C2) act is (A5), whereas (A6) represents the (A2)-(C2) type.

(A5) Okay, fine with me
(A6) No, I won't

A quite natural way of describing (A5) would be to use the verb TO GIVE IN (Dutch TOEGEVEN, which is ambiguous between 'to give in' and 'to admit') as in (D4). For (A6) one might use TO REFUSE (Dutch WEIGEREN), as in (D5).

(D4) *Sa* gave in (and went home with *Ha*)
(D5) *Sa* refused (to go home with *Ha*)

As with suggesting, there are no lexical gaps here.

381 In the case of advising, an additional complication arises.

(C3) The act performed by *Ha* is an act of advising, such as 'You'd better take your medicine'

Two types of positive and negative responses can be given to a piece of advice: one can either concentrate on the assertive aspect of advice, as in the responses (A7) and (A9), or on its directive aspect, as in (A8) and (A10).

(A7) I think you're right
(A8) Okay, I will
(A9) I don't think so; it's still too early
(A10) No, I won't

The verbs TO AGREE and TO DISAGREE can be used to account for (A7) and (A9), as in (D6) and (D7).

(D6) *Sa* agreed (with *Ha* on taking his/her medicine)
(D7) *Sa* disagreed (with *Ha* on taking his/her medicine)

In Dutch, the comparable verbials AKKOORD GAAN ('to agree') and NIET AKKOORD GAAN ('to disagree') could be used. The directive-oriented negative reply (A10) can be described by means of TO REFUSE (Dutch WEIGEREN), as in (D8).

(D8) *Sa* refused (to take the medicine)

A problem arises with the directive-oriented positive response: I did not succeed in finding a linguistic action verbial (apart from the passe-partout verb TO SAY) suited for the description of (A8). Here we seem to be confronted with a first gap.

382   Next in line is the speech act of inviting.

> (C4)   The act performed by *Ha* is an act of inviting, such as 'Would you like to come to my party tomorrow night?'

The positive (A1)-(C4) response could simply be (A11), and (A12) could be the negative (A2)-(C4) reply.

> (A11)   Yes, I would
> (A12)   No, I can't

To describe these two acts, the verbs TO ACCEPT (Dutch AANNEMEN) and TO DECLINE (Dutch AFSLAAN) might be used, as in (D9) and (D10).

> (D9)   *Sa* accepted (*Ha*'s invitation to come to the party)
> (D10)   *Sa* declined (*Ha*'s invitation to come to the party)

Again, all lexical slots are filled. (Notice that 'No, I wouldn't' cannot be regarded as an appropriate negative response to an invitation of the above type; it would count as an insult rather than as an act of declining the invitation.)

383   What about responses to requests?

> (C5)   The act performed by *Ha* is an act of requesting, such as 'Can you possibly give me a lift?'

Acts (A13) and (A14) are adequate replies of the (A1)-(C5) and the (A2)-(C5) types, respectively.

> (A13)   Sure
> (A14)   No, I'm afraid not

The negative response (A14) can be described as a refusal (using the verb TO REFUSE, Dutch WEIGEREN), as in (D11).

> (D11)   *Sa* refused (to give *Ha* a lift)

For the positive response, however, no adequate linguistic action verbial presents itself. Thus, (A1)-(C5) is our second lexical gap. Notice that the gap cannot be filled by means of such phrases as 'to comply with the request'; this phrase, just as 'to follow someone's advice' or 'to obey someone's order', indicates a positive behavioral response, not a positive linguistic response.

384   Similar to requests are orders and commands. According to the traditional accounts, they differ from requests mainly in that they require authority over the hearer on the part of the speaker. As far as the set of descriptive linguistic action verbials is concerned, the responses to both types of acts show an identical pattern. Consider (C6).

> (C6)   The act performed by *Ha* is an act of ordering, such as 'Come here, Michael!'

Acts (A15) and (A16) are possible responses of the (A1)-(C6) and the (A2)-(C6) types, respectively.

(A15) Okay
(A16) No, I won't

(A16) could be described by means of the verb TO REFUSE, Dutch WEIGEREN. Once more, an adequate linguistic action verbial does not present itself for the positive reply (A15).

385 At least two more types of directives deserve our attention: permissions and prohibitions.

(C7) The act performed by *Ha* is an act of giving permission, such as 'You can go home now'
(C8) The act performed by *Ha* is an act of prohibiting, such as 'You mustn't leave this early'

(A17) is an appropriate positive response to the permission; (A18) is a possible negative one.

(A17) Thank you
(A18) I'm not going now

The prohibition can be replied to positively as in (A19) and negatively as in (A20).

(A19) Fine with me
(A20) I'll do it anyway

(A17) is simply an act of thanking, for the description of which we have available the verb TO THANK, Dutch (BE)DANKEN. As a result, (D12) is an adequate account of (A17).

(D12) *Sa* thanked *Ha* (for the permission to go home)

But for (A18) through (A20) no descriptive verbials seem to be available.

386 SDC Table 2 summarizes the verbials available for the description of positive and negative responses to a number of directive speech acts. How can we explain the gaps? How can we explain the fact that some response types were 'forgotten' in the lexicalization process? I believe that a vague principle of *harmony of interaction* can show us why some responses to particular types of directives are cognitively less salient and, therefore, do not need to be lexicalized.

Acts of inviting, suggesting, and even insisting leave the hearer completely free to do as he/she chooses. These acts clearly indicate the speaker's preference with respect to the hearer's actions. But no matter what course of action the hearer takes, there is nothing unharmonious about the interaction. Therefore, both positive and negative responses can be expected with equal probability. As a result, both options got lexicalized.

The same reasoning applies to advising when its assertive aspect is focused

DUTCH	SEMANTIC DIMENSION	ENGLISH
akkoord gaan	[(A1)- (C1)]	to agree
afwijzen	[(A2) - (C1)]	to disagree
toegeven	[(A1) - (C2)]	to give in
weigeren	[(A2) - (C2)]	to refuse
akkoord gaan [(A7)	(A1) - (C3)	(A7)] to agree
ϕ [(A8)		(A8)] ϕ
niet akkoord gaan [(A9)	(A2) - (C3)	(A9)] to disagree
weigeren [(A10)		(A10)] to refuse
aannemen	[(A1) - (C4)]	to accept
afslaan	[(A2) - (C4)]	to decline
ϕ	[(A1) -(C5)]	ϕ
weigeren	[(A2) - (C5)]	to refuse
ϕ	[(A1) - (C6)]	ϕ
weigeren	[(A2) - (C6)]	to refuse
(be)danken	[(A1) - (C7)]	to thank
ϕ	[(A2) - (C7) ; (A1) - (C8) ; (A2) - (C8)]	ϕ

SDC Table 2

upon. But what happens if its directive component is envisaged? It seems to me that advising may be stronger as a directive than insisting because it implies some kind of authority (the kind that we have called 'knowledge authority' in the previous chapter; see paragraph **350**). It is assumed that the person giving the advice knows what the best course of action is. As a result, the hearer is expected to respond positively and not to disregard the advice. Since harmony of interaction can only be obtained if the response is positive, the positive response itself is taken for granted to such an extent that it loses its cognitive salience. This explains the absence of a verbial to describe (A8). On the other hand, the negative response is cognitively salient because—if it occurs—it disrupts the harmony of interaction.

Completely analogous accounts can be given for the gaps in connection with requests and orders. Complying with a request and obeying an order are the harmonious reactions expected. In the case of orders, the expectation results from the 'power authority' involved. Requests are quite compelling in spite of the absence of such authority.

387 What about permissions and prohibitions? Why are the negative responses to these types of acts not lexicalized, though they no doubt disrupt interactional harmony? A possible explanation is that in the case of prohibitions, negative responses are not only unexpected and disruptive but also rare because of the high degree of authority involved: a speaker who prohibits something is often in a position to actively prevent the hearer from doing what he/she prohibits him/her to do (whereas in the case of an order, such active intervention is usually harder because it is much more difficult to make somebody do something than to prevent him/her from doing it). On the other hand, permissions imply that the hearer wants to do what he/she is allowed to do; therefore, negative responses to permissions are rare as well. The *scarcity* of negative responses to acts of permitting and prohibiting deprives them of the cognitive salience they gained by being disruptive. Therefore, they are 'forgotten' in the lexicalization process.

388 A final question has to be answered. How is it that there *is* a verbial to describe the positive response to acts of permitting, even though that response is certainly the expected and harmonious one? Since permissions imply that the hearer wants to do what he/she is allowed to do, and since the speaker has authority over the hearer with respect to the act in question, the positive response is, not surprisingly, an expression of gratitude. And since expressions of gratitude also occur in other contexts and are generally called acts of thanking, it is only logical that the same name is given to the expression of gratitude following a permission. (It is quite possible that in an imaginary language in which gratitude were expressed only after obtaining a permission, there would be no word equivalent to TO THANK.)

6.3 FIXED ROUTINE RESPONSES

389 The responses studied in the previous section can either be positive or negative. There are also routine responses of a fixed formulaic nature that lack the positive-negative option. Some of these are easy to describe in English and in Dutch. Consider the response act (A1) uttered in the contexts specified by (C1) through (C3).

(A1) Thank you

(C1) The act performed by *Ha* is an act of congratulating, such as 'Congratulations on your birthday'
(C2) The act performed by *Ha* is an act of condoling with *Sa*, such as 'I'm terribly sorry that your father died'
(C3) The act performed by *Ha* is an act of welcoming, such as 'Welcome home'

In all these contexts, (A1) can be described by means of TO THANK, Dutch (BE)DANKEN, as in (D1).

(D1) *Sa* thanked *Ha*

Sa expresses his/her gratitude for *Ha*'s kind attitude toward him/her. Hence, (A1), in response to acts of congratulating, condoling, and welcoming, is not an obscure or empty routine. Its conversational meaning coincides with the lexical meaning of the words used.

390 A bit more complicated are the responses to greetings. In the context specified by (C4), several replies are possible, some of which are listed as (A2) to (A4).

(C4) The act performed by *Ha* is an act of greeting, such as 'How are you?'
(A2) Very well, thank you
(A3) Fine. How are YOU?
(A4) Very well, thank you. And you?

Though in (A2) the same formula, 'thank you', is used as in (A1), and though (A2) could be said to express appreciation (if not gratitude) for *Ha*'s interest in *Sa* or for his/her polite display of recognition (which is probably the essence of every greeting), (A2) can hardly be described as an act of thanking. Nor do we have any other linguistic action verbial at our disposal to describe the response act. Acts (A3) and (A4) are return greetings, describable by means of TO GREET, Dutch (BE)GROETEN.

391 Finally, there are a number of fixed routine responses for which no descriptive verbials exist at all. First, consider (A5) through (A9), uttered when (C5) obtains.

(C5) The act performed by *Ha* is an act of apologizing, such as 'I am sorry for having been so rude to you'
(A5) No harm done
(A6) Never mind
(A7) That's quite all right
(A8) Please don't worry
(A9) Forget it

For none of these acts do we have descriptive verbials.

392 Second, consider (A10) through (A14) uttered in a context in which (C6) obtains.

(C6) The act performed by *Ha* is an act of thanking, such as 'Thank you very much'
(A10) You're welcome
(A11) That's quite all right
(A12) Not at all
(A13) Forget it
(A14) Don't mention it

Again, no descriptive verbials seem to be available in English or in Dutch. Like 'Thank you' as a response to a certain type of greeting, 'You're welcome' as a response to an act of thanking is a forgotten routine, though TO THANK and TO WELCOME are linguistic action verbials. The reason is that the conversational meaning of the formulas does not coincide with the lexical meaning of the words used. Similarly, in many languages there are fixed routine responses to acts of thanking, which include an equivalent to the verbs TO PRAY, TO BEG, TO ASK: German, *bitte*; French, *je vous en prie*; Italian, *prego*; Hungarian, *kérem* (BITTEN, PRIER, and PREGARE mean 'to pray, to beg, to ask'; KÉRNI means 'to ask (for something)'). Yet these acts would never be described as acts of praying, begging, or asking.

Notice that (A7) is identical with (A11) and that (A9) is identical with (A13). This is possible by virtue of the fact that both apologizing and thanking express the speaker's feeling that he/she owes something to the hearer (cf. Coulmas' account of thanks and apologies in Coulmas 1981).

393 The material presented in this section is represented graphically in SDC Table 3, which is, so to speak, filled with gaps. The acts surveyed are all responses to expressive speech acts. The high proportion of lexical gaps should not surprise us, given the fixed, formulaic nature of these acts. The *automaticity* involved in their performance is extremely high, and therefore their cognitive salience can be expected to be low. It is only when the routine responses are not made with the expected accuracy and speed (as in the speech of a foreigner) that they come to mind.

The presence of a verb, TO THANK, to describe responses to acts of congratulating, condoling, and welcoming is due to their formal and semantic similarity to independent (i.e. nonresponse) expressions of gratitude.

Responses to greetings are no less automatic than replies to apologies and thanks. But they can often be described by means of TO GREET because of the frequent reciprocity of acts of greeting.

394 In the previous section it was suggested that the normal, expected, harmonious responses to speech acts are cognitively less salient and are, therefore, likely to escape lexicalization. This hypothesis may explain the many gaps in the area covered by this section. The routine responses under investigation, lacking the positive-negative option, are so compelling that they form part of a strong expectation pattern of harmonious interaction. One could almost say

THE SEMANTICS OF FORGOTTEN ROUTINES 203

DUTCH	SEMANTIC DIMENSION	ENGLISH
(be)danken	(A1) – (C1) (A1) – (C2) (A1) – (C3)	to thank
φ	(A2) – (C4)	φ
(be)groeten	(A3) – (C4) (A4) – (C4)	to greet
φ	(A5) – (C5) (A6) – (C5) (A7) – (C5) (A8) – (C5) (A9) – (C5)	φ
φ	(A10) – (C6) (A11) – (C6) (A12) – (C6) (A13) – (C6) (A14) – (C6)	φ

SDC Table 3

that acts of apologizing, thanking, and the like, are not complete unless an appropriate routine response follows. The responses are part of the act and hence, as separate speech acts, they tend to escape our attention.

6.4 CONCLUSIONS

395 This chapter is certainly not a complete overview of the gaps in the lexical frame associated with linguistic action. Its purpose was to draw attention to certain types of acts that, because of their routine character, are easily overlooked and that therefore require special study.

The complete parallelism between Dutch and English, which will be hard to find in other areas of linguistic action, shows that language, in particular the lexicon, does not even make forgetting into a totally whimsical activity. Such adherence to a kind of crosslinguistic systematicity lends our hypothetical explanations some strength. This is not to say that there is any universality to the findings of the extremely limited investigation presented. However, the apparent strength of the lexicalization principles involved, reflected in the complete parallelism between English and Dutch, makes the search for universals in this domain of the linguistic action verbials particularly tempting and compelling.

396 All the hypothetical explanations presented for the phenomena under investigation boil down to one basic principle: the gaps in the lexical frame associated with linguistic action are due to the low cognitive salience of the corresponding acts. This principle, if it is correct, proves that there is a relationship between the lexicon, or the lexicalization process, and habits of conceptualization. Hence, this chapter confirms our belief that studying and comparing the verbials available in different natural languages for the description of linguistic action may yield insights into people's language-specific and culture-specific conceptualization and experience of linguistic behavior and, therefore, into the nature of linguistic behavior itself.

397 In her somewhat misguided criticism of Searle's speech-act classification (based on the view that the taxonomy as such can be refuted by showing that linguistic action is conceptualized differently in some different culture), Rosaldo (1980) points out the important fact that for the Ilongot the so-called expressives 'have much more to do with social roles and bonds than with the inner feelings they apparently signify' (p. 30). In other words, they are there to satisfy social needs and to establish and maintain social relationships. With the classical speech-act definition of expressives in mind, one might conclude that what is happening in Ilongot culture is diametrically opposed to Western verbal behavior. Yet, a first glance at the types of conversational routines that are 'forgotten' in the lexicalization process in English and in Dutch, has led us to the hypothesis that the distinguishing trait of expressives is not the expression of a psychological state as such but the expression of a psychological state important to the hearer (see paragraph 374). Thus, social roles and bonds come into play and the differences between Ilongot and Western cultures suddenly become less pronounced— at least in the area of expressive verbal behavior. Whether comparable similarities underlie apparent contrasts in other areas should, once more, be subjected to further empirical-conceptual research.

PART III

THEORETICAL AND METHODOLOGICAL EPILOGUE

CHAPTER 7

PROVISIONAL CONCLUSIONS

7.0 INTRODUCTION

398 Not a single portion of this essay can be regarded as conclusive. The comparative lexical approach advocated in the first chapter is a line of research that will require large-scale investigations before it can be expected to lead to major new insights. Even the methodology proposed in the second chapter is merely tentative and will have to be refined. The previous four chapters are no more than a bunch of pilot studies. But I believe that they already show the feasibility and fruitfulness of a comparative lexical approach to linguistic action to be beyond doubt. Its comparative aspect has remained extremely limited: there was a comparison between only two closely related languages. Yet we have reached a number of more or less important insights. Silence was shown to be an integral part of linguistic interaction; we have learned about the nature of truth and the ways in which it can be deviated from; the verbials of directing have helped us to understand the directive function of language better; and even the absence of lexical items to describe certain types of routine utterances has turned out to be revealing in several ways (for instance, by laying bare the reasons why the members of the traditional class of expressive speech acts can be regarded as different from representative expressions of emotions or attitudes).

To make another comparison, the approach is like a psychoanalysis of language: put language on a couch and let it talk to get its unconscious out into the open. A belief in the sensibleness of the same kind of approach underlies the work on metaphor by Lakoff and Johnson (1980): metaphorical lexicalizations are taken as evidence for conceptualization habits.

399 Most detailed linguistic investigations display some tediousness. Therefore, I hope the somewhat monotonous nature of this essay (and especially of the four exploratory exercises) can be forgiven. My sincerest wish is that, however closely form and content may be related, the stylistic impediments have not made the reader stumble over the meaning I have been trying to convey.

In this brief chapter on provisional conclusions I want (a) to present a sketchy overview of the types of tentative results, with illustrations from Chapters 3 through 6, (b) to demonstrate how the semantic dimension approach can be applied in comparisons between 'equivalent' words in different languages, and (c) to indicate some more pitfalls of comparison.

7.1 TYPES OF TENTATIVE RESULTS

400 The major result of lexical, empirical-conceptual research in the domain of linguistic action so far is the gratifying conclusion that it was not a complete illusion to believe that a one-sided theoretical approach involved the dangers of inventing distinctions that may be theoretically valid but that are not necessarily 'out there' (see paragraph **401**), of neglecting aspects of linguistic behavior that *are* there, and very prominently so (see paragraph **402**), and of proposing theoretical constructs that may or may not reflect reality, but usually not in the symmetrical fashion proposed (see paragraphs **403** and **404**). Moreover, it has become clear that linguistic action verbials reflect cultural attitudes (see paragraph **405**) and are linked with matters of cognitive salience (see paragraph **406**).

401 First, on the most trivial level, it follows from lexical research that the categories of speech acts that are usually distinguished are not reflected, in any straightforward way, as conceptually distinct in the lexicalization of linguistic action in natural languages. The absence of diffuseness would not be defended even by the most ardent of theorists, but the extent to which nondiffuseness is absent becomes clear only when one takes a close look at sets of lexical items.

More interestingly, lexical research can offer evidence showing defects in common definitions of classes while suggesting improved versions at the same time. Consider, for example, the class of expressives the point of which is, according to Searle's (1976) definition, that a certain psychological state is expressed (which must be different from the belief expressed in assertives, the wish expressed in directives, and the intention expressed in commissives). But the expression of a psychological state in itself does not set expressives apart from other types of speech acts. Compare:

(1) I am sorry that you could not make it last night
(2) I am sorry for having been so rude to you
(3) I am sorry that your father died

Also compare the way in which these acts can be described:

(1') S said/stated/claimed that he/she was sorry that . . .

(2′) S apologized for having been rude
(3′) S commiserated/condoled H's father's death

Though all three are expressions of regret, act (1) is normally described as an assertive (there isn't even a way in English to describe (1) *as an expression of emotion* except with 'S expressed his/her regret that ...') whereas for (2) and (3) we have explicitly expressive descriptive verbs available. Studying the lexicalization versus nonlexicalization pattern of these and many other examples has led us to the hypothesis that what sets the traditional class of expressives apart from other speech acts is the extent to which the emotion or attitude expressed is relevant to the hearer. (See Chapter 6, paragraphs 367 to 378).

402 Second, linguistic action verbials draw our attention to aspects of verbal behavior that are usually neglected or even completely ignored in the linguistic and philosophical literature. The most striking example is probably the area of linguistic silence, the absence of speech. Natural language lexicalizations transform this seemingly marginal aspect of linguistic behavior into an essential one. There are hundreds of words and expressions to describe being silent. Silence is not just the absence of sounds. It is gradable and characterized by a certain intensity. Compare TO BE SILENT with TO BE SILENT AS THE GRAVE, or TO BE MUM AS AN OYSTER, NOT BREATHE A WORD, or TO FORSWEAR SPEAKING. Silence can have a propositional content so to speak: one can BE SILENT ABOUT SOMETHING, KEEP SOMETHING SECRET, KEEP SOMETHING IN PETTO, and SMOTHER SOMETHING. Linguistic silence occurs in a certain context: one can FALL SILENT or KNOCK IT OFF, or one can simply NOT GET A WORD IN EDGEWAYS. Silence has its causes and its motives, and it can be TOMBLIKE, SOLEMN, or even PREGNANT. It is, therefore, high time to study it more seriously than has been done so far (as in the few ethnomethodological studies of pauses in conversation). (See Chapter 3.)

403 Third, lexicalization patterns can show theoretical constructs concerning aspects of linguistic behavior to be wrong or misleading. For instance, in the area of deviations from the truth, there are not just simple acts of lying but also deviations along a quantity scale of truth (with at one end TO EXAGGERATE and at the other TO UNDERSTATE) and a quality scale of truth (with at one end TO SLANDER and at the other TO WHITEWASH). Theoretically, these four poles should be of equal importance. However, in the lexicalization of linguistic behavior, the understatement pole is underrepresented in comparison with the others; in fact, in some languages, such as Dutch, there is even a clear gap (which can only be filled with a pun on OVERDRIJVEN, the equivalent of TO EXAGGERATE, viz. the nonexistent word 'ONDERDRIJVEN'). This asymmetry in what looks like a symmetrical structure requires further investigation. (See Chapter 4, paragraphs 239 to 252.)

404 A second example is taken from the area of the directives. Often, it is claimed that WARNING is negative ADVISING. Upon closer examination, however, this symmetrical relationship on the directionality scale of directives (with attempts to direct someone toward doing something at one end and attempts to make the hearer not do something at the other) distorts reality. A first surprising fact about this scale is that the two extremes are not occupied by TO ORDER and TO PROHIBIT. These two are not exclusively positive and exclusively negative, respectively, because it is possible to order someone not to do something and to prohibit someone not to do something (which is equivalent to obliging him/her to do something). An exclusively positive directive would be TO INVITE (in its original sense of asking someone to come over to your house) and related acts; an exclusively negative one is TO VETO. TO ORDER and TO PROHIBIT are slightly closer to the center of the scale and could be called intrinsically positive and negative, respectively; TO ORDER is intrinsically positive because it is positive if combined with a complement with a positive propositional content and negative if combined with a negative propositional content; TO PROHIBIT is intrinsically negative because it is negative when combined with a positive propositional content and positive when combined with a negative propositional content. To come back to the acts of WARNING and ADVISING, whereas TO ADVISE describes an intrinsically positive directive (in the same sense as TO ORDER does), TO WARN is not in the same sense an intrinsically negative directive; the negativity of WARNING is not as strong as that of PROHIBITING, though it would probably be true to say that TO WARN may be more frequently used to describe negative directive acts than to describe positive directive acts. Thus, TO WARN is not just the negative counterpart of TO ADVISE; it has to be placed considerably further toward the center of the scale. (See Chapter 5, paragraphs **331** to **346**.)

405 That linguistic action verbials reflect *cultural attitudes* is hardly surprising. One illustration should be sufficient. Consider the following verbials: TO BACKBITE, TO BAD-MOUTH, TO BESMEAR, TO BESMIRCH, TO BLACKEN, TO CALUMNIATE, TO CAST A SLUR ON, TO CAST ASPERSIONS ON, TO DEFAME, TO DEFILE, TO DENIGRATE, TO DISPARAGE, TO DRAG THROUGH THE MUD, TO GIVE A BAD NAME, TO LIBEL, TO MALIGN, TO RUN DOWN, TO SLUR, TO SMIRCH, TO SPEAK ILL OF, TO SPEAK SLIGHTINGLY OF, TO SULLY, TO TARNISH, TO TRADUCE, TO VILIFY. All of these are associated, to varying degrees, with untruthfulness. In fact, apart from TO CRITICIZE and a few others, there are hardly any linguistic action verbials that contain 'to say something bad or unfavorable about someone or something' as part of their meaning, and that are not, in all or most of their uses, associated with untruthfulness. This is in sharp contrast with the large number of verbials meaning 'to say something good or favorable about someone or something' without being associated with a lack of truthfulness (such as TO PRAISE, TO LAUD, TO GLORIFY, etc.). Thus the lexicon reflects a usually unconscious value judgment that is entirely in keeping with Freud's observation that 'society makes what is disagreeable into what is untrue'. (See Chapter 4, especially paragraph **248**.)

406 There is also a clear link between the *cognitive salience* of certain forms of language behavior and the way in which they are lexicalized (or not lexicalized). For instance, every language contains a large number of routine expressions. For some of those, we have descriptive linguistic action verbials available, such as TO APOLOGIZE, TO COMMISERATE, TO CONGRATULATE, TO GREET, TO THANK, etc. But English does not offer words to describe others. Just think of expressions such as 'Never mind' (in response to an apology) or 'You're welcome' (in response to an act of thanking). Such forgotten routines are consistently less important (at least in the limited comparative data we have made available) in the lexicalization of linguistic action; an expression such as 'You're welcome', for instance, does not play a separate role; it is part of the thanking ritual as a whole. Thus, the lexicon does not even make forgetting into a totally whimsical activity. (See Chapter 6.)

7.2 APPLYING THE SEMANTIC DIMENSION APPROACH

407 In the methodological introduction of Chapter 2 (see especially paragraph **136**), our interest was emphasized in the discovery and analysis of the *semantic dimensions* along which linguistic action verbials can be compared—rather than in classifications of verbials. One of the advantages was said to be the possibility of presenting graphic representations of semantic patterns. Sufficient illustrations have been provided in the SDC Tables of Chapters 3 through 6. Those SDC Tables, however, always compared sets of verbials in the two languages under investigation along one single dimension of variation. The semantic dimension approach can also be applied to contrast and represent the meanings of a couple of 'equivalent' verbs along all or most of the dimensions of variation with respect to which their meaning is not neutral.

408 Let us illustrate this point with a comparison between the English directive TO SUMMON and three of its Dutch 'equivalents', DAGVAARDEN, ONTBIEDEN, and OPROEPEN. If we compare these four verbs along the dimensions of directivity, directionality, authority, and social setting (as defined and discussed in Chapter 5), which seem to be the main parameters in terms of which the differences between them can be described, the resulting picture is SDC Table 1.

409 The degrees of directivity along SD1 are based on purely intuitive judgments. Of more interest are the remaining three dimensions. It is clear that TO SUMMON in the sense of 'calling together', 'requesting to appear', or 'ordering to appear in court' describes an exclusively positive directive. And so do DAGVAARDEN, ONTBIEDEN, and OPROEPEN.

However, TO SUMMON can also mean 'to order to do something'. This second meaning is probably derivative of the first, and in this sense TO SUMMON is no longer exclusively positive, but only intrinsically positive. A similar se-

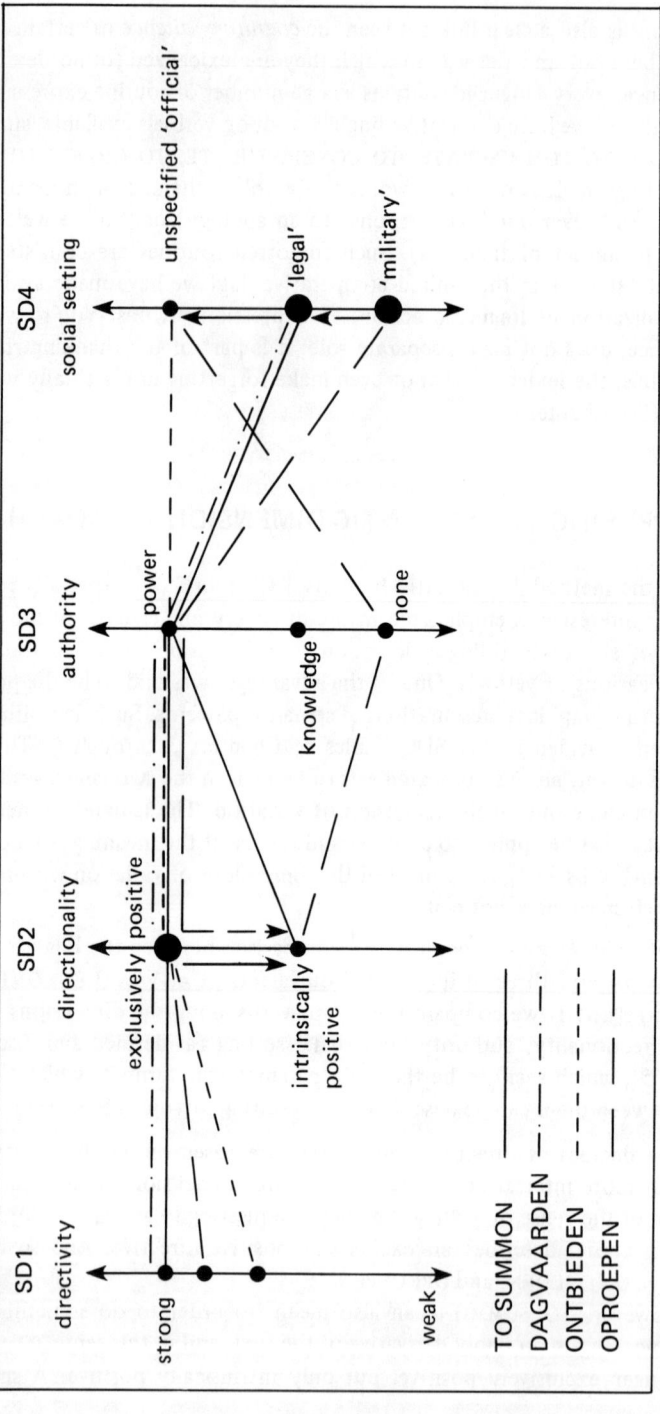

SDC Table 1

mantic extension is not possible for the Dutch verbs DAGVAARDEN and ONTBIEDEN, but it is for OPROEPEN.

All four verbs imply some sort of 'power' authority on the part of the speaker. But OPROEPEN, in its intrinsically positive sense, diverges from TO SUMMON, in the same sense, by not implying authority at all.

On the social-setting dimension, TO SUMMON is strongly associated with a legal setting, but it can be easily extended to other kinds of official settings. DAGVAARDEN is completely restricted to a legal context. ONTBIEDEN focuses on an unspecified official setting. And OPROEPEN is strongly associated with a military context, though easily extendable to the legal world, in its exclusively positive sense, but focuses on an unspecified official setting in its intrinsically positive sense.

410 This somewhat complicated mapping of equivalences and divergences between words that can be used as translations for each other would be hard to describe, and even harder to visualize, without explicit reference to semantic dimensions. Thus it seems that this approach should be pursued further. Much further, in fact. Also, the interdependence between different dimensions relevant to the analysis of meaning within (subfields of) the domain of linguistic action should be fully explored. Degree of directivity, for instance, is not independent of the authority involved, which, in turn, is largely determined by the social setting within which a directive linguistic act is performed. It would seem, then, that we have barely begun to scratch the surface of linguistic action, its conceptualization, and lexicalization.

7.3 MORE PITFALLS OF COMPARISON

411 In Chapter 2 (paragraph **140**) a problem was pointed out that almost necessarily distorts any comparison between (American) English and (Flemish) Dutch lexical items, because of the history and structure of the societies in which the two languages are spoken. In order to ward off some criticisms likely to be evoked by parts of the exploratory exercises, I want to bring to notice a related problem haunting attempts at contrastive lexical analysis.

412 The problem is this. Since the actual lexicalization of verbal behavior seems to lead to different conceptualizations, looking at linguistic action verbials in direct contrast with equivalents in other languages may be not only revealing but also—if one is not careful enough—misleading. The point was brought home to me when, during a discussion of verbials of directing in front of an American audience, the remark was made that including the verb TO DRAFT (as in paragraphs **318**, **325**, and **335**) was complete misplacement since it did not describe a *linguistic* activity at all. At first, I did not understand what was happening. After all, I would never have hesitated to translate sentence (1) as (2).

(1) *X* was drafted (into the army)
(2) *X* werd opgeroepen (voor militaire dienst)

In sentence (2) the verb OPROEPEN is used, which is also an equivalent of TO SUMMON (as discussed in paragraphs **408** and **409**) and hence a clear case of a linguistic action verb. How could this conflict be resolved?

413 After a while, it dawned upon me that the solution had to be found in institutional differences. If we have a look at the process of getting people into the army to do military service, we discern essentially two stages. The first stage is the *selection* procedure. The second is the resulting *notification*, which counts as an order to join up. Only the second stage of the overall process is linguistic in nature. Though TO DRAFT and OPROEPEN refer to the same general process or event (in such a way that they can be used as translations of each other), they concentrate on different aspects. TO DRAFT focuses on the selection procedure, which in an American context is the most relevant stage in the process since the outcome is not at all predictable; once the result of the lottery is known, the notification follows automatically. In a Belgian context, however, the selection process is largely irrelevant since the outcome is, in most if not all cases, known in advance; there is no lottery, only rules; therefore, the most relevant or salient aspect of the event is the notification, on which the verb OPROEPEN concentrates.

414 This frame analysis of the institutional facts involved shows that what had actually happened was that my knowledge of (Flemish) Dutch had interfered with my judgments about the semantics of an English verb. If it is true that TO DRAFT refers to the whole process, including the notification stage, then the resulting claims were not necessarily wrong. But a simple listing of the verb among other verbials of directing was at least misleading. Such problems will inevitably keep cropping up in comparative lexical research. All one can do is to make them explicit whenever possible. Whether the degree of difficulty will increase when comparing less closely related languages, or whether it will decrease (as a result of the remoteness, which eliminates blurring similarities) is a matter for experience to teach us.

7.4 CONCLUSION

415 Since many natural languages contain hundreds and some natural languages contain thousands of linguistic action verbials, the comparative lexical approach to linguistic action I advocate is intrinsically endless. In trying to outline a manageable topic of investigation, one can try to cover the whole field (or sizable subsections of it) for a very small number of languages. This approach was taken in this essay, which, as a result, consists mainly of a set of exploratory 'exercises' that raise more questions than they answer. An alternative—and for me the logical next step—is to extend the research in the sense of what Bolinger would call 'painting with a wider brush on a broader canvas'. How this can be done will be tentatively sketched in the last chapter of this book.

CHAPTER **8**

PERSPECTIVES: BASIC LINGUISTIC ACTION VERBS

8.0 INTRODUCTION

416 It seems clear that in order to maximize the comparative aspect of the empirical-conceptual approach, the topic of investigation needs to be restricted. In a programmatic statement (see section 8.1) I will suggest that wide-ranging comparisons are possible on the level of some sort of 'basic' linguistic action verbs. In sections 8.2 and 8.4 this level is operationally—albeit tentatively—defined. The resulting set of English basic linguistic action verbs is briefly discussed (in 8.5). The role of crosslinguistic evidence is touched upon (in 8.6), and some speculations are put forward as to where this next logical step may lead us. The task of constructing a preliminary coherent theory of pragmatics is again shown to be inevitable in a methodological afterthought (section 8.7).[10]

8.1 PROGRAMMATIC STATEMENT

417 An extension of the research in the sense of 'painting with a wider brush on a broader canvas' is possible if we restrict our object of investigation to a single level of the hierarchic structure that also characterizes the linguistic action part of the lexicon, namely the level of what could be called *basic linguistic action verbs* (which, as will be explained later, is vaguely comparable to the level of the 'basic color terms' in color terminologies or to the level of the 'life-form terms' in biological folk taxonomies).

---

[10] For a less tentative formulation of the operational criteria needed to identify the sets of basic linguistic action verbs in different languages, see Verschueren (1984).

216 PERSPECTIVES

418 By drastically reducing the object of investigation in this way, a very extensive investigation in two stages becomes possible:
1. A comparative investigation of the *sets of basic linguistic action verbs* available in a large number of languages, from which, it is hoped, 'synchronic implicational universals' can be deduced with respect to the development of the lexicalization of linguistic action (similar to those found for color terms in Berlin and Kay's *Basic Color Terms* and for plant and animal names in Brown's 'Folk botanical life forms' and 'Folk zoological life forms'[11].
2. A detailed comparison of the *semantic dimensions* needed for the description of the basic linguistic action verbs in a small number of languages (preferably representatives of the different stages of development which may, by then, have been discovered as synchronic implicational universals), from which *universal principles of the lexicalization of linguistic action* might be deduced. This would provide us with a key to the understanding of how linguistic action is conceptualized by speakers of natural languages all over the world.

419 The results of this wide-ranging investigation could later be employed as a universal starting-point for further detailed examinations of individual lan-

---

[11] The 'synchronic implicational universals' referred to are the following:

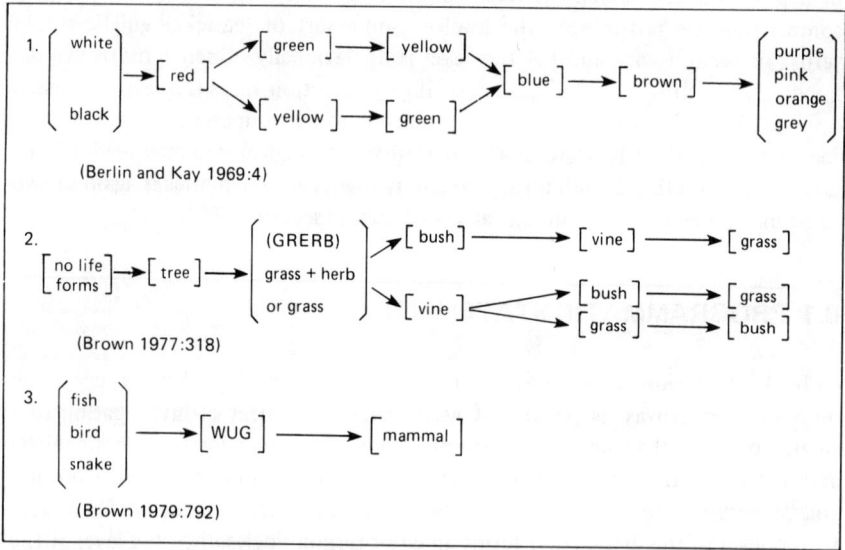

The universals are 'synchronic' because they are based on data from a wide range of languages as they are now. Yet they suggest universal patterns of development because they are 'implicational' in the sense that the occurrence of an item in languages implies the occurrence of another item or items but not vice versa; e.g., a language that has a term for 'grass' will also have one for 'tree'.

guages (with respect to their linguistic action verbials in general) and for small-scale comparisons.

The type of research proposed requires a clear notion of what basic linguistic action verbs are. The remainder of this chapter is largely devoted to a tentative operational definition of the concept. A disadvantage of operational criteria is that often they have to be chosen on the basis of their applicability rather than their inherent value. The resulting balance between intellectual integrity and practical workability is rarely satisfying. Yet, for lack of a magical formula, this approach is inevitable.

8.2 PRIMARY OPERATIONAL CRITERIA

8.2.0 Introduction

420 When trying to define 'basic linguistic action verbs', there are several sources of inspiration (one anthropological, another linguistic, and still another psychological) to draw on. I shall sketch them cursorily by way of introduction as there will be many occasions to refer to them in the ensuing discussion.

421 First, American linguistic anthropologists have been studying natural language taxonomies (which they call 'folk taxonomies' and which are viewed as reflecting 'folk theories') for many years. Biological folk taxonomies generally consist of at least five hierarchical levels (see Berlin, Breedlove, & Raven 1973): (a) a 'unique beginner' (e.g. plant or animal), which is rarely named; (b) a small number of 'life-form' terms (e.g. tree, grass, bird, snake, fish, mammal); (c) a large number of 'generic' terms (e.g. oak, pine, perch, robin, cat, dog); (d) a lower number of 'specific' terms (e.g. white fir, post oak); and (e) an even lower number of 'varietal' terms (e.g. baby lima bean, butter lima bean). Since we are looking for a taxonomical level that would make our subject matter manageable across a wide range of languages, our basic linguistic action verbs will have to be situated on a level similar to that of the life-form terms. In addition to botanical and zoological nomenclature, the favorites for lexical research by anthropologists have been the areas of kinship and color. Some color-term investigations may be of substantial help in determining our criteria for basic linguistic action verbs. Consider Berlin and Kay's (1969:6) four main criteria for inclusion of a word in the class of basic color terms:
1. 'It is *monolexemic*; that is, its meaning is not predictable from the meaning of its parts'. (See also Conklin 1962:43)
2. 'Its signification is not included in that of any other color term'.
3. 'Its application must not be restricted to a narrow class of objects'.
4. 'It must be psychologically salient for informants. Indices of psychological salience include, among others, (1) a tendency to occur at the beginning of elicited lists of color terms, (2) stability of reference across informants

and across occasions of use, and (3) occurrence in the idiolects of all informants'.

All of these are referred to when I propose similar criteria for inclusion of a word in the set of basic linguistic action verbs.

422 A second source of inspiration is Dixon's (1971) article on the distinction between the everyday variety and the mother-in-law variety (only spoken in the presence of certain taboo relatives) of Dyirbal, and its relevance for methods of semantic description. He observes that the everyday variety has a much more extensive vocabulary than the mother-in-law variety, which seems to be restricted to a kind of core vocabulary containing, as far as verbs are concerned, only 'nuclear verbs', i.e. verbs that can only be decomposed in terms of semantic features and that, unlike the nonnuclear ones, cannot be defined in terms of other verbs. Again, the relevance of these notions to our operational definition of basic linguistic action verbs is clarified later. (See also paragraph **109**).

423 Third, psychological studies of human categorization (e.g. Rosch 1977a) have shown that not all levels of the hierarchical structure of the lexicon are psychologically equally salient; in other words, there is a cognitively basic level (see also paragraphs **107** to **110**). This cognitive psychological notion of a basic-level term, though clearly serving as a source of inspiration, will be shown to be of minimal help— and even somewhat confusing—in our search for basic linguistic action verbs (which is not to dispute its relevance for other purposes, even within the empirical-conceptual approach to linguistic action). (See paragraph **438**.)

8.2.1 The Primary Structural Criterion

424 Linguistic action verbials have been defined as the verbs and verblike expressions used in natural language to describe (aspects of) linguistic action. It is clear that verblike expressions such as TO PUT ONE'S VETO UPON or TO SHOOT QUESTIONS AT are less basic than TO FORBID or TO QUESTION. Since it seems to be generally true that verbs are more basic than the verblike expressions, we should only talk, as we have done so far, about basic linguistic action *verbs*, not about basic linguistic action verbials. Such considerations lead us to the following criterion for inclusion of a lexical item into the class of basic linguistic action verbs:

    A. It is monolexemic.

425 As it stands, the criterion is identical to Berlin and Kay's first criterion for inclusion of a word into the class of basic color terms. However, they defined a word's being monolexemic in semantic terms: 'its meaning is not predictable from the meaning of its parts' (p. 6). Such a semantic definition would allow idiomatic verblike expressions into the set of basic linguistic action verb(ial)s: though the meanings of fixed expressions such as TO ADDRESS A WARNING TO or TO PRONOUNCE $X + Y$ HUSBAND AND WIFE are predictable from the meanings of their parts, this is not the case for idioms such as TO POP THE QUESTION (i.e. to ask someone to marry you) or TO DISH THE DIRT (i.e. to gossip), which are not really transparent. As a matter of fact, if we were obliged to place these expressions on a scale of 'basicness', most speakers of English would probably be inclined to put the transparent fixed expressions closer to the 'basic' pole than the idiomatic, nontransparent ones. Therefore, criterion A has to be interpreted in purely structural terms: a word is monolexemic if it consists of only one word with a lexical meaning; words with a grammatical meaning (or words that have no life of their own), such as particles, prepositions, reflexive pronouns, and the like, may be added.

8.2.2 The Primary Semantic Criterion

426 Our primary semantic criterion is analogous to Berlin and Kay's second criterion for inclusion of a word into the class of basic color terms, and it is related to Dixon's notion of 'nuclear verbs'. Its basic form is the following:

B. It cannot be defined in terms of a different linguistic action verb.

However, B has to be modified in several ways.

427 First, if the criterion were to be applied literally, there would be, for English, only two or three basic linguistic action verbs, TO SAY (SOMETHING), TO SPEAK, and maybe (depending on considerations to be made explicit later) TO TALK. Most, if not all, linguistic action verb(ial)s can be given a definition that includes the words TO SAY or TO SPEAK, which are linguistic action verbs themselves. The criterion cannot be kept completely analogous to the one for basic color terms since there are no color terms that can be applied to any color whatsoever, whereas there are linguistic action verbs that can be used to describe any type of linguistic action. Nor can basic linguistic action verbs, without qualification, be regarded as nuclear verbs; again, only TO SAY and TO SPEAK could be regarded as nuclear in the wider domain of action in general (which is united by the master notion TO DO SOMETHING); what we are looking for is a similar 'nuclear' level inside the area of linguistic action. These remarks lead us to a provisional rephrasing of criterion B in the following sense: a basic linguistic action verb cannot be defined in terms of a different linguistic action verb, except for the general ones TO SAY (SOMETHING) and TO SPEAK.

If TO SAY (SOMETHING) and TO SPEAK, as general linguistic action verbs, are excluded from the set of verbs the applicability of which in a definition of a different verb rules out the latter's being 'basic', then this must also be the case for TO EXPRESS, which has to be situated on an even higher level of generality (because it requires the further specification 'in words' or 'linguistically' to be fully precise in any definition of any type of linguistic activity).

428 However, a further modification is needed. Studies of folk taxonomies have shown that a word can recur on different levels of a single taxonomy. Thus the word PLANT functions as the 'unique beginner' in folk botanical classifications; but at the same time it can mean 'small plant' in contrast to the 'life-form' term TREE. Similarly, TO SAY (SOMETHING) and TO SPEAK (which are at the 'unique beginner' level for linguistic action, though they are not unique) also have more specialized meanings on a lower level of the hierarchy: at the 'unique beginner' level they both mean 'to use language'; but at a lower level TO SPEAK also means 'to utter linguistic sounds' (and thus TO WHISPER can be defined as 'to speak in a low voice or, technically speaking, without voice') and TO SAY (SOMETHING) also means 'to make a statement' (and thus TO ADMIT can be defined as 'to say that X is right in believing that P is true'). Therefore, criterion B can be reformulated as follows: a basic linguistic action verb cannot be defined in terms of a different linguistic action verb, except for TO SAY (SOMETHING) and TO SPEAK in their general sense of 'using language'. If TO SAY and TO SPEAK have a more specialized sense in the definition, the defined verb will not be regarded as a basic linguistic action verb; hence, TO WHISPER and TO ADMIT are excluded.

429 Third, the 'definition' referred to in criterion B has to be a definition *in natural language*, not to be confused with some linguistic or philosophical metalanguage. Consider the relationship between TO ASK and TO REQUEST in English. It is not unusual for linguists or philosophers to define a question or the activity of asking as 'a request for information'. From a theoretical point of view this is probably valid. But natural language—or at least English—reverses this relationship: TO REQUEST will be more naturally defined as 'to ask someone to do something', so that 'to request information' can be described as 'to ask someone to give information'; the difference in forcefulness that would have to be referred to in a complete definition of TO ASK and TO REQUEST does not change the definitional relationship. The conclusion is that TO ASK is more basic than TO REQUEST; since requesting can be defined in natural language as a type of asking, TO REQUEST cannot be regarded as a basic linguistic action verb; on the other hand, TO ASK is a basic linguistic action verb unless a further definition in terms of a linguistic action verb can be provided. As a result, a fuller formulation of criterion B would be: in natural language (as opposed to a philosophical or linguistic metalanguage), a basic linguistic action verb cannot be defined in terms of a different linguistic action verb, except for TO SAY (SOMETHING) and TO SPEAK (and their equivalents in other languages) in their general sense of 'using language'.

430 Fourth, the 'definition' referred to in criterion B does not have to be semantically exhaustive. As with Dixon's nonnuclear verbs, which may be equally distant from the focus of, and hence definable by, more than one nuclear verb, there may be nonbasic linguistic action verbs for which different definitions are equally plausible, either because the verb to be defined is polysemous (such as TO ADMIT, which means 'to say, in a statement sense, that someone is right' or 'to allow someone to enter') or because its signification is a mixture between two or more acts on a higher level of the hierarchy (such as TO NOTIFY, which may be a mixture between informing and warning). Even when only one definition is plausible, it does not have to be semantically exhaustive. Consider TO PROMISE, which can be described as 'to say (in its statement sense) that one will do something'; promising is certainly more than *just* stating that one will do something; yet, the definition can be expected to be plausible (perhaps with an additional reference to the obligation that the speaker takes upon him/herself) for most speakers of English, and therefore we may have to exclude TO PROMISE from the set of basic linguistic action verbs.

431 Fifth, a *reversed definition* does not count. For instance, though 'to say that one is grateful' is definitely TO THANK, it does not count as a good enough definition of TO THANK since the verb does not necessarily mean 'to say (in its statement sense) that one is grateful'; there are quite a few other (mostly formulaic) ways of thanking; note that the definition is acceptable in the general sense of TO SAY as 'to express linguistically' (which was rejected as irrelevant for the purposes of criterion B).

Related to this is the problem of *indirectness* (see paragraphs 7 and 21 to 23). Since an order can be given indirectly by means of a question or a statement, some *acts* of ordering can be described in terms of 'asking' or 'saying that'. Or, conversely, 'to say that the door is open' may be TO ORDER (to close the door). This does not mean, however, that the *verb* TO ORDER can be defined in terms of TO ASK or TO SAY.

432 Sixth, there is another type of definition against which the reader has to be warned. Consider TO THREATEN, of which it can be said that 'it is just like promising, except that the hearer would not like the speaker to do what he/she says he/she will do'. This type of definition implies that threatening *is not* really promising; hence, it is not possible to regard threatening as a subtype of promising (the two are simply contrasting subtypes of commissives, of which one is 'marked', the other 'unmarked'); in other words, TO PROMISE cannot be said to be more basic than TO THREATEN on the basis of their definitional relationship (though it might be for other reasons such as psychological salience and the resulting markedness relationships).

433 The following reformulation of criterion B incorporates most of the foregoing comments:

> B'. In natural language (as opposed to a philosophical or linguistic metalanguage), it is not possible to give a nonreversed definition (whether semantically exhaustive or not) of a basic linguistic action verb in terms of a different linguistic action verb, except for TO SAY (SOMETHING) and TO SPEAK (or their equivalents) in the general sense of 'using language' or 'expressing linguistically'.

A more positive, though somewhat less explicit, way to put this criterion might be the following: basic linguistic action verbs describe (aspects of) linguistic action and exclude each other in paraphrases.

In spite of all the built-in safeguards, it is still necessary to present some additional warnings, which will give rise to supplementary criteria. It should be clear that criterion B makes the verbs satisfying it *basic* because speakers of the language in question do not (habitually) regard the acts they refer to as subtypes of other types of linguistic action.

8.3 SOME WORDS OF CAUTION

8.3.1 The Whims of Folk Taxonomies

434 Theoretical attempts to discover 'basic speech acts' have usually been searches for speech-act types to which all others can be logically reduced (see, e.g., Van der Auwera 1980a). Such a neat few-to-many relationship is not to be found in the lexicalization of linguistic action. Most folk taxonomies are full of gaps. Folk zoological classifications, for instance, may have the generic terms for cat, dog, and horse, while lacking the corresponding life-form term 'mammal'. Similarly, there may be nonbasic linguistic action verbs for which there is no corresponding basic one. This is not a problem as long as there is another nonbasic linguistic action verb in terms of which the first one can be defined. But if there is not, which will always be the case for the one(s) on the level next to the 'basic' level in the hierarchy, then we are at a loss for a criterion to decide whether a verb is a basic linguistic action verb or not. (Note that the previous remarks imply that the definitions referred to in criterion B do not have to be definitions in terms of basic linguistic action verbs; any other linguistic action verb, on a level higher than the one to be defined, will do.) Since basic linguistic actions, as lexicalized in natural languages, are not necessarily those of which all others are subtypes, additional criteria are needed for the class of basic linguistic action verbs. Examples will be given while presenting these supplementary criteria. But first another problem needs to be pointed out.

8.3.2 The Problem of Synonymy

435 A second problem remains. Often we encounter linguistic action verbs that are synonymous, or nearly so. Consider TO TELL and TO REVEAL (in one of its senses), TO ORDER and TO COMMAND, TO REQUEST and TO DEMAND, TO ALLOW and TO PERMIT, TO PROHIBIT and TO FORBID, TO SPEAK and TO TALK. How do we decide which member of such pairs of synonyms is more basic than the other? Often, it may not be possible to take a decision, but at least for some cases criteria can be adduced.

8.4 SECONDARY OPERATIONAL CRITERIA

8.4.0 Introduction

436 Though I am inclined to say that *only* verbs satisfying criteria A and B can be regarded as basic linguistic action verbs, the primary operational criteria presented in the previous section are by no means fully automatic procedures for *accepting* a verb as a basic linguistic action verb. The following secondary operational criteria reflect additional important considerations that, on occasion, may overrule our central semantic criterion in order to cope with the whims of folk taxonomies and the problem of synonymy.

    C. It must be psychologically salient for informants.
    D. It should exclusively or primarily name linguistic actions.
    E. Its application must not be restricted to a narrow class of arguments.
    F. It should be the most neutral or unmarked choice available.

All of these require some extra clarification. Notice that the four criteria are not unrelated to each other. In fact, criteria D, E, and F all specify properties that influence, if not determine, the cognitive salience referred to in C.

8.4.1 Psychological Salience

437 The psychological salience criterion (i.e. criterion C) is identical to Berlin and Kay's fourth criterion for inclusion of a word in the class of basic color terms. The indices of salience that I have in mind are also similar. Put informally, the main question is, Does the verb in question figure prominently in the native speaker's (i.e. the informant's) conceptualization (as reflected in his/her lexicalization) of linguistic action? On the basis of this criterion, verbs such as TO BLESS, TO CHALLENGE, TO COUNT, TO CURSE, TO DAMN, TO QUOTE, TO SCOLD, TO SWEAR, etc., would probably have to be rejected if they were to pass our basic semantic test.

438 Though a lack of psychological salience may be adduced to exclude verbs that satisfy criterion B, it would probably be wrong to use its presence as an argument for including some that do not satisfy it, since this would distort the conceptual structure of the taxonomy. (An example would be TO PROMISE.) In other words, not all verbs that would be regarded as 'basic-level terms' (at least inside the area of linguistic action) by cognitive psychologists have to be basic linguistic action verbs. Many of them may be situated on a level lower in the hierarchy. The fact that not all cognitively basic words are situated on the same level results, in part, from what we have called the 'whims of folk taxonomies': it is clear that for languages lacking a life-form term for 'mammal' the cognitively basic ones will be the generic terms for cat, dog, etc.; moreover, even when there are no gaps, the psychologically most salient terms may be scattered over

different levels of the hierarchy since salience depends on knowledge, cultural importance, etc. (see paragraphs **107** to **110**). Without keeping this in mind, the cognitive psychological notion of 'basic-level terms' would be more a source of confusion than of inspiration for our first supplementary criterion.

8.4.2 Exclusiveness

439 If we are confronted with a pair of words such as TO TELL and TO REVEAL, exclusiveness (criterion D) is a good help to decide which one of the two is more basic than the other: since TO TELL has only or at least primarily linguistic action meanings, it is more basic than TO REVEAL, which, in addition to its linguistic action meaning, also signifies 'to open up to view.' In applying the criterion, the directional relationships between the different meanings of a word have to be taken into account. For instance, TO TELL also has a 'revealing' or 'mar   'Fossils tell much about the past', but this sense is clearly derived from or subordinated to the linguistic action meaning; thus, it remains true that TO TELL is primarily a linguistic action verb. The directional relationship in TO REVEAL is probably reversed; moreover, both meanings seem to be more or less of equal importance. In the case of TO REVEAL, the 'different meanings' referred to are degrees of generality rather than distinct senses. Really distinct senses are to be found in other examples to be excluded on the basis of criterion D, such as TO PUT FORWARD, the linguistic action meaning of which is metaphorical.

8.4.3 Applicability

440 For the use of all linguistic action verbs, appropriateness conditions can be formulated. For some verbs, however, these conditions impose very strong limitations on their applicability (criterion E); in other words, only a narrow class of arguments is appropriate for them. Consider TO PRAY (which requires God as a hearer), or TO BAPTIZE (which requires a priest as an agent, except in an emergency). Such verbs, which will usually be connected with a strong institutional frame, are excluded from the set of basic linguistic action verbs. (Note that this criterion is analogous to the third one for basic color terms.)

8.4.4 Markedness

441 Often, two or more linguistic action verbs will be synonymous, or nearly synonymous. In such cases a markedness criterion (F) can be handled that is closely related to the applicability criterion above: we can regard as more basic the member of a pair of synonyms that has the widest applicability and that can therefore be said to be the most neutral or unmarked choice available. Consider TO SPEAK and TO TALK. In general it may be true to say that talking is speaking informally, but it is not equally valid to say that speaking is talking formally. However, this relationship is reversed for TO SPEAK and TO TALK in the sense of 'conversing'. Therefore, in most of their meanings it can be said that TO SPEAK is more basic than TO TALK, whereas in the sense of conversing TO TALK is more basic than TO SPEAK.

442 Needless to say, this markedness criterion will not solve all synonymy problems. Sometimes, however, it may also help us to solve difficulties of a different nature. For instance, TO ALLOW can be described as 'not forbidding' in natural language, and TO FORBID as 'not allowing'. Even if, for both members of the contrasting pair, nonreversed natural language definitions in terms of a different linguistic action verb (such as the definition of TO FORBID as 'order not to do something' and the definition of TO ALLOW as 'to say, in a statement sense, that someone may do something/that one does not object') had not been possible, it would have been sufficient to enter only one of them in the set of basic linguistic action verbs since both verbs are definable in terms of each other. As with most contrast sets, the positive pole TO ALLOW seems to be unmarked and would, therefore, have been the better candidate for inclusion (see also paragraph 83).

443 There is another type of markedness in the lexicalization of linguistic action that may compel us to exclude some verbs from the set of basic linguistic action verbs. Remember that the semantic description of some linguistic action verbs requires conditions to be formulated with reference to properties of A, the act described, as well as with reference to D, the describing act (see paragraph 127). These Cd's usually concern the formality or informality of D (as in the case of TO PUMP and TO GRILL, meaning TO QUESTION) or Sd's value judgments about A (as in the case of TO NAG, meaning TO URGE). If a verb V is marked in the sense that its semantic description requires such C's attached to D in addition to those attached to A, it cannot be regarded as a basic linguistic action verb.

8.5 A PROVISIONAL LIST

444 On the basis of our set of criteria, we can construct a provisional list of basic linguistic action verbs in English. It cannot be stressed enough that this list, as it stands now, remains a *working hypothesis*. To arrive at a final version, much more is needed. For instance, extensive work with informants is necessary to apply most of the criteria we have formulated; for this purpose, elicitation procedures and psychological tests will have to be constructed. Moreover, the actual form of the criteria themselves, as well as of the procedures and tests, may require considerable adaptations for individual languages. In addition, evidence from different languages may even force us to change the hypothesis about English.

445 The tentativeness of the following proposals is somewhat attenuated by the fact that, in the case of English, we can rely on the products of centuries of dedicated lexicographical efforts. Particularly useful, as a starting point, is the list of approximately 2,000 'basic' words in terms of which the *Longman Dictionary of Contemporary English* (London: Longman, 1978) phrases all its definitions. This list contains 87 linguistic action verbs. Almost all of them can be excluded from the set of basic linguistic action verbs on the basis of our operational criteria. In order to demonstrate how this works in each individual case, I present the complete set of verbs with the natural language definitions that I consider to be plausible either because they occur in English dictionaries (in which case quotation marks are added) or because of my own intuitions (based in part on dictionary entries).

446 In the following list, a minus (−) indicates verbs to be excluded from the set of basic linguistic action verbs, and an asterisk (*) indicates verbs to be included).

−TO ACCEPT: to say that one accepts
−TO ACCOUNT FOR: to explain; to say what something means
−TO ADD: 'to say also' (e.g. 'I should like to add that . . .')
−TO ADDRESS: to speak/write to; 'to direct speech or writing to'
−TO ADMIT: 'to permit to enter'; 'to state or agree to the truth of'; to say that something is true
−TO ADVERTISE: 'to make (something for sale, etc.) known to the public'; to inform/tell the public that; 'to ask (for someone or something) by placing an advertisement in a newspaper, etc.'
−TO ADVISE: 'to tell what one thinks should be done'
−TO AGREE: to say that one is of the same opinion or that one is willing to do/accept something
−TO ALLOW: to say that someone may do something/that one does not object
*TO ANSWER: to say something in response to some other utterance
−TO APPOINT: to say that someone is to occupy a certain position
−TO APPROVE: 'to agree officially to'
−TO ARGUE: 'to provide reasons for or against'; to say why one believes something; 'to disagree in words'; to talk about something about which one disagrees
*TO ASK: 'to call on a person for an answer to'; say something to the effect that one wants to obtain information/some object/a favor, etc.
−TO BEG: 'to ask humbly for'
−TO BLAME: to say that one considers someone responsible
−TO BROADCAST: to tell/inform the public by means of radio or television
−TO CALL: to speak in a loud voice; to speak to over the phone

—TO CHARGE: 'to ask in payment'; 'to declare officially and openly (that something is wrong)'; 'to command'
—TO CLAIM: 'to ask for or demand as one's right'; 'to declare to be true'
—TO COMMAND: to tell someone to do something, with the right to be obeyed
—TO COMPLAIN: 'to express feelings of annoyance, pain, etc.'; to say that there are certain things one considers wrong, annoying, etc.
—TO COUNT: to mention/name/say the numbers in order
—TO CRY: to speak loudly
—TO CURSE: to wish that harm comes to someone; 'to use bad language'
—TO DARE: 'to say that (someone) is not brave enough (to do something)'
—TO DECLARE: 'to make known publicly or officially, according to rules, custom, etc.'; 'to state with great force so that there is no doubt about the meaning'
—TO DEMAND: 'to ask or ask for and not take "No" for an answer'
—TO DESCRIBE: to make statements so as 'to give a picture (of someone or something) in words'
—TO DIRECT: 'to tell someone the way to a place'; 'to order'; to tell
—TO DISMISS: 'to send away'; to tell to go away; 'to allow to go'
—TO ENCOURAGE: 'to urge on to fresh efforts'
—TO ENQUIRE: to inquire
—TO EXAMINE: 'to ask questions, in order to measure knowledge or to find out something'
—TO EXCUSE: 'to forgive for a small fault'
—TO EXPLAIN: to say what something means
—TO FORBID: 'to command not to do something'
—TO FORGIVE: 'to say that one is no longer angry about something and/or wishing to give punishment'
—TO GREET: 'to address in a friendly or respectful way'
—TO GUESS: to make a statement without knowing all the facts
—TO INFORM: to tell
—TO INQUIRE: to ask
—TO INSTRUCT: to tell how something is to be done
—TO INTERRUPT: to speak so as to break off someone else's speech
—TO INTRODUCE: to tell two people each other's names; to mention for the first time
—TO INVITE: to ask someone to a social occasion
—TO JUDGE: to say what one's opinion is about something
—TO MENTION: 'to say the name of'; to refer to
*TO NAME: 'to say the name of'; 'to give a name to'
—TO OFFER: 'to present for acceptance or rejection'; to ask whether someone wants something
—TO ORDER: to tell someone to do something

—TO PERMIT: to allow
—TO PERSUADE: to argue successfully
—TO PRAISE: 'say about someone/something (to someone) that it/he/she is praiseworthy'
—TO PRAY: 'to speak to God'
—TO PRETEND: 'to claim falsely that'
—TO PROMISE: to say that one will do something; (promise: 'a statement, which someone else has a right to believe and depend on, that one will or will not do something')
—TO PRONOUNCE: to speak/utter; to state/declare (officially)
—TO PROVE: to make statements that show something to be true
—TO QUESTION: to ask someone a question
—TO REASON: to argue
—TO RECOGNIZE: 'to admit (someone or something) as being real or having the right to be the stated thing'
—TO REFUSE: to say 'No' to a proposition/offer/request
—TO REMIND: 'to tell or cause (someone) to remember'
—TO REPLY: to answer
—TO REPORT: to tell of/make known
—TO REQUEST: 'to demand politely'
*TO SAY: 'to express (a thought, intention, opinion, question, etc.) in words'
—TO SCOLD: to speak to someone in an angry and complaining way, especially to blame
—TO SEND: to order to go
—TO SHOUT: to speak or say very loudly
*TO SPEAK: 'to say things; express thoughts aloud; use the voice; talk'
—TO STATE: to say that something is the case (especially formally)
—TO SUGGEST: to say what one thinks would be a good idea
—TO SWEAR: 'to promise formally or by an oath'; 'to state firmly'
—TO SUPPORT: 'to say that one approves of'
*TO TALK: to produce words, speak
*TO TELL: to make known in words
*TO THANK: to express gratitude
—TO TRANSLATE: to change from one language into another
—TO URGE: 'to beg or persuade with force'; 'to tell of with force'
—TO VOTE: 'to declare one's choice officially'
—TO WARN: 'to tell (of something bad that may happen, or of how to prevent something bad)'
—TO WELCOME: 'to greet a person when arriving in a new place'
—TO WHISPER: to speak in a low voice; 'to tell (a secret) widely'
—TO WISH: to express a want; to say what one wants
*TO WRITE: to use written language

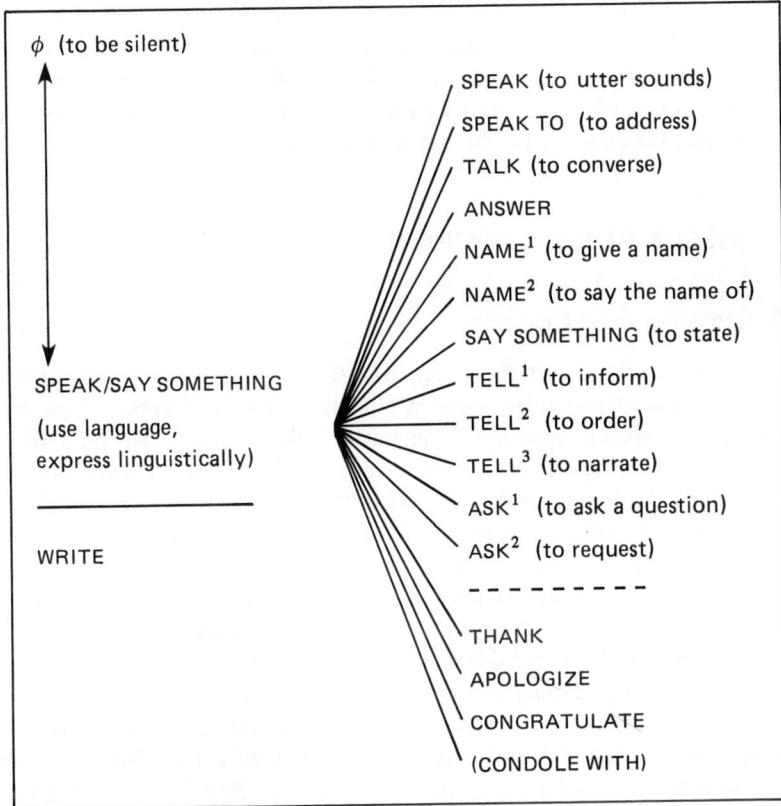

Figure 1 English basic linguistic action verbs (working hypothesis)

447 In the majority of cases, our decision to include or exclude a verb has been based completely on the central semantic criterion. One of the exceptions, however, is TO CURSE in the sense of 'using bad language', for which an acceptable natural language definition in terms of a different linguistic action verb (except for the 'unique beginner') seems hardly feasible. Its psychological salience can be expected to be so low that including it would probably be a mistake.

448 Starting from *Longman's* 2,000 basic words, and handling our operational criteria in a somewhat intuitive fashion, we end up with the following set of basic linguistic action verbs in English: TO ANSWER, TO ASK, TO NAME, TO SAY, TO SPEAK, TO TALK, TO TELL, TO THANK, TO WRITE. There are three more verbs that do not occur in *Longman's* list of 2,000 but that seem to satisfy our criteria: TO APOLOGIZE ('to express sorrow, as to a fault or causing pain'), TO CONGRATULATE ('to express praise and admiration for a happy event or something successfully done'), and TO CONDOLE WITH ('to express sympathy to (someone who has experienced sadness, sorrow, misfortune, etc.)'). This gives us a total of 12. They are presented schematically in Figure 1. (TO CONDOLE WITH is put between brackets because, in spite of its occurrence in all dictionaries, at least some speakers of English have a hard time figuring out how to use the verb so that, at least for them, its psychological salience must be really low.)

8.6 CROSSLINGUISTIC COMPARISON

8.6.1 Crosslinguistic Evidence

449 In spite of all the criteria at our disposal, we may be misled about the taxonomic status of particular words as long as we keep concentrating on one language or on separate languages. If linguistic anthropologists had found only languages lacking a life-form term for 'mammal', they could not have guessed that such a life-form term was possible and they might not have regarded the terms for cat, dog, and the like as generic ones. Similar things may happen with linguistic action verbs. A case in point is the set of expressive verbs separated from the other basic linguistic action verbs in Figure 1. The set of basic linguistic action verbs, as reflected in the tentative table, shows a striking discrepancy between the number of basic verbs devoted to the extremely wide areas of conversing, asserting, asking, ordering, and the like, and the number of verbs devoted to the relatively narrow class of expressive acts. Such a discrepancy may be deemed suspicious, and we should not be surprised to find languages in which there are more general terms covering the different English ones (the most general being something equivalent to 'expressing a feeling F in words'). If these were to be found, the taxonomic status of the verbs TO CONGRATULATE, TO APOLOGIZE, etc., might have to be reinterpreted. The only indication that I have found so far that such a suspicion might not be completely without grounds, is the fact that Hungarian lumps together some of the expressives in a—for us—pretty odd way: ÜDVÖZÖL means both greeting and congratulating, while KÖSZÖN means thanking as well as greeting. This suggests a conceptual relationship—at least for speakers of Hungarian—between thanking and congratulating as well as between these two types of acts and greeting (which disappeared from the basic linguistic action verb list for English because of its definition as 'to address in a friendly or respectful way'). That expressives are troublesome is emphasized again in the next section (8.6.2).

450 Crosslinguistic evidence may also be adduced to support markedness decisions (since markedness is frequently consistent across languages). Thus the neutrality of TO SPEAK versus TO TALK, in most of their senses, is supported by the fact that the Hungarian equivalent of TO TALK, viz. BESZÉLGET, is even morphologically marked in comparison with the neutral BESZÉL.

451 Finally, plain gaps can be brought to light by comparing with other languages. For instance, many languages have a verb fitting all the criteria for basic linguistic action verbs that describes the opposite of speaking, the absence of speech, linguistic silence (viz. Dutch ZWIJGEN, German SCHWEIGEN, French SE TAIRE, etc.). English does not. (See Chapter 3.)

8.6.2 Some Contrastive Speculations

452 Studies of metapragmatic terms in Afro-American and Caribbean communities (such as Abrahams & Bauman 1971; Kernan, Sodergren, & French 1977; Kochman 1972; Mitchell-Kernan 1971) and in non-Western societies (such as Finnegan 1969 and Rosaldo 1982) have generally shown that whereas our linguistic action lexicon focuses strongly on *personal intent*, 'folk' societies tend to focus on *interpersonal relationships* and *manner of speaking*. On the basis of these anthropological data, a possible expectation might be the following. Whereas synchronic implicational universals for color terms and life-form terms show a linear pattern of development (with a limited number of alternating paths), the sets of basic linguistic action verbs in Western (or, more generally, literate) societies and those in 'folk' societies might turn out to be completely different and to show totally unrelated patterns of development.

453 Though this is a real possibility, the differences may also turn out to be less radical than they seem at first sight. Our analysis of forgotten routines (Chapter 6), for instance, has demonstrated the need for a redefinition of the class of expressive speech acts: their crucial property is not the expression of a psychological state as such, but the expression of a psychological state deemed important for the hearer. Thus, *interpersonal relationships* seem to matter more than *personal intent*. Therefore, the emergence of 4 expressive speech-act verbs in the set of only 12 basic linguistic action verbs for English might not be so suspicious after all.

454 Similarly, the contrast between *personal intent* and *manner of speaking* or style may not be a function of the opposition between literate versus preliterate or 'folk' societies but rather between verbs and nouns in the lexicalization of linguistic action. Thus, Afro-American terms for speaking are usually discussed in the nominalized '-ing' form: SIGNIFYING, MARKING, LOUD TALKING, etc. And the major categories of speech distinguished by speakers of Tzeltal (as reported by Gossen 1974 and Stross 1974) are said to be 'ancient speech' versus 'recent speech' (a distinction that is entirely a matter of style). But if we ask members of mainstream Western cultures what types of speech there are (rather than what one can do with language), we are also likely to get manner-of-speaking distinctions rather than words focusing on personal intent. Speakers of English are likely to come up with things such as 'sweet talk,' 'baby talk,' 'shoptalk,' etc. And the basic distinction for Flemish speakers of Dutch would no doubt be

'ABN' ('Algemeen Beschaafd Nederlands', literally 'General Educated Dutch') versus 'dialect'. Conversely, Black English and Tzeltal *do* have linguistic action verbs contrasting types of personal intent in much the same way as ours do.

455 What all these observations and speculations amount to is a renewed realization that it would be wrong to approach the subject matter of linguistic action with only a preconceived framework of abstract and general concepts. What we need in addition is a thorough investigation of metapragmatic awareness. Studying the lexicalization of linguistic action as a reflection of its conceptualization is a first scratching of the surface. And all I have been able to do in this work is to provide some of the necessary tools and background notions to begin the task.

8.7 METHODOLOGICAL AFTERTHOUGHT

456 Two requirements emerge from the foregoing programmatic sketch of what we regard as the logical next step in the development of the empirical-conceptual approach to linguistic action. First, the results of the investigation should be such that they are psychologically relevant, because what we are after, ultimately, are reflections of conceptualization habits. Second, a high degree of universality is aimed at. How can these two requirements be satisfied in a balanced manner? In other words, remembering the principle proposed in our earlier discussion of abstractness in lexical semantics (see paragraphs **115** to **125**), how can the appropriate degree of abstractness be reached?

457 There are at least two tools at our disposal to obtain the required level of *psychological relevance*. First, the set of basic linguistic action verbs needs to be defined for each investigated language and culture separately, taking into account *language-specific and culture-specific definitional relationships*. That is why we need our primary semantic criterion for inclusion into the set of basic linguistic action verbs, as well as the supplementary considerations of psychological salience and related phenomena. Second, bearing in mind all kinds of language-specific phenomena such as *valence* (or 'case frame') and *word order, tense, aspect, modality*, etc., in the lexical semantic description of the selected verbs, may bring our findings closer to the psychologically real conceptualization patterns for the speakers of different languages.

458 In order to reach the required level of *universality* and thus the appropriate degree of *abstractness*, we need a *coherent pragmatic background theory*. The need for such a theory (an embryonic version of which is to be found in Verschueren 1985) as a *descriptive tool* has already been emphasized in our discussion of how to avoid circularity in lexical semantic analyses of linguistic action verbs (see Chapter 2). The central part of our lexical semantic strategy has been shown to be the formulation of the conditions under which a given verb can be used appropriately as a description of a given form of verbal behavior. If we do not want to get stuck with sets of conditions about which it is not clear what they are conditions on, and especially if we want to make crosslinguistic and crosscultural comparisons possible, such an essentially pragmatic approach can be successful only if it is based on a coherent background theory.

459 A second function of the pragmatic background theory, particularly relevant in the search for basic linguistic action verbs, is that of a *heuristic tool*. It can be used to construct testing procedures to find out whether the sets of basic linguistic action verbs discovered on the basis of the language-specific and culture-specific definitional relationships cover the entire domain of linguistic (inter)action.[12]

460 As predicted in the discussion of theoretical versus empirical-conceptual approaches (see Chapter 1), neither exists in its pure form. But even for the project outlined in this final chapter, for which the level of universality and the degree of abstractness aimed at in empirical-conceptual approaches to linguistic action is at its highest, the required background theory remains extremely limited. Unlike Searle's speech-act theory or Grice's conversational logic, it does not have to include rules for verbal behavior. Nor does it specify what types or classes there are. It is only expected to be an overview of the elements of speech situations as carriers of semantic dimensions along which linguistic action verbs vary (without making judgments about the relative importance of the dimensions in question—which cannot be avoided, for instance, in classifications). Thus, the enterprise remains true to its original aim. Only after the completion of a significant amount of empirical-conceptual research should we return to theorizing about linguistic (inter)action and close the hermeneutic circle—for a while.

---

[12] In Verschueren (1984) it has been used for the construction of a standardized set of speech events.

REFERENCES

Abrahams, R. D., and R. Bauman. 1971. Sense and nonsense in St. Vincent: Speech behavior and decorum in a Caribbean community. American Anthropologist 73.762-72.
Alford, Danny K. H. 1978. The demise of the Whorf hypothesis (A major revision in the history of linguistics). Proceedings of the Fourth Annual Meeting of the Berkeley Linguistics Society 485-99.
Allwood, Jens. 1976. Linguistic communication as action and cooperation: A study in pragmatics. (Gothenburg Monographs in Linguistics 2.) Department of Linguistics, University of Göteborg.
Allwood, Jens. 1978. On the analysis of communicative action. Gothenburg Papers in Theoretical Linguistics 38.
Allwood, Jens, and Erland Hjelmquist (eds.). (forthcoming) Foregrounding Background. Göteborg: Doxa.
Anscombre, Jean-Claude. 1980. Voulez-vous dériver avec moi? Communications 32.61-124.
Anscombre, Jean-Claude, and Oswald Ducrot. 1977. Deux "mais" en français? Lingua 43.23-40.
Austin, John Langshaw. 1962. How to do things with words. Oxford: Oxford University Press. (Second edition, 1975, Cambridge, MA: Harvard University Press.)
Ballmer, Thomas, and Waltraud Brennenstuhl. 1981. Speech act classification: A study in the lexical analysis of English speech activity verbs. Berlin/New York: Springer.
Baskett, Glen D., and Roy O. Freedle. 1974. Aspects of language pragmatics and the social perception of lying. Journal of Psycholinguistic Research 3:2.117-31.
Basso, Keith H. 1972. 'To give up on words': Silence in Western Apache culture. In P. P. Giglioli (ed.) 1972, 67-86.
Bauman, Richard, and Joel Sherzer (eds.). 1974. Explorations in the ethnography of speaking. Cambridge: Cambridge University Press.
Bendix, Edward Herman. 1966. Componential analysis of general vocabulary: The semantic structure of a set of verbs in English, Hindi, and Japanese. The Hague: Mouton.
Benveniste, Emile. 1966. Problèmes de linguistique générale. Paris: Gallimard.

Berlin, Brent, Dennis E. Breedlove, and Peter H. Raven. 1973. General principles of classification and nomenclature in folk biology. American Anthropologist 75.214-42.
Berlin, Brent, and Paul Kay. 1969. Basic color terms: Their universality and evolution. Berkeley/Los Angeles: University of California Press.
Berliner Gruppe (Thomas Ballmer, Waltraud Brennenstuhl, Konrad Ehlich, Jochen Rehbein). (n.d.) Sprachliches Handeln (Listen, Kategorien, Modelle). Ms.
Berrendonner, Alain. 1981. Zéro pour la question: Syntaxe et sémantique des interrogations directes. Cahiers de Linguistique Française (Genève) 2.41-69.
Blount, B., and M. Sanches (eds.). 1977. Sociocultural dimensions of language change. New York: Academic.
Bok, Sissela. 1978. Lying: Moral choice in public and private life. New York: Vintage Books.
Bolinger, Dwight. 1965. The atomization of meaning. Language 41:4.555-73.
Bolinger, Dwight. 1973. Truth is a linguistic question. Language 49:3.539-50.
Bolinger, Dwight. 1975. Aspects of language. New York: Harcourt.
Bolinger, Dwight. 1977. Neutrality, norm and bias. Distributed by Indiana University Linguistics Club.
Brown, Cecil H. 1977. Folk botanical life forms: Their universality and growth. American Anthropologist 79:2.317-42.
Brown, Cecil H. 1979. Folk zoological life forms: Their universality and growth. American Anthropologist 81:4.791-817.
Bruxelles, S., O. Ducrot, E. Fouquier, J. Gouaze, G. dos Reis Nunes, and A. Remis. 1976. MAIS occupe-toi d'Amélie. Actes de la Recherche en Sciences Sociales 6.47-62.
Chisholm, Roderick M., and T. D. Feehan. 1977. The intent to deceive. Journal of Philosophy 74:3.143-59.
Cohen, L. Jonathan. 1964. Do illocutionary forces exist? Philosophical Quarterly 14: 55.118-37.
Cohen, L. Jonathan. 1974. Speech acts. Current Trends in Linguistics 12.173-208.
Cohen, Ted. 1973. Illocutions and perlocutions. Foundations of Language 9.492-503.
Cole, Peter (ed.). 1978. Syntax and semantics 9: Pragmatics. New York: Academic.
Cole, Peter, and Jerry L. Morgan (eds.). 1975. Syntax and semantics 3: speech acts. New York: Academic.
Cole, Roger W. (ed.). 1977. Current issues in linguistic theory. Bloomington: Indiana University Press.
Coleman, Linda, and Paul Kay. 1981. Prototype semantics: The English word *lie*. Language 57:1.26-44.
Conklin, H. C. 1962. Lexicographical treatment of folk taxonomies. International Journal of American Linguistics 28.119-41. Reprinted in S. A. Tyler (ed.), 1969, 41-59.
Coseriu, Eugenio, and Horst Geckeler. 1974. Linguistics and semantics. Current Trends in Linguistics 12.103-71.
Coulmas, Florian (ed.). 1981. Conversational routine: Explorations in standardized communication situations and prepatterned speech. The Hague: Mouton.
Crumrine, Lynne S. 1968. An ethnography of Mayo speaking. Anthropological Linguistics 10:2.19-31.
Dallmayr, Fred R., and Thomas A. McCarthy (eds.). 1977. Understanding and social inquiry. Notre Dame/London: University of Notre Dame Press.
Davis, Steven. 1979. Perlocutions. In J. R. Searle, F. Kiefer, and M. Bierwisch (eds.), 1979, 37-55.
de Beaugrande, Robert. 1980. Text, discourse, and process: Toward a multidisciplinary science of texts. Norwood, NJ: Ablex.
Dixon, R. M. W. 1971. A method of semantic description. In D. D. Steinberg and L. A. Jakobovits (eds.) 1971, 436-71.

Ducrot, Oswald. 1973. La Preuve et le dire. Paris: Mame.
Ducrot, Oswald. 1980. Analyses pragmatiques. Communications 32.11-60.
Dumont, Louis. 1970. Homo Hierarchicus. Chicago: University of Chicago Press.
Feld, Steven, and Bambi B. Schieffelin. 1981. Hard words: A functional basis for Kaluli discourse. In D. Tannen (ed.) 1981.
Ferguson, Charles A. 1976. The structure and use of politeness formulas. Language in Society 5:2.137-51. Reprinted in F. Coulmas (ed.) 1981, 21-35.
Fillmore, Charles J. 1975. An alternative to checklist theories of meaning. Proceedings of the First Annual Meeting of the Berkeley Linguistics Society, 123-31.
Fillmore, Charles J. 1977. Topics in lexical semantics. In R. W. Cole (ed.) 1977, 76-138.
Fillmore, Charles J. 1978. On the organization of semantic information in the lexicon. Papers from the Parasession on the Lexicon, Chicago Linguistic Society, 148-73.
Fillmore, Charles J. 1979. Innocence: A second idealization for linguistics. Proceedings of the Fifth Annual Meeting of the Berkeley Linguistics Society, 63-76.
Finnegan, Ruth. 1969. How to do things with words: Performative utterances among the Limba of Sierra Leone. Man 4.537-52.
Fisiak, J. (ed.). 1976. Papers and studies in contrastive linguistics (vol. 6). Washington, D.C.: Center for Applied Linguistics.
Fortescue, Michael. 1979. Why the 'language of thought' is not a language: Some inconsistencies of the computational analogy of thought. Journal of Pragmatics 3:1.67-80.
Frake, Charles O. 1972. Struck by speech: The Yakan concept of litigation. In J. Gumperz and D. Hymes (eds.) 1972, 106-29.
Franck, Dorothea. 1981. Seven sins of pragmatics: Theses about speech act theory, conversational analysis, linguistics and rhetoric. In H. Parret, M. Sbisà and J. Verschueren (eds.) 1981, 225-36.
Fraser, Bruce. 1974. An analysis of vernacular performative verbs. In R. W. Shuy and C.-J. N. Bailey (eds.) 1974, 139-58.
Frege, Gottlob. 1892. Über Sinn und Bedeutung. Zeitschrift für Philosophie und philosophische Kritik 100.25-50.
Freud, Sigmund. 1917. Introductory lectures on psychoanalysis (1978, The Pelican Freud Library 1). Harmondsworth: Penguin Books.
Gadamer, H. G. 1975. Truth and method. New York: Seabury.
Garfinkel, Harold. 1972. Studies of the routine grounds of everyday activities. In D. Sudnow (ed.) 1972, 1-30.
Giglioli, Pier Paolo (ed.). 1972. Language and social context: Selected readings. Harmondsworth: Penguin.
Goffman, Erving. 1974. Frame analysis: An essay on the organization of experience. New York: Harper & Row.
Goodenough, Ward H. 1956. Componential analysis and the study of meaning. Language 32:1.195-216.
Goodenough, Ward H. 1965. Yankee kinship terminology: A problem in componential analysis. American Anthropologist 67:5.259-87. Also in S. A. Tyler (ed.) 1969, 255-88.
Gossen, Gary H. 1974. Chamulas in the world of the sun: Time and space in a Maya oral tradition. Cambridge, MA: Harvard University Press.
Gregersen, Kirsten (ed.). 1978. Papers from the Fourth Scandinavian Conference of Linguistics (Hindsgavl, January 6-8, 1978). Odense: Odense University Press.
Grice, H. Paul. 1975. Logic and conversation. In P. Cole and J. L. Morgan (eds.) 1975, 41-58.
Grice, H. Paul. 1978. Further notes on logic and conversation. In P. Cole (ed.) 1978, 113-27.
Gumperz, John J., and Dell Hymes (eds.). 1972. Directions in sociolinguistics. New York: Holt, Rinehart and Winston.

Habermas, Jürgen. 1979. Communication and the evolution of society. Boston: Beacon Press.
Harder, Peter. 1978. Language in action: Some arguments against the concept 'illocutionary'. In K. Gregersen (ed.) 1978, 193-7.
Harris, Roy. 1980. The language-makers. Ithaca, NY: Cornell University Press.
Hindelang, Götz. 1978. Auffordern: Die Untertypen des Aufforderns und ihre sprachlichen Realisierungsformen. Göppingen: Alfred Kummerle.
Hymes, Dell. 1974. Foundations in sociolinguistics: An ethonographic approach. London: Tavistock.
Jakobson, Roman. 1970. Main trends in the science of language. New York: Harper and Row.
Jessen, Heino. 1979. Pragmatische Aspekte lexikalischer Semantik: Verben des Aufforderns im Französischen. Tübingen: Günter Narr.
Johnson-Laird, P. N., and P. C. Wason (eds.). 1977. Thinking: Readings in cognitive science. Cambridge: Cambridge University Press.
Katz, Jerrold J., and Jerry A. Fodor. 1963. The structure of a semantic theory. Language 39:2.170-210.
Kay, Paul, and Chad K. McDaniel. 1978. The linguistic significance of the meanings of basic color terms. Language 54:3.610-46.
Kernan, K. T., J. Sodergren, and R. French. 1977. Speech and social prestige in the Belizian speech community. In B. Blount and M. Sanches (eds.) 1977, 35-50.
Kochman, Thomas (ed.). 1972. Rappin' and stylin' out. Urbana: University of Illinois Press.
Kockelmans, Joseph J. 1967. Some fundamental themes of Husserl's phenomenology. In J. J. Kockelmans (ed.), Phenomenology: The philosophy of Edmund Husserl and its interpretation. Garden City, NY: Doubleday and Company, 24-36.
Kuhn, Thomas S. 1962. The structure of scientific revolutions. Chicago: University of Chicago Press.
Lakoff, George, and Mark Johnson. 1980. Metaphors we live by. Chicago: University of Chicago Press.
Leech, Geoffrey. 1974. Semantics. Harmondsworth: Penguin.
Lehmann, Dorothea. 1976a. Untersuchungen zur Bezeichnung der Sprechaktreferenz im Englischen. (Forum Linguisticum 8.) Frankfurt am Main: P. Lang.
Lehmann, Dorothea. 1976b. A confrontation of *say, speak, talk, tell* with possible German counterparts. In J. Fisiak (ed.) 1976, 99-109.
Lehrer, Adrienne. 1974. Semantic fields and lexical structure. Amsterdam: North-Holland.
Leisi, Ernst. 1973. Praxis der Englischen semantik. Heidelberg: Carl Winter Universitätsverlag.
Leonard, H. S. 1959. Interrogatives, imperatives, truth, falsity and lies. Philosophical Studies 26.172-86.
Lessing, Gotthold Ephraim. 1778. Anti-Goeze. In G. E. Lessing 1965, Werke in Sechs Bänden 6: Philosophie/Theologie. Zürich: Stauffacher-Verlag, pp. 398-458.
Létoublon, Françoise. 1980. Le vocabulaire de la supplication en Grec: Performatif et dérivation délocutive. Lingua 52.325-36.
Levinson, Stephen C. 1981. The essential inadequacies of speech act models of dialogue. In H. Parret, M. Sbisà, and J. Verschueren (eds.) 1981, 473-92.
Lounsbury, Floyd G. 1964. The structural analysis of kinship semantics. In Proceedings of the Ninth International Congress of Linguists. The Hague: Mouton. Also in S. A. Tyler (ed.) 1969, 193-212.
Lyons, John. 1977. Semantics. Cambridge: Cambridge University Press.
Makkai, Adam. 1972. Idiom structure in English. The Hague: Mouton.
Malinowski, Bronislaw. 1954. Magic, science and religion, and other essays. Garden City, NY: Doubleday and Company.
McCarthy, Thomas. 1979. Translator's introduction. In J. Habermas 1979, vii-xxiv.

McCawley, James D. 1977. Remarks on the lexicography of performative verbs. In A. Rogers, Bob Wall, and John P. Murphy (eds.) 1977, 13-25.
McDaniel, Timothy. 1978. Meaning and comparative concepts. Theory and Society 6.75-92.
Metzing, Dieter. 1975. Formen kommunikationswissenschaftlicher Argumentationsanalyse. Hamburg: Buske.
Meyer-Hermann, Reinhard. 1978. Aspekte der Analyse metakommunikativer Interaktionen. In R. Meyer-Hermann (ed.), Sprechen-Handeln-Interaktion. Tübingen: Max Niemeyer, pp. 103-42.
Mihailă, Rodica. 1977. Le silence en tant qu'acte de langage. Revue Roumaine de Linguistique 22:4.417-21.
Miller, George A., and Philip N. Johnson-Laird. 1976. Language and perception. Cambridge: Cambridge University Press.
Minsky, Marvin. 1977. Frame-system theory. In P. N. Johnson-Laird and P. C. Wason (eds.) 1977, 355-76.
Mitchell-Kernan, Claudia. 1971. Language behavior in a black urban community. Monographs of the Language Behavior Research Laboratory, no. 2. (University of California, Berkeley).
Morgan, Jerry L. 1978. Two types of convention in indirect speech acts. In P. Cole (ed.) 1978, 261-80.
Nida, Eugene A. 1975. Componential analysis of meaning: An introduction to semantic structures. The Hague: Mouton.
Ochs Keenan, Elinor. 1976. The universality of conversational postulates. Language in Society 5:1.67-80.
Ortony, Andrew (ed.). 1979. Metaphor and thought. Cambridge: Cambridge University Press.
Parret, Herman, Marina Sbisà, and Jef Verschueren (eds.), 1981. Possibilities and limitations of pragmatics. Amsterdam: John Benjamins.
Perret, Delphine. 1976. On irony. Pragmatics Microfiche 1:7.D3.
Porzig, W. 1967. Das Wunder der Sprache (4th edition). Bern/München.
Pratt, Mary Louise. 1977. Toward a speech act theory of literary discourse. Bloomington: Indiana University Press.
Pratt, Mary Louise. 1980. The ideology of speech act theory. To appear in Centrum.
Reddy, Michael. 1979. The conduit metaphor—A case of frame conflict in our language about language. In A. Ortony (ed.) 1979, 284-324.
Riniker, Ursula. 1979. Some doubts about pragmatical theory. Journal of Pragmatics 3:1.59-66.
Rogers, Andy, Bob Wall, and John P. Murphy (eds.). 1977. Proceedings of the Texas Conference on Performatives, Presuppositions and Implicatures. Arlington, Virginia: Center for Applied Linguistics.
Rosaldo, Michelle Z. 1982. The things we do with words: Ilongot speech acts and speech act theory in philosophy. Language in Society 11:2. 203-37.
Rosch, Eleanor. 1977a. Human categorization. In N. Warren (ed.) 1977, 1-49.
Rosch, Eleanor. 1977b. Classification of real-world objects: Origins and representations in cognition. In P. N. Johnson-Laird and P. C. Wason (eds.) 1977, 212-22.
Rosch, Eleanor. 1978. Principles of categorization. In E. Rosch and B. B. Lloyd (eds.) 1978, 27-48.
Rosch, Eleanor, and Barbara B. Lloyd (eds.). 1978. Cognition and Categorization. Hillsdale, NJ: Erlbaum.
Sacks, Harvey, Emanuel A. Schegloff, and Gail Jefferson. 1974. A simplest systematics for the organization of turn-taking for conversation. Language 50:4.696-735.
Sapir, Edward. 1921. Language: An introduction to the study of speech. New York: Harcourt, Brace and World.

Sapir, J. David, and J. Christopher Crocker (eds.). 1977. The social use of metaphor: Essays on the anthropology of rhetoric. Philadelphia: University of Pennsylvania Press.

Schank, Roger C., and Robert P. Abelson. 1977. Scripts, plans, goals and understanding: An inquiry into human knowledge structures. Hillsdale, NJ: Erlbaum.

Schön, Donald A. 1979. Generative metaphor: A perspective on problem-setting in social policy. In A. Ortony (ed.) 1979, 254–83.

Schuetz, Alfred. 1967. Phenomenology and the social sciences. In J. J. Kockelmans (ed.), Phenomenology: The philosophy of Edmund Husserl and its interpretation. Garden City, NY: Doubleday and Company, pp. 450–72.

Schüle, Klaus. 1976. Sprechhandlungstheorie und Sprechtätigkeitstheorie. Wiesbaden: Vieweg.

Searle, John R. 1969. Speech acts: An essay in the philosophy of language. Cambridge: Cambridge University Press.

Searle, John R. 1975a. Indirect speech acts. In P. Cole and J. J. Morgan (eds.) 1975, 59–82.

Searle, John R. 1975b. The logical status of fictional discourse. New Literary History 6: 2.319–32.

Searle, John R. 1976. A classification of illocutionary acts. Language in Society 5:1.137–51.

Searle, John R. 1978. Literal meaning. Erkenntnis 13:1.207–24.

Searle, John R. 1979a. Expression and meaning. Cambridge: Cambridge University Press.

Searle, John R. 1979b. Metaphor. In A. Ortony (ed.) 1979, 92–123. Also in J. R. Searle 1979a.

Searle, John R., Ferenc Kiefer and Manfred Bierwisch (eds.). 1979. Studies in semantics and pragmatics. Dordrecht: Reidel.

Seitel, Peter. 1974. Haya metaphors for speech. Language in Society 3:1.51–67.

Seitel, Peter. 1977. Saying Haya sayings: Two categories of proverb use. In J. D. Sapir and J. C. Crocker (eds.) 1977, 75–99.

Shuy, R. W., and C.-J. N. Bailey (eds.). 1974. Toward tomorrow's linguistics. Washington, D.C.: Georgetown University Press.

Siegler, F. A. 1966. Lying. American Philosophical Quarterly 3:2.128–36.

Silverstein, Michael. 1979. Language structure and linguistic ideology. In The elements: A parasession on linguistic units and levels. Chicago: Chicago Linguistic Society, 193–247.

Steinberg, Danny D., and Leon A. Jakobovits (eds.). 1971. Semantics: An interdisciplinary reader in philosophy, linguistics and psychology. Cambridge: Cambridge University Press.

Stross, Brian. 1974. Speaking of speaking: Tenejapa Tzeltal metalinguistics. In R. Bauman and J. Sherzer (eds.) 1974, 213–39.

Sudnow, David (ed.). 1972. Studies in social interaction. New York: The Free Press.

Sweetser, Eve. 1981. The definition of *lie*: An examination of the folk theories underlying a semantic prototype. Ms., University of California Berkeley.

Tannen, Deborah (ed.). 1981. Proceedings of the Georgetown University Round Table. Washington, D.C.: Georgetown University Press.

Tannen, Deborah, and Piyale Cömert Öztek. 1977. Health to our mouths: Formulaic expressions in Turkish and Greek. Proceedings of the Third Annual Meeting of the Berkeley Linguistics Society, 516–34. Reprinted in F. Coulmas (ed.) 1981, 37–54.

Trier, Jost. 1931. Der deutsche Wortschatz im Sinn bezirk des Verstandes. Heidelberg.

Tyler, Stephen A. (ed.). 1969. Cognitive anthropology. New York: Holt, Rinehart and Winston.

Van der Auwera, Johan. 1980a. On the meanings of basic speech acts. Journal of Pragmatics 4:3.253–64.

Van der Auwera, Johan. 1980b. Indirect speech acts revisited. Distributed by Indiana University Linguistics Club.

REFERENCES

Van Valin, Robert D. 1976. Meaning and the Sapir-Whorf hypothesis. Ms., University of California Berkeley.
Vassilyev, L. M. 1974. The theory of semantic fields: A survey. Linguistics 137.79-93.
Vendler, Zeno. 1972. Res cogitans: An essay in rational psychology. Ithaca, NY: Cornell University Press.
Verschueren, Jef. 1977. The analysis of speech act verbs: Theoretical preliminaries. Distributed by Indiana University Linguistics Club. Reprinted as On speech act verbs (Pragmatics & Beyond, 4). Amsterdam: John Benjamins, 1980.
Verschueren, Jef. 1978a. Pragmatics: An annotated bibliography. Amsterdam: John Benjamins. (Annual supplements are published in the Journal of Pragmatics.)
Verschueren, Jef. 1978b. Reflections on presupposition failure: A contribution to an integrated theory of pragmatics. Journal of Pragmatics 2:2.107-51.
Verschueren, Jef. 1980. Konceptualisering en de sociale wetenschappen. Restant 8:2.121-30.
Verschueren, Jef. 1981a. Problems of lexical semantics. Lingua 53.317-51.
Verschueren, Jef. 1981b. Basic linguistic action verbs. Cahiers de Linguistique Française 2 (Les différent types de marqueurs et la détermination des fonctions des actes de langage en contexte, Actes du 1er colloque de pragmatique de Genève, 16-18 mars 1981, 1ère partie). 71-88.
Verschueren, Jef. 1981c. The lexicalization of linguistic action. Proceedings of the Seventh Annual Meeting of the Berkeley Linguistics Society, 328-35.
Verschueren, Jef. 1982a. The social psychology of background assumptions. In J. Allwood and E. Hjelmquist (eds.) (forthcoming)
Verschueren, Jef. 1982b. Abstractheid in het lexicaal-semantisch onderzoek. In Handelingen van het 23e Vlaams Filologencongres. Zellik, Belgium: Secretariaat van de Vlaamse Filologencongressen, 442-450.
Verschueren, Jef. 1983. Speech act classification (Review article). Language 59:1.166-75.
Verschueren, Jef. 1984. Basic linguistic action verbs: A questionnaire. Antwerp Papers in Linguistics 37.
Verschueren, Jef. 1985. Metapragmatics and universals of linguistic action. In J. Verschueren (ed.) 1985. (forthcoming)
Verschueren, Jef. (ed.). 1985. Linguistic action: Some empirical-conceptual studies. Norwood, NJ: Ablex.
Vincent, Jocelyne M., and Cristiano Castelfranchi. 1981. On the art of deception: How to lie while saying the truth. In H. Parret, M. Sbisà, and J. Verschueren (eds.) 1981, 749-77.
Warnock, G. J. 1971. The object of morality. London: Methuen.
Warren, N. (ed.). 1977. Studies in cross-cultural psychology. New York: Academic.
Weisgerber, L. 1962. Die sprachliche Gestaltung der Welt (3rd edition). Düsseldorf.
Whorf, Benjamin Lee. 1956. Language, thought, and reality. Cambridge, MA: M.I.T. Press.
Wierzbicka, Anna. 1972. Semantic primitives. Frankfurt am Main: Athenäum Verlag.
Wierzbicka, Anna. 1977. Mental language and semantic primitives. Communication and Cognition 10:3/4.155-79.
Wierzbicka, Anna. 1980. Lingua mentalis: The semantics of natural language. Sydney: Academic.
Winch, Peter. 1958. The idea of a social science and its relation to philosophy. London: Routledge and Kegan Paul.
Winch, Peter. 1964. Understanding a primitive society. American Philosophical Quarterly 1.307-24. Reprinted in F. R. Dallmayr and T. A. McCarthy (eds.) 1977, 159-88.
Witherspoon, Gary. 1977. Language and art in the Navajo universe. Ann Arbor, MI: University of Michigan Press.
Wittgenstein, Ludwig. 1953. Philosophische Untersuchungen. Oxford: Basil Blackwell.
Zenone, Anna. 1981. Marqueurs de consécution: Le cas de 'donc'. Cahiers de Linguistique Francaise (Genève) 2.113-39.

INDEX OF ENGLISH LINGUISTIC ACTION VERBIALS

Note: All numbers refer to paragraphs

TO ABANDON: 201, 221
TO ACCEDE: 337
TO ACCEPT: 382, 446
TO ACCOUNT FOR: 446
TO ACCREDIT: 306, 319, 329, 337
TO ACQUIESCE: 300, 337
TO ACT: 254
TO ACT/PLAY A PART: 254
TO ACT/PLAY THE HYPOCRITE: 254, 265
TO ADD: 446
TO ADDRESS: 446
TO ADDRESS A WARNING TO: 343, 425
TO ADJURE: 337
TO ADMIT: 428, 430, 446
TO ADMONISH: 312, 337
TO ADVERTISE: 317, 327, 335, 446
TO ADVISE: 293, 305, 337, 344, 350, 404, 446
TO ADVOCATE: 337
TO AFFECT: 254
TO AGGRANDIZE: 250
TO AGREE: 337, 379, 381, 446
TO ALLOW: 337, 435, 442, 446
TO ALLURE: 337
TO ANGLE FOR: 324, 335
TO ANSWER: 446, 448

TO APOLOGIZE: 368, 406, 448, 449
TO APPEAL: 308
TO APPEAL TO ONE FOR: 326, 337
TO APPLY FOR: 306, 326, 335
TO APPLY PRESSURE: 337
TO APPOINT: 306, 329, 335, 446
TO APPROVE: 335, 337, 370, 446
TO ARGUE: 89, 446
TO ASK: 79, 123, 291, 302, 305, 324, 330, 335, 337, 340, 352, 354, 392, 429, 431, 446, 448
TO ASK ABOUT: 324
TO ASK A QUESTION: 302, 324, 335
TO ASK FOR: 326, 330, 335, 340
TO ASPERSE: 247
TO ASSENT: 337
TO ASSERT/VINDICATE A CLAIM/ RIGHT/TITLE TO: 308
TO ASSIGN: 306, 312, 329, 335
TO ASSUME: 254
TO AUTHORIZE: 306, 337
TO BACKBITE: 247, 405
TO BADMOUTH: 70, 247, 405
TO BAN: 308, 325, 329, 334, 341
TO BAPTIZE: 440
TO BAR: 329, 341
TO BARGAIN: 317, 329
TO BEAR FALSE WITNESS: 258, 269

243

INDEX OF ENGLISH

TO BEAT AROUND THE BUSH: 68, 71, 80, 164, 165, 199, 217
TO BECOME MUM: 192
TO BE/BECOME MUM AS AN OYSTER: 172, 194, 402
TO BEG: 290, 300, 326, 337, 353-354, 392, 446
TO BEG LEAVE: 325
TO BELITTLE: 242, 249
TO BE MUTE: 164, 165, 184
TO BEND THE TRUTH: 246
TO BESEECH: 337
TO BE SILENT: 149, 150, 152-157, 164, 165, 167, 402
TO BE SILENT ABOUT: 150, 211, 402
TO BE SILENT AS A POST/STONE: 173
TO BE SILENT AS THE GRAVE/TOMB: 171, 402
TO BESMEAR: 247, 405
TO BESMIRCH: 247, 405
TO BESPEAK: 327, 335
TO BE THE SOUL OF DISCRETION: 197, 217
TO BID: 325, 335
TO BID COME: 325, 335
TO BITE ONE'S LIPS: 175, 194
TO BITE ONE'S TONGUE: 175, 194
TO BLACKEN: 247, 405
TO BLACKLIST: 306, 329, 341
TO BLACKMAIL: 292, 321, 326, 335, 337, 358
TO BLACK OUT: 205-206, 213
TO BLAME: 248, 446
TO BLESS: 437
TO BLOW UP: 250
TO BOAST: 80, 237
TO BOOK: 317, 327
TO BREAK OFF: 202
TO BRIEF: 337
TO BROADCAST: 446
TO BULLY (SOMEONE INTO DOING SOMETHING): 337
TO BURY: 162, 171
TO BUTTON ONE'S LIP: 163, 175, 194
TO BUTTON UP: 164, 165, 176
TO CAJOLE: 337
TO CALL: 322, 325, 335, 337, 446
TO CALL AWAY: 325, 335
TO CALL BACK: 325, 335
TO CALL FOR: 335
TO CALL FORTH: 335
TO CALL IN: 325, 335

TO CALL ON/UPON: 335, 337-338
TO CALL OUT: 322, 325, 329, 335
TO CALL THE SHOTS: 346
TO CALL THE SIGNALS: 346
TO CALL TOGETHER: 325, 335
TO CALL UP: 318, 325, 335
TO CALUMNIATE: 247, 405
TO CANT: 254, 265
TO CANVASS: 317, 319, 327, 335
TO CARICATURE: 268
TO CAST A SLUR ON: 247, 405
TO CAST ASPERSIONS ON: 247, 257, 405
TO CATECHIZE: 315, 324, 335
TO CAUTION: 343
TO CEASE: 162
TO CENSOR: 159
TO CENSURE: 315, 329, 341
TO CERTIFY: 306, 335
TO CHALLENGE: 337, 437
TO CHARGE: 306, 317, 327, 329, 335, 340, 446
TO CHECK ONE'S SPEECH: 199
TO CITE: 308, 325, 335
TO CLAIM: 260, 308, 310, 326, 335, 446
TO CLAMOR FOR: 335
TO CLAM UP: 172
TO CLASSIFY: 166, 168, 205, 213
TO CLOSE: 192
TO CLOSE ONE'S MOUTH: 163
TO CLOSE UP: 176
TO CLOSE UP LIKE A CLAM/AN OYSTER: 172, 229
TO COACH: 337
TO COAX: 337
TO COLOR: 239-240, 246, 277
TO COLOR A LIE: 277
TO COME TO AN END: 162, 192
TO COMMAND: 133, 290, 300, 305, 331, 333-334, 337, 342, 348-349, 435, 446
TO COMMISERATE: 368, 406
TO COMMISSION: 306, 317, 327, 329, 335
TO COMMIT PERJURY: 258
TO COMPLAIN: 446
TO CONCEAL: 162, 168, 195
TO CONCOCT: 279
TO CONDOLE (WITH): 368, 448
TO CONGRATULATE: 103, 368, 378, 406, 448-449
TO CONJURE: 316, 325, 335, 337
TO CONJURE UP: 316, 325, 335, 357

INDEX OF ENGLISH

TO CONSCRIPT: 318
TO CONSENT: 337
TO CONSULT: 354
TO CONVENE: 306, 325, 335
TO CONVINCE: 80
TO CONVOKE: 306, 325, 335
TO COOK UP: 279
TO COPY: 167
TO COUNSEL: 337
TO COUNT: 437, 446
TO COVER UP: 168, 205-206, 210, 213, 229, 233
TO CRAVE: 337
TO CRITICIZE: 248, 405
TO CROSSEXAMINE: 308, 324, 335
TO CROSSINTERROGATE: 308, 324, 335
TO CROSS-QUESTION: 308, 324, 335
TO CRY: 446
TO CURSE: 437, 446-447
TO DAMN: 437
TO DARE: 291, 337, 446
TO DECEIVE: 262
TO DECLARE: 446
TO DECLINE: 382
TO DECREE: 308, 337, 357
TO DEFAME: 247, 405
TO DEFILE: 247, 405
TO DEFY: 329, 337
TO DELIVER AN ULTIMATUM: 337
TO DEMAND: 302, 312, 325-326, 335, 337, 435, 446
TO DENIGRATE: 247, 405
TO DEODORIZE: 251
TO DESCRIBE: 446
TO DEVIATE FROM THE TRUTH: 246
TO DICTATE: 329, 335, 337
TO DIRECT: 446
TO DISCONTINUE: 166, 208
TO DISMISS: 446
TO DIRECT: 337
TO DISAGREE: 379, 381
TO DISALLOW: 342
TO DISAPPROVE: 370
TO DISCOURAGE: 342
TO DISGUISE: 233
TO DISH THE DIRT: 248, 425
TO DISPARAGE: 247, 405
TO DISSEMBLE: 254
TO DISSIMULATE: 254
TO DISSUADE: 342
TO DISTORT: 246

TO DRAFT: 318, 325, 335, 412-414
TO DRAG THROUGH THE MUD: 247, 405
TO DRAW THE LONGBOW: 250
TO DRESS UP: 242, 252, 270
TO DROP A HINT: 337
TO DROP A LINE: 165
TO DRY UP: 176, 184, 186, 187
TO DUMBFOUND: 151
TO DUMMY UP: 176
TO DUN: 327
TO EGG (ON): 337
TO ELICIT: 324, 335
TO EMBARGO: 319, 329, 341
TO EMBELLISH: 251, 257, 270
TO EMBROIDER: 242, 252, 270
TO ENCOURAGE: 337, 446
TO END: 162
TO ENDORSE: 337
TO ENJOIN: 308, 314, 345
TO ENQUIRE: 446
TO ENTICE: 337
TO ENTREAT: 337
TO ERR: 237
TO EVOKE: 325, 335
TO EXACT: 326, 335
TO EXAGGERATE: 240, 244, 250, 257, 266, 403
TO EXAMINE: 308, 320, 324, 335, 446
TO EXCOMMUNICATE: 315
TO EXCUSE: 446
TO EXHORT: 337
TO EXORCISE: 316, 325
TO EXPLAIN: 446
TO EXPOSTULATE: 341
TO EXPRESS: 427
TO EXTEND AN INVITATION: 325, 335
TO EXTORT: 321, 326, 335, 358
TO EXTRACT INFORMATION: 324, 335
TO FAIL TO MENTION: 191, 196, 210, 225, 229
TO FAKE: 254
TO FEIGN: 254
TO FABRICATE: 279
TO FALL SILENT: 152, 154, 164, 165, 176, 184-187, 402
TO FALSIFY: 274
TO FANTASIZE (ABOUT): 279
TO FIB: 239-240, 276
TO FILE AND FORGET: 166, 168, 205-206, 213

TO FINISH: 223
TO FINK/RAT/SNITCH/SQUEAL ON: 248
TO FISH FOR: 324, 335
TO FLATTER: 237, 262
TO FOMENT: 335
TO FORBID: 342, 424, 435, 442, 446
TO FORGIVE: 446
TO FORSWEAR SPEAKING/SPEECH: 174, 402
TO GAMMON: 254
TO GILD: 251, 277
TO GILD A LIE: 277
TO GIVE A BAD NAME: 247, 405
TO GIVE A COLOR TO: 246
TO GIVE A FALSE COLORING: 246
TO GIVE A FREE HAND: 335, 338
TO GIVE AN OPEN MANDATE: 306, 337
TO GIVE AN ORDER: 337
TO GIVE A PIECE OF ADVICE: 337
TO GIVE CARTE BLANCHE: 306, 337-338
TO GIVE FAIR WARNING: 343
TO GIVE FULL POWER: 306, 337
TO GIVE IN: 380
TO GIVE LEAVE: 325, 337
TO GIVE MOUTH HONOR TO: 256
TO GIVE NO SIGN OF LIFE: 162
TO GIVE OFFICIAL SANCTION: 306, 337
TO GIVE PERMISSION: 337
TO GIVE THE GO-AHEAD: 295, 335, 338
TO GIVE THE GREEN LIGHT: 335, 338
TO GIVE THE WORD (OF COMMAND): 337
TO GLORIFY: 248, 405
TO GLOSS (OVER): 251
TO GOAD: 337
TO GRANT: 337
TO GREET: 368, 390, 393, 406, 446
TO GRILL: 324, 335, 443
TO GUESS: 446
TO HAGGLE: 317, 329
TO HAIL: 248
TO HAVE LITTLE TO SAY: 186
TO HAVE LOST ONE'S TONGUE: 175
TO HEM AND HAW: 164, 165, 199, 217
TO HESITATE: 183, 223
TO HIDE: 168

TO HIGGLE: 317, 329
TO HINT: 337, 352
TO HOLD ONESELF ALOOF: 216
TO HOLD ONE'S PEACE: 179, 199, 217, 229
TO HOLD ONE'S TONGUE: 163, 179
TO HOLD OUT ON: 179, 196, 217
TO HUSH: 151
TO HUSH UP: 159, 207, 213
TO HYPERBOLIZE: 250
TO IMPETRATE: 337
TO IMPLORE: 337
TO IMPORTUNE: 327, 335, 337
TO IMPOSE: 335
TO IMPOSE ON ONE FOR: 335
TO IMPUTE: 255
TO INCITE: 337, 358
TO INDENT: 317, 327
TO INDUCE: 337
TO INFORM: 446
TO INFORM ON: 248
TO INHIBIT: 342
TO INQUIRE (AFTER): 324, 335, 446
TO INQUISITION: 324, 335
TO INSIST (ON): 302, 337, 352
TO INSTIGATE: 337, 358
TO INSTRUCT: 337, 351, 446
TO INTERDICT: 308, 314, 341
TO INTERPELLATE: 319, 324, 335
TO INTERROGATE: 320, 324, 335
TO INTERRUPT: 446
TO INTERVIEW: 322, 324, 335
TO INTRODUCE: 446
TO INVEIGLE: 337
TO INVENT: 279
TO INVITE: 303, 305, 325, 334-335, 337, 404, 446
TO INVOKE: 316, 325, 335
TO ISSUE A CAVEAT: 343
TO ISSUE A COMMAND: 337
TO ISSUE A WRIT/INJUNCTION: 308, 314, 345
TO JUDGE: 446
TO KEEP AT A DISTANCE: 216
TO KEEP BACK: 162, 179
TO KEEP BETWEEN US/THEM: 179, 197
TO KEEP BUTTONED UP: 164, 165, 179
TO KEEP CLOSE: 179
TO KEEP DARK: 179
TO KEEP FROM: 179, 209-210

INDEX OF ENGLISH   247

TO KEEP IN: 179
TO KEEP IN IGNORANCE (ABOUT): 179, 209-210
TO KEEP IN PETTO: 179, 203, 229, 402
TO KEEP IN THE DARK (ABOUT): 179, 209-210
TO KEEP IT A DEEP DARK SECRET: 179
TO KEEP IT UNDER ONE'S HAT: 179
TO KEEP MUM: 179
TO KEEP ONE'S DISTANCE: 216
TO KEEP ONESELF TO ONESELF: 179, 216
TO KEEP ONE'S MOUTH SHUT: 178, 179
TO KEEP ONE'S OWN COUNSEL: 179, 217
TO KEEP ONE'S TONGUE BETWEEN ONE'S CHEEK: 179
TO KEEP ONE'S TONGUE IN CHECK: 175
TO KEEP ONE'S TRAP/YAP SHUT: 175, 179
TO KEEP QUIET: 163, 178, 179
TO KEEP SECRET: 162, 179, 195, 210-211, 402
TO KEEP SILENCE: 179
TO KEEP SILENT: 155, 179
TO KEEP SOMEBODY OUT OF SOMETHING: 179
TO KEEP STILL: 179
TO KEEP TO ONESELF: 179
TO KEEP UNDER ONE'S HAT: 162
TO KEEP UNDER WRAPS: 168, 179
TO KEEP WITHIN THE BOSOM OF THE LODGE: 179, 197
TO KEEP WITHIN THESE WALLS: 179, 197
TO KID: 276
TO KNOCK IT OFF: 163, 222, 402
TO LAUD: 248, 405
TO LAY AN EMBARGO ON: 319, 341
TO LAY CLAIM TO: 308, 326, 335
TO LAY DOWN THE LAW: 308, 310, 337
TO LEAVE IN THE DARK (ABOUT): 179, 209
TO LEGALIZE: 308, 337
TO LET ON: 254
TO LEVY: 308, 327, 335
TO LIBEL: 247, 405

TO LICENSE: 306, 337
TO LIE: 103, 128-130, 236, 239-240, 245, 259, 262-263, 286
TO LIE FLATLY: 239, 245-246, 263
TO LIE LIKE A TROOPER: 239-240, 263, 271-272
TO LURE: 337
TO MAGNIFY: 250
TO MAINTAIN (A DEATHLIKE/TOMBLIKE/GOLDEN/SOLEMN/PREGNANT) SILENCE: 171, 179, 192
TO MAINTAIN A SECRET: 179
TO MAKE A PRETENSE: 254
TO MAKE A REQUEST: 337
TO MAKE A SHOW OF: 254
TO MAKE DEMANDS/A DEMAND: 326, 337
TO MAKE FALSE PRETENSES: 254, 270
TO MAKE INQUIRY: 324, 335
TO MAKE INQUISITION: 324, 335
TO MAKE MANDATORY/OBLIGATORY: 308, 337
TO MAKE NO SIGN: 162
TO MAKE REQUISITION: 308, 326, 335
TO MAKE RESERVATIONS: 317, 327, 335
TO MAKE SMELL LIKE ROSES: 251
TO MAKE THE RULES: 346
TO MAKE UP: 279
TO MALIGN: 247, 405
TO MANDATE: 308, 329, 335
TO MANIPULATE: 337
TO MANUFACTURE: 279
TO MEMORIALIZE: 306
TO MENACE: 345
TO MENTION: 446
TO MISQUOTE: 274
TO MISREPRESENT: 246
TO MUFFLE: 214
TO MUSTER: 325, 335
TO MUZZLE: 151
TO MUZZLE ONESELF: 175, 194
TO NAG: 443
TO NAME: 446, 448
TO NEGATIVE: 308, 341
NEVER LET ON: 176, 197
NOT BREATHE A WORD: 163, 174, 194, 402
NOT GET A WORD IN EDGEWAYS: 188, 402

NOT GIVE AWAY: 162, 197, 211
NOT HAVE A WORD TO SAY: 174, 186, 229
TO NOTIFY: 430
NOT LET A WORD ESCAPE ONE: 174
NOT LET IT GO FURTHER: 197
NOT LET OUT A PEEP: 174
NOT OPEN ONE'S MOUTH: 175, 178
NOT SAY ANYTHING: 155
NOT SAY A WORD: 164, 165, 174
NOT SAY 'BOO': 163-165, 174
NOT SPEAK: 149, 150, 156, 158, 235
NOT SPEAK ABOUT: 150, 156
NOT TALK: 149, 150, 235
NOT TALK ABOUT: 150
NOT TELL THE TRUTH: 235, 245
NOT UTTER A WORD: 163-165, 174, 178
NOT WRITE: 166, 167
TO OBTEST: 308, 325, 335, 337
TO OFFER: 446
TO OKAY: 57, 337
TO ORDAIN: 308, 314-315, 329, 337
TO ORDER: 6, 80, 88, 89, 300, 317, 327, 334, 335, 337, 342, 348-350, 404, 431, 435, 446
TO ORDER ABOUT/AROUND: 70, 318, 346
TO ORDER UP: 318, 325, 335
TO OUTLAW: 308, 329, 342
TO OVERCHARGE: 268
TO OVERCOMMEND: 256
TO OVERLAUD: 250, 256
TO OVERPRAISE: 250, 256
TO OVERSTATE: 250
TO OVERSTRESS: 250
TO PAUSE: 223
TO PERJURE ONESELF: 258
TO PERMIT: 294-295, 337, 348, 435, 446
TO PERSIST: 337
TO PERSUADE: 337, 446
TO PETITION: 306, 337, 353-354
TO PICK THE BRAINS OF: 324, 335
TO PLAY/CALL THE TUNE: 346
TO PLAY UP TO: 256, 269
TO PLEAD: 300, 337
TO POP THE QUESTION: 327, 335, 425
TO POSE A QUESTION: 324, 335
TO POSSUM: 254
TO POST: 306, 329, 335
TO PRAISE: 248, 405, 446

TO PRAY (FOR): 326, 337, 392, 440, 446
TO PRECONIZE: 315, 329, 335
TO PRESCRIBE: 322, 337
TO PRESENT A PETITION: 306, 337
TO PRESS: 337
TO PRETEND: 254, 446
TO PREVARICATE: 246
TO PRICK: 337
TO PROD: 337
TO PROHIBIT: 291, 300, 331, 333-334 342, 404, 435
TO PROMISE: 6, 52, 76, 80, 430, 432, 438, 446
TO PROMOTE: 317, 327, 335
TO PROMPT: 337
TO PRONOUNCE: 446
TO PRONOUNCE X AND Y HUSBAND AND WIFE: 68, 71, 80, 425
TO PROPOSE: 327, 335, 337
TO PROSCRIBE: 308, 329, 341
TO PROVE: 446
TO PRY/PRIZE OUT: 324, 335
TO PUBLICIZE: 317, 327, 335
TO PULL SOMEONE'S LEG: 276
TO PUMP (FOR INFORMATION): 324, 335, 443
TO PUT A BRIDLE ON ONE'S TONGUE: 175, 194
TO PUT A FALSE APPEARANCE UPON: 246
TO PUT A FLEA/BUG IN SOMEONE'S EAR: 337
TO PUT AN EMBARGO ON: 329
TO PUT A QUESTION TO: 324, 335
TO PUT FORWARD: 79, 439
TO PUT IN A CLAIM: 326
TO PUT IN A FALSE LIGHT: 246
TO PUT IN AN ORDER FOR: 317, 327, 335
TO PUT ON A (FALSE) FRONT: 254
TO PUT ON AN ACT: 254, 270
TO PUT ONE'S FOOT DOWN: 345
TO PUT ONE'S VETO UPON: 308, 341, 424
TO PUT ON THE GRILL: 324, 335
TO PUT ON THE INDEX: 315, 329, 341
TO PUT QUERIES: 324, 335
TO PUT THE BITE ON: 326
TO PUT THE LID ON: 168
TO PUT THE PRESSURE ON: 337

INDEX OF ENGLISH 249

TO PUT THE SCREWS TO: 337
TO PUT TO SILENCE: 151
TO PUT UNDER AN INJUNCTION: 308, 345
TO PUT UNDER AN INTERDICT: 308, 341
TO PUT UNDER THE BAN: 308, 341
TO PUT UP A FRONT: 254, 270
TO QUALIFY: 306, 337
TO QUERY: 324, 335
TO QUESTION: 324, 335, 424, 443, 446
TO QUESTIONNAIRE: 324, 335
TO QUIT: 201
TO QUIZ: 324, 335
TO QUOTE: 437
TO READ: 167
TO READ THE RIOT ACT: 308, 310, 329, 335, 341, 357
TO REASON: 446
TO RECALL: 325, 335
TO RECLAIM: 308
TO RECOGNIZE: 446
TO RECOMMEND: 327, 337
TO REFUSE: 380-381, 383-384, 446
TO REFUSE COMMENT: 176, 218, 224-225
TO REGULATE: 308, 337
TO REMAIN SILENT (ABOUT/AS TO): 179
TO REMIND: 446
TO REMONSTRATE: 341
TO RENDER/GIVE/PAY LIP SERVICE: 256
TO REPLY: 446
TO REPRESS: 176, 182, 214
TO REQUEST: 89, 123, 290-291, 302, 326, 337, 352, 435, 446
TO REQUEST THE PLEASURE OF SOMEONE'S COMPANY: 325, 335
TO REQUEST THE PRESENCE OF: 325, 335, 429
TO REQUIRE: 326, 337
TO REQUISITION: 308, 310, 326, 335
TO RESERVE: 317, 327
TO REVEAL: 435, 439
TO ROAST: 324, 335
TO RULE: 308, 337, 342
TO RULE AGAINST: 308, 342
TO RULE OUT: 342
TO RUN DOWN: 247, 405
TO SANCTION: 308, 337

TO SAVE ONE'S BREATH: 200
TO SAY (SOMETHING): 260, 365, 381, 427-428, 431, 433, 446, 448
TO SAY NEITHER YES NOR NO: 199, 218, 224-225
TO SAY NOTHING: 149, 150, 155, 156, 192
TO SAY NOTHING ABOUT: 150
TO SAY SOMETHING: 155, 156
TO SAY THE WORD: 337
TO SCOLD: 437, 446
TO SCREW: 321, 326, 335, 358
TO SEAL ONE'S LIPS: 175, 178
TO SECRETE: 162, 210
TO SEDUCE: 327, 335, 337
TO SEND: 446
TO SEND AFTER: 325, 335
TO SEND FOR: 325, 327, 335, 357
TO SET: 329, 335, 337
TO SET CONDITIONS: 337
TO SHAM: 254
TO SHOOT QUESTIONS AT: 324, 335, 424
TO SHOUT: 446
TO SHUT ONE'S BAZOO: 163, 175
TO SHUT ONE'S FACE/MOUTH/HEAD: 164, 165, 175
TO SHUT UP: 164, 165
TO SIC: 329, 335, 357
TO SILENCE: 151
TO SIMULATE: 254
TO SIT MUM: 179
TO SIT ON: 179, 205-206, 210, 213
TO SLANDER: 240, 247, 266, 403
TO SLANT: 246
TO SLUR: 247, 405
TO SMIRCH: 247, 405
TO SMOTHER: 176, 182, 214, 402
TO SOLICIT: 326-327, 335, 337
TO SPEAK: 80, 156, 427-428, 433, 435, 441, 446, 448, 450
TO SPEAK FALSELY: 245
TO SPEAK ILL OF: 247, 405
TO SPEAK SLIGHTINGLY OF: 247, 405
TO SPUR: 337
TO STAND ALOOF: 216
TO STAND MUTE: 164, 165, 175, 184, 185
TO STAND ON: 337
TO STATE: 80, 89, 90, 260, 446
TO STATION: 329, 335

TO STIFLE (SOMETHING): 176, 182, 214, 229
TO STIPULATE: 308
TO STIPULATE FOR: 326, 337
TO STOP: 162
TO STOP TALKING: 152
TO STORY: 270
TO STRAIN THE TRUTH: 246
TO STRETCH THE TRUTH: 246
TO SUBMIT: 335
TO SUBPOENA: 138, 308-309, 325, 335
TO SUBSCRIBE: 337
TO SUE (FOR): 326, 337
TO SUGGEST: 305, 337, 352, 446
TO SULLY: 247, 405
TO SUMMON: 138, 303, 308-309, 325, 335, 408-409, 412
TO SUPPLICATE: 326, 337
TO SUPPORT: 446
TO SUPPRESS: 176, 182, 214
TO SUSPEND: 306, 329, 341
TO SWEAR: 437, 446
TO TABOO: 315, 329, 341
TO TAKE A BREAK: 204
TO TAKE A SECRET INTO THE GRAVE: 189
TO TAKE UP/CARRY ON AN INQUIRY: 324, 335
TO TALK: 156, 427, 435, 441, 446, 448, 450
TO TALK ABOUT: 70
TO TALK IN SUPERLATIVES: 250
TO TALK OVER: 329
TO TARNISH: 247, 405
TO TELL: 90, 304-305, 337, 348-349, 435, 439, 446, 448
TO TELL A LIE: 245

TO TEMPT: 337
TO THANK: 371, 385, 388-389, 392-393, 406, 431, 446, 448
TO THREATEN: 79, 80, 292, 345, 432
TO TRADUCE: 247, 405
TO TRANSLATE: 446
TO TROUBLE SOMEONE FOR: 337
TO TRUMP UP: 279
TO TRY: 308, 320, 324
TO TWIST: 246
TO TWIST SOMEONE'S WORDS: 274
TO UNDERREPORT: 249
TO UNDERSTATE: 240, 249, 257, 266, 403
TO URGE: 76, 337, 443, 446
TO UTTER A CAVEAT: 343
TO VARNISH: 251
TO VEIL: 162, 168, 195, 210
TO VETO: 308, 341, 404
TO VILIFY: 247, 405
TO VOTE: 446
TO VOUCHSAFE: 306, 337
TO WARN: 293, 343-344, 350, 404, 446
TO WARN OFF: 325
TO WARP: 246
TO WARRANT: 306, 345
TO WASTE NO WORDS: 200
TO WELCOME: 392, 446
TO WHEEDLE (SOMETHING OUT OF A PERSON): 326, 337, 358
TO WHISPER: 80, 428, 446
TO WHITEWASH: 240, 251, 257, 266, 403
TO WISH: 371, 377, 446
TO WITHHOLD: 179, 211
TO WORM OUT OF: 324, 335
TO WRITE: 160, 446, 448
TO ZIP ONE'S LIP: 175, 194

INDEX OF DUTCH LINGUISTIC ACTION VERBIALS

Note: All numbers refer to paragraphs

AANBEVELEN: 327, 339
AANDIKKEN: 250
AANDRINGEN: 339
AAN EEN KRUISVERHOOR ONDER-
  WERPEN: 311, 324, 336
AANHITSEN: 329, 339
AANKLEDEN: 251-252, 270
AANMANEN (TOT): 312, 339
AANMOEDIGEN: 339
AANNEMEN: 382
AANPORREN: 339
AANPRATEN: 317, 327, 336
AANPREKEN: 339
AANPRIJZEN: 327, 339
AANRADEN: 339, 344, 350
AANREKENEN: 327
AANSPOREN: 339
AANSPRAAK MAKEN OP: 311, 326, 336
AANSTELLEN (TOT): 306, 329, 336
AANSTICHTEN: 339
AANSTOKEN: 339, 358
AANTIJGEN: 255
AANVRAGEN: 306, 326-327, 336
AANVUREN: 339, 358
AANWAKKEREN: 339
AANWIJZINGEN GEVEN: 339

AANWRIJVEN: 255
AANZEGGEN: 306, 339
AANZETTEN: 339
AARZELEN: 183, 223
ABRAHAMMETJE SPELEN: 199, 269
ACHTERHOUDEN: 162
ACHTERKLAPPEN: 247
ADVERTEREN: 317, 327, 336
ADVISEREN: 339
AFBEDELEN: 326, 336
AFBIEDEN: 329
AFBREKEN: 202
AFBRENGEN VAN: 342
AFDINGEN: 317, 329
AFDREIGEN: 292, 321, 326, 336, 358
AFDWINGEN: 326, 336, 358
AFFECTEREN: 254
AFKEUREN: 370
AFPERSEN: 321, 326, 336
AFPINGELEN: 317, 329, 336
AFRADEN: 342, 344
AFSLAAN: 382
AFSMEKEN: 326, 336
AFSTAPPEN VAN: 159, 162, 192
AFTROGGELEN: 326, 336, 358
AFWIJZEN: 379
AKKOORD GAAN: 379, 381

INDEX OF DUTCH

AUTORISEREN: 306, 339
(BE)DANKEN: 371, 385, 389
BEDELEN: 326, 336
BEDINGEN: 326
BEDREIGEN: 292
BEGRAVEN: 171
(BE)GROETEN: 390
BEKLADDEN: 247
BEKRACHTIGEN: 306, 339
BEKRITISEREN: 248
BELASTEN MET: 306, 329, 336
(BE)LASTEREN: 240, 247
BENOEMEN TOT: 306, 329, 336
BEPALEN: 339
BEPLEITEN: 339
BEPRATEN: 339
BESPREKEN: 317, 327, 336
BESTELLEN: 317, 327, 336
BEVELEN: 76, 339, 348-349
BEWEGEN TOT: 339
BEWEREN: 260
BEWIMPELEN: 251
BEZWALKEN: 247
BEZWEREN: 316, 325, 336, 339
BIDDEN (OM): 326, 339
BIJEENROEPEN: 306, 325, 336
BILLIJKEN: 339
BINNENROEPEN: 325, 336
BOE NOCH BA ZEGGEN: 163, 174
BORDUREN: 242, 252, 270
BOT STILZWIJGEN: 202
BRENGEN TOT: 339
BUITEN DE WET STELLEN: 311, 329, 342
CARTE BLANCHE GEVEN: 306, 339
CATECHISEREN: 315
CENSUREREN: 315, 329, 341
CHANTAGE PLEGEN: 321, 326, 336
CHANTEREN: 321, 326, 336
CHARGEREN: 250, 268
COMMANDEREN: 318, 339, 346
CONVOCEREN: 306, 325, 336
DAGVAARDEN: 138, 309, 311, 325, 336, 408-409
DECRETEREN: 311, 339
DE DISCRETIE IN PERSOON ZIJN: 197, 217
DE HANDEN IN DE MOUW HOUDEN: 180
DE HYPOCRIET UITHANGEN: 254, 265

DE KAARTEN DUIKEN: 217
DE LIPPEN OP ELKAAR DRUKKEN/KLEMMEN: 175
DENIGREREN: 247
DE PUBLIKATIE STOPZETTEN VAN: 166, 208
DE STILTE BEWAREN: 180
DE TONG VOOR DE TANDEN HOUDEN: 180
DE UITZENDING STOPZETTEN VAN: 208
DE WAARHEID GEWELD AANDOEN: 245
DE WAARHEID NIET ZEGGEN: 245
DE WAARHEID TE KORT DOEN: 246
DE WAARHEID VERDRAAIEN/VERKRACHTEN/VERWRINGEN: 246
DE WEG WIJZEN: 336
DE WOORDEN BLEVEN HEM IN DE KEEL STEKEN: 174, 184
DICHTKLAPPEN: 176
DICTEREN: 329, 336, 339
DOEN ALSOF: 254, 270
DOOR DE MAND VALLEN: 277
DOOR DE MODDER SLEUREN: 247
DOOR HET SLIJK HALEN: 247
DREIGEN: 292, 345
DRUK UITOEFENEN OP: 339
EEN AANVRAAG INDIENEN/DOEN: 306, 326, 339
EEN AANZOEK DOEN (OM): 327, 336, 339
EEN BEROEP DOEN OP: 336, 338
EEN BEVEL GEVEN: 339
EEN DIEP/GROOT GEHEIM VAN IETS MAKEN: 176
EEN DOODSE STILTE BEWAREN: 171, 180
EEN EIS INSTELLEN: 311-312, 326, 336
EEN EIS STELLEN: 339
EEN EMBARGO LEGGEN OP: 319, 329
EEN GEHEIM BEWAREN: 180
EEN GEHEIM MEE ONDER DE AARDE/IN HET GRAF NEMEN: 171, 189
EEN INTERDICT UITSPREKEN OVER: 314, 341
EEN KIKKER/ROGGESTAART IN DE KEEL HEBBEN: 184
EEN LIPPENDIENST BEWIJZEN: 256

INDEX OF DUTCH

EEN MEINEED AFLEGGEN: 258, 273
EEN ROL SPELEN: 254, 270
EEN SNAAR NIET AANROEREN: 199
EEN ULTIMATUM STELLEN: 339
EEN VALSE GETUIGENIS AFLEGGEN: 258, 269
EEN VERWRONGEN VOORSTELLING GEVEN VAN: 246
EEN VERZOEKSCHRIFT INDIENEN: 306, 339, 353
EEN VOORSTEL INDIENEN: 306
EEN VRAAG STELLEN: 302, 324, 336
EEN WAARSCHUWING GEVEN: 343
EINDIGEN: 162, 192
EISEN: 312, 326, 336, 339
ER EEN SCHEPJE OP DOEN: 250
ER GEEN WOORD TUSSEN KRIJGEN: 188
ERGENS EEN SPELDJE BIJ STEKEN: 204
EXAGEREREN: 250
EXAMINEREN: 320, 324, 336
EXCOMMUNICEREN: 315
FABRICEREN: 280
FANTASEREN: 280
FEMELEN: 254, 265
FINGEREN: 280
GEBAREN: 254
GEBIEDEN: 339
GEEN BEK/MOND OPENDOEN: 163
GEEN GELUID UITBRENGEN: 174
GEEN KIK GEVEN/LATEN: 174, 189
GEEN MOND/BEK OPENDOEN: 175
GEEN PIEP (MEER) GEVEN/LATEN: 174, 189
GEEN SLAG AAN DE BAK KRIJGEN: 176, 188
GEEN (STOM) WOORD (MEER) ZEGGEN: 174, 194
GEEN TEKEN VAN LEVEN GEVEN: 162
GEEN WOORDEN VOOR IETS HEBBEN: 174, 186
GEEN WOORD LOSSEN (OVER IETS): 174
GEEN WOORD OVER ZIJN LIPPEN LATEN KOMEN: 174
GEHEIMHOUDEN: 162, 195
GELASTEN: 306
GELUKWENSEN: 369, 378
GERESERVEERD BLIJVEN: 216
GOEDKEUREN: 339, 370
GOEDPRATEN: 240, 251
GOEDVINDEN: 370
GROETEN: 369
HEFFEN: 311, 327, 336
HET EERSTE WOORD OVER IETS NOG MOETEN ZEGGEN: 174
HET STILZWIJGEN BEWAREN: 180, 192
HET WOORD STIERF OP ZIJN/HEM OP DE LIPPEN: 174, 184
HUICHELEN: 254
IEMAND BIJ DE NEUS NEMEN: 176
IEMAND DE WET STELLEN: 346
IEMAND ERGENS BUITEN HOUDEN/ LATEN: 180
IEMAND HET MES OP DE KEEL ZETTEN: 339
IEMAND IETS IN DE SCHOENEN SCHUIVEN: 68, 255
IEMAND IETS IN HET HOOFD PRATEN: 339
IEMAND IETS OP HET HART DRUKKEN: 339
IEMAND IETS UIT HET HOOFD PRATEN: 342
IEMAND IN ZIJN EER/GOEDE NAAM AANTASTEN: 247
IEMAND LASTIG VALLEN MET: 339
IEMAND LELIJK/SLECHT MAKEN: 247
IEMAND NAAR DE MOND PRATEN: 256, 269
IEMAND OVER DE HEKEL HALEN: 247
IEMANDS HAND VRAGEN: 327
IEMAND VAN IETS ONKUNDIG LATEN: 180
IEMANDS WOORDEN VERDRAAIEN/ VERWRINGEN/VERVALSEN: 274
IEMAND VOOR IETS WINNEN: 339
IEMAND ZWART MAKEN: 247
IETS ACHTER DE ELLEBOOG HOUDEN: 180
IETS ACHTER DE HAND HOUDEN: 180
IETS ACHTER HOUDEN: 180, 196
IETS BEDEKT HOUDEN: 180
IETS BUITEN BESCHOUWING LATEN: 180
IETS DOODZWIJGEN: 171

INDEX OF DUTCH

IETS IN DE DOOFPOT LATEN/
  STOPPEN: 180, 207, 213
IETS IN PETTO HOUDEN: 180, 203
IETS MAAR BLAUWBLAUW LATEN:
  180
IETS MET DE MANTEL DER LIEFDE
  BEDEKKEN: 197
IETS NIET AAN IEMANDS NEUS
  HANGEN: 214
IETS TUSSEN DE TANDEN HOUDEN:
  180
IETS VOOR ZICH HOUDEN: 180
IETS IN DE MOUW HOUDEN: 180
IN ALLE/ZEVEN TALEN ZWIJGEN:
  176, 194
INBLAZEN: 339
IN DE BAN DOEN: 311
IN EEN VALS DAGLICHT STELLEN:
  246
INFORMEREN: 324, 336
INGEVEN: 339
INLIJVEN: 318
INROEPEN: 325, 336
INSTEMMEN MET: 339
INSTRUEREN: 339, 351
INTERPELLEREN: 319, 324, 336
INTERVIEWEN: 322, 324, 336
IN VERZOEKING BRENGEN: 336
INVITEREN: 325, 336
INVORDEREN: 311, 336
INWILLIGEN: 339
IN ZIJN ROL BLIJVEN: 254
JOKKEN: 276
KIK NOCH MIK GEVEN: 174
KLEINEREN: 242
KLEUREN: 239, 246
KWAADSPREKEN: 247
KWEZELEN: 254, 265
LATEN HALEN: 325, 336
LEGALISEREN: 311, 339
LEUGENS VERKOPEN: 245
LEUGENS VERTELLEN: 245
LIEGEN: 239, 245
LIEGEN ALS EEN ALMANAK: 239
LIEGEN ALS EEN KETTER: 239
LIEGEN ALSOF HET GEDRUKT
  STAAT: 239
LIEGEN DAT MEN HET ZELF
  GELOOFT: 239
LIEGEN DAT MEN ZWART/SCHEEL
  ZIET: 239

MACHTIGEN: 306, 339
MACHTIGING GEVEN TOT: 339
MANDATEREN: 311, 329, 336
MANIPULEREN: 339
MEELOKKEN: 325, 336
MEETRONEN: 325, 336
MET DE MOND VOL TANDEN STAAN:
  175, 186
MET SPEK SCHIETEN: 250
MET STOMHEID GESLAGEN ZIJN: 184
MET VERSTIJFDE TONG STAAN: 175,
  184
MISRADEN: 339
MOOIPRATEN: 251
NIET AKKOORD GAAN: 379, 381
NIET IN ZIJN KAARTEN LATEN
  KIJKEN: 217
NIET KIKKEN (VAN IETS): 174
NIET PRATEN: 157
NIET SCHRIJVEN: 166
NIETS LOSLATEN: 176
NIET SPREKEN: 157
NIETS ZEGGEN: 157, 192
NIET VAN ZICH LATEN HOREN: 162
NIET VEEL WOORDEN AAN IETS
  VUILMAKEN: 200
NIET VEEL WOORDEN VERSPILLEN:
  200
NIET VERKLAPPEN: 197
NIET VERRADEN: 197
OMPRATEN: 329, 345
ONDERDRUKKEN: 182
ONDERVRAGEN: 320, 324, 336
ONTBIEDEN: 138, 306, 309, 325, 336,
  408-409
ONTLOKKEN: 324, 336
ONTMOEDIGEN: 342
ONTRADEN: 342
ONTVEINZEN: 254
ONTWRINGEN: 324, 336
OPBLAZEN: 250
OP DE INDEX PLAATSEN/ZETTEN:
  315, 329, 341
OP DE ROOSTER LEGGEN: 324
OPDRAGEN: 306, 329, 339
OP EEN AFSTAND BLIJVEN: 216
OPEISEN: 326, 336
OPGEVEN: 201, 336
OPHITSEN: 339
OPHOUDEN: 223
OPJAGEN: 329, 336

INDEX OF DUTCH

OPKROPPEN: 176, 182, 214
OPLEGGEN: 329, 339-340
OPPEREN: 339
OPROEPEN: 316, 318, 325, 336, 339, 408-409, 412-413
OPRUIEN: 329, 336
OPSCHROEVEN: 250
OPSNIJDEN: 250
OPSTOKEN: 339
OPVRAGEN: 326, 336
OPZETTEN: 329
OP ZIJN MOND PASSEN: 199
OP ZIJN RECHTEN STAAN: 339
OP ZIJN TONG BIJTEN: 175, 194
OP ZIJN WOORDEN PASSEN: 199
OPZWEPEN: 339
ORDONNEREN: 306, 339
OVERDRIJVEN: 240, 250, 403
OVERHALEN TOT: 339
OVERREDEN: 339
OVERROEPEN: 256
PAF STAAN VAN: 184
PAUZEREN: 204, 223
PETITIONEREN: 306, 339
PLEITEN VOOR: 339
POTDICHT ZIJN: 172
PRECONISEREN: 315, 336
RAAD GEVEN: 339
RAADPLEGEN: 354
RECLAME MAKEN VOOR: 317, 327 336
RECLAMEREN: 326, 336
REGLEMENTEREN: 339
RESERVEREN: 317, 327, 336
RINGELOREN: 346
ROND DE POT DRAAIEN: 199, 217
SANCTIONEREN: 311, 339
SCHOOIEN: 326, 336
SCHORSEN: 306, 329, 341
SCHRIJVEN: 160
SIMULEREN: 254
SMEKEN: 339, 353
SOLLICITEREN NAAR: 306, 326, 336
SOMMEREN: 311-312, 339
SPRAKELOOS STAAN: 175, 184
SPROOKJES VERTELLEN: 270
STAAN OP: 339
STAKEN: 222
STILHOUDEN: 180
STILVALLEN: 176, 184, 186-187
STIPULEREN: 311, 339

SUGGEREREN: 339
TABOE VERKLAREN: 315, 329, 341
TARTEN: 339
TEGEN DE DKIPPEN/STERREN OP LIEGEN: 239, 271
TERUGEISEN: 326, 336
TERUGROEPEN: 325, 336
TERUGVORDEREN: 311, 326, 336
TERZIJDE LATEN: 180
TEVEEL AANREKENEN: 268
TE VOORSCHIJN ROEPEN: 325, 336
TOEGEVEN: 339, 380
TOELATEN: 339, 348
TOELATING GEVEN: 339
TOESTAAN: 339
TOESTEMMEN IN: 339
TOESTEMMING GEVEN: 339
TOEWIJZEN: 311-312, 329, 336
TOT STAKING OPROEPEN: 322, 329
TRONEN: 325, 336
UITDAGEN: 339
UITDRIJVEN: 316, 325, 336
UITHOREN: 123, 324, 336
UITNODIGEN: 325, 336
UITSLUITEN: 341
UITVINDEN: 280
UITVRAGEN: 324, 336
UIT ZIJN DUIM ZUIGEN: 280
UIT ZIJN ROL VALLEN: 277
VAN ADVIES DIENEN: 339
VAN ALLE KATTEN KWAAD WETEN: 272
VAN DE WAARHEID AFWIJKEN: 246
VAN EEN VLIEG/MUG/MUIS EEN OLIFANT MAKEN: 250
VAN EEN SCHEET EEN DONDERSLAG MAKEN: 250
VAN IEMAND KWAAD STOKEN: 247
VASTLEGGEN: 339
VEINZEN: 254
VERBANNEN: 311, 325
VERBERGEN: 195
VERBIEDEN: 342
VERBLOEMEN: 251
VERDICHTEN: 280
VERDRAAIEN: 246
VERFRAAIEN: 251, 270
VERGOELIJKEN: 251
VERGROTEN: 250
VERGULDEN: 251
VERGUNNEN: 339

VERGUNNING GEVEN/VERLENEN: 339
VERHOREN: 311, 320, 324, 336
VERKEERD VOORSTELLEN: 246
VERKLAREN: 260
VERKLEINEN: 240, 242, 249
VERLEIDEN: 327, 336
VERLOKKEN: 336
VEROORLOVEN: 306, 339
VERORDENEN: 311, 339
VERSMOREN: 182, 214
VERSTOMD STAAN VAN: 175, 184
VERSTOMMEN: 184
VERVALSEN: 274
VERWRINGEN: 246
VERZINNEN: 280
VERZOEKEN: 325, 339
VERZWIJGEN: 157, 195
VISSEN NAAR: 324, 336
VOET BIJ STUK ZETTEN: 339
VOLMACHT GEVEN: 306, 339
VOORGEVEN: 254
VOORSCHRIJVEN: 322, 339
VOORSLAAN: 339
VOORWAARDEN STELLEN: 339
VOORWENDEN: 254
VORDEREN: 311, 326, 336
VRAGEN: 324, 330, 336, 339-340, 354
VRAGEN AFVUREN OP: 324, 336
VRAGEN OM: 326, 330, 340
WAARSCHUWEN: 343, 350
WAT AFLIEGEN: 272
WEGTRONEN: 325, 336
WEIFELEN: 183
WEIGEREN: 380-381, 383-384
WENSEN: 371
WERVEN: 317, 319, 327, 336
WETTIGEN: 311, 339

WIT WASSEN: 251
ZEGGEN: 260
ZICH ERGENS BUITEN HOUDEN: 180
ZICH KOEST HOUDEN: 180, 199, 217
ZICH OP DE LIPPEN BIJTEN: 175, 194
ZICH OP EEN AFSTAND HOUDEN: 216
ZICH VAN DE DOMME HOUDEN: 254, 273
ZICH VERONTSCHULDIGEN: 369
ZICH WENDEN TOT: 339
ZIJN DEELNEMING BETUIGEN: 369
ZIJN MOND/BEK/BAKKES/BABBEL/ RAMMEL/SNATER/SNOET/SNUIT/ TOET HOUDEN: 163, 180
ZIJN MOND/BEK/BAKKES NIET OPENDOEN: 175
ZIJN PIJPEN IN DE ZAK HOUDEN: 180
ZIJN TONG GEWELD AANDOEN: 194
ZIJN TONG IN BEDWANG/TOOM HOUDEN: 175, 180, 194
ZIJN TONG VERLOREN HEBBEN: 175
ZIJN VETO UITSPREKEN OVER: 311, 341
ZIJN WOORDEN AFMETEN: 199
ZO DICHT ZIJN ALS EEN POT/BRIEF: 172
ZO GESLOTEN ZIJN ALS EEN GRAF: 171
ZO GESLOTEN ZIJN ALS EEN OESTER: 172
ZO GESLOTEN ZIJN ALS EEN POT/ PEPERDOOS/BRANDKAST: 172
ZWIJGEN: 157
ZWIJGEN ALS EEN MOF: 172
ZWIJGEN ALS HET GRAF: 171
ZWIJGEN ALS VERMOORD: 171
ZWIJGEN OVER: 157, 164

AUTHOR INDEX

NOTE: All numbers refer to pages. Italics indicate bibliographic citations.

A
Abelson, Robert P., 45, *240*
Abrahams, R. D., 26, *235*
Alford, Danny K. H., 20, *235*
Allwood, Jens, 25, *235*
Anscombre, Jean-Claude, 9, 25, *235*
Austin, John L., 4*n*, 14, 22, *235*

B
Bailey, C.-J. N., *240*
Ballmer, Thomas, 10, 25, *235*
Baskett, Glen D., 123, *235*
Basso, Keith H., 73, 121, *235*
Bauman, Richard, 26, *235*
Bendix, Edward H., 40, *235*
Benveniste, Emile, 25, *235*
Berlin, Brent, 45, 46, 217, *236*
Berrendonner, Alain, 6, *236*
Bierwisch, Manfred, *240*
Blount, B., *236*
Bok, Sissela, 123, 147, *236*
Bolinger, Dwight, 23, 31, 37, 63, *236*
Breedlove, Dennis E., 45, 217, *236*
Brennenstuhl, Waltraud, 10, 25, *235*

Bruxelles, S., 9, *236*
Brown, Cecil H., *236*

C
Castelfranchi, Cristiano, 123, *241*
Chisholm, Roderick M., 123, *236*
Cohen, L. Jonathan, 6, 24, *236*
Cohen, Ted, 7, *236*
Cole, Peter, *236*
Cole, Roger W., *236*
Coleman, Linda, 47, 123, 147, *236*
Conklin, H. C., 217, *236*
Coseriu, Eugenio, 41, *236*
Coulmas, Florian, 187, *236*
Crocker, J. C., *240*
Crumrine, Lynne S., 26, *236*

D
Dallmayr, Fred R., 13, *236*
Davis, Steven, 7, *236*
de Beaugrande, Robert, 9, *236*
Dixon, R. M. W., 218, *236*
dos Reis Nunes, G., *9*, *236*
Ducrot, Oswald, 9, 25, *235*, *236*, *237*
Dumont, Louis, 17, *236*

AUTHOR INDEX

F
Feehan, T. D., 123, *236*
Feld, Steven, 26, *236*
Ferguson, Charles A., 187, *237*
Fillmore, Charles J., 33, 45, 46, 51, *237*
Finnegan, Ruth, 26, *237*
Fisiak, J., *237*
Fodor, Jerry A., 37, *238*
Fortescue, Michael, 37, 38, *237*
Fouquier, E., 9, *236*
Frake, Charles O., 26, *237*
Franck, Dorothea, 8, *237*
Fraser, Bruce, 22, *237*
Freedle, Roy O., 123, *235*
Frege, Gottlob, 6, *237*
French, R., 25, *238*
Freud, Sigmund, 130, *237*

G
Gadamer, H. G., 19, *237*
Garfinkel, Harold, 19, *237*
Geckeler, Horst, 41, *236*
Giglioli, Pier Paolo, *237*
Goffman, Erving, 45, *237*
Goodenough, Ward H., 36, 41, *237*
Gossen, Gary H., 26, 231, *237*
Gouaze, J., 9, *236*
Gregersen, Kirsten, *237*
Grice, H. Paul, 60, 60*n*, 136, 144, *237*
Gumperz, John J., *237*

H
Habermas, Jürgen, *238*
Harder, Peter, 6, *238*
Harris, Roy, 22, *238*
Hindelang, Götz, 185, *238*
Hjelmquist, Erland, *235*
Hymes, Dell, 26, *237, 238*

J
Jakobson, Roman, 18*n*, *238*
Jakobovits, Leon A., *240*
Jefferson, G., 19, *239*
Jessen, Heino, 25, *238*
Johnson, Mark, 21, 207, *238*
Johnson-Laird, P. N., 38, 40, 60, *238, 239*

K
Katz, Jerrold J., 37, *238*
Kay, Paul, 45, 46, 47, 123, 147, 217, *236, 238*
Kernan, K. T., 25, *238*
Kiefer, Ferenc, *240*

Kochman, Thomas, 26, *238*
Kockelmans, Joseph J., 18, *238*
Kuhn, Thomas, 20, *238*

L
Lakoff, George, 21, 207, *238*
Leech, Geoffrey, 52, *238*
Lehmann, Dorothea, 25, *238*
Lehrer, Adrienne, 41, *238*
Leisi, Ernst, 58, *238*
Leonard, H. S., 123, *238*
Lessing, Gotthold E., *238*
Létoublon, Françoise, 25, *238*
Levinson, Stephen C., 8, *238*
Lloyd, B. B., *239*
Lounsbury, Floyd G., 36, 41, *238*
Lyons, John, 37, 41, *238*

M
Makkai, Adam, 33, *238*
Malinowski, Bronislaw, 17, *238*
McCarthy, Thomas A., 13, 16, *236, 238*
McCawley, James D., 22, *239*
McDaniel, Chad K., *238*
McDaniel, Timothy, 15, 17, 46, *239*
Metzing, Dieter, 9, *239*
Meyer-Hermann, Reinhard, 25, *239*
Mihailă, Rodica, 73, 120, *239*
Miller, G. A., 38, 40, 60, *239*
Minsky, M., 45, *239*
Mitchell-Kernan, C., 26, *239*
Morgan, J. L., 11, *236, 239*
Murphy, J. P., *239*

N
Nida, E. A., 40, *239*

O
Ochs Keenan, E., 73, 121, *239*
Ortony, A., *239*
Öztek, Piyale C., 186, *240*

P
Parret, H., *239*
Perret, D., 8, *239*
Porzig, W., 44, *239*
Pratt, M., 8, 22, *239*

R
Raven, Peter H., 45, 217, *236*
Reddy, M., 26, 27, 53, *239*
Remis, A., 9, *236*

Riniker, U., 8, *239*
Rogers, Andy, *239*
Rosaldo, M., 22, 24, 26, 185, 204, *239*
Rosch, E., 45, 49, 218, *239*

S
Sacks, H., 19, *239*
Sanches, M., *236*
Sapir, E., 21*n*, 44, *239, 240*
Sapir, J. David, *240*
Sbisà, M., *239*
Schank, Roger C., 45, *240*
Schegloff, E. A., 19, *239*
Schieffelin, Bambi B., 26, *237*
Schön, Donald A., 15, 21, *240*
Schuetz, Alfred, *240*
Schüle, Klaus, 8, *240*
Searle, John R., 7, 8, 9, 11, 14, 22, 60, 60*n*, 61, 149, 188, 208, *240*
Seitel, Peter, 25, *240*
Sherzer, Joel, *235*
Shuy, R. W., *240*
Siegler, F. A., 123, *240*
Silverstein, Michael, 20, 21, *240*
Sodergren, J., 25, *238*
Steinberg, Danny D., *240*
Stross, Brian, 24, 26, 73, 120, 231, *240*
Sudnow, David, 19, *240*
Sweetser, Eve, 123, *240*

T
Tannen, Deborah, 186, *240*
Trier, Jost, 44, *240*
Tyler, Stephen A., 13, 20, *240*

V
Van der Auwera, Johan, 222, *240*
Van Valin, Robert D., 10, 20*n*, *241*
Vassilyev, L. M., 41, *241*
Vendler, Zeno, 22, *241*
Verschueren, Jef, 3*n*, 10, 21, 23, 25, 37, 38, 60, 136, 148, 215*n*, 232, 233*n*, *239, 241*
Vincent, Jocelyne M., 123, *241*

W
Wall, B., *239*
Warnock, G. J., 123, *241*
Warren, N., *241*
Wason, P. C., *238*
Weisgerber, L., 44, *241*
Whorf, Benjamin Lee, 20, 44, *241*
Wierzbicka, Anna, 37, 38, 54, *241*
Winch, Peter, 15, 16*n*, 17, 18, 19, *241*
Witherspoon, Gary, 18, *241*
Wittgenstein, Ludwig, 19, 58, *241*

Z
Zenone, Anna, 9, *241*

SUBJECT INDEX

NOTE: All numbers refer to pages.

A
Abstractness, 53-58, 232-233
Adjective, 34, 46, 50, 115-116
Adverb, 34
Advice, 150, 178, 185, 196, 198-199, 209-210
Agreement, 195-196
Ambiguity, 120
American English, 67-69
Analyzability, 54
Apache, 73, 121
Apology, 188-189, 191, 201, 202
Appropriateness conditions, 8, 58-63, 76, 224, 232-233
Approval, 189-190, 193
Arbitrariness, 42, 46-47
Argumentation, 9
Article, 52
Assertives, 9, 134, 146, 150, 184, 192-193
Atomic concept, 36-37, 53
Atomic predicate, 38
Authority, 180-183, 185, 190, 199-200, 211-213
  knowledge, 181-182, 185, 199
  power, 181-182, 185, 200, 213
  reversal of, 182
Automaticity, 187, 202
Azande, 17-18

B
Basic-level term, 45, 48-51, 218, 224
Belizian City Creole, 25
Black English, 231

C
Categorization, 45-48, 218
Challenge, 149
Circularity, 58-63
Code, 61, 83-89, 119
Cognition, 46-51 (see also Psychological salience)
Collocation, 30-31
Color terms, 46, 50, 215-219, 223, 231
Command, see Order
Commissives, 9, 150-152, 184, 185
Communication type, 60, 75-82, 119
Componential analysis, see Lexical decomposition
Conceptual area, 41-42
Conceptual field, 41-42
Conceptualization, 16-21, 223
  and lexicalization, 19-21, 63, 185, 207, 213-214, 216, 232

SUBJECT INDEX

Conceptualization *(cont.)*
  and nonlexicalization, 187-214, 211
Conceptualization habits, 20-21, 32, 48, 58, 204, 207
Condolence, 188-189, 201
Congratulation, 188-189, 194-195, 201, 230
Context, 51, 62, 75-82, 116-118
Conversational logic, 233 (*see also* Maxims of conversation)
Conversational routines, 24, 186-214, 207, 211
Cultural attitudes, 208, 210

D
Declarations, 9
Definition, 56-57, 219-221, 226, 232-233
  ostensive, 58, 74, 123
  reversed, 221
Delocutivity, 25
Dialect, 68, 232
Dictionary, 54-55, 226
Directives, 9, 24, 65-66, 148-185, 195-200, 207, 209-214
  directionality of, 170-180, 210-213
  directivity of, 153-155, 211-213
  double. 183
  goals of, 164-170
  negative, *see* Directives, directionality of
  positive, *see* Directives, directionality of
  and social setting, 155-164, 211-213
    commercial, 161
    educational, 164
    industrial relations, 164
    legal, 157-159, 211-213
    media, 164
    medical, 164
    military, 161-162, 184, 211-213
    official, 155-156, 211, 213
    political, 162
    religious, 159-161
Disagreement, *see* Agreement
Disapproval, *see* Approval
Discourse, 9
  literal and serious, *see* Literalness, Seriousness
  parasitic forms of, 8
Distinguisher, 37
Duration, 89, 94-96, 119
Dyirbal, 50, 218

E
Effect, *see* Perlocutionary effect
Erklären, 13
Ethnography of speaking, 26
Ethnomethodology, 19
Explicit performatives, 5, 10-11, 12, 136
Expressives, 9, 188-195, 200-204, 208-209, 231
Extralinguistic reality, 45, 51, 60

F
Felicity conditions, 5, 7-9, 12
Fixed formulae, 30
Flemish Standard Dutch, 67-69, 231-232
Folk taxonomy, 215-217, 219-220, 222, 223
Forgotten routines, 186-204, 211, 231
Formality, 68-69, 87, 225
Formulaic expression, 186
Frame, 45, 51-52, 74-75, 124, 152-153
  lexical, 52, 75, 124, 130, 143, 187
  linguistic, 45, 52
French, 68, 80, 202, 231

G
German, 80, 202, 231
Grammatical forms, 10, 12
Greek, 80
Greeting, 188-189, 201, 202, 230

H
Harmony of interaction, 198-200, 202
Haya, 25
Hearer, 60, 108-111, 164-170, 183-185, 192-193, 209
  delayed, 183
Hermeneutic circle, 20, 233
Hermeneutics, 19
Hungarian, 56, 202, 230

I
Idiom, 30, 33, 35, 218-219
Illocutionary act, 4, 149
Illocutionary act types, *see* Speech-act classification
Illocutionary force, 4, 6-7, 10, 12, 24, 118, 134-137, 148-185
Illocutionary force indicating devices, 5, 7
Illocutionary point, 7
Ilongot, 26, 185, 204

SUBJECT INDEX 263

Imagination, 144-145
Immediacy, 87
Indirectness, *see* Speech act, indirect
Insisting, 196, 198-199
Intensity, 89-94, 119
Interlocutor, *see* Hearer, Speaker
Invitation, 165-166, 172-174, 197, 198
Italian, 202

J
Japanese, 57

L
Language, 60
   natural, 220
'Langue', 36
Latin, 74, 75, 80
Lexical decomposition, 36-41, 44-45,
     47-48, 53-55
Lexical domain, *see* Lexical field
Lexical field, 41-45, 47, 52
   complex, 42, 52
   paradigmatic, 41
   syntagmatic, 42
Lexical gap, 42, 187-214, 222, 231
Lexical hierarchy, 49-51, 215, 218,
     222-224
Lexical item, 30-33, 75
Lexical semantics, 29-69
Lexicalization, 30, 45, 75, 203-204
     (*see also* Conceptualization, and
     lexicalization)
   complex, 30-33, 76, 123
   simple, 30, 80, 120
Life-form terms, 215-217, 220, 230, 231
Linguistic action, 14-15, 27, 58, 73-75,
     87, 119, 194-195, 213-214, 224
   the comparative lexical approach to,
     22-28, 207-211, 213-214
   the empirical-conceptual approach to,
     22-28, 58, 63, 69, 208, 211,
     232-233
   the theoretical approach to, 22-23, 208-
     209, 233
   universals of, 15, 28, 204, 216
Linguistic action verbials, 35, 58-60,
     63-67, 73-233
   formation of, 87, 119
Linguistic action verbs (*see also* Linguistic
     action verbials)
   basic, 215-233

Linguistic adaptation, 63
Linguistic anthropology, 41, 45
Literalness, 7-8, 11
Locutionary act, 6
Lying, 24, 122-147, 209
   motives for, 146-147

M
Magic, 17-18
Manner of speaking, 231
Markedness, 11, 36-37, 76, 224-225, 230
Maxims of conversation, 60, 74, 104, 119,
     144-146
Meaning, 6, 12, 75-82
   the checklist approach to, 45, 47-48
   literal, *see* Literalness
   logical analyses of, 56
   nonpropositional, 115-116
   shared, 16
Meaning component, *see* Semantic feature
Mentiendum, 123
Mentiens, 123
Metaphor, 21, 26-27, 32-33, 207
   conduit, 26-27, 53
Metapragmatic awareness, 232
Metapragmatic terms, 28
Metapragmatics, 28
Monolexemicity, 218-219

N
Navajo, 18
Neutrality, *see* Markedness
Noun, 34, 46, 50, 231-232
Noun phrase, 61

O
Order, 171-172, 174-176, 180-181,
     197-198, 200

P
'Parole', 36
Perception, 46-47
Performative verbs, 5, 23, 35
Performativity continuum, 23
Perlocutionary act, 4, 7, 12
Perlocutionary effect, 4, 7, 111, 146
Perlocutionary intent, 136, 138-141
Permission, 150-151, 153, 175, 181, 198,
     200
Phenomenology, 18

SUBJECT INDEX

Politeness formula, 186
Possessive pronoun, 52
Pragmatics, 27-28, 59-63, 232-233
Presupposition, 61
Prohibition, 149, 168, 171-174, 177-178, 198, 200
Propositional content, 4, 6-7, 10, 24, 111-115, 122-147
Prototype, 45-48, 51, 61-62, 65
Psychological relevance, 54, 56-58, 232
Psychological salience, 187-188, 198-200, 202, 204, 208, 211, 218, 223-224, 229

Q
Question, 149, 154-155, 164-165, 172-174, 177

R
Rationality, 17-18
Refusal, 196-198
Representatives, see Assertives
Request, 154-155, 174-177, 197, 200
Response, 195-200
  routine, 200-203

S
Scene, 45, 51-52
Semantic class, see Taxonomy
Semantic dimension, 47, 65-67, 211-213
Semantic dimension comparison table, 65-67
Semantic feature, 36-37, 53-56
Semantic field, see Lexical field
Semantic marker, 37
Semantic pattern, 66
Semantic primitive, 37-38, 53-55
Semantic space, 63-67
Sentence structure, 61
Sequencing, see Speech-act sequences
Seriousness, 7-8
Silence, 24, 73-121, 207, 209, 231
  causes of, 96, 101
  motives for, 101-108
Social action, 12-21, 152-153, 155-164, 184
  the conceptualization of, see Conceptualization
  the empirical-conceptual approach to, 13-17, 19-21
  the meaningfulness of, 16

the theoretical approach to, 13-17
universals of, 13-16
Sound features, 61, 89-96, 119
Speaker, 60 (see also Tacens)
Speech act, 4, 61, 73
  basic, 10, 222
  indirect, 5, 10-11, 12, 221
Speech-act classification, 9-10, 12, 65, 152, 184, 188-195, 204, 208-209
Speech-act rules, 4-5
Speech-act sequences, 8-9
Speech-act theory, 3-12, 14-15, 22-23, 233
Speech-act types, 61 (see also Speech-act classification)
Speech-act verbs, 5, 10, 25-26, 35, 38-40, 47, 231
Speech activity theory, 8
Structuralism, 41-45
Style, 61
Suggestion, 195-196, 198
Synchronic implicational universals, 216, 231
Synonymy, 222, 224-225

T
Tacendum, 75, 77, 111-115
Tacens, 74, 96-110
Taxonomy, 65, 75, 82
Text, 9, 61, 141-143, 195
Thanking, 190-191, 193, 198, 200-203, 211
Threat, 149-150
Topic, 111-115, 146-147
Truth, 122-147, 207
  gradability of, 125, 145
  quality scale of, 125-133, 145, 209
  quantity scale of, 125-133, 145, 209
Tzeltal, 26, 73, 120-121, 231

U
Unique beginner, 217, 220
Units of analysis, 9
Universal mental language, 37-38
Universality, 53, 55-57, 232-233 (see also Linguistic action, universals of; Social action, universals of; Synchronic implicational universals)

V
Value judgments, 143-144, 146-147, 184, 210, 225

Variability, 47, 48, 50, 52-53
Verb, 34, 38, 46, 50, 231
  nuclear, 50, 218-220
  quality-diminishing, 126, 127, 129-130, 132, 135, 140
  quality-increasing, 126, 130-132, 135, 140
  quantity-diminishing, 125, 130-131, 135, 140, 146
  quantity-increasing, 125, 130-132, 135, 140
Verba cessandi, 76-82, 116-118
Verba mentiendi, 123-147
Verba reticendi, 75-82, 88-89, 111-115, 121, 122
Verba silendi, 75-82, 119
Verba tacendi, 74-121, 123
  basic, 76-82, 94, 119, 120

Verbial, 34-35
Verbials of directing, 148-185
  basic, 153-155
Verbials of distorting, 128-129, 130
Verbials of lying, 128, 130
Verstehen, 13-14, 19

W

Warning, 150, 178, 185, 209-210
Welcoming, 201
Wish, 190-191, 194-195
Word, 30, 61
  and concept, *see* Conceptualization and lexicalization
Word boundaries, 42, 47
Word classes, 34
Word group, 33